The DC: 0-3 Casebook

A Guide to the Use of
ZERO TO THREE's *Diagnostic Classification
of Mental Health and Developmental Disorders of
Infancy and Early Childhood* in
Assessment and Treatment Planning

Editors
Alicia F. Lieberman,
Serena Wieder, and
Emily Fenichel

Foreword by Stanley I. Greenspan

ZERO TO THREE: National Center for Infants, Toddlers, and Families

This publication was made possible by the generous support of the Ittleson Foundation, Inc.

Published by: ZERO TO THREE: National Center for Infants, Toddlers and Families
2000 M Street, NW, Suite 200
Washington, DC 20036-3307
telephone: (202) 638-1144
fax: (202) 638-0851

Additional copies may be ordered from:
ZERO TO THREE Publications
toll-free: (800) 899-4301
www.zerotothree.org

Jacket and Text Design: Susan Lehmann, Washington, DC

ISBN 0-943657-38-5
Library of Congress Catalog Card Number: 97-061588

Printed in the United States of America
First Edition, Second Printing (September 2003)

Acknowledgments

Like all undertakings of ZERO TO THREE: National Center for Infants, Toddlers and Families, this *Casebook* is the product of collaboration among many dedicated and talented people. We express our gratitude first of all to the 25 authors, who took considerable time from their demanding daily work to reflect on their practice, articulate their clinical reasoning, and work patiently with us to make each chapter, and the *Casebook* as a whole, as useful as possible to a broad audience of readers. Secondly, we acknowledge the steadfast support of ZERO TO THREE President, Jeree H. Pawl; the Diagnostic Classification Task Force chaired by Joy D. Osofsky; our Board of Directors; and staff, led by Matthew E. Melmed, Executive Director.

It is with special gratitude that we thank the Ittleson Foundation, Inc. and Anthony C. Wood, Executive Director, for both financial and moral support of this work. They saw merit in our original conception of the *Casebook* and encouraged us to proceed as the work became more ambitious and complex.

Above all, we acknowledge the families about whom and for whom this *Casebook* is written. Although all details that might identify particular families have been changed, the strength of each family's efforts to understand, grow, and heal is clear. As allies in these efforts, professionals learn from each child and family with whom we work, and we hope that as our understanding increases, we become ever more effective partners.

The Editors

About ZERO TO THREE

ZERO TO THREE's mission is to promote the healthy development of infants and toddlers. We are America's leading resource on the first 3 years of life and work to strengthen the critical roles of professionals, policymakers, and parents in giving all of our children the best possible start.

We focus on the first 3 years of life because this is the time of greatest human growth and development. It is also the time when caring adults have the greatest opportunity to shape a child's future.

Matthew E. Melmed, *Executive Director*

Contents

Foreword

Stanley I. Greenspan, M.D.

ZERO TO THREE's system for diagnostic classification of mental health and developmental disorders of infancy and early childhood encourages clinicians to try to understand the full richness and complexity of the developmental process in the earliest years of life. *Diagnostic Classification of Mental Health and Developmental Disorders of Infancy and Early Childhood (DC: 0-3)* (ZERO TO THREE, 1994) is designed to help clinicians: a) recognize individual differences in the ways infants and young children process sensation, organize experience, and implement action; b) observe and understand the child's interaction with key caregivers; c) explore the impact of family, cultural, and community patterns on the child's development; and d) capture the quality of a child's adaptive processes, as well as the developmental challenges the child faces. This volume, the *DC: 0-3 Casebook,* shows how clinicians from a range of professional disciplines are using the developmentally based *DC: 0-3* system in a variety of service settings in the United States and Canada.

DC: 0-3 conceptualizes the diagnostic process as a continuous one, which permits deeper and deeper levels of understanding and modification of diagnostic conclusions as the clinician gains fuller awareness of the child and family. Any experienced infant/family professional, regardless of discipline, will recognize the wisdom of this approach. Because complexity and continuous, rapid change are the very essence of early development, hurried judgments or overly reductionistic approaches to intervention are likely to be inadequate—often dangerously so. Unfortunately, clinicians today are under enormous pressure to reach conclusions too quickly, often on the basis of inadequate information. One source of pressure comes from efforts to contain costs in health, mental health, child development, and social service settings by limiting the number of sessions or restricting the sources of information a clinician can use to learn about a child and family. A second source of pressure is conceptual, as clinicians trained in currently orthodox theoretical frameworks tend to look only at presenting symptoms or biological indicators in diagnosing mental health and developmental disorders in infants and young children. As so many of the chapters in this *Casebook* illustrate, to overlook an infant or young child's relationships, family patterns, and complex interactive dynamics with the important people in his life during the assessment process is to risk the likelihood of serious misdiagnosis, with costly and potentially life-altering consequences. In contrast, a thoughtful assessment based on a strong alliance with parents and other key caregivers will not only lead to more appropriate treatment planning, but in some cases may also point to changes in the caregiving environment sufficient to restore the child's developmental momentum with a minimum of professional intervention.

As conceptualized in *DC: 0-3*, therefore, the assessment and diagnostic process must allow the clinician to learn about and, to the greatest extent possible, observe directly all the critical dimensions of a young child's life. This process would usually include meeting with parents to hear in some detail their observations of the child's current strengths and difficulties in physical, cognitive, language, social, emotional, and family functioning, as well as their observations of the child's development and their experience as parents from pregnancy onward. Time with parents and other key caregivers should include ample opportunity for the clinician and family members to discuss family issues and patterns, identifying together areas of strength as well as challenges. Most importantly, the assessment process should include one or more lengthy observations of the infant or young child interacting spontaneously with his or her parents and other key caregivers. In order to observe the child's highest levels of functioning, the clinician should, when possible and appropriate, suggest ways in which the caregiver might facilitate the interaction. To explore further the child's capacities to use support from the environment, the clinician may also wish to interact with the child.

Other important sources of information include observations of the child in his or her child care or therapeutic programs and reports from child care professionals, early interventionists, and primary care clinicians. Consultations from specialists such as occupational therapists, neuropsychologists, endocrinologists, and nutritionists and assessment of specific areas of functioning, such as speech and language or sensory processing, should be included in the assessment process to answer questions that arise from discussion with parents and observational sessions—not as part of a "standard" assessment protocol, which can often undermine a beginning alliance with parents.

As the chapters in this *Casebook* reveal, an assessment process based on *DC: 0-3* will yield rich, complex information about the child's current strengths and challenges, his or her developmental history, and the resources and concerns of family and community. *DC: 0-3*'s multi-axial approach to diagnosis and the guidelines to selecting the appropriate diagnosis are designed to assist the clinician in organizing this information. The resulting narrative and diagnostic profile guide the clinician's discussion with caregivers and intervention planning, and identify remaining questions. If interventions are indicated, new levels of understanding emerge from the child and family's experience with intervention, and initial diagnostic formulations can be revised.

Each chapter in the *Casebook* provides a picture of how a particular clinician or team of clinicians in a particular setting develops an understanding of a particular child and family, and uses the framework of *DC: 0-3* to inform and articulate this understanding. As the reader will observe, depending on the reporting clinicians' training and theoretical orientation, the mission of the service setting in which assessment occurs, families' priorities, and other factors, some chapters in the *Casebook* may focus in relatively more depth on one or another aspect of the child and family's functioning (for example, presenting problems in the child, family dynamics, or individual differences and developmental stages). Over time, we will likely observe an equal emphasis on all the relevant areas of functioning. Just as the field of infancy and early childhood is growing, so is our approach to assessment and diagnosis.

Readers are likely to find many ways to use the case studies in this volume, which should ideally be read with a copy of *DC: 0-3* close at hand. Some readers will use case studies of each diagnostic category in *DC: 0-3* to enrich their understanding of the diagnostic categories themselves. Other readers may use the chapters to test their own diagnostic acumen, imagining themselves as the clinician and asking themselves, as various stages in the assessment process are described, what kinds of additional information they might want, and how further information might modify their preliminary diagnostic hypotheses. Still other readers may focus their attention on descriptions of the assessment/intervention process itself—a process that should be continuous, but which, given the complexities and constraints of current service systems and family circumstances, often involves interruptions, barriers to care, and less than optimal choices.

DC: 0-3 is a dynamic system that attempts to capture an even more dynamic process—development in the earliest years of life. The process of understanding, diagnosing, and intervening with infants and young children must always be seen as an ongoing endeavor. The diagnostic categories and approach to assessment and diagnosis that are identified in *DC: 0-3* and illustrated in this *Casebook* are designed as tools for understanding a variety of infants, young children, and families, and for organizing appropriate interventions to support and enhance their development. We hope that these tools will prove to be useful ones, for there is much work to be done.

Introduction

It is a great pleasure to introduce this collection of case studies as a companion volume to ZERO TO THREE's *Diagnostic Classification of Mental Health and Developmental Disorders of Infancy and Early Childhood (DC: 0-3)*. The diagnostic manual has already attained widespread recognition and praise for its usefulness in providing clear and comprehensive clinical criteria for categorizing mental health disturbances in the earliest years of life. This casebook has the goal of illustrating how the diagnostic categories are used clinically to organize the information that emerges in the course of the assessment, develop working hypotheses about etiology and prognosis, and guide the choice of treatment. The intent is to foster the development of a common vocabulary that includes the regular use of all aspects of a comprehensive assessment, an agreed-upon set of diagnostic categories, and a well-defined process for organizing observations and other information obtained during the assessment so that they form the rationale for a coherent and individualized intervention plan. The case illustrations are meant as guideposts to enhance the clinician's understanding of the diagnostic categories and to aid in their accurate use during the assessment and treatment process.

ZERO TO THREE's diagnostic classification system and this casebook are organized around three primary principles. One principle is that children's psychological functioning unfolds in the context of their relationships. Children's sense of self and of their place in the world is shaped at its very core by the interactions with those who have major responsibility for their care. A second principle is that individual differences in temperament and constitutional strengths and vulnerabilities play a major role in how children experience and process what happens to them, and must always be kept in mind in assessing a child's functioning. At the same time, the caregivers' response to the child's individual characteristics and their acceptance, care, and skill in responding to areas of difficulty can modulate and even transform early challenges or risk factors so that they do not handicap the child's overall developmental course. The transactional processes by which child and caregivers communicate and help each other grow are fundamental in conceptualizing our approach to assessment and treatment. A third principle is the importance of the family's cultural context in understanding the child's functioning and developmental course.

One important corollary of this position is that we assess individuals and relationships, but we classify disorders rather than people (Emde, in press 1996; Rutter & Gould, 1985). It is essential to remember that people are not defined by their psychiatric diagnoses. Individuals may have a disorder, but they also passes a core human dignity as well as areas of experiences where they function flexibly, competently, and creatively. In addition, stressful and even pathogenic life circumstances can provide the motivation to develop coping strategies that spur individuals towards a richer and more multilayered sense of themselves. This can be just as true for infants and young children as it is for adults because children's functioning is profoundly influenced by the quality of their emotional relationships and by the characteristics of the different settings in which they spend time. A child with a particular diagnosis can behave quite differently in different settings depending on the level of emotional support, cognitive stimulation, age-appropriate or -inappropriate forms of discipline, and overall sense of well-being versus stress experienced by the child in each of these settings.

Children's sensitivity to the specific characteristics of individual relationships and situations dictate our approach to the general format of the diagnostic process. Assessments in the first years of life need to involve direct observations of the child with their primary attachment figures and childcare providers in the context of settings where they spend time on a regular basis, and across a span of several weeks. Only this kind of comprehensive, observation-based assessment can provide an accurate picture of the child's range of skills, areas of resilience and vulnerability, developmental course, and variations in level of functioning. A thorough exploration of all these factors is essential in arriving at an accurate diagnosis and in understanding the relative place of the disorder in the child's overall functioning.

Precisely because young children's functioning is influenced in essential ways by the nature of their primary relationships, the genuine collaboration of parents and caregivers is a prerequisite for an accurate diagnosis. Nobody knows the child more intimately than the primary caregivers, even if they are not aware of this knowledge and need the assessor's guidance in eliciting it. A working relationship between the assessor and the child's primary caregivers is the crucial foundation for a useful assessment, and the time and effort devoted to developing it should by no means be considered either a chore or a waste of time. Rather, the process of building a working relationship needs to be regarded as an integral component of the assessment process and a useful avenue for learning about the caregivers' perceptions of the child and about the personal strengths and vulnerabilities that caregivers bring to the relationship with the child.

Although the importance of enlisting the parents' trust and collaboration is widely accepted by clinicians, this point is worth repeating because it is easy to underestimate how anxiety-arousing an assessment of their child can be for the parents. As Bowlby (1988) observed, "parents, especially mothers, are much maligned people." Parents seem to intuitively understand this, and they enter the assessment process with feelings of guilt, shame, and self-doubt that compound their worries about the child's condition. Unless alleviated in the course of the parents' interactions with the assessor, these feelings may lead to the omission or distortion of crucial information as an attempt at self-protection from the assessor's perceived criticism. Helping the parents understand that they are partners in the assessment process rather than culprits responsible for their child's condition is not only humane and clinically sound but also pragmatic because this approach increases the chances of obtaining complete and accurate information about family history and current circumstances that might be essential for understanding the child's condition.

Parents, like children, function in the context of the cultural, socioeconomic, familial and psychological conditions in which they live. The Spanish philosopher Jose Ortega y Gasset (1957) captured vividly the inextricable interconnection between the individual and his or her life conditions when he said: "I am myself and my circumstances." What parents can offer to their children, both materially and psychologically, is shaped, conditioned, made possible, and also circumscribed by the circumstances in which they find themselves. A full appreciation of the possibilities and limitations of the family's material and psychological conditions is very helpful in keeping at bay a tendency to blame the parents for the child's disorder and in facilitating the development of a realistic treatment plan. In the same vein, unfortunate and potentially damaging misunderstandings can be prevented by the assessor's efforts to learn and understand the world view and childrearing values instilled by the parents' cultural background, and the implications of these values for their relationship with the child. In addition, this culturally informed perspective can enrich the assessor's repertoire in developing and implementing the treatment plan.

Diagnosis needs to be an ongoing process involving periodic re-evaluations of the child and caregivers. Children change, parents change, and their circumstances change. In addition, the goal of treatment is to promote and support positive movement towards increased child-caregiving reciprocity and a more adaptive child emotional, social, and cognitive developmental course. Only an open-ended approach to diagnosis can be flexibly responsive to this dynamic developmental and interactional picture.

The cases presented in this casebook illustrate our approach to assessing the child in the context of his or her primary relationships and over several sessions. The case presentations also rely on a variety of sources of information, including direct observation of the child and the parents or other caregivers, parental reports, reports from other important caregivers, medical reports, and standardized testing when clinically indicated. Although the authors may differ in their theoretical orientation and clinical methods, the chapters themselves do not focus on theory. Rather, the emphasis is on description of the child and family functioning and relationships. This descriptive approach mirrors the descriptive nature of the diagnostic categories themselves.

Like the diagnostic classification system on which it is based, this casebook should be considered a work in progress, open to revision as clinical and research knowledge accumulates and expands. This perspective is particularly timely due to the inevitable constrictions of illustrating a diagnostic category with only one or at most two clinical examples. Each case is unique in terms of the following characteristics of the child and the family: ethnic and cultural background; socioeconomic conditions; family composition including the child's birth order, number of siblings, presence or absence of both parents, and nuclear or extended family structure; parents' intellectual and emotional functioning and the presence or absence of a psychiatric condition; child's age, temperament, level of development functioning, and ways in which the caregivers adjusts to the child's unique characteristics; and a myriad other variables that may mediate the particular manifestations of the child's disorder.

In addition, each chapter represents the assessment practices of the particular clinical setting in which the child was seen. The setting might be a hospital, mental health clinic, or private practice office, and the sessions may take place in the home, in the clinical setting, or in a combination of settings. The assessment itself might be carried out by a multidisciplinary team or by a single assessor, who may be a psychologist, psychiatrist, pediatrician, or social worker, and who brings to the process the particular viewpoints and skills of his or her discipline. The format of the sessions might be unstructured, involve the use of standardized procedures and instruments, or a combination of both methods. As a result of this variety of approaches, each assessment procedure described in the casebook represents a particular professional subculture, which might provide a different pathway into the complex phenomenon of the child's condition.

The same is true of the approaches to treatment described in the different chapters. Some settings prefer to use a seamless integration of the assessment and treatment process, with assessment and treatment blending into each other from the very first sessions. Others choose a clear delineation between assessment and treatment, with one modality being formally replaced by the other at some time in the process. The chapters vary as well in the extent to which the course of treatment is described because in some cases the family chose to enter treatment until its completion, and in other cases, the recommendations for treatment could not be implemented for a variety of reasons. In every case, the clinician has had to work with what was possible in assessment and treatment without forgetting to strive for what might have been ideal. This tension between what is optimal and what is attainable applies not only to the family's willingness to collaborate in the process but also to the financial considerations that are part of all clinical interventions whether in the private or the public sectors.

ZERO TO THREE's diagnostic classification system (*DC: 0-3*) and this casebook provide a unique and much needed window for understanding the mental health and developmental disorders of infancy and early childhood. Their purpose is to provide a common vocabulary that will enhance communication among professionals, to facilitate the development of clearly articulated assessment and treatment plans, and to serve as an instrument for the accumulation and refinement of clinical and research knowledge as well as for securing much-needed insurance coverage for the assessment and treatment of young children. The classification system has already generated much attention and enthusiasm among clinicians working with young children and their families, who find it an important tool both for organizing their thinking and for communicating with each other. Extensive use in a variety of new settings and with a variety of children and their families should add to the system's already established clinical usefulness and teach us more about the validity and reliability of the specific diagnostic categories.

References

Bowlby, J. (1988). *A secure base: Clinical applications of attachment theory.* London: Routledge.

Emde, R. N. (in press). Thinking about diagnostic classification in early childhood. *Devenir.*

Ortega y Gasset, J. (1957/1994). *El hombre y la gente.* Mexico: Editorial Porrus.

Rutter, M. & Gould, M. (1985). Classification. In Rutter and L. Hersov (Eds.), *Child and adolescent psychiatry: Modern approaches* (pp. 304-321). London: Blackwell Scientific Publications.

Using DC: 0-3 To Guide Assessment and Treatment Planning for Infants and Young Children

It is the responsibility of any clinician who is charged with doing a full diagnostic work-up and planning an appropriate intervention program for an infant or young child to take into account all the relevant areas of a child's functioning, using state-of-the-art knowledge in each area. These areas include:

• presenting symptoms and behaviors;

• developmental history—past and current affective, language, cognitive, motor, sensory, family, and interactive functioning;

• family functioning and cultural and community patterns;

• parents as individuals;

• caregiver-infant (child) relationship and interactive patterns;

• the infant's constitutional-maturational characteristics; and

• affective, language, cognitive, motor and sensory patterns.

In addition, it is important to consider the family's psychosocial and medical history, the history of the pregnancy and delivery, and current environmental conditions and stressors.

The process of gaining an understanding of how each area of functioning is developing for an infant or toddler usually requires a number of sessions. A few questions to parents or caregiver about each area may be appropriate for screening, but not for a full evaluation. A full evaluation usually requires a minimum of three to five sessions of 45 or more minutes each. A complete evaluation will usually involve:

• taking the history;

• direct observation of functioning, including observation of family and parental dynamics, caregiver-infant relationship and interaction patterns, the infant's constitutional-maturational characteristics, and language, cognitive, and affective patterns; and

• hands-on interactive assessment of the infant, including assessment of sensory reactivity and processing, motor tone and planning, language, cognition, and affective expression.

Standardized developmental assessments, if needed, should always build on the clinical process described above. Such assessments may be indicated when they are the most effective way to answer specific questions, and when the child is sufficiently interactive and can respond to the requirements of the test.

A clinician conducting a diagnostic evaluation and formulating an intervention plan should have considerable experience in assessing all the areas of functioning described above and in integrating the assessment findings into a cohesive formulation. If necessary, a clinician should call upon colleagues with appropriate expertise to help assess specific areas of functioning. When a team, rather than a single clinician, is responsible for conducting an assessment and formulating the diagnosis and intervention plan, at least one member of the team should have considerable expertise in integrating the different elements of the assessment into a coherent understanding of the nature of the difficulty and the type of intervention(s) most likely to be helpful. Discussion with this kind of experienced clinician is also important when the person conducting the assessment is a trainee working under supervision or a less experienced practitioner.

The chapters in this casebook portray the efforts of clinicians who assess and treat infants and young children in a variety of practice settings. Although they have changed names and identifying characteristics of children and families in order to protect confidentiality, clinicians otherwise present in candid detail the reasons for the referral, the assessment process, assessment findings, the diagnosis, the discussion of the diagnosis and treatment planning with the child's family or caregivers, the course of intervention (including, in some cases, reformulation of the diagnosis), and the prognosis.

Readers of the casebook are encouraged to become familiar with *Diagnostic Classification of Mental Health and Developmental Disorders of Infancy and Early Childhood (DC: 0-3)* (ZERO TO THREE, 1994) and to refer to it often. For readers' convenience, guidelines to selecting the appropriate diagnosis, an overall outline of the *DC: 0-3* classification system, and the Parent-Infant Relationship Global Assessment Scale (PIR-GAS) are included here.

Axis I: Primary Diagnosis

The primary diagnosis should reflect the most prominent features of the disorder. Some maladaptive behaviors observed in infants and young children are described in more than one of the various categories identified as primary disorders in Axis I. Because an infant or young child, in comparison with an adult, is capable of only a limited number of behavioral patterns or responses to various stresses or difficulties, such as somatic symptoms, irritability, withdrawal, impulsivity, fears, and developmental delays, some overlap is inevitable. The following guidelines will assist the clinician in determining which diagnosis takes precedence:

1. Traumatic stress disorder should be considered as a first option if it is clear that the child's disordered behavior or emotions would not be present without the stress of a specific overwhelming episode or multiple repeated trauma.

2. Regulatory disorders should be considered if there is a clear constitutionally or maturationally based sensory, motor, processing, organizational, or integration difficulty.

3. Adjustment disorder should be considered as a diagnosis if the presenting problems are mild and of relatively short duration (less than four months), and are associated with a clear environmental event.

4. Disorders of mood and affect should be considered where there is neither a clear constitutionally or maturationally based vulnerability, nor a severe or significant stress or trauma, and when the difficulty is neither mild nor of short duration.

5. Multisystem developmental disorders and reactive attachment deprivation/maltreatment disorder, which involve chronic patterns of maladaptation, should take precedence over other categories, such as regulatory disorders or traumatic stress disorders. In other words, these two disorders are exceptions to the general rules listed above.

6. Relationship disorder should be considered where a particular difficulty occurs only in relationship to a particular person.

7. Do not use Axis I if the **only** difficulty involves a relationship and there are no symptoms independent of that relationship.

8. The diagnosis of reactive attachment deprivation/maltreatment disorder should be reserved for **inadequate**, basic physical, psychological, and emotional care.

9. Common symptoms such as feeding and sleep problems require assessment of the underlying basis for these difficulties—for example, acute trauma, adjustment disorder, or regulatory disorder. Feeding and sleep may be problems in their own right.

10. On rare occasions, a child may have two primary conditions.

11. When it is difficult to make a decision between two or more Axis I diagnoses—that is, when a good case could be made for a second diagnosis as a first choice—a second diagnosis may be indicated as a "rule-out" diagnosis.

Prominent features of each Axis I diagnosis are presented in outline form below. In addition, a brief narrative description of each diagnosis appears at the beginning of the case report which illustrates the diagnosis. For fuller descriptions, the reader should consult *DC: 0-3*.

100. Traumatic Stress Disorder

A continuum of symptoms related to a single event, a series of connected traumatic events, or chronic, enduring stress.

1. Reexperiencing of the trauma, as evidenced by
   a. Posttraumatic play.
   b. Recurrent recollections of the traumatic event outside play.
   c. Repeated nightmares.
   d. Distress at reminders of the trauma.
   e. Flashbacks or dissociation.

2. Numbing of responsiveness or interference with developmental momentum.
   a. Increased social withdrawal.
   b. Restricted range of affect.
   c. Temporary loss of previously acquired developmental skills.
   d. A decrease in play.

3. Symptoms of increased arousal.
   a. Night terrors.
   b. Difficulty going to sleep.
   c. Repeated night waking.
   d. Significant attentional difficulties.
   e. Hypervigilance.
   f. Exaggerated startle response.

4. Symptoms not present before
   a. Aggression toward peers, adults, or animals.
   b. Separation anxiety.
   c. Fear of toileting alone.
   d. Fear of the dark.
   e. Other new fears.
   f. Self-defeating behavior or masochistic provocativeness.
   g. Sexual and aggressive behaviors.
   h. Other nonverbal reactions, e.g. somatic symptoms, motor reenactments, skin stigmata, pain, or posturing.

200. Disorders of Affect

Focuses on the infant's experience and on symptoms which are a general feature of the child's functioning rather than specific to a situation or relationship.

201. Anxiety Disorders of Infancy and Early Childhood

Levels of anxiety or fear, beyond expectable reactions to normal developmental challenges

1. Multiple or specific fears.

2. Excessive separation or stranger anxiety.

3. Excessive anxiety or panic without clear precipitant.

4. Excessive inhibition or constriction of behavior.

5. Lack of development of basic ego functions.

6. Agitation, uncontrollable crying or screaming, sleeping and eating disturbances, recklessness, and other behaviors.

    Criterion: Should persist for at least two weeks and interfere with appropriate functioning.

202. *Mood Disorder: Prolonged Bereavement/Grief Reaction*

1. The child may cry, call, and search for the absent parent, refusing comfort.

2. Emotional withdrawal, with lethargy, sad facial expression, and lack of interest in age-appropriate activities.

3. Eating and sleeping may be disrupted.

4. Regression in developmental milestones.

5. Constricted affective range.

6. Detachment.

7. Sensitivity to any reminder of the caregiver.

203. *Mood Disorder: Depression of Infancy and Early Childhood*

Pattern of depressed or irritable mood with diminished interest and/or pleasure in developmentally appropriate activities, diminished capacity to protest, excessive whining, and diminished social interactions and initiative. Disturbances in sleep or eating.
Criterion: At least two weeks.

204. *Mixed Disorder of Emotional Expressiveness*

Ongoing difficulty expressing developmentally appropriate emotions.

1. The absence or near absence of one or more specific types of affects.

2. Constricted range of emotional expression.

3. Disturbed intensity.

4. Reversal of affect or inappropriate affect.

205. *Childhood Gender Identity Disorder*

Becomes manifest during the sensitive period of gender identity development (between approximately 2-4 years).

1. A strong and persistent cross-gender identification
    a. Repeatedly stated desire to be, or insistence that he or she is, the opposite sex.
    b. In boys, preference for cross-dressing or simulating female attire; in girls, insistence on wearing stereotypical masculine clothing.
    c. Strong and persistent preferences for cross-sex roles in fantasy play or persistent fantasies of being the opposite sex.
    d. Intense desire to participate in the games and pastimes of the opposite sex

e. Strong preference for playmates of the opposite sex.

2. Persistent discomfort with one's assigned sex or sense of inappropriateness in that gender role.

3. Absence of nonpsychiatric medical condition.

206. Reactive Attachment Deprivation/Maltreatment Disorder of Infancy

1. Persistent parental neglect or abuse of a physical or psychological nature, undermines the child's basic sense of security and attachment.

2. Frequent changes in, or the inconsistent availability of, the primary caregiver.

3. Other environmental compromises which prevent stable attachments.

300. Adjustment Disorder

Mild, transient situational disturbances related to a clear environmental event and lasting no longer than four months.

400. Regulatory Disorders

Difficulties in regulating physiological, sensory, attentional, motor or affective processes, and in organizing a calm, alert, or affectively positive state. Observe at least one sensory, sensory-motor, or processing difficulty from the list below, in addition to behavioral symptoms.

1. Over- or underreactivity to loud or high- or low-pitched noises.

2. Over- or underreactivity to bright lights or new and striking visual images.

3. Tactile defensiveness and/or oral hypersensitivity.

4. Oral-motor difficulties or incoordination influenced by poor muscle tone and oral tactile hypersensitivity.

5. Underreactivity to touch or pain.

6. Gravitational insecurity.

7. Under- or overreactivity to odors.

8. Under- or overreactivity to temperature.

9. Poor muscle tone and muscle stability.

10. Qualitative deficits in motor planning skills.

11. Qualitative deficits in ability to modulate motor activity.

12. Qualitative deficits in fine motor skills.

13. Qualitative deficits in auditory-verbal processing.

14. Qualitative deficits in articulation capacities.

15. Qualitative deficits in visual-spatial processing capacities.

16. Qualitative deficits in capacity to attend and focus.

Types of Regulatory Disorders

401. Type I: Hypersensitive

Fearful and Cautious
Negative and Defiant

402. Type II: Under-reactive

Withdrawn and Difficult To Engage
Self-Absorbed

403. Type III: Motorically Disorganized, Impulsive

404: Type IV: Other

500. Sleep Behavior Disorder

Only presenting problem; under three years of age; no accompanying sensory reactivity or sensory processing difficulties. Child has difficulty in initiating or maintaining sleep; may also have problems in self-calming and dealing with transitions from one stage of arousal to another.

600. Eating Behavior Disorder

Child shows difficulties in establishing regular feeding patterns with adequate or appropriate food intake. Absence of general regulatory difficulties or interpersonal precipitants (such as separation, negativism, trauma).

700. Disorders of Relating and Communicating

1. DSM-IV conceptualization, Pervasive Developmental Disorder or
2. Multisystem Developmental Disorder

Multisystem Developmental Disorder (MSDD)

1. Significant impairment in, but not complete lack of, the ability to form and maintain an emotional and social relationship with a primary caregiver.
2. Significant impairment in forming, maintaining, and/or developing communication.
3. Significant dysfunction in auditory processing.
4. Significant dysfunction in the processing of other sensations and in motor planning.

701. Pattern A

These children are aimless and unrelated most of the time, with severe difficulty in motor planning, so that even simple intentional gestures are difficult.

702. Pattern B

These children are intermittently related and capable of simple intentional gestures some of the time.

703. Pattern C

These children evidence a more consistent sense of relatedness, even when they are avoidant or rigid.

Axis II: Relationship Disorder Classification

Axis II should be used only to diagnose significant relationship difficulties. Relationship problems may co-occur with symptomatic behaviors in the infant but are not synonymous with them. This means that serious symptoms maybe apparent in an infant without relationship pathology, and relationships may be pathological without overt symptoms in the infant. Thus, clinicians should realize that an infant with a primary diagnosis (Axis I) need not have a relationship diagnosis (Axis II). Relationship problems may derive from within the infant, from within the caregiver, from the unique "fit" between infant and caregiver, or from the larger social context.

In deciding whether a relationship disorder is present, the clinician should consider three aspects of a relationship:

• the behavioral quality of the interaction, reflected in the behavior of each member of the dyad;

• affective tone characteristic of the dyad; and

• psychological involvement, or the meaning of the child's behavior to the parent.

901. Overinvolved relationship

Physical and/or psychological overinvolvement

1. Parent interferes with infant's goals and desires.
2. Over-controls.
3. Makes developmentally inappropriate demands.
4. Infant appears diffuse, unfocused, and undifferentiated.
5. Infant displays submissive, overly compliant behaviors or, conversely, defiant behaviors.
6. Infant may lack motor skills and language expressiveness.

902. Underinvolved relationship

Sporadic or infrequent genuine involvement

1. Parent insensitive and/or unresponsive.
2. Lack of consistency between parent's expressed attitudes about infant and quality of actual interactions.
3. Parent ignores, rejects, or fails to comfort infant.

4. Parent does not reflect infant's internal feeling states.

5. Parent does not protect infant adequately.

6. Interactions under-regulated.

7. Parent and infant appear to be disengaged.

8. Infant appears physically and/or psychologically uncared-for.

9. Infant delayed or precocious in motor and language skills.

903. Anxious/Tense relationship

Tense, constricted, with little sense of relaxed enjoyment or mutuality

1. Parent overprotective and oversensitive.

2. Awkward or tense handling of infant.

3. Some verbally/emotionally negative interactions.

4. Poor temperamental fit.

5. Infant very compliant or anxious.

904. Angry/Hostile relationship

Harsh and abrupt, often lacking in emotional reciprocity

1. Parent insensitive to infant's cues.

2. Handling of infant is abrupt.

3. Infant frightened, anxious, inhibited, impulsive, or diffusely aggressive.

4. Infant's behavior defiant or resistant.

5. Demanding or aggressive behaviors in infant.

6. Fearful, vigilant, and avoidant behaviors in infant.

7. Tendency toward concrete behavior in child.

905. Mixed relationship

Combination of the features described above.

906. Abusive relationships

    a. Verbally abusive relationship
    b. Physically abusive relationship
    c. Sexually abusive relationship

Axis III: Medical and developmental disorders and conditions

Axis III should be used to note any physical (including medical and neurological), mental health, and/or developmental diagnoses made using other diagnostic and classification systems. These systems include the American Psychiatric Association's *Diagnostic and Statistical Manual (DSM IV)*, *International Statistical Classification of Diseases* (ICD-10), the American Academy of Pediatrics' *Diagnostic and Statistical Manual for Primary Care (DSM-PC) Child and Adolescent Version*, and specific classifications used by speech/language pathologists, occupational therapists, physical therapists, and special educators.

Axis IV: Psychosocial stressors

This axis is included to help clinicians take into account various forms and severity of psychosocial stress that are directly or indirectly present in the life of an infant or young child. The ultimate impact of a stressful event or enduring stress depends on three factors:

• the severity of the stressor (its intensity and duration at that level of intensity, the suddenness of the initial stress, and the frequency and unpredictability of its recurrence);

• the developmental level of the child (chronological age, endowment, and ego strength); and

• the availability and capacity of adults in the caregiving environment to serve as a protective buffer and help the child understand and deal with the stressor.

The clinician should identify the source or sources of psychosocial stress on the child (for example, foster placement, medical illness, parental illness, poverty, violence in the environment) and rate the overall impact of psychosocial stressors on the child as:

• No obvious effect.

• Mild effects—cause recognizable strain, tension, or anxiety but do not interfere with infant's overall adaptation.

• Moderate effects—derail child in areas of adaptation but not in core areas of relatedness and communication.

• Severe effects—cause significant derailment in core areas of adaptation.

Axis V: Functional Emotional Developmental Level

This axis addresses the way in which the infant organizes affective, interactive, communicative, cognitive, motor, and sensory experience, reflected in his/her functioning. Seven developmental levels are offered, each characterized by an essential process or capacities. The age range at which each ability begins to develop is also indicated. It is important to note that while the processes that constitute various developmental levels initially emerge in a developmental progression, once an infant or young child is past the expected age for a process to be evident, the child may show these processes to different degrees. The levels are:

Mutual attention (all ages)

Capacity of the infant or young child to show interest in the world by looking and listening; the ability of the dyad to attend to one another and remain calm and focused.

Mutual engagement (readily observable between 3 and 6 months)

Capacity for joint emotional involvement, seen in looks and other gestures that convey a sense of pleasure and affective engagement.

Interactive intentionality and reciprocity (6-18 months)

Capacity for cause and effect interaction, where the infant signals and responds purposefully to another person's signals; involves sensorimotor patterns and a range of emotional inclinations.

Representational/affective communication (over 18 months)

Capacity to use mental representations, as evidenced in language and play, to communicate emotional themes.

Representational elaboration (over 30 months)

Ability to elaborate in pretend play and symbolic communication a number of ideas that go beyond basic needs and deal with more complex intentions, wishes, or feelings; ideas need not be logically connected.

Representational differentiation I (over 36 months)

Ability to deal with complex intentions, wishes, and feelings in pretend play and symbolic communication in which ideas are logically related; ability to distinguish and switch between reality and fantasy.

Representational differentiation II (over 42 months)

Ability to elaborate complex pretend play and symbolic communication, characterized by three or more ideas, logically connected and informed by concepts of causality, time, and space.

Assessment of the infant or young child's functional emotional developmental level should be based on observations of the infant interacting with each of his or her parents or other significant caregivers. Toward the end of the evaluation, the assessor should also evaluate the quality of his/her own interaction with the child, and indicate levels reached.

In evaluating the infant or young child's functional emotional developmental level, the clinician should consider the levels the child has reached, whether these levels are age-appropriate, how long they can be sustained, and the conditions required for the child to be fully engaged in them. The clinician should consider the following questions for each level (e.g., mutual attention, mutual engagement):

• Has the infant reached his or her expected age capacities with regard to the functions of this level?

• Can the infant respond at age-appropriate levels under a variety of conditions, including various affect states or under stress?

• Can the infant respond more appropriately when the parent supports the interaction by providing sensory-motor facilitation?

• Can the infant respond more appropriately when the parent reduces the level of potentially stressful or confusing stimulation in the environment?

• Does the parent need to be especially gifted to elicit age-appropriate interactions?

The PIR-GAS

The Parent Infant Relationship Global Assessment Scale (PIR-GAS) provides a continuously distributed scale of infant-parent relationship functioning, ranging from "well adapted" (90) to "grossly impaired" (10). This measure was derived from the model of relationship disturbances described by Anders (1989), which includes relationship perturbations, disturbances, and disorders. PIRGAS ratings **below** 40 qualify for a relationship diagnosis.

90 Well adapted

Relationships in this range are functioning exceptionally well. They are not only mutually enjoyable and unusually conflict free, but they are also growth promoting for both partners' development.

80 Adapted

Relationships in this range of functioning evidence no significant psychopathology. They are characterized by interactions that are frequently reciprocal and synchronous and are reasonably enjoyable. The developmental progress of the partners is not impeded in any way by the pattern of the relationship, which is "good enough" for both partners.

70 Perturbed

Relationships in this range are functioning less than optimally in some way. The disturbance is limited to one domain of functioning, and overall the relationship still functions reasonably well. The disturbance lasts from a few days to a few weeks. For example, an infant with a minor physical illness sleeps poorly for several nights, exhausting his parents; or parents moving into a new house are less attentive to their infant, who is less able to self-regulate in the unfamiliar surroundings.

60 Significantly perturbed

Relationships in this range of functioning are strained in some way but are still largely adequate and satisfying to the partners. The disturbance is not pervasive across a large number of domains but rather is limited to one or two problematic areas. Further, the dyad seems likely to negotiate the challenge successfully and the pattern not to be enduring. The disturbance lasts no longer than a month. Caregivers may be stressed by the perturbation, but they are generally not overconcerned about the changed relationship patterns, instead considering it within the range of expectable responses that are likely to be relatively short-lived. For example, a toddler develops food refusal for the first time following the birth of a new sibling.

50 Distressed

Relationships in this range of functioning are more than transiently affected, but they still maintain some flexibility and adaptive qualities. One or both partners may be experiencing some distress in the context of the relationship, and the developmental progress of the dyad seems likely to be impeded if the pattern does not improve. Caregivers may or may not be concerned about the disturbed relationship pattern, but overt symptoms resulting from the disturbance in either partner are unlikely. For example, a child is distressed frequently when her mother ignores her cues to slow down during feedings and face-to-face interactions. Other domains of functioning show no interaction problems or child distress.

40 Disturbed

Relationships in this range of functioning appear to place the dyad at significant risk for dysfunction. The relationship's adaptive qualities are beginning to be overshadowed by problematic features of the relationship. Although not deeply entrenched, the patterns appear more than transient and are beginning to adversely affect the subjective experience of one or both partners. For example, parent and child engage in excessive teasing and power struggles in multiple domains, including feeding, dressing, and bedtime. Although parent and child attempt pleasurable interactions, they often go too far, leaving one or both partners distressed.

30 Disordered

Relationships in this range of functioning are characterized by relatively stable, maladaptive interactions and distress in one or both partners within the context of the relationship. Rigidly maladaptive interactions, particularly if they involve distress in one or both partners, are the hallmark of disordered relationships. Although generally conflicted, interactions in disordered relationships may instead be grossly inappropriate developmentally, without overt conflicts. For example, a depressed parent repeatedly seeks comfort from his or her infant, actively recruiting caregiving behavior from the child.

20 Severely disordered

Relationships in this range of functioning are severely compromised. One or, more likely, both partners are significantly distressed by the relationship itself. Maladaptive interactive patterns are rigidly entrenched, appear to be relatively impervious to change, and seem to be of relatively long duration, although the onset may be insidious. A significant proportion of interactions is almost always conflicted. For example, a father and his toddler frequently interact in a conflicted manner. The father sets no limits until he becomes enraged, and then he spanks the toddler vigorously. The toddler is provocative, and the father feels angry with him all the time.

10 Grossly impaired

Relationships in this range of functioning are dangerously disorganized. Interactions are disturbed so frequently that the infant is in imminent danger of physical harm.

References

American Psychiatric Association. (1994). *Diagnostic and statistical manual of mental disorders*, Fourth Edition. Washington, DC: American Psychiatric Association.

Anders, T.F. (1989). Clinical syndromes, relationship disturbances and their assessment. In A. J. Sameroff & R. N. Emde (Eds.), *Relationship disturbances in early childhood* [pp. 125-162]. New York: Basic Books.

Wolraich, M.L. (Ed.). (1996). *The classification of child and adolescent mental diagnoses in primary care: Diagnostic and statistical manual for primary care (DSM-PC) child and adolescent version*. Elk Grove Village, IL: American Academy of Pediatrics.

World Health Organization. (1992). *International Statistical Classification of Diseases and Related Health Problems* (ICD-10), 10th Revision. Geneva World Health Organization.

ZERO TO THREE. (1994). *Diagnostic classification of mental health and developmental disorders of infancy and early childhood*. Arlington, VA: ZERO TO THREE: National Center for Clinical Infant Programs.

100. Traumatic Stress Disorder

Theodore J. Gaensbauer, M.D.

Traumatic Stress Disorder refers to the characteristic symptomatology observed in children who have experienced either single or multiple traumatic events. Symptoms include traumatic reexperiencing; numbing of responsiveness or interference with developmental momentum, or both; increased arousal, various nonverbal reactions, and increased fearfulness or aggression, or both. The case of Austin presents the situation of a child whose development was proceeding uneventfully until he was traumatized as a result of medical illness and treatment.

Reason for referral

At age 2 years 10 months, Austin was referred following what had been expected to be a routine consultation with a plastic surgeon related to a hand injury he had sustained 18 months earlier. When the surgeon entered the room, Austin screamed in panic and physically resisted any approach. Based on this extreme reaction, the surgeon recommended a psychiatric consultation.

Assessment process

Initially the therapist met with Austin's parents to gather information about his injury, his medical treatments, and his symptoms and adjustment from the time of the injury to the present. The therapist also obtained developmental and family history in order to put Austin's reactions to the injuries in the context of his overall development and the family system. Following the parental interview, the therapist met with Austin for two office sessions, observing him both in spontaneous play and in structured play situations. Structured situations were utilized to facilitate reenactments of his traumatic experiences in ways which would allow assessment of his emotional reactions. One or both of Austin's parents, usually his mother, participated in all of the evaluation and treatment sessions.

Assessment findings

History of medical illness and treatments

At 15¹/₂ months, Austin was hospitalized for a cellulitis on his leg. As he was receiving intravenous antibiotics, fluid began infiltrating into the soft tissues on the back of his hand. Because of extensive wrapping, the infiltration was not discovered for several hours. By this time, his hand and arm were extremely swollen and "rock hard." Emergency interventions included puncturing his hand over 40 times with a needle and syringe, both to allow fluid to escape and to inject chemicals designed to neutralize the burning. Swelling receded gradually, and Austin was discharged three days later. Unfortunately, tissue necrosis developed at the infiltration site, requiring oral medications and repeated outpatient office treatments for cleansing and debridement. Two weeks later, Austin was rehospitalized for a surgical debridement extending to the depth of bone and tendons. Two days later, a skin graft from his thigh to the back of his hand was performed. Both procedures were done under general anesthesia. (Further details regarding these procedures are provided as they emerged in the therapy.)

Austin was required to wear a neoprene glove for the next eight months to keep the skin graft in place. The hand eventually healed with a thick 2-inch-square scar over the top of his hand, allowing normal strength and full range of motion. The prognosis for future function was excellent. There was uncertainty, however, about whether surgical revision of the scar would be required at some future time to allow his hand to grow normally. It was at the meeting with the plastic surgeon who was to evaluate this question that Austin had become so severely upset.

Symptomatology

Austin's parents described a number of psychological symptoms following his injury and treatments. He was extremely fussy and clingy during the next several weeks, wanted to be held constantly, and was difficult to soothe. He was also limp and withdrawn, and lost interest in the kinds of activities that he had previously greatly enjoyed. His parents commented that "nothing made him happy." He also developed significant sleep difficulties. Prior to the injury, he had been sleeping through the night. After the injury and treatments, he showed frequent distressed awakenings and did not sleep a whole night through for the next several months. It took approximately a year before he was consistently able to sleep the entire night in his own bed. His parents recalled one apparent nightmare, when he suddenly awoke crying and wanted his mother, although he did not describe any specific imagery. He also exhibited developmental regressions in walking and talking. Prior to the injuries he had been walking on his own and speaking single words; following the injuries he wanted to be carried everywhere and seemed less coordinated when he began walking again. He gave up learning new words for a month or so, and mostly whined for his parents.

Austin also showed an increase in aggression. Whereas previously he had been very social and shown little anger, he began to have temper tantrums and episodes of angry defiance. At day care, there were a number of instances where he threw toys and hit and bit his playmates. He bit his parents on their shoulders while being held, or on their legs if he wanted to be held. His play also became more disorganized. He seemed more distractible and less able to sustain his play activities. As a result of his increased aggression and difficulties in being calmed, Austin required more discipline than in the past, resulting in increased tension between him and his parents. His mother commented that getting him to wear his neoprene glove was a constant battle.

In addition to these more general symptoms, Austin showed traumatic reexperiencing in a number of forms. His panic reaction at the plastic surgeon's office appeared to express his fear that his previous painful encounters with doctors would be repeated. Whenever doctors were mentioned he would exclaim, "I don't need to go to the doctor!" He also became fearful whenever the family drove by the hospital where he had been cared for. Fearful associations of a more indirect nature were also seen. For example, whenever his parents cautioned him about being "burned" (as on the stove), he would become very fearful and back away.

Reenactment play involving his hand was seen in the form of a recurrent game he played with his mother, consisting of her "fixing his hand" by putting bandages on it and kissing it to make it better. This bandaging activity had generalized to the point where he liked to put band-aids and stickers on "every little bump"—his fingers, head, ears, and even his teeth. Austin was also very sensitive about his hand and manifested a sense of vulnerability when attention was drawn to it. Whereas previously he had used both hands interchangeably, he stopped using his injured hand for activities such as drawing or throwing. He would hide it under his other arm whenever someone asked him about the scar or conceal it between his own body and a parent's body when he was being held. Recently, as his mother was putting sunscreen on his hand, he said to her: "It's gross, isn't it, Mommy?"

Austin's parents had attempted to help him with his symptoms and feelings through their increased availability and by physical and emotional comforting. They said they had not talked directly to Austin about his injuries because they had been told by his doctors that he was too young to experience pain or to remember the events, and that it would therefore be better not to bring them up. Nonetheless, they felt that Austin was a very observant child with an excellent memory and that he may very well have overheard them talking about his medical problems.

Developmental history

Austin was the well-loved, only child of a young, high-functioning couple. His conception was planned, and he was the product of a normal pregnancy, labor, and delivery. His father was successfully employed in business. His mother remained home with him for three months and then returned to three-quarter-time work. For his first two years he was cared for in a home day care setting with a few other children. At age 2 he was enrolled in a small preschool. Austin was described as a very easy, good-natured, and highly social baby. His parents recalled very little fussing. Feeding and sleeping routines had been established easily. By 6 months of age he was sleeping through the night. Developmental milestones had all been observed within normal time frames. He was crawling by 8 months of age and walking by one year. At 15 months his language attainment involved multiple single words. Following the one-to-two-month regression in language described above, he regained his momentum quickly and was speaking in complete sentences by age 2 years. Socially, Austin had been exposed to adults at his day care and during frequent visits with his parents' extended family. He had shown only low levels of anxiety around unfamiliar people and occasional, mild separation distress when left by his parents. Prior to his injury he had responded well to limit setting; temper tantrums or significant anger had not been observed. When he developed temper outbursts following his injury and medical treatments, his parents had not been sure if the upsurge in anger was related to his traumatic experiences or simply marked the onset of the developmentally expectable "terrible twos." In retrospect, they dated the onset to the time of his treatments. Apart from the problems with his hand and several mild ear infections, Austin's health had been excellent.

At the time of the initial evaluation, other than the symptoms described above, Austin's parents felt that for the most part he had regained the predominantly happy, energetic, and sociable disposition that had been characteristic of his first 15 months of life.

Observations from evaluation sessions

In the first session, Austin presented as an appealing, well-cared-for child who appeared advanced in his overall development. He smiled when the therapist greeted him in the waiting room but entered the playroom cautiously and somewhat fearfully, holding his mother's hand. Prior to the session, he had been told he was going to see a doctor who would talk to him about his hand. He had responded that he didn't need to go to a doctor and did not want to talk about his hand. Nevertheless, within several minutes of his arrival he became more comfortable and was able to show the therapist his scarred hand. He said a nurse "didn't turn it" and that it had hurt. When asked how he felt when it hurt, he responded, "Good." He denied having felt sad or scared.

As the session progressed, the therapist brought out a box containing play hospital equipment and began setting the play materials out on the table. With Austin's participation the therapist identified a specific doll figure to represent Austin. Austin initially stayed away from the hospital furniture being laid out but explored other play materials in the same boxes. Some tiny play medicine bottles caught his interest. He recognized them as medicines and then spontaneously put one of the bottles over the hand and then in the mouth of the boy doll designated as Austin. Together Austin and the therapist identified which dolls were to represent his parents and the doctors and nurses. Austin then put the little boy doll in an area away from the hospital equipment, surrounding it with several pieces of toy furniture like a fort, and placed the mother and father dolls nearby.

During this initial exploratory play, one noteworthy reaction was his avoidance of the concept of shots. As the various play items were brought out—soaps, medicines, scissors—he was able to identify each one. When the therapist pulled out a tiny play injection syringe (one-half inch in length), however, he refused to identify it. He hesitated, and then said it was a pen. When the therapist observed that it looked like something for shots and asked if he didn't like it, Austin replied that the boy didn't want shots. He was clearly tense at that moment.

As the session progressed Austin became more and more engaged in the hospital play. He placed the boy in the hospital bed and placed a toy crutch next to the boy's leg. His mother said that after his skin graft, to protect an intravenous site, he had been placed in a splint which extended down the side of his leg. Finding a play knife, he spontaneously poked it into his own hand and then poked the therapist, saying, "It's all better." Somewhat later, he found another boy doll and put it in a toy cupboard in such a way that the boy's hand was squeezed by the cupboard door. Austin commented that "[the doll's] hand is caught" and that "he has a hole in his hand"; there was indeed a small tear in the doll's arm. Taking a small plastic thermometer, he poked the hand of the little boy doll (rather than the arm where the hole actually was) and showed his mother the "hole." He wanted to put bandages on the doll's hand, which he and the therapist did using paper tissues and scotch tape, and then said again "It's all better." Following this "hole in the hand" play, Austin became somewhat wild. He pointed a toy rifle at the therapist and ran at him with the gun aimed directly at his genital area.

In the second evaluation session, Austin returned to the materials used in the previous session, remembering and naming all of the items. He put a baby doll in bed and said the baby was sick, and then said the baby was all better. He then said a "nurse" doll was sick, put that doll in bed, and wanted to put a "bandage" on her hand. Serving as his helper, the therapist asked Austin if we should give the nurse any medicines. This question made him anxious. He interrupted the play, jumped up and down in an agitated way, and became rather aggressive. He pointed a gun at the nurse, then took a truck and smashed all of the hospital equipment from the table onto the floor.

Later, he returned to the hospital play and found the boy doll with the "hole in the hand" from the previous session. He wanted to put a bandage on the boy doll's hand, but instead brought out some surgical knives which he pressed against the back of the boy's hand. As this play was proceeding, the therapist again pulled out the tiny toy injection needle. Austin immediately became anxious, asking, "What's that?" and moved closer to his mother. Clearly the play had lost its "pretend" quality at that moment. Reassured by his mother and the therapist, he became more relaxed. The therapist empathized with how frightened he was of shots and how much he hated them.

Following each of the evaluation sessions, there was a transient upsurge in symptoms similar to those seen following the original injuries, including regressed behavior, whininess, and disorganized hyperactivity. After the second session, his mother felt he was "almost out of control." Later that day he hit two playmates and bit a third at his preschool, actions which had not been seen for several months.

Diagnosis

The therapist judged that Austin's symptoms were consistent with the diagnosis of Traumatic Stress Disorder. His traumatic experiences involved both the original injury to his hand and the series of painful medical treatments and surgeries that followed. Symptoms observed by his parents included: a) traumatic reexperiencing, manifested by reenactment play involving preoccupation with his hand, distress at exposure to reminders such as doctors and hospitals, and avoidance both of situational reminders of his injury, such as places where he might be "burned," and of physical reminders, reflected in the hiding of his hand; b) numbing of responsiveness and interference with developmental momentum, manifested by social withdrawal and constriction in play, temporary disruption in the skills of walking and talking, and a dampening in the capacity for pleasure; c) symptoms of increased arousal, including sleep difficulties, increased fussiness that was difficult to soothe, and disorganization and distractibility in his play; and d) generalized signs of increased anxiety and aggression. Acute symptoms were observed for several months and then gradually diminished over the next year. Nevertheless, symptoms of traumatic reexperiencing and increased arousal were still present 18 months later.

Austin's reenactment play in the evaluation sessions revealed his continued anxious preoccupation with his injured hand, the depth of his unresolved anger, and the impressive extent of his memory about his injury and treatments. While verbally denying having been frightened or sad, his initial avoidance of the hospital scene and his hiding the boy doll away from the doctors and nurses gave evidence of his fearfulness. He was able to play out many specific aspects of his experience, such as taking medicines, having a splint on his leg, being poked in the hand with a knife "to make it all better," and bandaging the boy doll with a "hole in his hand." Unresolved fears related to "shots" were very evident in his reaction to the toy syringe. Poorly modulated anger, especially toward doctors and hospitals, was evident in his gun play, his smashing of the toy hospital scene, and his direct attack on me.

In light of his normal development prior to the injury and the direct relationship between his hospital experiences and his symptoms, the diagnosis of Traumatic Stress Disorder seemed straightforward. The painful, frightening nature of his medical experiences and the duration of his symptoms made the diagnosis of an Adjustment Disorder inappropriate. The therapist was not able to identify earlier developmental experiences or parental influences which might have placed Austin at increased risk for emotional disturbance following a traumatic event. On the contrary, his solid early development and strong parental support appeared to be protective in ameliorating the severity of his symptoms. At the time of the evaluation, there was increased conflict in the family concerning limit setting and disciplinary issues. While it was possible that this might have become a developmental issue in any case, since Austin's parents were indulgent by nature, it appeared that the conflicts derived primarily from the events surrounding the hand injury. Austin's parents had given him extra love and attention in attempting to console him for his suffering. On the other hand, they had been required to impose a variety of painful medical procedures on him that had provoked anger and resistance. The overall result was that Austin appeared to have a lower frustration tolerance for being disciplined than he had shown previously. While creating strain, the interactional conflicts did not seem severe enough to merit an additional diagnosis, such as a relationship disorder.

Diagnostic Summary

Axis I: Primary Diagnosis
Traumatic Stress Disorder.

Axis II: Relationship Disorder Classification
No diagnosis.

Axis III: Medical and Developmental Disorders and Conditions
Third degree burn of the back of hand with necrosis of underlying tissues (OCD-9 944.46).

Axis IV: Psychosocial Stressors
Hospitalization for cellulitis, infiltration of back of hand with subsequent necrosis, numerous painful debridements, two surgeries for debridement, and a skin graft.
Overall effects: moderate to severe in nature, though circumscribed in time.

Axis V: Functional Emotional Developmental Level
Age-appropriate representational elaboration with focal areas of emotional vulnerability related to the trauma. Had fully reached mutual attention, mutual engagement, interactive intentionality and reciprocity, and representational/affective communication.

PIR-GAS: 90 (Well-adapted)

Discussion with caregivers and treatment planning

Based on the formulation described above, the therapist recommended a course of psychotherapeutic treatment utilizing play therapy techniques and parental participation similar to the approach described in the two evaluation sessions. Given the relatively manageable nature of the trauma, the good

prognosis for normal functioning of his hand, his optimal early development, and solid parental support, the therapist expected Austin would have
a good response to therapy.

Through the psychotherapeutic work, the therapist hoped to facilitate a
re-experiencing of the various traumatic events within a safe environment in
order to reduce the intensity of the posttraumatic affects and to help Austin
develop a sense of mastery over the entire experience. Since the events had
occurred at such a young age and in rapid succession, the therapist also
hoped to help Austin develop a more coherent understanding of what happened to him and why, so that the experience could be lifted out of the realm
of what he would have perceived as unpredictable and personalized attacks.
Developing a meaningful narrative seemed the predominant therapeutic
challenge, given the fact that the traumatic events had occurred prior to the
onset of language fluency. By providing opportunities for the communication of his nonverbal understanding, the therapist hoped to help him con-
vert his preverbal sensory, behavioral, and affective representations into verbally accessible memories and feelings. The goal was to connect Austin's various traumatic feelings to the specific traumatic events which had evoked
them, instead of having them be expressed in generalized regressive behavior
and diffuse anger. The therapist anticipated working collaboratively with
Austin's parents throughout the therapy, identifying together how Austin's
current functioning was continuing to be affected by his earlier traumas and
developing constructive approaches to help him in the home environment.

Intervention

The therapist met with Austin for 14 additional sessions during the next 4
months, initially for two sessions per week, then weekly for several weeks,
and eventually biweekly. For the most part, initiative rested with Austin in
regard to the particular play materials and themes that were the subject of
focus. At the same time, however, the therapist was active in introducing
reenactment situations and themes which seemed important to deal with.
Austin's drive to rework and integrate his unresolved posttraumatic feelings
was most impressive. In each of the next 10 sessions Austin spontaneously
sought out the hospital play materials at the beginning of each session. The
format of the sessions involved moving back and forth between interactions
with Austin around play themes and reenactments, and discussions with his
parents both about the events being played out in the sessions and his behavioral adjustment at home.

While difficult to summarize in a neat package, several phases of the
therapy can be highlighted. Initially, Austin's play seemed to focus on the
most immediate physical aspects of his painful treatments, such as shots,
debridements, and the taking of medications, relatively isolated from any situational contexts. Eventually his mother and the therapist were able to help
place these painful experiences in some perspective by following through
with a sequential narrative organized around the original intravenous infil-

tration and the second hospitalization and surgeries two weeks later. Toward the end of the therapy, the impact of the trauma on the larger developmental issues of his aggression and his sense of bodily integrity became areas of focus.

Therapeutic process

One of the initial therapeutic goals was to assist Austin's parents in their understanding of the different ways in which Austin's posttraumatic feelings were being manifested and to help them look beyond his overt behavior to the meaning behind it. In the interpretive hour, the therapist attempted to highlight the relationship between the posttraumatic themes elicited in the two evaluation sessions and the "wildness" that immediately followed. An opportunity to further explore the relationship between Austin's overt behavior and his underlying feelings occurred in the first session following the interpretive hour. The preceding weekend Austin had stayed with close relatives while his parents were away. Following his parents return, Austin was hyperactive, whiny, and defiant. At one point, holding a toy gun, he said he wanted to "shoot mommy dead." His parents had tended to respond concretely to his misbehavior rather than to the underlying feelings. For example, his mother's response to his expressed wish to "shoot mommy" was guilt inducing: "If you shoot me dead, who will take care of you?" As she reviewed Austin's reactions with the therapist in the session, his mother was able to see the underlying feelings of anxiety and abandonment which had fueled his anger and was able to connect them to his increased sense of vulnerability in his parent's absence as a result of his hand injury and treatments. She recalled an occasion after his surgeries when Austin had been left with relatives with whom he was very familiar and had been frightened by a minor event which previously would not have bothered him.

Austin's play in this session corroborated the association between parental separation and increased fearfulness. It also illustrated his preoccupation with the experience-near physical aspects of his painful treatments, in this case the repeated debridements. As his mother and the therapist were talking, he played out that the "father" doll was cut on the foot with a knife. Then a baby doll's leg was cut, followed by a boy doll who got a cut on the hand. While telling the therapist that the boy's hand hurt, he unconsciously wrapped his own hand inside his T-shirt. The therapist interpreted his actions to mean that Austin feared something bad might happen to him while his mother and father were away and he was angry at being left. Austin denied verbally that he was scared or angry, but appeared to confirm the interpretation in his actions. He first knocked over the mother and father dolls, and then all the rest of the hospital play materials. As described below, his fears about being separated became much more understandable as the circumstances surrounding his two surgeries were clarified.

In the next session, a play interaction focused around the taking of medication illustrated Austin's continued preoccupation with the experience-near details of his treatment, as well as a therapeutic approach that seemed helpful in bringing out his feelings. After saying that one of the boy dolls with a mark on his foot was hurt, he pulled out the toy medicine bottles. Austin assigned the therapist the part of the boy. As a way of communicating understanding about Austin's anger at all the medical procedures that had been forced on him, the therapist pretended he did not want to take the medicines. Austin was surprised, then delighted with this idea. He immediately wanted to change roles and be the boy who was refusing the medicines. He and the therapist repeated a sequence of the therapist offering a medicine and his refusing it seven or eight times, using every one of the bottles in the toy kit. The first time he played the boy role he screamed: "I don't like it!" with great intensity, conveying the very real distress associated with being forced to take unpleasant medicines. With each sequence his tone became lighter, so that by the end of the repeated cycles we were both laughing at the boy's audacity and success at resisting.

Shortly after, however, Austin's conflicted feelings about his anger were revealed when he took a toy gun and wanted to shoot the boy doll who was refusing the medicines. This play allowed his mother and the therapist to validate his anger about all of the medical interventions and also to empathize with his feelings that he was not supposed to be angry. His mother remembered how they had encouraged Austin to be a good boy when they were getting him to take his medicines. Austin then carried out a gesture that seemed to express his past submission to his treatments by bringing over some stickers for the therapist to place on his hand and wrist. At the end of the session, however, Austin again expressed anger by smashing the hospital toys to the floor with a truck. He nodded in agreement when the therapist commented that he didn't like hospitals and doctors.

Prior to the next session, clearly preoccupied by fears of what might happen to him in the therapist's office, Austin had asked his mother if the therapist was the doctor who was going to fix his hand. During the session his mother and the therapist were able to utilize role playing to help him master these fears and to conceptualize other feelings he had not been allowed to express. He found a toy doctor kit and began to examine the therapist with a stethoscope. Playing the role of the frightened patient, the therapist drew a red mark on the back of his hand, and offered it to Austin for treatment while pretending to be very scared. Austin held and rubbed the back of the therapist's hand in the process of examining it, saying, reassuringly, "It won't hurt." The therapist said he knew it would. Austin then turned to examine his mother's hand. She, too, pretended to be afraid that it would hurt, despite Austin's assurances. Austin seemed at a loss as to how to respond to his therapist's and mother's insistence that it would hurt. It was as if he had not assimilated the possibility of expressing such a feeling, having identified with the repeated reassurances that he had received from parents and medical personnel.

Having played out the various intrusive and painful medical treatments over the course of several sessions in the absence of any context, it seemed an appropriate time to systematically take him through the actual sequence of events in order to help him put his experiences into their proper setting. The therapist asked Austin's mother to go over exactly what happened to him at the time of the initial infiltration. As she was describing the events the therapist drew the scene on paper with Austin's active participation. In an effort to mitigate Austin's anger by helping him to recognize that his parents were very distressed as well, the therapist explicitly asked his mother to describe their feelings and then drew his parents looking very worried and sad. To emphasize the idea of his swollen hand, the therapist made a tracing of his hand on the paper and drew a large red mark on the back of it. Austin promptly grabbed the pen and wanted to trace his own hand. However, instead of tracing the periphery of his hand as the therapist had done, he moved the pen in an up and down "poking" motion, making short marks along the side of each of his fingers. His mother was immediately reminded of how Austin's hand and fingers had been punctured with needles in order to release the fluid in his hand.

This poking gesture was striking in its suggestion that a specific detail of his experience had been retained in Austin's mind 20 months later. Memory for this kind of specific detail had been previously demonstrated when he placed the crutch/splint along the side of his leg in the second session. Another example of the possible reenactment of a specific memory occurred in a later session. After putting the boy doll in a hospital bed, Austin placed the mother doll at the foot of the bed and pushed the bed over to a play swing set and slide that he had set up on another part of the table. His parents remembered that during his initial hospitalization they had on several occasions taken Austin in a wheelchair to an area of the hospital where similar play equipment was available.

Having reviewed the events around the original injury, in a subsequent session the therapist asked Austin's mother to describe the follow-up hospitalization for the surgical debridement and skin graft. She felt this was the most stressful time for everyone. Prior to this moment his treatments had been limited to his hand, and his parents had been able to be with him throughout. For each of his surgeries he was taken from his parents and carried by a nurse to the operating room, screaming all the way. His mother recalled that when they rejoined him in the recovery room following the debridement procedure, he was struggling desperately to get out of his restraints. Following the skin graft procedure, Austin was immobilized as well, with three limbs bandaged and one arm tied over his head.

This was clearly the most difficult experience for Austin to explore. As his mother began to talk about this period and drew the operating scene on paper, Austin developed a "tummy ache" and wanted to go to the bathroom. When they returned, his mother resumed her drawing. Austin immediately stated he had another tummy ache and became very distressed and whiny, pulling on his mother and falling to the floor when she did not want to take him to the bathroom again. He then took a truck and ran it across his mother's drawing, saying that he did not like that picture any more. After empathic discussion of his intense fearfulness about these events he let his mother tell the story using the doll figures and play materials he and the therapist had used previously. As his mother set up the operating room scene, Austin handed the therapist the baby boy doll, wanting him to draw the baby's hand red. His mother then took the boy doll out of the "nurse" doll's arms and carried him to the operating table. Following the operation, he and the therapist bandaged the doll on three of his limbs and carried him to his hospital bed with his arm over his head. In an obvious wishful fantasy, Austin hid the boy doll behind some plastic screens, which served as dividers between the hospital beds. He said the baby was hiding from the nurse. Austin then had the nurse doll give the boy doll to the father doll, saying she did not want the baby anymore. He then put the mother, father, and baby dolls all together behind the screen with the nurse doll searching for all of them. When the nurse doll finally found them, he had the father doll push the nurse doll, saying "You go away." He repeated this sequence several times. His mother and the therapist talked about how scared and angry he had been about the nurse taking him to the surgery, and that his parents wished they could have sent the nurse away as well.

Austin's unresolved feelings about the surgeries were reflected by several distressed awakenings that occurred for the next several nights. He complained that he was afraid of monsters and needed to sleep in his parents' bed. His parents at this point were very attuned to the meanings of his regressive behavior and were able to interpret his fearfulness in relation to the events being discussed in therapy. They talked with him frequently during the next few days about his feelings about the surgeries with a resultant calming effect. Both in the sessions and at home, Austin seemed able to modulate the amount of information he could handle by indicating when it was "too scary" or saying he had a tummy ache when he had talked enough. For example, in a subsequent session when focused on the baby doll on the operating table surrounded by the doctors and nurses and away from his family, the therapist commented, "The baby is scared." With a very serious look on his face, Austin repeated verbatim, "The baby is scared," and then immediately told his mother he had a stomach ache.

Reenactment play related to the surgeries continued for several sessions. Austin's play became progressively less affectively charged and more light-hearted, as well as more creatively expansive in its themes. He began to focus less on the little boy, for example, and spent time identifying dolls to represent his many relatives, including a number who were not actually at the hospital. He found chairs for each doll, took them to the bathroom, and played the "I don't like medicines" game with them. As his fearfulness diminished, he became less anxious at bedtime and was able to sleep through the night without needing his parents to be with him. He also became more comfortable about attention being drawn to his hand, no longer hid it under his arm, and began to use it for activities such as drawing and throwing.

During the latter part of the therapy, as his fearfulness in relation to the hospital scenes diminished, two issues relating to the impact of the traumas on his more general development came into focus. The first related to his anger about all of the painful experiences and its influence on the control of his aggression. In one session, he had the therapist draw a red mark indicating an injury on the hand of one of the doctor dolls. Looking determined and with great force, he pressed the play scalpel into the doctor's hand, nodding when the therapist commented that now the doctor would know how much it hurt. At times Austin's anger would be expressed by a generalized wildness, such as throwing toys or coming close to "accidentally" hitting his mother or the therapist, which would require limit setting. Over and above anger about the specific traumatic events being reenacted, there was a conditioned tendency toward heightened arousal which appeared to have grown out of the repeated mobilization of "fight-flight" physiological mechanisms of alarm. This tendency toward heightened arousal contributed to making his anger more intense and destructive than it might otherwise have been. His parents noted tendencies toward overexcitement even in happy situations. They commented that this excessive excitement often led to conflict because of his inability to respond to their attempts to calm him.

As discussed earlier, his parents were inclined to be permissive by nature. However, because of the intensity of his feelings they were required to be more strict and to administer more frequent punishments than they would have liked. At one point Austin himself commented with frustration and sadness about the amount of time he was spending in "time out." Because the maintenance of a balance between firmness and patient understanding was taxing to the parents, the therapist spent considerable time sharing his understanding and providing support to them around this issue. The combination of the parents' work with Austin at home and his opportunity to express angry feelings directly toward specific people and situations in the therapy sessions resulted in a gradual reduction in anger intensity.

The second developmental concern that emerged toward the end of treatment related to more general fears about bodily integrity, over and above his specific posttraumatic fears. On one occasion Austin spontaneously said to his mother in a frightened tone that he didn't want her to go to the doctor because he was afraid the doctor would cut off her hand and she would die. His anxiety about the loss of a body part was also reflected in his intense preoccupation with a children's story about a fox who had lost its tail. At the surface level the fears were obviously related to fantasies of losing his hand. There were also, however, several indications that these fantasies carried over to fears about his genital integrity. One bit of evidence was the fact that on several occasions, including the very first session, when he became aggressive in the midst of a discussion of his medical treatments he attacked the therapist's genital area. Another indicator was seen in an early session as the original hospital experience was being discussed and the therapist had drawn a picture of a little boy with an intravenous bottle and pole alongside. To enlist Austin's participation, the therapist asked him where the therapist should place the intravenous line. Rather than pointing to his leg, where the line had actually been, he pointed to the boy's genital area. Another time, while his mother was describing his skin graft during his second hospitalization,

Austin watched with particular intentness as the therapist drew a red mark on the side of the boy doll's thigh where the graft had been taken. His confusion about what had been done to him, particularly during the skin graft, had contributed to anxiety about whether his genitalia had also been damaged. This concern was becoming more prominent as he was entering the developmental phase where sexual differences were beginning to be understood. This issue was discussed with both Austin and his parents. Austin was probably too young to completely incorporate reassurances about his body and his genitals. The therapist hoped at least to make his parents aware of this issue so they could help him with any concerns that might arise during the next several years as issues of sexual differentiation and gender identification became even more prominent.

With the significant improvement in his symptomatology, Austin's parents felt that termination was appropriate. The therapist would have preferred to continue a little longer, but, nevertheless, felt optimistic that the major traumatic experiences had been opened up for reworking and that his parents had a good understanding of the various issues and how to help Austin with them. In addition to the symptomatic improvements previously described, there were several other indications that the traumatic feelings had been significantly reduced. Austin's hospital play had become less affectively charged and more playful. He was also much less preoccupied with doctor/hospital issues. In the last sessions he did not immediately proceed to the hospital toys, but found other items to play with.

Perhaps the most telling indicator of improvement was Austin's response to two medical appointments, one involving a routine visit to his pediatrician and the other a dental examination because of a chipped tooth. Both of these occurred toward the end of therapy. In the therapy sessions prior to the actual visits Austin was able to play out in an anticipatory way what was going to occur. This seemed helpful. Although he was anxious throughout, he was able to handle both situations well. It was not necessary to contact the doctors' offices directly to discuss with them ways to alleviate Austin's anxiety. (The therapist would have done so had he been less confident that Austin could handle the situations on his own.)

From a symptom standpoint, one area that had not been fully worked through was Austin's anger. As discussed above, although the therapist would have preferred to have had this pattern under better control prior to termination, he believed that the issue had been effectively opened up for discussion and continued reworking. He also believed that Austin's increased aggression related not only to specific anger about the various medical procedures, but to the carryover of generalized anger and over-arousal into various day-to-day situations. Thus, it appeared that internal control of these feelings would ultimately have to be worked out over an extended period of time in the context of repeated disciplinary interactions with his parents. Though the therapist had some concerns about the risk of a negative interactional cycle, he had a basic confidence in the parents' ability to provide a consistent, nonpunitive disciplinary structure and also felt that Austin's anger was not of an intensity that would prevent him from being responsive to his parents' disciplinary efforts.

In the last session the therapist, Austin and his mother reviewed the various experiences and feelings that had been touched on during the therapy. Austin acknowledged that it was still hard for him to talk about his hand because it made him feel bad. Questioned about specific feelings, he nodded in an ambiguous way when asked about sad feelings, but nodded in a very definitive way when asked about mad feelings. He was clearly both sad and angry about the termination and did not want to leave at the end of the session. He kept insisting he wanted to play with one more toy and refused to say good-bye.

Follow-up

The therapist saw Austin and his parents for a brief follow-up meeting nine months after the termination, just prior to his fourth birthday. Overall, his parents felt that he was doing well and that the therapy had accomplished the goals originally set for it. They said he had a clear understanding of his traumatic experiences and was comfortable discussing them without anxiety or anger. In particular, he was no longer self-conscious or defensive when attention was drawn to his hand. His father commented: "He's fine with it. It's part of him." Use of his injured hand had continued to expand to the point where he had returned to his previous level of ambidexterity.

Some persisting symptoms were noted, but at a much reduced affective intensity compared to before the therapy. His symptoms also seemed available to ongoing interpretation and amelioration, since both Austin and his parents were aware of their origins. He was continuing to show anxiety related to doctors and hospitals, for example, but within a manageable degree. During a recent visit to a hospital emergency room after his fingers had been squeezed in a door, he had been quite anxious but had been able to accept the doctor's reassurances and allowed the examination to be carried out. There had also been an episode of acute anxiety when he felt physically threatened by a peer at his preschool. He had been able to tell his parents and his teachers about his fears and had been effectively comforted. Intermittent episodes of aggressiveness persisted, including temper outbursts toward his parents when he didn't get his way, and occasional biting or pinching of playmates. His parents were continuing to handle his anger with patience and limit-setting and felt that he was "getting it."

One significant new symptom described by his parents was a "fixation" on knives and swords. Austin had begun to want to carry a knife in his pocket and would go through the kitchen drawers bringing out whatever knife he could find, to the point where his parents had put away all of the sharp knives. On several occasions, when angry, he had made threats while holding a knife. For example, at a recent picnic outing he had taken a plastic knife and threatened to cut another boy's hand. When watching movies, he was attracted to characters who carried swords, and was particularly fascinated with Captain Hook from *Peter Pan*. This character, having experienced the loss of one hand and carrying a sword in the other, seemed to exemplify both sides of Austin's conflict: fear of the loss of a body part and angry identification with the aggressor. The symptom suggested that Austin's anger about the medical procedures had not been fully resolved. In the midst of a developmental period when boys typically are engrossed in activities involving aggressive play with phallically representative toys, such as cars, guns, and missiles, these unresolved feelings were significantly coloring Austin's preoccupations. As with his other symptoms, Austin was quite conscious of the connection between his interest in knives and swords and his surgical experiences, and was able to talk about it.

Prognosis and discussion

In summary, there was considerable cause for optimism regarding Austin's long-term adjustment. The symptoms that brought him into therapy appeared to be resolved or reduced to manageable intensities. Those areas where symptoms were persisting seemed to be accessible to ongoing parental influence. Nonetheless, it was evident that the trauma had had important influences on Austin's development and was continuing to make itself felt. The appearance of the new symptom involving knives was a dramatic reminder that, although traumatic stress disorder symptoms may appear to be resolved, new or recurrent symptoms, or both, may emerge at later points in time and can significantly affect subsequent developmental issues. Therapists and parents should be aware that further therapy is often indicated.

200. Disorders of Affect

201. Anxiety Disorder

Robin C. Silverman, Ph.D.
Alicia F. Lieberman, Ph.D., and
Judith H. Pekarsky, Ph.D.[*]

Anxiety Disorder is characterized in young children by a pervasive affective experience of anxiety or fear when they are involved in ordinary daily interactions and routines or challenged by normative developmental tasks. Symptoms include pronounced mood dysregulation, excessive difficulties during separations and transitions, and recklessness and aggression directed to the self or others. In the case of Andy, ongoing difficulties in his relationship with his mother resulted in a chronic anxious state evidenced in reckless and defiant behaviors.

Reason for referral

Andy was referred to our clinic by his mother at the suggestion of a community social worker. Andy's mother Jan perceived her 22-month-old son as "out of control." He demonstrated extreme recklessness and aggression, and injured himself frequently, requiring trips to the emergency room. He bolted away from his mother for long distances without looking back, and ran in front of moving cars, to be yanked out of the way in the nick of time.

Difficulties in transitions, separations, or changes in routine frequently resulted in Andy's screaming, crying, and crashing about uncontrollably with his body. Andy's tantrums included head-banging, throwing himself on the floor, and breaking his furniture and toys The tantrums were so extreme that in the course of a single week he broke his mother's necklace, a typewriter, and the family television set. These tantrums often lasted for more than an hour.

[*] A version of this paper was presented at ZERO TO THREE's 10th National Training Institute in Atlanta, Georgia, December, 1995. Robin Silverman was the infant-parent therapist in this case, Alicia Lieberman the clinical supervisor, and Judith Pekarsky assisted with the conceptualization and writing of this paper. The authors wish to thank Maria St. John, Carina M. Grandison, and Charles Zeanah for their thoughtful readings of and commentary on versions of this paper.

In response to these tantrums, Jan became angry and demanded that Andy stop screaming and crying. She either yelled and slapped him, or ignored him. None of these attempts was successful in diminishing the tantrums, which ended when Andy collapsed in exhaustion and fell asleep. Jan reported that after waking from a tantrum-induced sleep, Andy would be withdrawn and emotionally brittle for hours.

Assessment process

Our clinic considers a 4-to-8 week assessment essential in the forging of a working alliance that will provide important information about the family. The evaluation includes both a developmental assessment and weekly home visits. During these initial home visits the therapist utilizes observation of and intervention with the family to provide a relatively seamless transition into ongoing treatment, when indicated.

In the case of Andy, the focus of the assessment was to gather information about Andy's reported symptoms and overall functioning as well as to learn more about Andy's relationships with his mother and his 6-month-old sister. At the end of the assessment period, infant-parent psychotherapy was agreed upon and commenced.

Assessment findings

History and background

The circumstances surrounding Andy's birth were quite difficult for both Jan and Andy. Jan dropped out of high school and left home at sixteen. She moved around to different adolescent crisis shelters or stayed with friends. Around this time she began to date Andy's father. Once Jan became pregnant, Andy's father left her. Jan gave birth to Andy at seventeen and then took care of him on her own. Several months after Andy's birth, Jan met and fell in love with Kenny. They moved in together quickly and Jan hoped that for the first time someone would take care of both her and Andy. Soon afterwards Jan became pregnant with Dee. Andy was 16 months old when Dee was born.

Jan reported that while she was living with Kenny she was depressed to the point that she could not get out of bed. Jan said that Kenny hit her. Kenny was also extremely critical of her parenting of both children, accusing her of allowing them to be "filthy," by which he meant they were unbathed and wearing dirty diapers. The extent and nature of the physical abuse to which Andy was exposed and personally subjected to at this time is unclear.

At 18 years old, Jan took her two children, 22-month-old Andy and 6-month-old Dee, and left Kenny. Jan soon felt overwhelmed by the unpredictable, extreme, and unmanageable quality of Andy's tantrums and she began to worry that Andy would "grow up to be like Kenny."

Developmental evaluation

The developmental evaluation comprises a brief interview with the mother, administration of the Bayley Scales of Infant Development, and a free-play observation period. During the interview, Jan reported that Andy was a full-term baby and that the birth was uncomplicated. Jan said that she did not drink alcohol or use other substances during her pregnancy with Andy.

From the information Jan provided it seemed that Andy met all of his developmental milestones on time and that, in spite of the environmental turmoil, he showed no indication of developmental delay. However, as an infant, Andy had difficulty falling asleep on his own and he cried inconsolably for no apparent reason. These difficulties persisted into his second year in the form of refusals to go to sleep and severe tantrums.

At 22 months, Andy had a sturdy, athletic body and carried himself like a little tank. He was an affectionate, serious, intelligent, and sensitive child with a well-developed capacity to understand many complex ideas. His affect was often intense and accompanied, it appeared to the therapist, by equally strong ideas about things that he could not yet articulate. His face was expressive and he demonstrated a wide range of affective responses.

During the administration of the Bayley Scales of Infant Development, Andy did not sit still or remain focused long enough to complete the structured tasks. When Andy did focus momentarily on a particular task he could complete it easily, indicating that he was generally within the normative developmental range and even had some skills that were advanced for his age.

For the most part, however, Andy moved around the room rapidly, climbed on the furniture, pulled all the objects off the shelves that were within his reach and established his own agenda, from which he could not be distracted. Because it was impossible to redirect him, the assessor ended the structured part of the assessment early and observed Andy for 30 minutes in free play.

While he was highly active, Andy was simultaneously acutely tuned in to his mother's conversation with the assessor. He was also vigilant in tracking the assessor's comings and goings and (as will be elaborated in the treatment section) during his free play he appeared preoccupied with certain themes which included spankings, separations, and deprivations.

Home visits

Home visits during the assessment period consisted of weekly one-hour sessions over a 60-day period. The visits focused on learning more about the relationships between Jan, Andy, and Dee, and their individual functioning in the context of the home environment. More specifically, the therapist tried to understand how the interaction and affective tone between Jan and Andy could explain aspects of Andy's worrisome behavior. At the same time, the therapist implemented case management efforts to improve the basic living conditions for the family and alleviate some of the external stressors.

Jan lived with her two young children in a barely habitable two-room unit. The stove and the heater were broken, the plaster was peeling off the walls, the plumbing was inconsistent at best, and the atmosphere was damp and dark.

Jan was proud that the in-law unit, despite its problems, was in a safe area. The neighborhood was cheerful and centrally located, with a school and. playground in the near vicinity. Jan's satisfaction with the safety of the neighborhood was somewhat ironic, however, since she did not leave her house for fear that Kenny would harm her or "steal Dee." As a result, active 22-month-old Andy was kept confined with his mother in this small space for days at a time.

Throughout the day, Andy was exposed to his mother's extreme fear and worry regarding both her and her infant daughter's physical safety. In every session Jan described how Kenny was trying to intimidate her. She said that he harassed her by phone and waited outside her door to follow her in his car as she walked. Jan reported he routinely violated the restraining order she had obtained against him.

Jan was convinced that Kenny would continue to harass her and perhaps physically harm her unless she relinquished her custody of Dee. Dee was a quiet, passive six-month-old who usually either slept during the sessions or sat on her mother's lap. Whenever Dee played on the floor, Andy harassed her, hit her, and took her toys away.

Throughout the assessment period, Jan spoke again and again of her frustration and the urgency of their situation—no money for food or diapers, Kenny's stalking her, no stove, no heat. The litany of difficult circumstances that Jan recounted was accompanied by extremely troubling interactions between Jan and Andy. Attempts on the therapist's part to talk with Jan about Andy and Dee were quickly dismissed as were various case management suggestions and efforts.

Mother-child relationship

Andy was excessively active in the small space in which the visits occurred and Jan repeatedly restricted, redirected, or reprimanded him. After a few sessions it became evident that unless the therapist responded precisely enough and empathically enough to Jan's distress, her provocations of and punitive interactions with Andy escalated.

Jan teased and tantalized Andy with her overt, unabashed affection for Dee. Jan punished Andy unpredictably. She held unrealistic expectations of him and refused to see him in a way other than that he was intentionally making life hard for her. She treated each of his assertions or requests as unreasonable and she labeled his behaviors in ways that reaffirmed his destructive tendencies. In response, Andy became more and more anxious as manifested in increasingly reckless and defiant behavior.

There were many incidents in which Jan conveyed to Andy that he was aggressive or dangerous. In one instance, Andy was playing with a baby doll, rolling it around in a stroller. The doll fell out of the stroller and Jan repeated several times, "You killed her, you killed baby doll." Andy picked the baby doll up and said urgently, "You see, not dead."

Throughout the assessment period Jan stopped Andy from doing something that he wanted to do (turn on the television, play with a toy, open a door) by saying, "It's broken, you broke it." This appeared to be Jan's most relied upon method of attempting to control Andy's assertions. This gave Andy a constant sense that he had done something wrong.

Jan also conveyed to Andy that he was a dangerous little boy through constant comparisons to Kenny. Jan was convinced that Andy was going to grow up to batter his wife and children. She said several times in every session, "You see, he's doing it right now, acting like Kenny. He's going to be just like Kenny." The behaviors to which Jan was referring were often provocations on Andy's part toward Dee that stemmed from his desperate efforts for his mother's attention, comfort, and approval. However, Jan could not see Andy's need for her or his anxiety about her unavailability or disapproval. She could only perceive him as a bad, dangerous child.

This attitude on Jan's part placed Andy in a terrible bind. Jan withheld from and frustrated Andy until he screamed with rage and then she labeled his response as aggressive or dangerous. In these moments, Andy felt dismayed and humiliated because he could not please his mother, worried about her anger toward him, and fearful of yet dependent upon her.

Jan ignored or misread kind impulses and actions on Andy's part which defied her more negative expectations of him. Because he craved responses from his mother of being seen and known by her, Andy's internal sense of himself was developing in a way that was congruent with Jan's perceptions of him: he was becoming a destructive person. However, Andy was also acutely aware that his mother was frightened of his anger and this made him exceedingly worried about his inability to control himself.

By the end of the assessment period the therapist was able to begin to identify and discuss with Jan the nature of the interactions between Jan and Andy that led to the extreme behaviors on Andy's part. At this early point in the treatment the therapeutic alliance remained tenuous. Jan's faith that the therapist could be helpful to her vacillated from week to week depending upon the degree to which the therapist was available to assist Jan in concrete ways. In addition, Jan expressed feelings of mistrust toward the therapist who she felt could "turn on [her] and take [her] kids away." Although Jan voiced her reservations candidly, she agreed to continue meeting on an ongoing basis.

Diagnosis

The following Axis I primary diagnoses were considered and ruled out: Traumatic Stress Disorder, Reactive Attachment Deprivation/ Maltreatment Disorder, and Mixed Disorder of Emotional Expressiveness.

Although Andy experienced ongoing stress which included exposure to and continuing threats of violence in his environment, Traumatic Stress Disorder was ruled out. Traumatic Stress Disorder is indicated when troubling behaviors occur that are associated with an identifiable traumatic event or series of traumatic events. Andy's difficulties were more generalized and pervasive.

Andy's day-to-day experience was one of ongoing struggle. His relationship with his mother was pervaded by tension and conflict, which left him in a state of constant arousal while providing him with little support or containment.

No discernible themes of particular traumatic events were identifiable in Andy's play. Rather, his play was characterized by pervasive restlessness, disorganization, and worry. Additionally, there was no evidence of the numbing of responsiveness that is one of the criteria for Traumatic Stress Disorder. Andy demonstrated a full range of affect, with predominant elements of anxiety and agitation.

The diagnosis of Mixed Disorder of Emotional Expressiveness was ruled out because the diagnostic criteria include restricted range of affect as well as absence or near absence of a specific type of affect. Neither of these symptoms was present in Andy's interactions. Andy did meet two of the criteria for this diagnosis: He displayed disturbed intensity of emotional expression as well as affect inappropriate to the situation. However, both of these symptoms were understood in light of Andy's experience of anxiety and his defense against it.

Reactive Attachment Deprivation/Maltreatment Disorder was considered as a possible diagnosis because Andy was exposed to a great deal of parental neglect and physical maltreatment. However, what began as difficulties in Andy's relationship with his mother had become for Andy a generalized way of experiencing the world. More specifically, the predominant affective experiences of anxiety and fear associated for Andy with his early attachment to his mother now pervaded his experience of himself and others.

Diagnostic Summary

Axis I: Primary Diagnosis
Anxiety Disorder of Infancy and Early Childhood.

Axis II: Relationship Disorder Classification
Mixed Relationship Disorder as characterized by anxious/tense relational patterns which result in physically abusive relational interactions.

Axis III: Medical and Developmental Disorders and Conditions
No medical or developmental concerns.

Axis IV: Psychosocial Stressors
Violence in environment, abuse—physical, poverty, abrupt changes in living situation, birth of a sibling.
Overall effects: severe and enduring.

Axis V: Functional Emotional Developmental Level
Has attained age-appropriate levels of mutual attention, mutual engagement, interactive intentionality and reciprocity. Age-appropriate level of representational/affective communication, but vulnerable to stress, and with predominantly angry affect.

PIR-GAS:10 (Grossly impaired)

Intervention

Treatment consisted of ongoing weekly visits in the family's home and included infant-parent psychotherapy, intensive case management, and concrete support. The following sections emphasize how the infant-parent therapist focused on both the difficulties in the relationship between Jan and Andy and the environmental stressors that contributed to Andy's troubling behaviors. Certain pivotal moments during the early, middle, and later phases of infant-parent treatment are reviewed.

Early phase of treatment

In one of the initial sessions Jan was telling the therapist about her many worries when Andy came into the room, took the therapist's hand, and insistently pulled at her to follow him. He led her near the kitchen area and pointed into the kitchen. She got down so that they were face to face and asked what he was showing her. He pointed again. She asked again, "What is it?" Andy pointed a third time, and said "Mommy pow-pow me and Dee." He was clearly telling her about their physical punishment.

Jan came up behind Andy, suddenly furious. She grabbed him by the arm, said, "Are you hungry, is that what you're saying?" Jan lifted Andy into the air and then placed him down on the counter. She then began to shovel boiled egg into his mouth. Andy choked a little, pushing the egg out of his mouth with his tongue and began to cry. As Andy struggled to get loose from her grip, Jan tightened her hold on him and continued to force feed him.

The therapist could identify immediately several possible reasons for Jan's angry response. Jan felt betrayed by Andy's seeking out the therapist's protection from her; Jan experienced the therapist as aligning herself with Andy and against her; and the therapist had abandoned Jan, in the middle of Jan's account of her despair, to follow and pay close attention to Andy.

Additionally, Andy, by asking the therapist for help so directly, had surprised his mother with the level of his understanding of her behavior. This exposure threatened Jan's sense of herself as a good mother. It challenged her conviction that Andy was, as she often portrayed him, "a perpetrator just like Kenny." And it suggested instead that Andy was a vulnerable little boy who was very worried about his mother's anger toward him.

Attempts to talk about this with Jan resulted in her feeling further implicated and enraged. Therefore, the therapist attempted to remedy this interaction between Jan, Andy and herself by springing into action about the practical issues that were preoccupying Jan. In the following weeks the therapist located legal consultation and advocacy and advised Jan about ways to both maneuver through the welfare system and discuss difficulties with the landlady. The therapist was present during one dispute in which she actually attempted to negotiate for Jan with her landlady.

The therapist also began to look for day care subsidy and transitional housing space, and to focus her attention on Jan, often to the exclusion of Andy and Dee, who were also vying for the therapist's attention. All of these

interventions were intended to demonstrate to Jan that the therapist understood the urgency that she was feeling, that the therapist was there for her as
well as for Andy and Dee, and that she would do what she could to assist Jan
in her efforts to become stable and safe.

Many sessions passed without any helpful results from these case management efforts. Jan was not answering her phone so it was impossible for
agencies to reach her. There was some confusion with her mail delivery as
well, because her unit was illegal and actually not listed with the post office.
The services the therapist tried to implement generally took time and Jan
was often impatient and rejecting of the therapist, suggesting that the therapist was somehow responsible for the lack of a timely outcome and ignoring her own contribution to the lack of progress in getting the services she
demanded.

During these sessions, Andy was consistently aggressive toward Dee. He
protested immediately when Jan gave Dee her bottle and stole the baby's bottle whenever he could. Severe tantrums followed when Jan took the bottle
from Andy, insisting that he could not have a bottle, returning it to Dee.

In each of these sessions Andy fell hard several times. He banged his
head, his elbow, and his hand. He climbed all over the furniture, grabbed
toys away from his sister and then threw them at her. Each week Andy had
a new bruise or cut. Some weeks he had gone to the emergency room for
more severe injuries. Jan reported that Andy routinely bolted for long distances without looking back.

As Andy became more attached to the therapist he began to strongly
protest her departures. When his protests failed, he "bolted" out the door as
she was leaving and took off down the block. Jan ran after him and caught
him. Andy screamed and cried and tried to get away. Jan carried him back
to the house, with Andy kicking, screaming, and throwing his head around.
Many of these early sessions ended with Andy trying to get away from his
mother and Jan feeling humiliated and enraged.

The therapist was initially unable to intervene in any way which might
call attention to the distress that Andy was feeling and that resulted in his
wanting to run away. Jan was not capable at this point in the treatment of
considering Andy's emotional needs or struggles and perceived his behavior
as intentionally defiant or hostile toward her. Attempts to sensitize Jan to
Andy's vulnerabilities or needs were met with indignation and increased tension as Jan felt predominantly misunderstood and blamed.

Rather than attempt to explore the meaning behind Andy's behavior, the
therapist used developmental guidance by suggesting that Jan hold Andy at
the end of the session and explain to him that the therapist was saying good-
bye for now and that she would be back next week.

This worked well for the first four sessions. On the fifth departure, however, Andy struggled free of his mother's grip and ran out the door and into
the road. Immediate action was clearly needed. The therapist ran after Andy
and stopped him. She got down to his level, and, holding his shoulders so
that they were face to face said, "Andy, it's very scary when you run away.

Your mommy and I are afraid you will get hurt. We don't want you to run away anymore." Holding Andy firmly and looking right at him, she repeated this one or two times with a serious and worried tone. Andy calmly put his arms up for the therapist to carry him and she picked him up and carried him back to his mother.

At the end of the next session Andy himself suggested a new departure routine. As the time for the therapist to leave approached, he requested that she carry him to her car. With Jan's approval, the therapist carried Andy as Jan and Dee walked to her car. The therapist then put Andy down on the sidewalk next to his mother. Jan, holding Dee, took his hand and the therapist got into her car and drove away while the three of them stood watching her. The family adopted this approach as the routine for many subsequent departures.

Three months into treatment, Jan requested a letter from the therapist for an upcoming meeting. Kenny had called the police and made an unfounded child abuse report against Jan which resulted in a surprise visit to her house by the police. He also sent Jan a copy of the letter he had submitted to Child Protective Services accusing Jan of severely neglecting and abusing Andy and Dee. Jan asked timidly if the therapist would write a letter on her behalf. The letter was to state that she was in therapy and that she was working hard to get back on her feet. Typically, Jan wanted this to be done right away: she asked for the letter the day before it was required for the meeting with the Child Protective Service caseworker.

In spite of the short notice, the therapist wrote a letter to Child Protective Services which demonstrated an affirmative stance toward Jan as a mother and as a person. She wrote that they had been meeting regularly, that Jan was committed to the therapy, that she was a dedicated parent who appeared emotionally invested in her children as they were in her. The letter also stated that it was the intention of the Infant-Parent Program to assist this family in remaining together, and in achieving close and satisfying relationships with each other.

The therapist hand-delivered the letter to Jan the next day and Jan took it to the social worker. The meeting was brief and inconsequential. It is unclear whether the social worker even reviewed the letter. But what was clear was that Jan had herself read the letter and for her this vote of confidence made a significant difference in the degree to which she felt she could trust the therapist.

As a result, the quality of the therapeutic relationship changed markedly. Jan was warm and available with both the therapist and Andy. She sought the therapist for advice about parenting and other concerns and she became open to ideas and suggestions that the therapist might have as to why Andy behaved in the ways that he did.

Middle phase of treatment

During the middle phase of treatment, the therapist witnessed a very severe tantrum that occurred, predictably over Andy wanting Dee's bottle. In the park earlier, where they had for the most part a calm and pleasant meeting, Andy had tried to steal Dee's bottle a few times, but managed then to divert himself to other activities. When they returned to the house he immediately reached for a bottle that was sitting on the counter. The following is an excerpt from the therapist's notes on that session:

Andy disappears into the kitchen and Jan follows him. He reaches for a bottle on the counter top. Jan tells him that he cannot have it. Andy begins to cry, then to scream, and he is quickly in a full blown tantrum. Jan walks out of the kitchen toward me; she is clearly upset. I asked her if there is anything she can give him in place of the bottle. Jan tries toys, cookies, crackers. Andy has been screaming now for several (maybe 10) minutes. Jan and I try to engage him, distract him, offer him alternatives. Andy rejects our overtures and screams louder. He then throws himself on the floor and starts kicking his feet.

Jan says, "This is where I get pissed off and just give him what he wants."

I say, "What happens if you hold out?"

Jan says, "He eventually falls asleep, then when he wakes up he's irritable and he still wants the bottle."

I ask, "How long will he cry like this?"

Jan says, "A long time, an hour or longer."

Andy is screaming and coughing. Jan warns him that he'll make himself sick. Andy screams louder, falls to the ground and starts to bang his head against the floor.

I say, "Would you consider holding him?"

Jan says, "I can't. He bites me and kicks and hits me."

I say, "Can I show you something that has worked for me before?"

Jan says, "Go ahead."

I walk behind Andy and as I reach for him I say, "I'm going to hold you now." Andy is screaming and hitting his head. I pick him up from behind. He wiggles and screams and throws his fists around. I sit down on the floor with Andy's back to me and hold him close to my chest. I wrap my arms around him and put one leg over his legs. Then I rock him and talk to him. I tell him that I am holding him to help him to calm down, that I don't want him to hurt himself. He resists for some time, continuing to cry. Jan is sitting with us and she and I talk about this as it is happening.

After Andy calms down I say, "Okay, I'm gonna let you go now." I let him go and he quickly scoots on his bottom to a few feet away from me. He is much calmer, but he is very angry at me, with furrowed brow and tightly clenched lips. Andy throws a broom handle down between us. I sit with him and tell him that I held him so that he wouldn't hurt himself. After the second or third time that I repeat this he seems to understand what I am saying and his whole demeanor towards me relaxes. Then he looks up at Jan who is sitting on a chair nearby holding Dee on her lap,

Andy says, "Go."

Jan says, "Go where?"

Andy repeats, "Go."

Jan says, "Go where?"

Andy says loudly, "Go!"

Jan laughs and says, "Andy, go where, where, where do you want me to go?"

Andy screams, "Go."

Jan says, "Me, me go?"

I say to Jan, "He wants Dee to go. He can't stand it that you're holding her on your lap when he needs you so badly to comfort him."

Jan puts Dee down. Andy immediately jumps up and holds his arms out for his mother to pick him up. Jan picks Andy up and holds him on her lap. Within moments, he is chatting to her absorbedly, interacting with her in a lively and affectionate way.

In the following session the struggle around the bottle resumed. Andy was again trying to inconspicuously remove the bottle from Dee. He had actually invented some rather ingenious methods of getting the bottle from his sister in such a way that a long time would pass before anyone would even notice. On this day the therapist watched him distract Dee with another toy and then slide the bottle out of her line of vision.

Jan spotted Andy and screamed. Her scream startled Andy who was concentrating very hard on the execution of his plan and he jumped. Partly excited by her own realization and partly desperate to avoid another tantrum, the therapist blurted to Jan, "The bottle is you." This comment brought both Jan and Andy to a stand still. Jan responded, "'You're really weird." The therapist and Jan laughed at this exchange. The humorous, mildly devaluing exchange at the therapist's expense allowed Jan and Andy to have a playful relationship to the interpretation. This made the idea of the meaning behind the bottle feel less imposed and threatening and, therefore, easier to consider. The charge around the bottle dissipated for both Andy and Jan.

Although nothing more was said at the time, this exchange had an enduring effect. When the therapist returned the following week Jan had purchased a special cup for Andy with a colorful twisting and turning straw. He was very proud of the cup and he showed it to the therapist immediately when she arrived. The struggle around the bottle never recurred.

Around this time, the family was finally able to move into transitional housing which provided a supportive, safe, and stable environment for Jan and her children while Jan pursued her trade degree. In addition, subsidized day care came through for both children. This meant that they could be among other children in a stimulating and secure environment during much of their day.

Late phase of treatment

In the later phase of treatment, the therapist videotaped a 60-minute free play between Andy, Jan, and Dee. In the following session Jan and the therapist met alone to watch and discuss the videotape. Jan said in this session that she had made an appointment with a psychiatrist and that she was taking antidepressants. Jan cried through most of the meeting and said that she felt bad all the time. She was more aware of the ways in which she wished things had been different and expressed deep sadness over the losses in her life.

As Jan talked about her own experience, she and the therapist simultaneously watched some of the videotape. Jan was completely taken with Andy. She watched with some amazement, commented on how smart he was and talked for the first time about what she called her "meanness" toward him.

Jan said that Andy was the only one in the world that was really hers and she referred to him as her "true buddy." Jan said that she treated Andy the way she was feeling about herself. These ideas were precipitated by the therapist asking Jan if she thought that Andy's agitation might be a way that he responded to her depression. The therapist suggested that Andy became frightened and would provoke Jan or make her angry so that she would not withdraw from him.

This line of exploration had an effect similar to the earlier comment about the bottle as it offered Jan an alternative way of understanding the meaning behind what she perceived in Andy as difficult behavior. Jan was increasingly able to allow for the possibility that Andy's incessant demands and agitated behaviors were an expression of his need to be loved, cared for, and close to her.

In the months that followed, exploration along these lines continued, while Jan, Andy, and Dee became stable in their home and in their respective daytime routines. The therapist attended meetings with Andy's day care teachers to ensure that Andy's difficulties were understood and were sympathetically addressed. Jan was also active and involved in Andy's preschool, attending meetings, talking with his teachers at the end of every day, and attempting to practice the same limit-setting methods with Andy at home as was done in school.

Andy was able to make friends with his peers and to elicit fondness and affection from his teachers. In fact, as subsidy for day care grew increasingly precarious, teachers and administrators rallied on behalf of this family to ensure their continuing financial support.

After a long and stressful battle, a family court judge ordered Jan and Kenny to participate in counseling in order to facilitate their co-parenting of Dee. Jan and Kenny complied with this order and Kenny was eventually granted visits with Dee that gradually increased to include overnights, weekends, and trips. As Jan felt less vulnerable and afraid of Kenny, she was able to tolerate increased contact with him that revolved around sharing in Dee's parenting.

Once a withdrawn and passive infant, Dee was thriving in her new home and her new daycare. Her vocabulary was increasing as was her ability to take pleasure in both solitary and interactive play. With her mother's thoughtful and increasingly balanced support, Dee was more and more able to assert herself with Andy and to fight back when she felt bullied or overridden. More confident that his mother would assist him, Andy was able to ask for help from his mother to negotiate with Dee rather than to angrily impose his will upon her.

As Jan released Andy from the negative projections that previously constricted her relationship with him, she experienced him more presently and spontaneously. Being with Andy in this way allowed Jan to recognize not only the ways in which Andy was difficult, but the ways in which he was quite adorable, funny, eager to please, and protective of her. Jan's increasing ability to focus on and respond to Andy had a calming and organizing effect on him, and his anxiety and agitation abated.

Andy responded to Jan's more nurturing receptivity toward him by expressing his affection for and dependency upon her directly while behaving less destructively in general. When, during sessions with the therapist, Jan told Andy that he broke something, the therapist would encourage Jan to invite Andy to "fix" it. Jan responded to this suggestion with indifference until she saw that Andy responded to her by wanting to fix everything whether it was broken or not. Andy's enthusiasm and cooperative spirit pleased Jan and she began to recognize and encourage his reparative impulses on her own.

Prognosis and discussion

Infant-parent treatment was conducted with this family for two years. During the termination phase the therapist's case management efforts were minimal as Jan required little assistance in managing the logistics of her own and her children's lives. Sessions were instead devoted to conversations regarding the nature of the family's relationships and interactions. Jan continued her individual treatment with her psychiatrist and met with the infant-parent therapist for a follow-up visit three months after termination when Andy was four years old.

Jan continues to pursue her trade degree. She has managed to maintain a stable and safe environment for herself and her children for more than a year and she has become an involved and valued member of her transitional housing program. She no longer spanks Andy because she says it is a method of discipline that "won't work for very long." Jan says instead, "It's better to rely on our relationship. He likes to make me happy."

Andy has had no accidents in a year. He is well liked by both peers and teachers in his day care setting. He can stay with a particular task for an extended period of time and takes pleasure in many different activities. Still quite strong-willed, Andy now responds with apparent trust in negotiative processes to attempts on the part of his mother and others to navigate charged situations with him. This allows for more mutual interactions and diminishes Andy's sense of being forced against his will. His tantrums occur less frequently, last shorter periods of time, and can be positively affected by Jan's responses to them. At four, Andy is becoming a nicely social preschooler who talks with his mother about all kinds of feelings and thoughts as they occur.

200. Disorders of Affect

202. Mood Disorder: Prolonged Bereavement/Grief Reaction

Alicia F. Lieberman, Ph.D.

The diagnostic category Prolonged Bereavement/Grief Reaction is based on the premise that the loss of a primary caregiver, such as a parent, is almost always a serious problem for an infant or young child because most young children do not have the emotional and cognitive resources to deal with such a major loss. The cases of Turner and Joey (see Tidmarsh, this volume) are presented to illustrate the variety of manifestations of Bereavement/Grief Reaction depending on the infant's age and developmental capabilities.

Reason for referral

Turner, a 9-month-old boy, was referred to the Infant-Parent Program (IPP) by his child welfare worker at the San Francisco Department of Human Services (DHS). Reasons for the referral were Turner's incessant crying, poor appetite, and little interest in his surroundings. When he was not crying, he often stared silently. He seldom smiled and made few vocalizations. The child welfare worker reported that this child's foster parents had been considering adoption when Turner was placed with them, but were expressing reservations as a result of Turner's behavior. They were concerned that Turner might be developmentally delayed or otherwise "damaged." They requested an assessment to rule out chronic disabilities that would preclude their adoption of Turner.

Assessment process

The assessment and intervention consisted of five sessions, and one telephone consultation with Turner's pediatrician. The first session involved a detailed interview with the child welfare worker and a review by the worker and the assessor of Turner's DHS chart. Two subsequent sessions involved home visits to observe Turner with his parents and to elicit their impressions and feelings towards him. The fourth session involved administering the Bayley Scales of Infant Development. The child welfare worker was apprised of the findings through telephone calls and a written report at the end of the intervention. A telephone follow-up with the foster parents took place 6 weeks after the final session.

Assessment findings

History and developmental course

The most notable aspect of Turner's recent history was that he had been moved from a previous foster home where he had been since birth to his current, potentially adoptive foster home 6 weeks prior to the referral. Neither the child welfare worker nor the two foster families involved—Ms. Burton and Tanya and Jimmy Anderson—had given much thought to the possible consequences of the move because they assumed that Turner was "too young to mind." As a result, they did not set up a transitional period when Turner and his new caregivers could get to know each other before beginning to live together. Turner's new parents agreed to take Turner after observing him with his foster mother for 45 minutes at the DHS visiting playroom and being told about his family background and birth history. By their report, they felt an "immediate chemistry" with him and were confident that they could provide him with a loving and caring home. Turner went to live with the Andersons one week after this meeting.

Efforts to learn about Turner's behavior prior to the move were met with only very general answers. Observing babies and understanding their likes and dislikes, their temperamental styles and their way of being in the world require specialized skill, and many people still consider it quaint to talk about babies as if they had distinct personalities or even feelings that are more than transitory responses of pleasure or displeasure. Turner's former foster mother, Ms. Burton, with whom he had been placed at birth, was clearly very fond of him and missed him after he left. However, she explained during a lengthy telephone conversation that she had been a professional foster mother for many years and made it a point to remind herself periodically that her mission in life was to care for babies only until a permanent home was found for them. This allowed her to let them go when the time came without, in her words, "falling apart afterwards."

Perhaps as a result of this attitude, Ms. Burton used general categories rather than specific examples to describe Turner during the time she took care of him. However, her descriptions were full enough to provide a picture of the child prior to his move to the Andersons. She explained (and the medical records confirmed) that Turner had been exposed to cocaine prenatally and as a newborn had some tremors and was difficult to console when he cried. However, by the time he was 3 months old, he had become a quiet baby who smiled often and liked to be held. Ms. Burton reported that, although a widow, she had a busy family life, with several children and grandchildren who liked to play with Turner when they came to visit. Ms. Burton also took care of three other foster children, ranging in age from 6 to 12, who called Turner their "baby." When asked if Turner preferred anybody in particular, Ms. Burton reported without hesitation that he liked her "best of all" and, just prior to the move, had started crying when she left the room. Ms. Burton considered this a sign that he was getting "spoiled' (a term she used fondly rather than critically) and thought it was important to move him to a permanent home before his feeling of belonging in the Burton family developed any further.

Ms. Burton reported that Turner's developmental milestones had been met on schedule. He started sleeping through the night at about 4 months, began to feed himself finger foods at 7 months, could sit up on his own at about 6 months and began crawling at 7 months. She could not remember any specific games but recalled with pleasure that he moved his head in rhythm to the music the older children listened to, and smiled and laughed when they took him in their arms to dance with him.

This description suggests that Turner was developing along expectable lines in the Burton household, that he had formed an attachment to Ms. Burton, and that he enjoyed interacting with the other children in the family. Whatever constitutional vulnerabilities he might have experienced as a result of intrauterine cocaine exposure seemed not to interfere with his overall development.

Cognitive functioning

The picture of a basically adequate developmental course was substantiated by the results of the Bayley Scales of Infant Development. Although he was slow to warm up and rather hesitant in his approach to the items, Turner's performance placed him squarely at age level, with an MDI=98 and an age-appropriate distribution of items passed and failed. He vocalized little, but his receptive language was adequate, as evidenced by his turning in response to his name and stopping an action when told, "No." While performing adequately, Turner showed little pleasure in experimenting with the test items, and protested only briefly when an object was removed. His facial expression was attentive but sober, and he did not seem to grow increasingly more socially engaged with the assessor in the course of the testing. He looked at the assessor to monitor her movements but with no sign of social engagement. For such a young baby there was an oddly business-like quality to his behavior; he behaved as expected, but seemed emotionally detached from the experience.

Home observations

Turner's behavior at home with Mr. and Ms. Anderson was quite different from his demeanor during the administration of the Bayley Scales. At home, he seemed like a younger baby, prone to wailing at the slightest frustration. When Ms. Anderson picked him up to soothe him, he held himself stiffly in her arms and arched away from her, pointedly avoiding eye contact while continuing to cry inconsolably. Nothing seemed to help him: singing, rocking, or patting rhythmically. Frustrated and angry, Ms. Anderson eventually resorted to leaving him alone in his crib, where he often cried himself to sleep. A brief moment of intimacy occurred when, during a calm interval, Ms. Anderson gave Turner a toy and they exchanged a short-lived smile. Otherwise, mother and child were quite detached from one another.

As they spoke about their difficulties with Turner, Mr. and Ms. Anderson also spoke about their own relationship and how they came to decide on adopting a baby. This was the second marriage for Mr. Anderson, who had grown children by his first wife. Ms. Anderson, in her late thirties and 10 years younger than her husband, had deeply wanted children but sought a spiritual meaning in this situation and thought it was their duty to give their love and economic resources to a child who did not have a home. When told that Turner's parents had abandoned him at birth and that he was exposed to cocaine, they wanted to help him and opened their hearts to him.

Unfortunately, Turner had not reciprocated their eagerness to form a bond with him. Although the incessant crying did not start until three days after placement, Ms. Anderson remembered feeling from the beginning that Turner was not the cuddly, responsive baby she had hoped for. She found herself irritated by his lack of joy and his failure to respond with glee to her efforts to play with him. When the crying began, she found herself suppressing the wish to shake him to make him stop. Her husband was affectionate and supportive, but he did not share her anguish at this situation. He thought it was only a matter of time until Turner got used to them and began to love them, and referred to his own experience as a father in support of this view. This made Ms. Anderson feel patronized, angry at him, and alone. She also felt guilty that she was not being more patient and loving with both Turner and her husband. In particular, she felt like a bad person because she was having second thoughts about wanting to adopt him.

Diagnosis

The relationship between Turner and his foster mother was primarily tense and constricted, with episodes of angry mutual withdrawal. This situation was not the reason for Turner's symptoms but rather the result of the child's developmentally appropriate protest and distress at the loss of his prior foster mother, who had become his primary attachment figure. Ms. Anderson's eager anticipation of a loving, cuddly baby; Turner's failure to live up to that image; and her resulting disappointment at what she perceived to be Turner's rejection of her became major obstacles to Ms. Anderson's ability to understand the baby's reaction and to remain empathically available to him. Her inexperience in taking care of babies and her feeling of being patronized by her husband's assurances added to Ms. Anderson's sense of failure and isolation. In addition, the child welfare worker's inability to anticipate Turner's response to the move and to plan for a more gradual transition compounded Ms. Anderson's reaction because she had been led to believe by a presumably knowledgeable and experienced professional that Turner would not be adversely affected by the change in caregivers.

Given the clear-cut circumstances surrounding the onset of Turner's symptoms, the diagnosis of Prolonged Bereavement/Grief Reaction was the most appropriate. The possibility of a Regulatory Disorder was briefly entertained when Turner was described as having tremors and being difficult to console as a very young baby, but this diagnosis was dismissed because he had clearly outgrown these difficulties by three months of age. The diagnosis of Reactive Attachment/Deprivation/Maltreatment was ruled out because Turner's symptoms were preventing the formation of an attachment to his new caregiver, rather than being the result of a maladaptive relationship.

Diagnostic Summary

Axis I: Primary Diagnosis
Prolonged Bereavement/Grief Reaction.

Axis II: Relationship Disorder Classification
No relationship classification; marked tendency towards alternating anxious/tense and angry/hostile relationship.

Axis III: Medical and Developmental Disorders and Conditions
In utero exposure to cocaine.

Axis IV: Psychosocial Stressors
Moderately severe. Sudden loss of primary attachment figure and of sibling figures.

Axis V: Functional Emotional Developmental Level
By report, had achieved age appropriate levels of mutual attention, mutual engagement, and interactive intentionality and reciprocity, but lost richness and flexibility of relatedness, and currently showed those levels only with support.

PIR-GAS: 45 (Between Distressed and Disturbed)

Discussion with caregivers and treatment planning

The feedback session with Mr. and Ms. Anderson consisted of a description of what the assessor learned about Turner's and the Andersons' experiences in the course of the assessment. Much emphasis was placed on the gap between the Andersons' hopeful expectations and their good intentions and what had actually happened, and the feelings of guilt, worry, and mutual estrangement that resulted from this discrepancy. The assessor explained that this was a common experience among adoptive parents, and that their feelings of anxiety and stress were a testimony to how devoted they were to being good parents to Turner. The parents' experience served as a framework to explain Turner's situation from the perspective of a baby who does not have the cognitive or emotional skills to anticipate the sudden loss of those he loves and to know how to cope with the loss. The assessor described Turner's response of withdrawal and grief as evidence that he was a little boy already capable of loving deeply, who could remember those he loved and pine for them.

Ms. Anderson sobbed as she became aware of Turner's behavior as an expression of suffering rather than of rejection, and she asked whether he would be capable of loving again. The assessor explained that he would need support and reassurance in order to take this risk, and asked the parents how they imagined they could help him. Ms. Anderson said she thought he needed to be held lovingly when he cried instead of being left in his crib, and Mr. Anderson supported this idea. Ms. Anderson said, crying: "He must feel so alone and unloved!" The assessor commented that it is hard to keep trying when a child does not respond to one's efforts, and Ms. Anderson replied, "Now that I know why he does it, I am not going to give up."

She then asked if Turner would profit from seeing Ms. Burton again. This was a difficult question, because while Turner would certainly recognize Ms. Burton, her presence might confuse him and raise the expectation of going back with her. As the parents and the assessor discussed together how difficult it was to know, Mr. Anderson suggested that Ms. Burton might send photographs of herself and the children for Turner to look at. The assessor said this sounded like an excellent compromise because Turner was at an age where he could recognize photos of people he knew. Ms. Anderson expressed amazement at this capacity in such a young baby.

At the end of the session, the assessor invited the parents to decide whether they wanted to meet further, or to keep in contact as needed. After a brief moment of indecision and consultation with each other, they decided that they had learned what they needed to know and felt prepared to cope with Turner's difficulties on their own. They said they would call if they had questions or concerns. It was agreed that there would be a telephone conversation in six weeks to see how things were going.

Intervention

Six weeks after the final session, the assessor called the Andersons to find out how they were. Mr. Anderson answered the phone and said that things were much better for all concerned. Chuckling, he said that his wife had become a veritable "mother hen," very protective of Turner, and quite confident of her authority when making statements about what the child needed. He then called her to the phone. Ms. Anderson spoke with a new confidence. She informed the assessor that Turner was doing just fine and that he had "gotten over" the loss of Ms. Burton.

Now almost 12 months old, Turner was saying "mama" and "dada" to Mr. and Ms. Anderson, cried when they left, greeted them when they came back, and busily brought them toys and insisted on their attention. Ms. Anderson's pride and joy were apparent in the ease and spontaneity with which she described Turner. When the assessor asked if there were any behaviors that raised questions in her mind, she said Turner still woke up crying two or three times during the night, but was easily calmed by their talking to him and patting him until he settled down. In a suddenly serious voice, she said: "I think he wants to be sure we will be there. He doesn't want to lose us, too." The assessor commented that she really knew her child, and she replied, as if it were self-evident, "Of course."

Prognosis and discussion

Ms. Anderson's response showed that she had come a long way in her self-confidence and her commitment to her child. Turner, for his part, seemed to be responding well to Ms. Anderson's newly found responsiveness and empathy. The behaviors Ms. Anderson described indicated that he had established a solid attachment to his new parents. These behaviors also suggest that Turner had recovered from the responses of grief and bereavement caused by the loss of Ms. Burton, although the long-term implications of this early experience for his personality formation cannot be predicted at this time.

200. Disorders of Affect

202. Mood Disorder:
Prolonged Bereavement/Grief Reaction

Lee Tidmarsh, M.D. FRCPC

Prolonged Bereavement/Grief Reaction is a disorder that occurs after a loss of a primary caregiver or attachment figure, such as a parent. For young children whose emotional and cognitive development does not yet provide the resources for coping with such a major stress, this loss becomes intolerable. Manifestations of this disorder may include any stage of the sequence of protest, despair, and detachment.

The case of Joey illustrates the process of identifying this disorder in a toddler whose developmental problems could have been attributed to other factors, and of planning treatment designed specifically to address the implications of a diagnosis of Prolonged Bereavement/Grief Reaction.

Reason for referral

Joey, a 21-month-old boy of West Indian origin, was living with his second foster family at the time of referral. He had been placed in this home at the time of the birth of his half-sister, Susie, five months earlier. Joey's mother signed adoption papers for Joey but not Susie and subsequently left Canada. Joey's biologic father was no longer involved with him and lived in another city.

Joey was referred for a mental health assessment because he had not adjusted well to his second foster family. The foster parents did not know how to cope with his temper tantrums and unpredictable behavior, which were upsetting the whole family, including the foster parents' three biologic children, ages 12, 11, and 4.

The assessment process

The entire family was invited to attend a meeting with the evaluator, but the foster parents, Mr. and Ms. Atwood, chose to bring only Joey. They were accompanied by a social service nurse who had known Joey from birth. The initial visit was primarily to gather information about Joey and his current foster family, as well as to get a general impression of the level of development of the child and the way the child and parents interact.

The evaluator arranged a second visit to observe Ms. Atwood and Joey in a free play situation in order to focus on his interaction with his foster mother and his level of play. After this visit, concerns about Joey's motor and language development led the evaluator to arrange for formal testing with the developmental psychologist. Finally, to complete the assessment, the evaluator observed Joey in his family home.

Assessment findings

History of present problem

Joey had been placed in foster care at birth, from the hospital, because his mother was a cocaine user and "had no plans to stop." Joey was black; he went to a family consisting of a black mother and a white father, two biologic children, and other foster children. The placement was planned for one year, after which time a reassessment of the situation would tell whether he could be adopted or not.

At the end of the year, Joey's mother signed adoption papers, and his foster family agreed to adopt, although they had not planned originally to do so. By all accounts, Joey was growing and developing well, and there was no cause for concern. He was described as a smiling, cheerful baby. However, the social service agency thought that a better racial match should be found —that is, a family with two black parents. At this time, Joey's biological mother gave birth to Susie, who also required placement. After a few months, agency staff succeeded in finding the current foster family, the Atwoods, headed by a father, age 33, who worked as a factory cutter and went to school and a mother, age 31, who was at home with the couple's three children. This family agreed to foster both children, planning to adopt them eventually. The first foster family did not object strongly. The social service nurse also felt that the first family could not manage both Susie and Joey. Therefore, a family who could take both siblings seemed more suitable.

Plans were made for integration into the new family. Joey visited daily with his sister at his new foster parents' home. There were no behavioral difficulties or signs of distress during these visits. After two weeks of daily visits, 15-month-old Joey was permanently placed, along with Susie, with the Atwoods. He had no further contact with his first foster family.

The Atwoods expected a certain period of adjustment and were not initially concerned about Joey's crying and tantrums. However, five months passed and he had not adapted. It was at this time that the infant mental health service was consulted.

In the initial interview with the evaluator, Ms. Atwood described Joey as being very hard to read. She said that she never knew what his response to a situation would be. He could be calm and happy, or he might have a huge tantrum. When he was upset, he would back up into a corner and isolate himself. This might last half an hour. Joey was hard to console. Some mornings he would wake up crying in bed and no one could soothe him. He had a favorite stuffed toy, the only possession that accompanied him in the changeover. He used this at night, but not during the day. If the toy was offered to him during a tantrum, he would throw it. Ms. Atwood said that during angry episodes Joey would avoid the gaze of his foster parents, and didn't listen. On other occasions, he would bang his head. At times, he would sit staring blankly, as if in another world.

The Atwoods said that Joey spoke about 30 words and that his language comprehension seemed normal to them. However, he walked unsteadily and was clumsy. Mr. Atwood said that Joey was very intelligent and that they had a nice time together on "good" days.

The foster parents said that Joey fell asleep easily and slept about 12 hours a night. His appetite was enormous, and he ate voraciously. However, he was not putting on a lot of weight.

Ms. Atwood said that she had cared for children since the age of 12 and was a teacher and had never seen a child behave the way Joey did. His behavior was affecting the whole family. She became very upset when her 12-year-old son said that the family had been happy before Joey came.

Four weeks prior to this assessment, Joey was scalded in the bathtub. When Mr. Atwood wasn't watching, Joey had turned on the hot water tap and burned the side of his face. The social worker had discussed the incident with the family and believed it was an accident. Additionally, Ms. Atwood had recently discovered that she was pregnant, and would be having her fourth child five months hence.

Birth and social history

Joey's mother had no prenatal care. He was born full term, by vaginal delivery, with Apgar scores of 9/9. His birth weight was 3,460 grams, which was in the 50th percentile, his length was in the 90th percentile; but his head circumference was only in the 5-to-10th percentile. No investigations of this discrepancy were considered necessary. According to the pediatrician who had followed him from birth, Joey had been jittery for a few months after birth, presumably due to his cocaine exposure in utero, but had had no other early difficulties.

Joey's postnatal growth was good, and he had no medical problems. Developmental milestones were early: he sat at $5^{1}/_{2}$ months and walked at 10 months. He was always very alert and responsive. There was no history of feeding or sleeping problems. He thrived in his first foster family and was attached to the foster mother and one of the other foster children.

Observational findings

The first visit with Joey and his foster parents revealed an attractive little boy with very big eyes and a slight build. He had no affective expression and merely stood by a toy table looking at the evaluator, not speaking or moving. When invited to play, he shook his head. After the initial settling period, when it was clear that Joey would not move without encouragement, his father left his chair and moved across the room to play with him. He got down on the floor, spoke to Joey in a cheerful tone, and showed him a toy.

Joey listlessly took the toy but did not continue to play. He didn't interact with his foster father, although Mr. Atwood remained on the floor with him. He approached his father to hug him when his father asked. Joey never expressed any joy and kept a serious look on his face throughout the session. Ms. Atwood remained in her seat and seemed discouraged by Joey's apathy. She said that he would come to use her for help, but not for play or fun.

The evaluator arranged a second visit with Ms. Atwood and Joey in order to have a closer look at his developmental skills, and observe their interaction. Joey again took time to warm up and never smiled once. He rarely approached his foster mother, who was sitting in a chair looking tired (she was now about 6 months pregnant). When she offered him a toy, he approached dutifully and took it but hardly played with it. In fact, he spent most of the time moving from one toy to the next without engaging in any one game. When I suggested that Ms. Atwood try a puzzle with him, he attempted it but was unable to manage the pieces and became frustrated. He threw a piece at the wall, whereupon his foster mother reprimanded him. He never went to her or touched her until the end of the session, when he took her hand to leave.

Joey was very awkward in his gross and fine motor development. He would get off balance easily, and bang into things. He never got upset when this occurred. His manipulation of objects appeared uncoordinated as well.

During a home visit, Joey repeated patterns we had seen in the office. Joey was serious and stared for 10 minutes, then warmed up slowly. He needed a lot of encouragement to engage in play, but as the visit progressed he became more mobile and interactive. He spoke only an occasional word, such as "no" or "Susie," his sister's name. Upon request, he showed the evaluator his bedroom, and did so obediently. The evaluator pointed to a toy Mickey Mouse on his bed, asking who that was. He smiled for the first time, which changed his face and demeanor completely. He took the toy and hugged it and said some words which were unclear. For a moment, he was like a different child. He then put "Mickey" down, and his serious, impassive expression returned.

Joey related very little to his foster mother during the visit, though she was on the floor and available to him. His sister, who was now 7 months old, was sitting near the foster mother, who offered her toys to hold. Joey would often approach his sister and had a somewhat protective attitude toward her.

Ms. Atwood expressed regret that she could not understand Joey better. She was ashamed of her impatience with him. She seemed very willing to try a little harder with him, though it was clear she needed support.

Observations during both office and home visits suggested that Joey had suffered an emotional setback and had shut down his affective expression, except for rare occasions (for example, his use of the Mickey Mouse transitional object). His passivity indicated either that he did not know how to engage anyone (unlikely in light of the report that he had been attached to his first foster mother and to one of the children in that home) or that he had given up and was reluctant to engage with anyone for fear of being let down. Of concern was the distance between Joey and his foster parents. Everyone, including Joey, seemed paralysed by his difficulties, and helpless about what to do to help him feel better.

Developmental testing

The Bayley Scales of Infant Development were administered by a developmental psychologist. Once again, Joey was sober and unenthusiastic but moderately compliant. He stopped tasks before completion once or twice and put his head down on the desk. He smiled when the examiner offered him a candy, which helped him complete the testing. During this session he went to his foster mother, who comforted him and encouraged him to return to the tasks.

Joey's test scores revealed an overall developmental age of 16 months (his chronological age was 22 months.) The developmental quotient (MDI) was 70. His earliest failure was at a task involving using two different words appropriately, a skill most 12-month-olds can usually demonstrate. Indeed his expressive language was the most severely delayed. He also was unable to put pegs in a board, which is a task most 16-month-olds can manage.

During the testing, Joey showed little enthusiasm for beginning tasks or persistence in trying to complete them. He made few attempts to engage the examiner socially. Because of Joey's depressed affect and lack of interest, the examiner was concerned that Joey's low developmental scores did not indicate his true potential. A neurological examination of Joey was normal, and an EEG and CT scan showed no abnormalities.

Diagnosis

Given Joey's history of cocaine exposure in utero and small head relative to the rest of his body, a biologic etiology to his developmental problems could be considered. His withdrawn, depressed behaviour was similar to that of infants with Regulatory Disorder (Type II: Underreactive). However, before the change of foster placement, Joey had achieved normal developmental milestones and had given no evidence of the worrisome current behavior described by the second foster parents.

Joey suffered a great loss in the change of foster families. He was apparently well adjusted and thriving; the change created an unhappy, distressed boy who ate voraciously, as if trying to fill a void. His depression manifested itself in his flat affect and lack of joy, unexpected crying, staring episodes, and withdrawn behavior.

Although Joey's new foster family had very good intentions, they were having trouble repairing the damage due to other family demands and were becoming frustrated and angry themselves. We observed an element of rejection in the foster mother's attitude toward Joey, which exacerbated his sadness. In addition, due to his high degree of distress in the past five months, he had not been able to make use of the caregiving that was available to him and had lost some ground in his developmental progress. Joey seemed to have good cognitive abilities and receptive language, but because of the lack of social interaction and high emotional stress, his expressive language had remained at the 12-to-15-month level. His development seemed to have stopped when he lost his primary attachment figure.

Diagnostic Summary

Axis I: Primary Diagnosis
Prolonged Bereavement/Grief Reaction.
R/O Regulatory Disorder: Type II Underreactive.

Axis II: Relationship Disorder Classification
Underinvolved Relationship Disorder.

Axis III: Medical and Developmental Disorders and Conditions
Rule out neurological effects of intrauterine cocaine exposure with developmental delay.

Axis IV: Psychosocial Stressors
Change in foster placement and loss of attachment figure; current foster mother pregnant and emotionally unavailable; physical trauma, in utero drug exposure.
Overall effects: severe and enduring.

Axis V: Functional Emotional Developmental Level
Has not achieved current expected level of representational/affective communication, but, with encouragement, is capable of prior levels, including mutual attention with encouragement, mutual engagement, and interactive intentionality, and reciprocity.

PIR-GAS:30 (Disordered)

Discussion with caregivers and treatment planning

The first step in the treatment process was to meet with the social worker and foster parents to discuss the difficulties Joey was having and the reasons underlying them. A critical question was whether the foster family was willing to keep this child. Factors against keeping him were the distress he created in the parents and other children, as well as the fact that mother was pregnant and would have less, not more, time to give to this boy in the future. In addition, the foster father was planning to start attending school full time in order to acquire a better job. This meant that the family would be on social assistance, involving a decrease in family income, and the father would be less available. Despite all these considerations, the Atwoods did not want to give up on this child. They felt that they needed to keep their commitment, and try to help him. Indeed, no one wanted to change Joey's placement again after seeing the disastrous effects on him of the previous move. Nor was it possible for him to return to the first foster family, as they had taken in other children. The Atwoods did make it clear to the social worker that they did not want to adopt him at this time as that would mean they would lose the social support they needed to work with him. Once adoption was legalized, the child would no longer be under state guardianship and the family would no longer automatically receive social assistance, financial or therapeutic. The family would have to apply for help as did other families, and face the possibility of waiting lists.

When it was clear that the Atwoods would keep Joey, a plan was made to involve Ms. Atwood and Joey in parent-child therapy on a regular basis, in order to help her understand his mood and behaviors, and to give her ideas as to how to stimulate him to speak and develop some motor skills. An occupational therapy evaluation was arranged so that the therapist could for-mulate suggestions for helping Ms. Atwood assist Joey in his development. The family arranged to have Mr. Atwood's mother come to live with them to help take care of the children. Ms. Atwood found this very helpful and was much relieved.

Unfortunately, winter and the mother's pregnancy delayed implementa-tion of the treatment plan. Travelling became very difficult, and viral illness in one child or another in the family caused cancellations. Home visiting by the therapist on a regular basis would have been desirable but was not pos-sible due to the distance and time required. The social worker visited fre-quently but merely to monitor the situation. The infant mental health ther-apist kept in regular telephone contact.

The initial evaluation and discussion with the foster parents seemed to help them develop a more understanding attitude toward Joey. They were also able to look at their limitations and make arrangements to get support from the grandmother. Gradually, Joey had fewer crying episodes and reports from the social worker indicated that he was able to play with the other children in the home, spoke more, and showed some signs of pleasure. His parents found him less difficult to handle. It appeared he had adjusted and settled into his new family. Ms. Atwood gave birth to her fourth child in the spring. Plans for parent-child therapy were suspended until the baby was a few months old and the mother had more time.

Follow-up assessment

During the summer, Ms. Atwood brought Joey for an occupational therapy evaluation but went to the wrong place and missed her appointment. The occupational therapist then left the program to return to school. Because of budget cutbacks, her replacement did not arrive until the fall. Thus, it was not until a full year after Joey's initial evaluation that a follow-up occupa-tional therapy assessment took place, prompted by the infant mental health specialist's continuing concerns about Joey's development.

Ms. Atwood was now working outside the home because the family was in need of money. She was even less available to Joey, who was spending his days with Mr. Atwood's mother, who still lived with the family, his sister Susie, and the new baby.

When Ms. Atwood brought Joey for the assessment, she described him as much better. However, she felt he was an "odd" child and still difficult to understand. She observed, for example, that whenever he was asked if he wanted to do anything, his initial response was to shake his head, "No," but he would then comply with the request. He still ate as much as he was allowed, but he played quietly, sometimes with his sister, and was not as difficult to manage as he had been.

During the evaluation, Ms. Atwood looked fed up with Joey and spoke to him in a negative, somewhat angry manner. She offered no support or encouragement for his activities. If he was not complying with the occupational therapist, she would tell him to "be a good boy." Joey was wary of his foster mother and never approached her during the session. Nor did he smile. When the occupational therapist left the room, he stood immobile, holding a ball, staring at his foster mother. He held this frozen position for about three minutes. When the therapist returned to the room, he moved toward her as if magically unfrozen, and stood very close to her, indicating that he wanted to play again. The therapist later reported she felt Joey was trying to get some warmth from her.

Developmental test results were discouraging. After a year with no direct intervention, Joey, now 34 months old, was further delayed in gross and fine motor development, and he still spoke very little. He seemed to hear well and understand, but his expressive language, according to his foster mother, was limited to two-word sentences at most. On the Peabody Developmental Motor Scales, his gross motor functioning was at the 16-month level, while fine motor functioning was at the 18-month level. Perceptual motor development was also at an 18-month level, with play skills at a 15-month level. Joey was not interested in representational play.

Because of Joey's observed lack of interaction with his foster mother, a play assessment was arranged to see how he could relate to the evaluator in free play. Ms. Atwood could not attend the session, and Joey was brought to the office, with his sister, by the nurse who had known him since birth. Joey willing took the evaluator's hand to go to the playroom, but on entering the room, became immobile. He stared at the evaluator as he had stared at his mother during the earlier assessment. His sister sat on the floor. Both children looked depressed. The evaluator explained that this was a time to play with whatever he wanted. After a few minutes with no response from Joey, the evaluator asked if he liked to play ball, and offered a soft ball to him. He took it and threw it back. He then began to move. He went to the toys and chose a dump truck. He took a black doll mother-figure and put her in the truck, along with two little cars. He spent much of the session pushing this truck around. He said nothing. He looked at the evaluator occasionally but never sought help or shared a toy. He was very aware of his sister and protective of her. If she dropped a toy he would retrieve it for her quickly. Finally, he found a box of tissues and proceeded to blow his and his sister's nose repeatedly until the whole box was empty. Susie never complained. In fact, her lack of play or response to her brother's intrusion was another concern for the evaluator. She was hard to engage and never made a sound. She spent the entire session mouthing one or two toys and never referred to the evaluator.

Updated diagnostic summary (34 months)

Axis I: Primary Diagnosis
Reactive Attachment Disorder.
R/O Depression of Infancy and Early Childhood.

Axis II: Relationship Disorder Classification
Underinvolved Relationship Disorder.

Axis III: Medical and Developmental Disorders and Conditions
Intrauterine cocaine exposure.
Possible mental retardation.
R/O neurological or metabolic causes of developmental delay.

Axis IV: Psychosocial Stressors
Similar past stressors including intrauterine cocaine exposure and loss of attachment figure.
Overwhelmed foster parents, financial insecurity, birth of new foster sibling.
Overall effects; severe and enduring.

Axis V: Functional Emotional Developmental Level
Unchanged from previous assessment.

PIR-GAS: 20 (Severely Disordered)

The new diagnosis reflected the evaluator's impression that Joey had recovered somewhat from the initial distress of losing his first foster mother. He demonstrated this by being less tearful and having fewer temper tantrums. In the presence of his foster siblings, he was more capable of play and spent less time in isolation. The staring spells were gone. However, it appeared that he had failed to make a new attachment to his foster mother, due to her emotional and now physical unavailability. Joey seemed depressed, and rarely smiled. Understimulated in his home environment, he was falling further behind in development. It was unclear whether Joey's delays were the outcome of the cocaine exposure or some other underlying process, were induced by the caregiving environment, or resulted from the interaction between constitution and environment. At the follow-up assessment, Joey's foster mother seemed willing to care for him, but she did not seem to enjoy his company and had little interest in playing with him. It also looked as if his sister might be suffering from similar deprivation.

Revised plan and implementation

The social worker was informed of our concern about Joey's development and poor relationship with his foster mother. On her next home visit, she discussed the need for Joey to receive more help than he had been getting. She once again explored with the parents whether they were capable of providing the time and attention Joey would need. They were still willing to keep him, and thought they could manage to bring Joey to appointments with doctors and therapists.

However, at a placement conference, arranged by the social service agency to discuss this difficult case and attended by the infant mental health therapist, the agency social workers agreed that this placement was inadequate to meet the needs of both Joey and his sister. But would leaving the children in the home be worse than changing the environment once again, with an uncertain outcome? A very difficult decision was taken—to look for a new foster home, with a caregiver who could be more available emotionally to these children and become actively involved in the intervention efforts they needed. The feeling among the professionals was that the current foster home was already overburdened and could not provide these children with enough of the special nurturing they would require to resume healthy growth. Until a new foster family was found, the children would be placed in a child care setting capable of providing them with appropriate attention and stimulation. The children would continue in the child care setting wherever they were next placed in foster care.

At what was to be a meeting to make a final decision about placement for Joey and his sister, the options seemed limited and generally unsatisfactory. The nurse who had known the children from birth was ready to take the children herself if no better solution could be found. Finally, someone remembered a family who had submitted their name for long-term foster placement during the previous year but had then decided to delay taking children. The family is white, with four biologic children aged 9, 8, 7, and 5 years. Staff contacted the family, who agreed to undergo evaluation as a foster home for Joey and Susie. Janet, the foster mother, said she was happy that her own children were all in school but that she was "tired of doing lovely dried flower arrangements" at home. The family was ready to care for more children.

Joey and Susie's transition from the Atwoods to their new foster home was accomplished over two days. The Atwoods were very distressed at losing the children and had pulled further away emotionally from them. The nurse facilitated the transition, spending a full day with the children and the new foster mother. The children settled into their new home without any signs of distress at the change of environment. Joey, however, was initially aggressive with the other children and once broke a glass on the head of the seven-year-old boy. However, Janet was not overly disturbed by this and handled the situation calmly.

At a home visit one month after the new placement, the infant mental health therapist found a remarkable change in Joey and Susie. It was as if a magic wand had been passed over them, bringing them alive again. When the therapist arrived with the nurse, both children stayed very close to Janet. In contrast to previous times she had seen them, they were wary of her. However, once they were comfortable with the therapist's presence, they began to play. Joey spoke more than the therapist had ever heard before. He brought out toys he liked and showed them to the nurse. His level of activity was higher than before, and his movements seemed more fluid. When the family's four children returned from school, enthusiastic bedlam ensued, which excited and delighted Joey. The two boys took over Joey and played horse on the floor. When Joey kicked one of them, Janet calmly removed him from the scene until he settled down a few minutes later. She said that incidents like this were happening less often than when he first arrived. The girls went to Susie; their fussing over her brought huge smiles to her face. The relaxed, happy atmosphere contrasted sharply with the Atwood family.

Two months postplacement, the nurse described visits in which Joey would not approach her at all but stayed very close to Janet. In the previous foster home, he would run to the nurse and happily go away with her.

Prognosis and discussion

Joey still has problems that will require further attention. Janet is aware that he may have some long-term developmental or behavioral problems and is willing to work with Joey. For example, although Joey is gaining ground fast, he is still delayed in motor and language development. In consultation with an occupational therapist, Janet will work at home with Joey to further his motor skills. Joey's language will be re-evaluated in a few months to look at progress and plan for further intervention if needed. Child care plans have been put on hold, as Joey and Susie need time to form an attachment to Janet and her family.

Joey's story demonstrates one way in which the loss of an important stable attachment figure interacts with other factors in a very young child's situation to profoundly affect development. Joey's distress made it impossible for him to reach out to a new caregiver and, unfortunately, his caregiving environment could not reach out to him. This deprivation exacerbated his predicament. In addition, the near-cessation of Joey's language development and his fine and gross motor difficulties further compromised his ability to engage with others. The picture of bereavement was changed as the child habituated to the new environment and because of improved understanding and acceptance by the foster parents. However, he continued to experience an environment with very little stimulation and warmth and gradually gave up hope of a close relationship, making attachment very hard. The fact that Joey trusts and relies on his new foster mother, after waiting 14 months for someone to latch on to, is encouraging. With this emotional security, he can concentrate his efforts on learning.

200. Disorders of Affect

203. Mood Disorder: Depression of Infancy and Early Childhood

Molly Romer Witten, Ph.D.

The diagnosis of Depression of Infancy and Early Childhood is reserved for infants and young children who exhibit a pattern of depressed or irritable mood with diminished interest and/or pleasure in developmentally appropriate activities, diminished capacity to protest, excessive whining, and a diminished repertory of social interactions and initiatives. These symptoms may be accompanied by disturbances in sleep or eating, including weight loss. Symptoms must be present for a period of at least two weeks.

Since infant depression may influence many domains of development as well as physiological processes, focusing solely on presenting symptoms of physiological difficulty or developmental delay can obscure the complex relational and environmental factors provoking the condition. The *DC: 0-3* guidelines for selecting an appropriate diagnosis (pp. 19) are helpful here, advising the clinician to consider Traumatic Stress Disorder, Regulatory Disorders, and Adjustment Disorders as possible explanations for symptoms before diagnosing a Disorder of Mood or Affect. However, when these conditions can be ruled out, and Depression or another mood disorder emerges as a likely explanation of the child's difficulties, the diagnostic work lies in understanding the interplay between the environmental determinants of the infant's relationships, both historically and in the present, context, and physical determinants of the infant's physiological and regulatory capacities.

The following case history describes the process of integrating the relationship issues and physiological factors that led to a diagnosis of Depression in a toddler who had previously been diagnosed as pervasively developmentally delayed—an apt illustration of the way in which symptoms of infant depression may be misinterpreted. The case history will necessarily focus on the diagnostic process rather than on the treatment and resolution processes. Only those aspects of treatment that served to confirm the diagnosis will be highlighted.

Reason for referral

Margaret (Meg) and Robert (Rob) Dunbar first contacted a private practice group of clinical psychologists when their only son Donny was 29 months old. In her initial phone call, Meg explained that their son had been diagnosed three months earlier as having a pervasive developmental disorder. She stated that he did not seem to be making progress after three months of early intervention. They wanted to understand why no progress was occurring. She noted emphatically that she and her husband enjoyed Donny tremendously. Rob and she had noticed a change when he was about 24 months old. His speech fell off, and he showed increased frustration and fewer attempts to communicate his needs. She reported that he most often recoiled from interaction with other children. She summed up her worry by explaining that he had been evaluated by the public school special education team but that she believed that he did not belong in special education. She and her husband wanted to learn where he did belong, and what interventions would help him develop normally.

Assessment process

DC: 0-3 recommends three to five sessions of 45 or more minutes each for a full evaluation of how each area of functioning is developing for an infant or toddler and to explore the myriad factors that provoke a depression in infancy. The assessment of Donny and his family involved five office visits, which included observation of play between parent(s) and child, and, infrequently, a few activities involving the clinician, as well as coming to understand the family's background and present arrangements.

Assessment findings

First session

In the first session Donny presented as an appealing, but somber toddler, wearing jeans, a preppy sweatshirt, and cartoon-illustrated multicolored sneakers. He was on the small side for his age, with a slight, almost delicate build. He had light brown, curly hair and a very fair complexion. He seemed subdued, possibly shy, with little indication of his feelings. His movements were measured: he seemed to move slowly, as if hesitant about interacting with the environment. He appeared to mold comfortably while being carried by his father, and as his father sat down with him.

As the adults talked, Donny sat on his dad's lap. He did not intrude on the "adult" conversation with his needs, impulsiveness, or childish exploration. He did not make demands for his parents' attention. He did not suck his fingers or content himself with other self-soothing behavior, as one might expect in a strange environment. Except for his furtive glances at the clinician, or his clinging when his parents encouraged him to explore, he did not initiate interaction. Because the clinician was expecting a child showing the behaviors associated with a Pervasive Developmental Disorder (PDD) diagnosis, she expected more rigidity, and a higher physical tension level than that which Donny presented. Her very first impression of him included a sense of surprise that he was not more tense and uncomfortable. Nevertheless, he seemed uninterested, in fact opposed to, exploring the room with all the toys available.

Both parents had direct gaze themselves, and welcoming, firm handshakes. They presented the information that they wanted considered in an organized manner. Their anxiety and somberness seemed appropriate to their worry about their son. As they spoke, Meg and Rob communicated a strong sense of purpose, providing the clinician with the information they thought she needed.

In the room, the clinician had put out a few toys that might interest a child diagnosed as having some sort of developmental disorder, including a Nerf ball, some bubble-making solution and a bubble wand, two toy telephones and a small xylophone. His father tried to put Donny down and get him to look at the toys, but he clung to his dad's lap. When Rob insisted, Donny just went from father to mother, whining uncomfortably. His parents became observably tense as Donny began whining. Worrying that his discomfort might escalate rapidly, the clinician invited his mother to entice him into her big black leather chair, which spins. Once Donny was in the chair, his father came over and spun him, and Donny's face registered interest. His father stopped spinning him, and asked, "Again?" Donny looked directly at his father and nodded, but did not speak. When, after the next spin his father asked, "More?", Donny looked at him and said "More," quietly, without inflection. While not highly animated and involved in the game, Donny did seem interested, and gestured to both his mother and the clinician to join in spinning him. By the end of this interaction, he was soberly but spontaneously saying, "More spin, fast," or "More spin, slow," thereby controlling the spinning game with his parents. This interactive sequence suggested that the original diagnosis of Pervasive Developmental Disorder, reported by the mother, was incorrect.

When the spinning stopped, Donny lost all traces of affect and sat motionless in the chair, as if in suspended animation. His mother took up the bubbles and wand, called to him, and blew some bubbles to him. Donny got up, went over to where his mother was sitting and began popping bubbles. He spoke quietly to his mother, using language that was more or less age-appropriate: "Look Mummy—I popped it." Although Donny's use of the pronoun "I" suggested an age-appropriate level of self-awareness, it was unclear how aware of himself he actually was, because he invested the statement, "I popped it" with no feelings of pride or satisfaction. As Meg blew the bubbles, Rob pointed to them one by one, and Donny then popped each bubble in turn. As the bubble blowing continued, everyone in the family seemed very attuned to each other and exchanged nonverbal cues. The clinician was impressed by a curious lack of enjoyment in the bubble play, but at this point, wondered if the family's lack of emotional expression had more to do with her observing them than with any intrinsic aspect of their interactions.

When the clinician asked whether Donny's level of language functioning that we had observed together just now was typical, Meg responded that Donny did not usually warm up this quickly! Clearly, she found his language to be so typical of him as to not warrant comment. She added that he was talking the way he did at home, more or less. Asked to expand on her comment, with the hope of understanding what the differences were between Donny's language at home and in other settings, Meg became affectively flat, in a way similar to Donny. Rob, quickly supporting his wife, explained that they did not know what to make of the differences between his behavior at home and in other settings. The teacher at his preschool said that he seemed "closed down." Sometimes he acted lethargic, lying on the floor; other times he just seemed "lost in space." Dad reported that Donny seemed to have little ability to follow directions or to interact at school. At home, while he didn't seem to follow directions, he was interpersonally engaged most of the time and seemed content to sit on his father's lap while he worked at the computer or go along with his mother on her errands. When they read to him, he seemed attentive, although he was predominantly nonverbal in all contexts. Rob reiterated that he and his wife felt perplexed by their observation of Donny's behavior when he was at home and his behavior in interaction with others.

During this conversation, Donny tentatively explored the room, wandering from toy to toy, not really playing. As we watched him together, the clinician asked his parents about his play. They said that he did not play, that he needed them to be with him all the time, and even then, he simply imitated whatever they showed him. Meg proceeded to enact this phenomenon by trying to play with him. She took a phone and said, "Oh, Dad wants to speak to you," and held one phone receiver out to Donny while she held the other to her ear. Donny took the phone and imitated her actions, putting the receiver to his ear, but he did not continue the play. He dropped the receiver and went wandering about aimlessly.

The clinician suggested that we try to discover what prompted Donny to initiate interactions, or respond to interactions, or to shut off. At this, Meg perked up, and smiled, asking, "So you see what we're saying?" The clinician assured her that she did, and thought together they might figure out what was going on over the course of three or four more meetings. She told them she understood what worried them about Donny's behavior and that it might be painful to acknowledge their worry as appropriate, or that they might feel some relief that she understood what they were describing. The clinician also noted it would be important for them to understand what Donny's behavior means to them as his parents. The clinician was careful not to limit her concern to just Donny, but to include Meg and Rob.

Noticing the careful wording, Meg's head went down, and she seemed to recoil into herself, acting as if she had been chastised. The clinician thought the parents wanted her to focus on identifying accurately Donny's developmental strengths and vulnerabilities and ways for them to help him to overcome his vulnerability around interaction with peers, and not focus on their relationship with him or their feelings directly. (While many parents feel relieved that the clinician notices not only the behaviors in their child that are worrisome, but also their parental experience of worry, others draw back, as this couple did, not understanding that their own experiences and understanding are vital to an accurate diagnosis.) Meg's response meant that the clinician's proposed exploration of the parents' relationship with Donny was threatening.

Both parents then seemed weary, sad, and quiet. The clinician empathized with how hard it must be for them to watch Donny, who had seemed engaged a little bit earlier in the session, be simply empty most of the time. During this first meeting, most of the clinician's attempts to reflect back their feelings, or inquire about what either parent might be feeling met with an uninformative response, or polite silence and a change of subject. Meg and Rob seemed to be very private people, unused to or uncomfortable sharing their feelings. When the clinician acknowledged that Donny's behavior must sadden them, commenting "that it must be difficult for you to watch Donny struggle and seem so isolated when he clearly is connected to you at other times," Meg's eyes welled up with tears. Rob jumped in and immediately shifted the focus away from those painful feelings, saying "What should we do for Donny?"

As so often happens in work involving parents and a baby, Rob had shifted our focus from his own issues and the clinician's concern for him and Meg to his child's behavior. The clinician's impression at that moment was clearly that he and Meg functioned as one unit. Perhaps they hoped that if the clinician stopped talking about feelings, the painful feelings would go away. The clinician noticed her own hesitancy to probe further . It suggested to the clinician that maybe Donny's parents avoided awareness both of shared feelings, as well as their own individual and differentiated emotional experiences.

While the clinician did not yet understand the parent's behavior, she was aware of their distance from her. In this first session, the clinician did not yet see how to bridge the distance, which seemed to prevent them from openly discussing the emotional involvement in their relationship with their son, so she focused on procedures. The clinician explained that the diagnostic process entailed meeting with the parents and Donny three or four more times, in a way similar to the present meeting, and that she would also want to meet with them without Donny to talk in detail about his life with them. They scheduled these visits, and Donny and his parents left.

Second session

The next diagnostic session began with free play. Meg and Rob proceeded to completely structure activities for Donny. He was given no choices, and he did not seem interested in initiating play based on his own ideas. He simply echoed his parents' words. For example, if his mother asked, "Donny, what does the dog want to do, does he want to eat hamburger?" Donny repeated, "He want to eat hamburger." Meg did not pick up the subtle difference in his inflection, which signaled an affirmative answer to her question.

The parents seemed bored by the play, and repeatedly asked what they should do next. The clinician encouraged them to include Donny in figuring out what to do. It never happened, though. The few times they asked for his input, they got no response. He would stop moving as if considering their statements, look around randomly, as if uncomprehending, and then flit from one toy to another, picking up and dropping them randomly. Meg and Rob did not verbally encourage Donny to explore further, and he did not initiate any purposeful play. Nor did they try to share their enthusiasm for a toy or entice him with a toy they found interesting.

Whenever Donny gave the least indication that he might be ready to move on, whichever parent was interacting with him would make the transition for him instantly by anticipating his choice and acting as if he had chosen, not themselves. They did this without waiting to see what he actually wanted to do next or stating that they recognized his cues. The clinician needed to discover if, given the interpersonal support and time, Donny could communicate his intentions and desires. The clinician needed to learn whether the parents' behavior was driven by Donny's limitations in executing his own ideas or their overinvolvement. This information would help the clinician know the extent to which Donny might have difficulty regulating his attention and organizing more purposeful behavior, which preempted his possible next steps, and the extent to which his ineffective approach occurred because his parents were misinterpreting his cues, to which he responded by moving and avoiding their "help." Since he had been diagnosed with a pervasive developmental disorder, this distinction was central to diagnosis. It was crucial to find out what Donny's intentions were.

Therefore, the clinician asked Meg and Rob to wait before changing activities until Donny gave a hearty cue that he no longer was interested in what he had initiated. She also encouraged them to speak for him when he seemed ready to change focus, saying something like "Donny says, I think I'll try . . ." Meg perceived this suggestion as creating unnecessary tension for Donny. She matter-of-factly said she didn't see why she had to "create uncomfortable situations for Donny." Her opinion was that "Donny just doesn't understand how to get what he needs," and that confusion "had happened often enough already in his life." Rob added, resolutely, that he and Meg tried to "help Donny navigate all the nuances of interaction" that they thought he didn't understand. It was not clear at this point what Donny didn't "understand," but his parents seemed to assume that, at some level, he did not comprehend his surroundings. The clinician wondered if they were only working trying to help Donny or if they were so overinvolved and enmeshed in their relationship that they could not allow him to make any moves on his own. Most children, no matter how severe or pervasive the extent of disability may be, provide cues about their desires or impulses. But as long as the parents preempted his expression with their own, the clinician could not learn Donny's language, or cues, for communicating his needs and desires.

Third session

Donny began the third session by telling his mother firmly that she should call him "Holly." This exchange perplexed the clinician, who asked Meg and Rob to explain. Meg said, "What Donny likes to do the most is take out some toy trains and use them to dramatize (from memory) the words of one of his books that we have read together. Donny also likes to tell me that his name is Holly or Adam (characters in the same book series) or other fantasy characters from books that we have read to him. He insists that we address him by these names and also gives us names and insists on calling us by these other names." The names—sometimes girls' names, sometimes boys' names, sometimes the names of objects—always came from books his parents had read to him.

When the family reenacted these dialogues in the office, the voices they used had an uncharacteristically full range of affect. This was not pretend play in which Donny experienced new feelings of his own and used the play to develop solutions in an emotional problem-solving strategy. Donny's play was fixed and rigid, admitting no alteration from the scripts he had been read. It was in the reenacting of the scripts that Donny retrieved his parents' best affective communications, borrowed from the stories they read to him. Meg's informative explanation showed that the naming phenomenon was not indicative of Donny's own ideas, but rather, complex imitation of scripts he remembered. Donny insisted on replicating the dialogue with them, inflections as well as words, and assumed the identities of the characters he could predict. The affect each expressed was not spontaneous or responsive to their ideas and feelings, but remembered and reenacted. Instead, they shared sequences of affect and action heard or viewed rather than spontaneous interaction. Donny seemed to use complex imitation as a way of recapturing a shared emotional experience with his parents. Since Meg and Rob preempted Donny during in-the-moment interactions, he had little or no opportunity to experience an emotional agenda of his own with them, except by engaging them in this unvarying reenactment of storybook plots.

Meg and Rob said that they didn't want to be left out of his world, so they allowed Donny to spend whole days using different names for all of them. The clinician expressed ignorance of this unusual naming and gently prodded him by addressing him as Donny. When Donny asked to be called "Holly," the clinician asked, "Who is Holly? I don't know Holly, tell me who Holly is, I want to know who you are." The parents were intrigued by the results: Donny answered to "Donny" with the clinician. While the clinician felt uncomfortable calling him by another name, she wasn't trying to get them to stop their name substitution with him; if Donny needed those other names, she didn't want to take them away from him. The clinician wanted to understand what fueled his expectation that he be called by a name other than Donny, and encouraged Meg and Rob to tell him that they liked using his name best, even while they were using the name he insisted they use.

It is noteworthy that the following week, when Meg and Rob came to see the clinician alone, they reported with some pleasure that Donny's demands for alternative names had decreased significantly following our discussion, for the first time in weeks. When asked how they explained this change, Meg and Rob together said they thought that this change in Donny's behavior occurred as a result of their telling Donny what they liked about his name. They told him that his name reminded them of his great-grandfather back in Scotland, for whom he was named, and how pleased that great man would have been to know that their Donny was such a fine lad. This outcome showed us that Donny didn't seem compelled to engage in the naming, except as a means of creating an emotionally satisfying interaction with his parents. His observed flexibility was an important characteristic in considering a differential diagnosis.

Another significant prognostic finding of the third session was that Donny's parents followed through on exchanges we had during sessions. For the purposes of treatment planning, as well as diagnosis, this was important information to have. It suggested that Meg and Rob engaged in our discussions seriously, thought about their interactions with Donny, and had the self-awareness and motivation to alter their own behavior when they felt it was appropriate to do so.

Fourth session

The fourth session involved only Donny's parents. As we talked about Donny's social and developmental history, the family values that guided Meg and Rob's parenting behavior became clearer. In describing their own childhoods, Meg and Rob helped the clinician understand how the cultural values from their ethnic heritage influenced their parenting style, their coping strategies, and their understanding of Donny's behavior. The clinician believed that cultural characteristics, including emotional reserve and intergenerational loyalty patterns, (McGoldrick, Pearce & Giordano, 1982) influenced how much these two parents could openly share their feelings. Additionally, Rob's family seemed to use academic strivings to create boundaries between the children of the family and the outside community.

Rob is 36 years old and was born in Scotland. He comes from a two-parent, Episcopalian family in which all five children are successfully established in their own lives. He is the only one of his siblings to marry. Rob said that growing up, his family was never "interested in social adaptation." He explained that they were all bookworms, eschewed friendships, and focused on achievement. He described his family's style of dealing with feelings: "We were taught to keep it in. If one of us felt bad, we were not to tell it." The clinician understood that family conversations focused on facts and any show of emotion was ignored as embarrassing and a demonstration of incompetence. The clinician asked Rob why there was no acknowledgment of feelings during his childhood. His reply indicated that there were no feelings expressed by anyone in his family. Asked if his family had feelings about his move to the United States, he shrugged his shoulders and said he guessed they were very happy for him and proud of him. The topic had never come up for discussion.

Meg is 36 years old and was also born in Scotland, in a small town near the one in which Rob's family lived. She is the "baby," the youngest of five siblings, also from a two-parent, deeply religious Episcopalian family. Her mother died when she was eleven, and she was raised essentially by her older sisters, with whom she remains close. When asked her how her family had dealt with her mother's death, Meg explained that her family's way was to keep on going, no matter what. She proudly reported that she had not missed a day of school on account of her mother's illness, death, or funeral. She described her four older siblings as organized and successful, but she reported that she is the most educated. When asked how they showed their feelings in her family, like anger or joy, Meg looked stunned. Her comment was "no one in my family ever gets angry. We are fun-loving, but quiet about it."

Both Rob and Meg came from families with strong kinship ties and strong ties to their church. Both families prized intelligence, hard work, and achievement. Rob described his family as very peaceful, very calm. Meg described hers as more demonstrative than Rob's. Neither parent could remember ever being punished. When asked how they learned family rules of behavior, Meg explained that she was quiet, sensitive, and smart, and it only "took a look" to put her back in line. Rob seemed very amused with the question, and chuckled, "It is a mystery to me, I don't remember anything more severe than a verbal rebuke, and even these were infrequent."

Except for Meg and Rob, the family members continue to live within a couple of miles of each other. Each parent denied family history of chronic illness, mental illness, alcoholism, addictions, suicide, or eccentricity. When the clinician challenged their idealized perceptions, by commenting that it was quite unusual for there to be no member on either side of any family with any health, financial, or interpersonal problems, Rob explained by saying that both families were close-knit, and mostly without friends outside the extended family.

Both Meg and Rob put forth a view that they came from families who emotionally and materially gave them all that they needed, even though in describing their experiences it seemed evident that feelings were customarily denied expression or affirmation. Their behavior and responses made it plain that they did not want to engage in looking at their families' functioning, and wanted the clinician to believe that there was nothing psychologically ineffective or problematic in their backgrounds or behavior.

In taking this position they seemed to be avoiding exploration of their own feelings around familial style of denial of their feelings and dreams, interpersonal loss, and geographical displacement. The clinician had the strong sense that, along with all the positive facets of their families and their courage to immigrate, their loyalty to their families disallowed their awareness of negative feelings. The insistence on togetherness in their families obscured their experiences of being separate and differentiated. Though neither Rob nor Meg had a hidden agenda in their presentation, nor were they trying to consciously withhold information , Rob's answer about his family being close-knit was a non sequitur. He did not attend to or address the comments the clinician made referring to limits of their families' support. Rather, he shifted the conversation to an idealized perception of his experience that not having his affect acknowledged or affirmed somehow provided support to make his own way. This hard-to-follow explanation coming from two competent, highly functioning people, seemed psychologically simplistic.

Meg and Rob told me that they had been married while both were in college. Because Rob seemed unlikely to be able to pursue his career interests at home, the couple decided to emigrate to the United States to seek further professional education and work for Rob. The original move to the United States occurred about eight years ago, after Meg finished her medical degree and residency. The Dunbars have lived in this city for the last five years. Rob holds a tenured professorship at a local university.

Meg hasn't worked as a physician since coming to the States and now does not work at all outside the home. Although she did some research prior to immigration, there were nuances in the licensing rules which she overlooked. In order for her to practice medicine, she would have had to reenter a full-time residency program, which she had already completed in Scotland. She did not realize this facet of the licensing laws and found the prospect unacceptable. She reported that she felt stunned when she couldn't get licensed, but then she became resigned to not working. When the clinician explicitly asked Meg about her career plans for the future, she said that Donny was her career now. She said that she had aspirations of having a large family but she and Rob found it took longer to get pregnant than they anticipated. She reported feeling at loose ends prior to Donny's birth, and that these feelings lessened considerably after he came. She said that she found energy once she was engaged in her role as mother and expressed great satisfaction in caring for her son. She said that her dream for more children was "unthinkable" given Donny's needs.

Both parents said that they had few social relationships outside of Rob's colleagues. They observed that for most of their lives their families had provided the social support and nurturing that they needed, and they had not had the experience of their family reaching outside of itself for support or help. On the contrary, the family value, more in Rob's family than in Meg's but somewhat in both, was to present a picture of self-sufficiency to the world outside the family, and to live as if this ideal were real, as much as possible, within the family.

In describing their backgrounds, Meg and Rob seemed uninterested in exploring or describing the emotional complexity of raising a child, or thinking about their childhoods and experience of being parented. Trying to understand how Meg and Rob understood their parenting tasks, the clinician asked them to describe the difficulties they experienced in Donny's behavior. They remained vague, alluding to inability to communicate, though Donny did communicate in an age-appropriate manner; lack of initiative and spontaneous behavior, which they seemed to choose consciously to prevent; and inability to play with peers, though, as he didn't seem to play with anyone, why were they focusing on peers only? In constructing an idealized version of their own childhoods, they preserved their family loyalty and avoided having to experience the tensions and emotional discomfort engendered in caring for a baby in isolation, in a foreign, sometimes incomprehensible, country. They could only express their sense that all was not well through their worries about their child. The parents' blocking off of negative affect supported a diagnosis of infant depression of their son.

Birth and developmental history

Meg stated that Donny, born Donald Michael, "was eagerly and joyously anticipated" by his parents, and the product of a planned, normal pregnancy. There was often a discrepancy between what Meg and Rob reported feeling about their experience and their actual demeanor. As they described this joyousness there was no hint of it in remembering it. Meg reported that his delivery, however, was complicated by a breech presentation that necessitated a cesarean section. Rob said that they were given only a few hours to prepare for the surgical birth. My queries about how they had coped with this unexpected crisis brought forth only silence. Finally, Rob dismissed the subject (and any feelings) by saying, "Well, we got through it, didn't we? What more is there to say?" From both of their perspectives, there was nothing to do but "forget the difficult experience of Donny's birth, and just take him home and love him." As Rob explained this perspective, Meg listened attentively, nodding in agreement. They said they did not perceive Donny's birth as difficult or highly charged, simply uncomfortable in its emergency nature. Their apparent discomfort with looking at their feelings around the highly charged delivery and their unwillingness to share those feelings provided information about how Meg and Rob organized their experiences regarding Donny's birth.

Donny weighed 7 pounds, 5 ounces at birth. His Apgar scores were 7 at one minute, and 8 at five minutes. He had no major or chronic illnesses during his infancy. He sat without support at 3 months, crawled at $6^{1}/_{2}$ months, and walked at 12 months. He acquired words at around 14 to 16 months and even spoke in sentences before regressing to echoing rather than spontaneous communication at around 2 years. While superficially this pattern seems to match that found in many children diagnosed as having a pervasive or multisystem developmental disorder, it differed in two important respects: Donny had a lot of language, not just a few words, when speaking "stopped"; and his language really didn't "stop" at all. His language with anyone other than his parents stopped; in relationship with his mother and father, he occasionally showed appropriate language but it was never observed by the outside world. On a visit back to Scotland, Meg and Rob noticed his apparent speech delay during prodding from their families, and when they compared him to their nieces and nephews who were about the same age as Donny.

The speech evaluation done at the local university-affiliated hospital when Donny was 26 months confirmed his parents' fears of an apparent developmental delay. On the Peabody Picture Vocabulary Test Donny scored at a 15-month level. On the Vineland Adaptive Behavior Scale he scored between 11 months (socialization) and 18 months (skills of daily living). His language score was at 12 months. His Adaptive Behavior Composite was at the .3rd percentile rank. The examiner's notes indicated that he "didn't interact spontaneously with anyone in the room, he did not follow single step directions, he became easily distracted and wandered from activity to activity. He seemed to listen to his parents, and he liked hugs." A report from his early intervention speech therapist indicated that Donny's difficulties were not with oral-motor functions, semantics, or articulation, but rather with the pragmatic, turn-taking, give-and-take aspects of language. He seemed limited and uncomfortable in his ability to stay focused in exchanges with her.

His parents stated that Donny was a very finicky eater, accepting only yogurt, pizza, cereal, bread, orange juice, milk, donuts, and pretzels. Meg reported that she gave him snacks whenever she was hungry, and since he didn't ask for snacks, she didn't really know if he wanted them at other times. His parents initially stated that Donny was very easygoing about sleep routines—that is, if they were all out late, he seemed content to stay up with them until he fell fast asleep, regardless of his surroundings. He didn't get cranky or signal a need to be settled down for sleep. However, at home in his own bed, Donny had great difficulty falling asleep, although once asleep he seemed to stay asleep until morning. The difficulty seemed to be that he lay awake in his bed for a long time after he was tucked in. Recently, falling asleep had become a problem. He demanded that one of his parents stay with him. If the parent got up to leave, he awoke and demanded that they lay back down.

Donny was still wearing diapers at the time of the evaluation. Meg explained that she had not attempted to toilet train him because she felt that he could not control himself, and he did not understand concepts of time and propriety enough to understand the concept of using a toilet. Meg and Rob reported that, at age 2^1/$_2$, Donny had never gone through the "terrible two's" and was always pleasant, easy-going and accepting of whatever his parents did for him.

Meg reported that Donny had not experienced any separations from either parent for more than a few hours. Although he was in a mother-child transitional preschool program, as well as a gymnastics program, he did not actively participate in either program, preferring to sit with his mother and watch the other children, or wander around aimlessly.

Fifth session

By the fifth diagnostic play session, Donny still had not shown any clear play or focused exploratory behavior, and Meg and Rob had not identified a toy with which Donny clearly wanted to play. Donny seemed unable to use his parents' examples in an imitative way. It was another bit of data that led differentially away from Pervasive Developmental Disorder (PDD) and toward a diagnosis of Depression. A child with PDD would have attempted to imitate perhaps more than Donny did. He was clearly communicating that he would only interact around their affect, not objects. Donny did use language to connect with his parents as when he asked his father to spin him more in the big black chair. However, their interactions occurred with little emotional expression. His cues for affect were often muted, or not observable at all. He didn't even spontaneously bang objects or manipulate them with intent. He seemed disconnected from expression of his impulses except in interaction with his parents around basic needs, other than concrete responses to his parents' requests. Interestingly, Meg and Rob observed that they had seen a subtle but noticeable change in his behavior at home over the course of the five diagnostic sessions. It seemed to them that he was initiating interaction with them more and using verbal language more.

Diagnosis

Axis I: *Primary Diagnosis:* One of the most important markers of development is a child's ability to have a repertoire of feelings with which to express his impulses. He uses these feelings as the basis for exploring his world. It is a child's feelings that create the structure for communication and learning during the early years. Donny did not express feelings, whether he was using words or not. He predominantly behaved in a sober manner, with very little range of affect. When he wanted something, he waited for his parents to notice his tentative cues, or their own sensations that initiated an interaction with him. Also, he did not provide cues as to whether they had understood his needs accurately. His expression of feeling occurred in the context of a parent-initiated interaction. There did not seem to be any depth to his pleasure, nor did his pleasure act as a bridge to maintain interpersonal or intersubjective connection. After each interaction, he returned to either a somber or shut-down state.

Donny's flat affect and severely constricted range of affect were the prominent characteristics of his disturbance. His functional inability to use toys as an expression of his internal impulses, lack of spontaneous play, restricted food preferences, and a repertoire limited to only whininess and lack of protest in response to environmental impingements fulfilled the criteria for a diagnosis of Depression.

Prior to considering the evidence that supported a diagnosis of Depression, the clinician considered Multisystem Developmental Disorder, Regulatory Disorder, Developmental Delay, Anxiety Disorder, Traumatic Stress Disorder, Reactive Attachment Disorder, and Mixed Disorder of Emotional Expressiveness.

The diagnosis of Pervasive Developmental Disorder made by the previous assessor seemed to miss the mark on several counts. First, this diagnosis seems to have been based on the fact that Donny appeared to have stopped talking and on observations of delays in communication, cognitive performance, and social interaction. However, Donny was not delayed in sensory integration, motor planning, or muscle tone, all domains in which difficulties are typically present when a child has a regulatory or multisystem (pervasive) developmental disorder. Secondly, the depth of involvement with his parents that Donny demonstrated was not consistent with a diagnosis of PDD or Multisystem Developmental Disorder (MSDD). Young children with MSDD most often seem isolated or distant in interactions with their parents; the quality of Donny's relationship with his parents seemed enmeshed (Minuchin, 1974) and overinvolved (Kerr and Bowen, 1988). The "lack of progress in early intervention" that worried Donny's parents might have been a marker for developmental delay. But this alternative, while logical in theory, became implausible because Donny's verbal exchanges with his parents, however infrequent, and his ability to imitate his parents' actions so accurately indicated quite a bit of age-appropriate functioning.

The very exclusivity of Donny's relationship with his parents could have indicated the presence of an anxiety disorder. But if Donny was experiencing heightened separation anxiety, he would have expressed strong feelings when his parents were not involved with him. Instead, he seemed to "shut off" emotionally when his parents were uninvolved with him, as though a switch had been flipped. Had Donny been experiencing separation anxiety, we would have expected to see interest in play, primarily with his parents, when they were close by and, in contrast, difficulty exploring the environment on his own and evidence of anxiety in his relationship with the clinician or when his parents introduced novelty into the interaction. This was not the case. Donny did seem occasionally interested in relating to the clinician, and he initiated no play at all, with his parents, with the clinician, or with toys. He waited for an adult to engage in play; then he imitated the adult's actions until he began flitting again.

If Donny had become upset when either the clinician or his parents did not follow his lead in using alternative names, there would have been cause to wonder why he had to find alternative personae. The clinician would have wondered if he was trying to protect himself from some painful memory or awareness. She also would have explored what the conditions were that triggered the naming phenomenon, looked for traumatic reenactment, and considered the possibility of traumatic stress or past traumatic experience as the source of the naming behavior. But his use of alternative names was easily modified once his parents provided a clear preference to call Donny by his own name. His alternative naming diminished substantially over the course of the evaluation process.

His parents' anxious response to his cues effectively blocked Donny from experiencing a range of feelings, or having a range of intensity of feeling. Donny's impulse expression developed without differentiation of various affects, and resulted in a muted quality in his affect expression. When his parents read the muted cues inaccurately, and failed to reflect back an accurate meaning to his cues, they effectively prevented him from learning how to cue more robustly. A diagnosis of Reactive Attachment Disorder would adequately reflect the effect of their behavior on aspects of Donny's behavior, but this diagnosis would not accurately reflect the parents' concern and active help-seeking. It addressed only the symptom behavior in the child, that of failure to initiate social interactions. This diagnosis would not reflect the concern and consistent care Meg and Rob showed: they were not neglecting their baby and were trying to provide him with the very best care possible. The difficulty with their care lay not in their level of attention to their son's needs, but in their confusion about how to interpret and respond to his cues regarding his needs.

Finally, although Donny's behavior did reflect some characteristics of Mixed Disorder of Emotional Expressiveness, this diagnosis did not capture the global nature of his affect constriction. A mixed disorder of emotional expressiveness is characterized by an "absence or near absence of one or more specific types of affects that are developmentally expectable"; a "range of emotional expression that is constricted in comparison to developmentally appropriate expectations"; and "disturbed intensity of emotional expression, inappropriate to the child's developmental level" (*DC: 0-3*, pp. 25-26). It implies that while the child's affect is expressed in constricted or atypical ways, he or she does initiate expression of affect. Donny's behavioral repertoire showed a nearly complete absence of initiating impulse expression, an avoidance of affect awareness, and a severely limited range of feelings. He did not express age-appropriate affects such as exuberance, enthusiasm, curiosity, self-assertion, negativism, joy, or even sleepiness. The clinician observed not a diminished range of expected behaviors or atypical intensity or expression of feeling, but rather a child apparently unused to spontaneous expression of any kind. His affect was consistently sober. Even when spinning, when the movement stopped, so did his expression of affect. And, what affect he did express in the spinning game was muted, showing increased interest, not enjoyment or even alarm. In addition, the diagnosis of Mixed Disorder of Emotional Expressiveness did not address or describe his emotionally "shut down" interaction quality or his lack of play. Depression seemed to be the most apt diagnosis for Donny.

Axis II: *Relationship Disorder Classification:* The quality of Donny's relationships with his parents seemed to constitute a major contributing factor to his depression. Meg and Rob's relationships with him reflected their reluctance to express their own feelings or share them with Donny. Each parent attended to almost every nuance of Donny's cues. But, neither parent acknowledged the feelings that went along with the cues or reflected back to him what his cues and actions might mean, testing out their interpretation. Because Donny's cues were tentative, he never gave them a robust response that would let them know whether they had gotten the cue right or not. For example, if a child's hand is outstretched, a mother might comment, "Oh, you want something to eat, don't you?", thereby giving the child feedback about how she interprets his actions as a cue to communicate about a feeling (hunger). For his part, the baby might keep reaching, if food was not what he wanted. In the Dunbar family, Meg and Rob were more likely to give Donny the food before his hand was gesturing for anything. And, if they gave him anything at all, he did not respond spontaneously with sturdy cues that they had given him what he actually wanted. Their exquisite anticipation of his impulses as well as their lack of verbal interpretation prevented him from learning to identify, express, and act on impulses. He did not seem to differentiate affects into separate feelings. When his parents were wrong in reading his cues, Donny simply became tense and distractible. His lack of experiencing impulses and affect, as well as providing muted cues, was observable as a diminished repertoire of social interaction and initiative, and diminished capacity to protest.

Also, Meg and Robert seemed to confuse Donny's needs, expressed through his behaviors with their needs, fueled by their complex personal histories and adult roles: they did not differentiate Donny's needs from theirs. Rather than trying to understand what provoked Donny's desire to use alternative names, for example, they simply complied with his request. They seemed inexperienced in reading the affective cues of their son. They interpreted his cues to have the same meaning as if they had given the cues. Because Donny's cues were nonverbal for the most part, as well as muted, his parents did not explore alternative interpretations, or look to his response for confirmation that they had understood his cues. This lack of interpersonal differentiation raised the probability that they might also distort Donny's cues and be unaware of his impulses as separate or different from their own. This lack of differentiation constituted an over-involvement between the parents and Donny.

Although Meg and Rob were overinvolved, overinvolvement did not completely characterize the quality of their anxiety about Donny's feelings. For example, they said that they didn't want Donny to experience any feelings that would increase his level of tension. Childhood in their estimation should be a time of unself-conscious, undiluted pleasure, without tension or worry. Meg and Rob worked anxiously to anticipate his every need. In doing this, they created an organization for him so that he would not experience anxiety. Theirs, however, was an organization he did not create for himself. Meg and Rob's relationship with Donny looked like an anxious attempt to protect their son from experiencing tension in any form, even when some tension seemed appropriate to the situation and, from the clinicians perspective at least, experiencing the tension would have been growth-promoting for Donny.

Since the purpose of diagnosis is to provide a readily understandable form for describing the quality of interaction between an infant and his family, more than one quality of relationship may be appropriate. Description of the complex quality of interaction between Donny and his parents necessitated using two categories. Here was a family in which the relationship between the baby and parents was tense, anxious, and overinvolved.

Axis III: *Medical and Developmental Disorders and Conditions:* Axis III provides an opportunity to note Donny's communication difficulties, which could have easily played some role in his parents' developing such exquisite ability to read his cues (Wetherby & Prizant, 1996). Given that he had ongoing speech therapy, it was important to note and highlight that. As his early intervention speech therapist had reported, his difficulties were with the pragmatics of speech, not comprehension, processing, or oral-motor skills.

Axis IV: *Psychosocial Stressors:* The purpose of Axis IV is to help clinicians take into account various forms of psychosocial stress that are influencing factors in disorders of infancy and early childhood. The clinician must distinguish the severity of a specific stressor from its ultimate impact on the child, which will be modified by the response of the environment (*DC: 0-3*, p. 58). The situation of the Dunbar family illustrates this chain of influence. The psychosocial stressor with the most significant impact on Donny's condition was each parent's depression.

Although they did not explicitly report feeling depressed, Meg and Rob each demonstrated symptoms of depression. For example, while they expressed an intense desire to help their son, Rob and Meg volunteered little information about themselves or their feelings not directly related to their concerns about Donny. On numerous occasions the clinician attempted to talk with them about topics they had identified as important to them. While each parent showed a range of feelings greater than Donny's, they nevertheless also seemed constricted in their expression of feelings.

Another impression that led the clinician to think Donny's parents were depressed involved Meg's expression of anxiety. On several occasions, Meg called the clinician after a session to clarify some part of the previous session that had led her to feel anxious. The first time this happened, the clinician was truly taken by surprise, and felt remorseful that she had not observed Meg's anxiety and helped her with it during the session. When Meg called after each of two more sessions to challenge her around a worrisome issue, the clinician asked her what kept her from showing how she felt during the session. Her response was that she often didn't know that she felt in a given way until some days after the session had occurred. It took her a long time to recognize the feelings that she experienced in a session, and longer to share them. She explained that she often felt confused by her feelings, uncomfortable in her awareness of her feelings, and fearful that the clinician would perceive her as stupid or unintelligent if she expressed her feelings. The clinician came to understand Meg's silences during sessions as indications that she had some feeling that needed to be explored further, but in its own good time.

For his part, Rob did not talk very much at all, and kept his eyes downcast unless he was explicitly interacting with the clinician. He mostly entered conversations to support his wife's statements or add factual material. Often, when the clinician addressed a question or comment to one of the parents, the other would answer, as if protecting the spouse from the painful feelings engendered by the question. When asked, Meg and Rob denied feeling depressed and said explicitly that they were quite content and that their lives "were more than they had imagined they could be." While respecting their expressed contentment, the clinician still experienced them as behaving in a depressed manner.

A number of factors could have fueled their depressions, most especially their experience of immigration, which included a sense of loss of their families back in Scotland. Even the parents' unresolved feelings about Donny's difficult birth and Meg's childhood loss of her mother were affected by the major stressor of immigration.

Each of Donny's parents experienced a multidetermined depression, framed by their cultural and family legacies, which severely restricted acknowledgment of affect and expression of feelings. Their depressions were exacerbated by their loneliness and sadness at being so far from their families and Scottish culture. They felt uncomfortable with the expressive "American exuberance and openness" with which they had to deal every day. They both reported feeling a sense of relief every time they went back to Scotland for a visit. They stated that they both slept better and ate better on their visits to Scotland. Their immigration contributed powerfully to their sense of familial loss and isolation, creating a desire to stay away from their painful feelings.

Perhaps because it was traumatic, Meg and Rob did not integrate their feelings regarding Donny's unexpected cesarean delivery. The delivery seemed to have created additional uncomfortable feelings that neither parent had been able to organize or resolve and that contributed to their apparent desire to avoid acknowledgment of feelings in general. The enduring stress of not knowing if something was wrong with their son, how permanent the difficulty was, or how they could organize help for his development was yet another source of painful tension. This unacknowledged anxiety about not knowing may have led Meg and Rob to accept, initially, the diagnosis of pervasive developmental disorder.

Meg's personal history of loss of her mother at age eleven, a loss that was barely acknowledged, much less mourned, sensitized her to Donny's level of frustration and her desire to protect him from being lost "in nuances of interaction that he doesn't understand." (Main & Hesse, 1990) Meg acknowledged that she had compensated for the loss of her professional identity (another result of immigration) by becoming completely invested in Donny's care. We may further hypothesize that attempting to adapt to her loss of professional status by focusing on Donny as her main concern also represented Meg's effort to cope with the loss of other important parts of her self—her mother, her family, and her culture—as well as her work.

Axis V: *Functional Emotional Developmental Level:* Axis V provides a description of the child's current level of emotional functioning. Given Donny's inability to play or represent his feelings with his parents, he was not functioning emotionally at an appropriate age level. When Donny's feelings were "switched on," he seemed organized around interacting with his parents, and attempted to follow their model, both in behavior as well as in expression of affect. When his feelings were "switched off," he functioned at a younger developmental level. At these times his characteristic emotional functioning was at the level of interactive intentionality and reciprocity.

The clinician completed separate Functional Emotional Developmental Level (FEDL)ratings for Donny with his mother, father, and herself. With his mother, during the interactions that occurred when he used his alternative names, it seemed that Donny's capacity for representational/affective communication was emerging. Donny achieved this level also with his father. His FEDL rating in interaction with the clinician remained at the level of interactive intentionality and reciprocity, with constriction. Although Donny's interactions with her were scant, they did allow the clinician to see him shift into a less mature way of functioning. Donny had not reached the expected level of emotional functioning for his age, and, for the levels he had attained, he demonstrated constricted range of functioning. He had not achieved current expected level, but did achieve some prior levels, such as mutual attention, mutual engagement, and interactive intentionality and reciprocity.

Diagnostic Summary

Axis I: Primary Diagnosis
Mood disorder: Depression of Infancy.

Axis II: Relationship Disorder Classification
Overinvolved Relationship; Anxious/Tense Relationship.

Axis III: Medical and Developmental Disorders and Conditions
Speech and language delay.

Axis IV: Psychosocial Stressors
Depression in each parent, resulting from their emigration and linked specifically to the mother's inability to engage in her chosen work, enduring effect. Unresolved feelings about a difficult birth experience, enduring effect. Mother's childhood loss of a parent, enduring effect.
Overall impact: severe.

Axis V: Functional Emotional Developmental Level
Functional Emotional Developmental Level—Has achieved expected age levels of mutual attention, mutual engagement, interactive intentionality and reciprocity, and representational affective communication with mother, father, and therapist, but with constrictions.

PIR-GAS:30 (Disordered)

Discussion with caregivers and treatment planning

After the five diagnostic sessions, Meg and Rob met with the clinician, who offered her diagnostic impressions of Infant Depression. Meg and Rob were politely thoughtful, and then they suggested a diagnostic formulation of their own. They did not share the clinician's concern regarding Donny's extremely limited range of affect and the constricted quality of his expression of feeling. Rob and Meg did, however, share her concern about Donny's lack of play and believed this was the most worrisome aspect of his behavior. They understood the value of play for future academic success. They felt that Donny didn't play because he had difficulty focusing his attention.

As they viewed matters, Donny's problems did not have to do with his feelings or his relationship with them. They did not see themselves as depressed; they thought that Donny was "temperamentally vulnerable from birth" (as if the two perceptions were mutually exclusive). The clinician said that "temperamental vulnerability" was an excellent way of describing Donny's pattern of providing low-key, muted cues, rather than strong expressions of his impulses. She explained that it made excellent sense to conclude that if Donny was in fact "temperamentally vulnerable from birth," his vulnerability had prevented him from developing the robustness of cue-ing needed to express his impulses firmly. She acknowledged that the low-key nature of his cues, and the muted quality of his cueing spoke directly to his temperamental vulnerability. However, his vulnerability did not explain how he came to be so shut down. They seemed to ignore the clinician's logic. Meg and Rob tactfully disagreed with the diagnosis and stated they thought Donny had an issue with shared attention. Their demeanor and words indi-cated that they did not want to discuss further the clinician's diagnostic impressions, recommendations, or goals.

It seemed that Meg and Rob were seeing diagnosis as a "label"—possibly even as a "life sentence," although one that might be mitigated by "treat-ment." The clinician realized that she sees relationships as both determining behavior and capable of change, but Meg and Rob's experience with rela-tionships was clouded by loss. Given their experiences, it was understandable that they might not perceive relationships as changeable, only "lose-able." If Meg, Rob, and the clinician could understand Donny's behavior in the con-text of his relationship experience, they could justify the hope that a shift in the quality of his relationships could fuel a recovery of function and devel-opmental pace. It was important for our therapeutic alliance that the clini-cian maintain her position without expecting Meg and Rob to accept it or understand it immediately. The clinician, of course, maintained her respect for their perspective, as well. Fortunately, we could acknowledge an essential shared reality: we all wanted Donny to get better.

To help us move forward, the clinician observed how helpful to her understanding of Donny their full engagement in the diagnostic process had been, and commented on the diligence with which they had tried promising caregiving strategies discussed during their sessions. Meg then commented that our diagnostic process was not what she had expected, adding that she and Rob felt more comfortable with it than with previous diagnostic processes.

The clinician picked up on their implied discomfort and asked what they thought about therapy in general and about previous therapeutic interventions with Donny. Meg answered that, frankly, they had mistrusted earlier recommendations because they had not been asked their opinions about their son's situation. In response to the clinician's recommendation that both they and Donny receive psychotherapy, they said that they liked her style of letting them "be the therapists with Donny," and added that they wanted to continue treatment, following the format of the diagnostic sessions. Meg and Rob seemed uninterested in the clinician's goals separate from their desire to continue the changes they had seen during the evaluation period. We set up weekly appointments for the next month.

The diagnostic and feedback process showed that, initially at least, the clinician needed to focus on helping Meg and Rob help their son. Their interest seemed to focus on his increasing ability to initiate interaction with them. They did not want to discuss any other goals the clinician might have formulated. In figuring out how to help Donny, the clinician believed, they would begin to address feelings about which they could not yet speak directly, and find resolution for their own painful dilemmas.

Intervention

During the first month of treatment, Meg and Rob brought up issues of body regulation in sleep and feeling lonely in the process of falling asleep. Donny's parents began to look at their own childhood patterns and related Donny's sleep difficulties to their own history of never being without family members around. Meg and Rob also began to ask Donny open-ended questions to encourage him to express himself through language. At the end of the first month, they said they wanted to keep on going and asked for an estimate of how many months it would take before Donny was "OK."

During the second and third months his parents worried about getting Donny to mind them. By the fifth treatment session, Donny had begun asking questions. They weren't sure they wanted their child belatedly going through the "terrible two's." The clinician encouraged them to become playful and give Donny opportunities to say "No" lots of times with his parents' acknowledgment and blessing, when it didn't matter.

The clinician invited them to get playful with the concept of "No." They stated flatly that they didn't understand. So the clinician played a game with Donny and his mother. The clinician pointed to Donny's nose and said, "Show me your elbow." Donny smiled and said, "No, that's my nose." Then the clinician invited his mother to point to a part of his body, to misidentify it in an obvious way, and invite him to respond. Donny smiled, became focused and excited and thought this game was very funny. Meg commented that this activity was silly. Donny knew the parts of his body, and this play wasn't going to fool him that it was OK to say "No." The clinician agreed and explained that the object was not to fool anyone. The point of the game was to give Donny a chance to say "No" lots of times and with his mother's acknowledgment and blessing, without any harm coming to anyone. The clinician knew they were getting somewhere when, the following week, Meg and Rob came back and Meg demonstrated the word game she and Donny were playing.:

Meg: Donny, are you Adam?

Donny: No! (smiling)

M: Donny, are you Holly?

D: No! (somewhat louder)

M: Donny, are you Daddy?

D: No! (yelling animatedly)

M: Are you Mommy?

D: NO! I'm Donny, silly! (and he got up and danced around the room, with both parents looking on, chuckling out loud).

The clinician congratulated Meg and Rob on helping Donny learn to say "No," she asked them what they thought Donny felt about saying "No" to them. The clinician fully expected Meg to answer that Donny felt great about it (since we had all just experienced that feeling), but Meg did what she usually did when asked questions about feelings. She looked downcast, became subdued, and withdrew from interaction with the clinician. Robert began playing with Donny, and tried to change the focus of the conversation. The clinician stayed with the topic, and asked Meg how she felt about saying "No" to Donny. She looked away, then back toward the clinician with a certain measured annoyance. This time she didn't withdraw, but firmly answered, "No, I don't want to capriciously say 'No' to Donny just so he can experience it."

The clinician wanted to help her begin to think about reasonable limits on his behavior, so she talked about what children might feel when they had a clear understanding of behavior limits. Meg asked if she was doing something wrong. The clinician assured her that Donny seemed very connected to Meg and that she wasn't implying or saying that Meg had done anything wrong.

Trying another approach, the clinician asked if there was any situation in which Meg wished Donny would behave differently. Meg said, "Yes, at gymnastics." She wished he'd stop crying and being irritable the whole time. She knew that he didn't like to follow the instructor's directions: he preferred to watch the other kids play. His mother, of course was allowed to stay with him. Asked if she had ever asked Donny to stop crying, she said with quite a look of surprise, "I would have thought he'd stop crying when he could stop crying." When asked if anything would be lost if she asked Donny to tell her he was scared in words rather than crying, she said she'd try it.

In the middle of the week, Meg left a phone message that she needed to talk about this "No" business. When the therapist called back, Meg got right to the point. She was worried that the clinician was offended, thinking Meg didn't take her suggestions seriously when she flatly refused to say "No" to Donny. Again she wanted to know if she was doing something to harm Donny. The clinician asked her if saying "No" to her had upset Meg. Meg was thoughtful a moment and said, Yes, she thought it had. "Were you trying to get me to say 'No' ?" she asked, suspicious of the clinician's motives. The clinician made it clear that she was not trying to get her to do anything specific, had not been trying to trick her, but had hoped to have a discussion with her about setting reasonable limits on Donny's behavior, that both parents could feel comfortable with. That conversation seemed to set us on a more even course. The silly games first played in the office were expanded at home. Eventually Donny, Meg, and Rob were using "No" in all sorts of silly but important ways.

The clinician encouraged Donny's parents to set limits by acknowledging his feelings while clearly staying with their own positions. As Donny developed awareness of his feelings, and as his parents reflected back to him their understanding of his feelings, his language took on a more interpersonal quality, with more intonation and spontaneity. He also began to reenact remembered feelings. These reenactments were similar to the retelling of stories from the books his parents read to him that had occurred earlier in the diagnostic sessions, but now he was remembering real experiences with his parents.

Eventually, by the fourth month, Donny began to play with some characters and the doll house. He choreographed play scenarios between himself, his father, and his mother, and gave them spontaneous alternative identities in play. These scenes were only moments long, but they were pleasurable, and all three family members expressed animated affect during the play. Also at the beginning of the fourth months, Meg and Rob asked to meet with the clinician to go over goals for the treatment, and to begin to think about what they ultimately could hope to accomplish. Meg and Rob seemed invested in their son's growing competence.

By the fifth month of treatment, Meg began to toilet train Donny, now that she felt that he had the capacity to control himself. Until that point she hadn't dared try to toilet train him because she hadn't wanted to "set him up for failure," since it was her assumption that he was "too vulnerable" to understand the concepts around toileting. Meg decided to talk with him about when he would want to be a big boy like his father and his school friends. Talking about his bodily sensations became an extension of discussing feelings. Donny did not need to understand time or issues of propriety, just how his body felt. Within one week Donny accomplished bladder and bowel control during the day. He was trained completely within another week.

The clinician congratulated Meg on the smoothness with which she had accomplished the toileting goal with her son. The conversation led to pondering how lonely she probably felt trying to do all these tasks of mothering in isolation from her family. Meg acknowledged fleetingly how lonely she sometimes felt. Immediately thereafter, she took the clinician to task for not appreciating "how easy you have it," working as a professional woman in her own country. No one, she asserted, questioned the clinician's legitimacy or credibility as a professional. Her loneliness seemed to have been quickly transformed into anger at the clinician. As the clinician empathized with how painful her situation must be for her, and explored with her some of the moments in which she must feel reminded of her losses, Meg became more reflective. As the session progressed, she seemed more able to tolerate awareness of her losses. She began to show more range of emotional expression in the sessions, especially with Donny.

In the very next weekly session Donny engaged in sustained symbolic play for the first time. In other words, as Meg began to acknowledge her own feelings, she did not have to protect herself quite as much from Donny's expression of feelings. The quality of their relationship changed, allowing Donny to become more engaged in expressing his feelings through play.

Donny's symbolic play powerfully represented the psychological struggle going on for the three of them around the issue of loss and interpersonal connection, especially in the marriage. In the twenty-third session Donny requested that I get out the doll house and he asked, "Where's Jam, Helen, and Gwen?" (some doll-house figures he had been using for a few weeks). He handed the appropriate figures to his parents. He had a clear plan for his play. The process and quality of the play was spontaneous and new, the story material definitely relevant.

(Donny is Jam, a cat figure; Robert is Helen, a woman figure;
Meg is Gwen, a girl figure)

Donny: Gwen can't come. She's sad because she can't come. Jam wants to have a picnic. What shall we do, Helen?

Meg: I'm a bit sad because I'm here all by myself. I want to come. Can I come too, Jam?

Robert: I wonder where Helen and Jam will go. Where would Jam like to go?

D: Jam wants to go for a ride in the van. Oh, no, the van's broken down. Jam can't go anywhere.

R: Why don't you call Gwen and see if she can fix it?

D: No, she can't fix it, she doesn't know how. Jam will whistle for Gwen. (Donny laughs. His parents explain that he is laughing because he knows that his parents and he whistle for his dog at home. He is amused by this turnabout with Jam whistling for Gwen.)

M: (putting Gwen on the roof of the doll house, she says with affect) Help me, help me, I'm stuck.

D: Jam will save Gwen from the fire in her house. She's stuck in the house. She doesn't know how to get down. (Donny moves Jam away from where he had been going to save Gwen and stands resolutely away from the doll house, near the van, and says) Me not help! Me Not Help!

R: Oh Jam, Gwen's asking, Help me, help me!

D: (moving Jam around animatedly as if speaking for him) Come down, climb down, Gwen you can do it ("You can do it, Donny, I know you can" is what his mother says to him when he gets stuck and asks for help.)

M: Help me, help me!

D: I'm coming. Get down by yourself. Just go like this (Donny makes a hand motion to slide off the roof of the house.)

Clinician: (interjecting, attempting to clarify the theme) Gwen's stuck, and she can't seem to get down by herself just now.

R: That's 'cause she climbed up there by herself, and it was dangerous, and now she has to get down by herself.

D: Jam will climb up and show her how to get down (Takes Helen away from Rob and hands the figure to Meg) Helen's tired, she can't help Gwen get down. (Donny takes Gwen from Meg, slides her down the roof of the doll house, and puts her in the baby crib in the house). Gwen's a baby, now. She's in the crib.

Finally, and relatively quickly, Donny was using play the way young children typically use it—to work on emotional issues important to him. The change in Meg's emotional capacity to engage in satisfying interactions with Donny, and the immediate shift in his ability to engage in symbolic expression of feelings which generalized to play with his father as well, confirmed the diagnostic impression that the quality of the relationship, fueled by the parents' depressions had powerfully, but temporarily, derailed Donny's development.

After six months of hard work, involving parental persistence in the face of their own doubts, as well as the building of therapeutic relationships among all of the participants, Donny was finally playing in a constricted but age-appropriate way. While six months of weekly parent/child sessions may seem a lengthy course of treatment in the time frame of current managed care protocols, given the severity of Donny's initial presentation, his condition resolved quickly. The connection between his parents' increasing abilities to own their authentic feelings, not simply present a social facade, and their capacity to engage in interactions satisfying to their son, and Donny's subsequent but immediate developmental shifts confirmed the diagnoses of depression, and overinvolved, anxious relationship disorder.

The sixth month of treatment was spent with Donny, his mother, and his father in rich, pretend play. Although his parents still did not acknowledge or express their feelings in verbal discussion, they played in an open, authentic manner. In their play they began to respond to their son's expressions of feelings and even began to address their own relationship issues. Meg and Rob began to clarify how hard it was for them to understand the other's comments and feelings. They were too isolated from each other to be a comfort for each other. Without that comfort they did not have the resources to allow Donny's exploration of his feelings. They used Donny's behavior as the vehicle for discharging their own emotional tensions. Through their play with Donny, however, Rob and Meg began to address their relationship issues. As they became involved in this play, their interpretation of Donny's behavior shifted to reflect Donny's actual affect in response to his experience. Interestingly, at this point Rob reported that Donny had started "eating everything." Beginning with food, Donny was venturing out to explore the world. He also began asking for friends to come over and play.

Even after it became apparent that Donny's functioning was well within the typical range, Meg and Rob elected to continue treatment. The Dunbars continued to come as a threesome for play therapy with the clinician for another year. Meg also initiated individual treatment, requesting a weekly hour "of her own" to explore her experiences separate from Donny or Rob.

Prognosis and discussion

As we come to understand Donny's apparent developmental "shut-down," we see a connection between relationship experience, factors of temperament, and depression in infancy. Primary to Donny's disorder were relationship issues as well as his own "vulnerable temperament" and muted cueing system. His parents' depressions fueled distortions in interpretation of Donny's cues, as well as a temporary inability to separate his needs from theirs. Their misinterpretation and lack of understanding of his cues prevented him from developing complexity in his affect, or robustness in his response style. A depression in infancy entails the inhibition, prohibition, and/or lack of acknowledgment of a child's impulses and expression of feelings. The infant responds to this debilitating lack of attunement by stopping and waiting for someone to answer his cues with reflective responses.

Without acknowledgment of feelings there is no reason to act, no way to release tension, no problems to solve, no satisfaction in relationship. In short, developmental progress does not go forth. When Donny experienced the authentic acknowledgment, reflection, and understanding of his cues and impulses, within the context of his relationships with his parents, his development regained its pace and reliability.

References:

Kerr, M.E., & Bowen, M. (1988). *Family evaluation: An approach based on Bowen theory.* New York: W.W. Norton.

Main, M., & Hesse E., (1990). Parents' unresolved traumatic experiences are related to infant disorganized attachment status: Is frightened and/or frightening parental behavior the linking mechanism? In M.T. Greenberg, D. Cicchetti, & E.M. Cummings (Eds.), *Attachment in the preschool years: Theory, research and intervention* (pp. 161-182). Chicago: University of Chicago Press.

Main, M., & Weston, D. R. (1981). The quality of the toddler's relationship to mother and father:Related to conflict behavior and the readiness to establish new relationships. *Child Development, 52,* 932–940.

McGoldrick, M., Pearce, J.K., & Giordano, J. (1982). *Ethnicity and family therapy.* New York: Guilford.

Minuchin, S. (1974). *Families and family therapy.* Cambridge: Harvard.

Seligman, S.P. & Pawl, J.H., *Impediments to the formation of the working alliance in infant-parent psychotherapy.* preprint.

Wetherby, A. M.& Prizant, B.M. (1996) Toward earlier identification of communication and language problems in infants and young children. In E. Fenichel, & S.J. Meisels (Eds.), *New visions for the developmental assessment of infants and young children* (pp. 289-312). Washington, DC: ZERO TO THREE: National Center for Infants, Toddlers, and Families.

ZERO TO THREE. (1994). *Diagnostic classification of mental health and developmental disorders of infancy and early childhood.* Arlington, VA: ZERO TO THREE: National Center for Clinical Infant Programs.

200. Disorders of Affect

204. Mixed Disorder of Emotional Expressiveness

Jean M. Thomas, M.D., M.S.W.

Mixed Disorder of Emotional Expressiveness focuses on the child's ongoing difficulties expressing developmentally appropriate emotions. The diagnosis implies that the child's affective experience or behavioral expressiveness, or both, lacks specific expectable affects or is constricted, disturbed in intensity, inappropriate to the situation, or all these. As with other Disorders of Affect, the child's affective symptoms reveal themselves as interactive difficulties, often arising in the context of the child's relationship with the primary caregiver. These interactive difficulties have generalized over situation and time to characterize the child's interactive style and expectations of both self and external relationships.

This case report illustrates the use of *DC: 0-3* in an evolving diagnostic process. The initial diagnostic profile guides treatment planning. As the intervention process reveals new information, the initial diagnosis may be revised and treatment goals and approaches modified accordingly. Thus our initial Axis I diagnosis of Adjustment Disorder (rule out Mixed Disorder of Emotional Expressiveness) was later revised to Mixed Disorder of Emotional Expressiveness, and the Axis II diagnosis was revised as well. This case report also illustrates how using the *Diagnostic and Statistical Manual of Mental Disorders, Fourth Edition* (DSM-IV) (APA, 1994), a clinician may misunderstand complex, affective symptomatology that is reported as hyperactive and disruptive behavior, and may misdiagnose Attention-Deficit/ Hyperactivity Disorder (ADHD).

Reason for referral

Carrie had just turned two when her mother, Ms. Hartman, called the Department of Psychiatry at the city's children's hospital because Carrie was "jealous," having "temper tantrums," and "throwing things." Three weeks following the birth of Dominic, her fourth child, Ms. Hartman was hospitalized for depression. Calling from the psychiatric hospital, Ms. Hartman detailed her concerns about Carrie and herself. "Carrie doesn't listen to me when I try to discipline her. She hits a lot and wants to sleep in my bed every night." Ms. Hartman was afraid that she had not been "handling Carrie's behavior well" before her hospitalization. She wanted help urgently, as soon as she was discharged.

Assessment/intervention process

One week after Ms. Hartman's discharge from the hospital, when Carrie was 26 months old and Dominic was 8 weeks old, a comprehensive assessment/intervention was conducted during four consecutive weekly sessions of two hours each. All sessions were conducted and videotaped in the hospital's child psychiatry clinic. The interdisciplinary team included an attending child psychiatrist, a child psychiatry resident, a developmental pediatrician, a psychologist, a family therapist, a speech/language specialist, an occupational therapist, and a physical therapist. The child psychiatrist and child psychiatry resident guided the process throughout and created continuity for the family and for the team. As different team members worked with Ms. Hartman and Carrie, varied members of the interdisciplinary team observed the sessions live via a video monitor and discussed their impressions among themselves both during and immediately after the sessions. Throughout the entire assessment/intervention process, Ms. Hartman, Carrie, and Dominic were all present.

During the first assessment/intervention session, the child psychiatrist and child psychiatry resident clarified Ms. Hartman's concerns and simultaneously observed the interactions among family members. Following this interview, the psychologist tested Carrie, using the Stanford Binet Intelligence Scale. The second session included a screening conducted by the speech/language specialist and an examination by a developmental pediatrician. The third session was devoted to occupational and physical therapy assessments. This session also included a family free-play session, followed by a discussion of that process between Ms. Hartman, the child psychiatrist, and the child psychiatry resident. This discussion focused on comparing this session to Ms. Hartman's experiences with Carrie at home and on the child's and the family's strengths. Before the fourth session, the interdisciplinary team met to synthesize their findings and hypotheses. Then, the child psychiatrist, psychiatry resident, and family therapist met with the mother to create a treatment plan.

Assessment findings

Presenting concerns

Ms. Hartman described a change in Carrie's behavior following Dominic's birth. She said that Carrie was jealous of her brother and was having increasingly frequent temper tantrums. Carrie was "out of control" and "aggressive." Ms. Hartman was concerned about her ability to discipline Carrie properly because of her own experiences with an abusive father. Ms.

Hartman did not want Carrie to remember her childhood as an unhappy experience, as she herself did. When she found herself beginning to say something to Carrie that reminded her of her own father, Ms. Hartman backed off and did not discipline Carrie.

Ms. Hartman described three recent stresses in addition to Dominic's birth: (a) three months before Dominic's birth, her own mother had died; (b) just three days before the birth, Carrie had had bilateral myringotomy tube placement; and (c) following Dominic's birth, Ms. Hartman had taken Xanex "to calm [her] nerves" as she became increasingly overwhelmed and depressed. Both depression and overuse of prescribed Xanax had precipitated Ms. Hartman's psychiatric hospitalization, which lasted four weeks, during which time Carrie stayed with family friends and Dominic stayed with his father. (Ms. Hartman's oldest child had been given up for adoption; her second child was in his father's custody.) Ms. Hartman felt that in association with these stresses, Carrie had become "aggressive" and "out of control." She blamed herself for Carrie's behavior and worried about the impact of her depression on Carrie.

Developmental and medical history

Ms. Hartman said that she did not know the identity of Carrie's father. She said that although she had used cocaine at one time, she had not used any drugs during her pregnancy with Carrie. Ms. Hartman received appropriate prenatal care, and the pregnancy was unremarkable. She said, however, that delivery had been complicated by a period of decreased oxygen to the fetus, resulting in an emergency delivery with suction. Carrie was born at 42 weeks gestation, weighing 7 pounds, 12 ounces.

Ms. Hartman said that Carrie's developmental milestones had been on target, with crawling at 5 months, standing at 7 months, walking at 10 months, and language beginning at 11 months. By 26 months, at the time of the assessment, Carrie was speaking in short sentences and had just begun toilet training.

Carrie began having ear infections at 5 to 6 months; myringotomy tubes were placed at 8 months. During this time, she began to insist on sleeping with her mother. Carrie's temper tantrums began at age 20 months, in the midst of another series of ear infections. Placement of a second set of myringotomy tubes occurred when Carrie was 24 months old, three days before the birth of her brother and approximately six weeks before her mother's call for help.

Family/social history

Ms. Hartman, an attractive 33-year-old woman who was receiving Aid to Families with Dependent Children, had been married twice. Her first marriage, at age 18, lasted only one month but functioned to help her escape from her childhood home. The son who was a product of this marriage had been given up for adoption at birth. The second marriage, when Ms. Hartman was age 21, had produced another boy, Tommy, who had been in the custody of his father since the marriage broke up when Tommy was four. At the time of the assessment, Tommy, age 11, was visiting his mother weekly. Carrie and Dominic were born out of wedlock and each had a different father.

Carrie was her mother's only daughter and the only child her mother had not at least considered giving up for adoption. (Ms. Hartman had considered giving up custody of Dominic before his birth, but she had changed her mind in the delivery room because "she could not handle another loss," especially given the recent death of her mother.) Ms. Hartman's ambivalence about Dominic continued. She dealt with her ambivalence by arranging for him to stay with his father frequently.

Ms. Hartman said that she had no current relationship with a man and was living only with Carrie and Dominic. She said that she was using Valium, which she had obtained by prescription, for "jitters" related to her effort to stop smoking. She also mentioned her "fear of being on Valium" and concerns about her short-term memory.

Observations and additional assessments

Session I: *Family interview:* At 26 months, Carrie was a highly energetic, impulsive, and moody child. Her speech was well developed (she used simple sentences and asked questions), and her articulation was readily understood.

With her mother, Carrie was alternately clingy and avoidant, attentive and distracted, engageable and irritable, and altruistic and aggressive. During the first interview, Carrie was initially tentative and clingy. When her mother fed Dominic, Carrie became subdued and played mostly at a distance from her mother. When she isolated herself, Carrie focused her attention on feeding a baby doll while remaining sensitively attuned to her mother and the interviewer. Later, Carrie responded to her brother's extended periods of crying by going to get his bottle for him. Although Carrie's affect was often blunted and sad, when she approached her mother with Dominic's bottle she smiled and was easily engaged. Occasionally, Carrie returned to actively seek the attention of her mother and the interviewers. Carrie's attention shifted and her level of activity and irritability increased when her mother was critical or preoccupied. She repeatedly challenged her mother's restrictions and had tantrums involving crying, yelling, and hitting when she was unable to get what she wanted. Once, as Carrie tried to pull her mother down to the floor to play, she and her mother struggled. Carrie yelled and hit her mother. Ms. Hartman responded with apparent frustration and embarrassment, indicating to the team through her glances and body language that she felt helpless in trying to quell Carrie's aggressive and demanding behavior.

Often, Ms. Hartman responded to Carrie's demands warmly and sensitively, she appreciated Carrie's help with Dominic, and she provided fairly consistent limits and did not reinforce tantrums. However, when preoccupied with Dominic, she missed Carrie's approach with a doll and later with a truck. She was also critical of Carrie's withdrawn, sullen behavior and felt helpless when Carrie was aggressive.

Psychological testing and observations: During the administration of the Stanford Binet Intelligence Scale, Carrie impressed the psychologist as a very active and impulsive child as she moved frequently from her chair or reached to get a toy and needed redirection. Despite her short attention span and the presence of an unfamiliar examiner, she scored a mental age of 2 years, 6 months, with a resulting IQ of 106. The examiner observed that although Carrie showed no stranger anxiety, she was difficult to engage and her interest in the test materials was fleeting. She seemed excited, unfocused, and, at times, clearly oppositional.

Session 2. *Speech and language screening:* A speech and language specialist administered the Fluharty Preschool Speech and Language Screening Test to Carrie while Ms. Hartman sat with Dominic a short distance away. Carrie demonstrated advanced or age-appropriate skills in most areas. Her articulation and comprehension were advanced for age; her skill at identifying objects was at age level; her ability to repeat words and phrases was below age level. The latter two scores may have reflected Carrie's oppositionality during the testing.

Developmental pediatric examination and hearing screening. Although she was very active, Carrie was more cooperative with this examination than with others. The team wondered if Carrie was more cooperative with the pediatrician because he was a man. All the other evaluators had been women. She engaged in multiple independent activities, returning to her mother intermittently and at one point asking for her pacifier. When the pediatrician asked her to identify her body parts, she was able to label all correctly, but surprised the pediatrician when she identified herself as a boy.

Carrie's height was in the 50th percentile and her weight in the 75th percentile for her age. Her physical examination and hearing screening were normal, except for mild, bilaterally decreased hearing sensitivity apparently associated with a recurrent ear infection, despite recent myringotomy tube placement.

Session 3. *Occupational and physical therapy evaluations:* With Ms. Hartman and Dominic close by, the occupational and physical therapists performed a structured screening assessment as part of the standard comprehensive assessment/intervention. They found Carrie's fine and gross motor skills to be age-appropriate; they thought sensory integration testing was not needed. Carrie responded well to the evaluators' verbal praise, and she repeatedly attempted more difficult tasks.

Family play: Carrie, Ms. Hartman, and Dominic were present. As before, Carrie at first played at a distance from her mother and brother, with her back to them. Ms. Hartman sighed, apparently in frustration, and moved to be closer to Carrie, who remained standoffish. Ms. Hartman then tried verbally to cajole Carrie to bring her the baby doll. Gradually, Carrie approached her mother. As her mother's invitation became playful, Carrie became transiently more animated. The interaction was interrupted by Ms. Hartman's response to Dominic's cry and Carrie's returned to solitary play with blocks. Throughout the play session, Carrie's affect was predominantly blunted and sad. Her mother appeared both discouraged by Carrie's minimal response and distracted by the baby. The observing team noted that Carrie was less demanding and aggressive than during the initial interview. They agreed that this change in Carrie appeared related to Ms. Hartman's increased comfort and wondered if this was because Ms. Hartman was more familiar with the assessment/intervention process.

After the free-play period, Ms. Hartman told the child psychiatrist and resident that she felt bad that she had very little time to play with Carrie at home. As her mother spoke, Carrie approached the child psychiatrist with a truck. The psychiatrist responded with interest and warmth but decided not to extend the play at that time in order to return her focus to listening to and supporting Ms. Hartman. Ms. Hartman commented on Carrie's short attention span and apologized for her lack of parenting skills. She felt that she was making very deliberate efforts to find time for Carrie, despite the demands of caring for a new baby, but that Carrie did not want to play with her. The team felt Ms. Hartman's self-effacing comments were related to her ongoing depressive mood.

Session 4. *Case conference and treatment planning session:* The entire team met to discuss the assessment results, differential diagnoses, and treatment planning. Following the team's conference, the child psychiatrist, the child psychiatry resident, and the family therapist met with Ms. Hartman to discuss their diagnostic impressions and to plan treatment collaboratively.

Diagnosis

Our comprehensive assessment of Carrie revealed a child with average cognitive abilities and motor skills and above-average verbal abilities, despite chronic ear infections. Several team members felt that Carrie's distractibility, impulsivity, excitability, irritability, and disturbed affective intensity might reflect the beginnings of Attention-Deficit/Hyperactivity Disorder (ADHD) as described in DSM-IV. However, ADHD was not diagnosable at this time, nor did this diagnosis help to describe what appeared to be the interactive origins of Carrie's ongoing symptoms.

The team found that the *DC: 0-3* system offered an age-appropriate diagnostic framework for assessing 26-month-old Carrie. The team considered Adjustment Disorder to be the most appropriate Axis I diagnosis because Carrie's symptoms appeared mild, of less than four months' duration, and related to specific stressors. However, by the end of the comprehensive assessment period, Carrie's disturbed intensity of emotional expression and wide mood swings no longer appeared mild and had continued over almost four months. Carrie seemed almost chronically excited, irritable, jealous, and angry. Moreover, she tended to have an intermittently constricted expression of pleasure in learning, and a response to her mother that alternated between constricted and exaggerated. Because of Carrie's constricted and unusually intense expression of emotion, Mixed Disorder of Emotional Expressiveness was listed as a rule out diagnosis.

In observing the relationship between Carrie and her mother, the team identified a mixed pattern of overinvolved, underinvolved, anxious/tense, and angry/hostile interactive behavior between mother and daughter that appeared more than transient. Ms. Hartman ignored or had trouble recognizing Carrie's appropriate bids for attention and got into power struggles with the little girl, who would often strike her mother. This pattern of inconsistency in parenting and excitable, negativistic behavior in the child suggested that the problematic features of their relationship might be generalizing over situation and time. The team's PIR-GAS rating of 40 (Disturbed) meant that the team did not make an Axis II diagnosis but did note a tendency toward a Mixed Relationship Disorder. The team also wondered whether Carrie's behavior might reflect a disorganization seen in some insecure attachments or whether this disorganization was better understood as an acute response to severe stressors.

Axis V, the Functional Emotional Developmental Level, describes the child's capacity to organize experience. Carrie had reached the expected developmental level, Representational/Affective Communication, as demonstrated by her warm and appropriate caregiving with the doll. Her verbal communication of her feelings was somewhat constricted despite her advanced language skills. This placed her functional development at the expected level but with constrictions.

Aware that the team's understanding would deepen over time and that Carrie's diagnostic profile might need to be revised, the child psychiatrist, child psychiatry resident, and family therapist met with Ms. Hartman. Together they planned treatment around: (a) reducing the family stress; (b) defining the developmental needs of Carrie and her mother; (c) setting limits and avoiding power struggles; and (d) exploring the influence of Ms. Hartman's past experiences on her current parenting style.

Diagnostic Summary (27 months)

Axis I: Primary Diagnosis
Adjustment Disorder.
Rule out Mixed Disorder of Emotional Expressiveness.

Axis II: Relationship Disorder Classification
No diagnosis.
Tendency toward a Relationship Disorder - Mixed (Overinvolved, Underinvolved, Anxious/Tense, Angry/Hostile).

Axis III: Medical and Developmental Disorders and Conditions
Decreased oxygen during delivery; recurrent ear infections.

Axis IV: Psychosocial Stressors
Moderate effects.

Axis V: Functional Emotional Developmental Level
Has achieved age-expected levels of mutual attention, mutual engagement, and interactive intentionality and reciprocity. Shows age-appropriate levels of representational/affective communication, but with constrictions, and vulnerable to stress.

PIR-GAS:40 (Disturbed)

Treatment goals, recommendations, and treatment planning

Treatment goals

Axis I: Adjustment Disorder
Treatment goals: decrease stressors:
A. Mother's mood and substance use problems
B. Family constellation changes, living environment, and finances

Axis II: Tendency toward a Relationship Disorder—Mixed (overinvolved, underinvolved, anxious/tense, angry/hostile)
Treatment goals:

A. Target the parent-child relationship interactions:
1. Define the child's developmental needs for independence and closeness, which vary with her sense of security.

2. Define the mother's developmental needs in her roles as parent, breadwinner, and adult friend.

3. Support the mother's setting limits and avoiding power struggles.

4. Support mutual interactive enjoyment.

B. Target the mother's psychological involvement:

1. Explore the mother's identification with Carrie, her only daughter.

2. Explore how current relationship themes of overinvolvement, underinvolvement, anxiety/tension, and anger/hostility parallel those in the mother's family of origin.

The diagnosis of Adjustment Disorder implies that symptoms will respond to a reduction of the specific stressors that led to the child's symptoms. In Carrie's family, as is frequently true, the mother's responses to stressors in her own life (mood disorder symptoms and self-medication for these symptoms) became stressors in their own right for the child. The team hoped that supportive treatment of the mother would reduce her depressive and substance-related symptoms so that she could gain increased control over the family living situation, including finances and allocation of time to meet both Carrie's needs and those of the new baby.

The team's identification of a disturbed relationship between Carrie and

Ms. Hartman implied that healing in Carrie and in her mother would be parallel and interdependent processes. The team believed that as Ms. Hartman felt supported, she would be better able to support Carrie. And it also hypothesized that a transactional process was involved—that is, as Ms. Hartman gained increased control over external stresses, her general sense of control would increase, enabling her to increase her actual control over other areas, such as Carrie's behavior. This success would lead, in turn, to even more effective coping with external stressors.

The goal of improving the parent-child relationship involved recognizing developmentally expectable tensions in relationships between parents and toddlers. A mother who has a tendency to be overinvolved with her toddler may feel abandoned in the face of the child's alternating bids for independence and closeness. The clinician can help to define appropriate developmental expectations for the child and the mother, and to provide specific assistance in setting limits, avoiding power struggles, and increasing mutual enjoyment of interactions.

Treatment was also designed to reach Ms. Hartman's psychological involvement with Carrie—that is, her attitudes and perceptions, and the meaning to her of Carrie's behavior to her. Ms. Hartman clearly identified with Carrie, her only daughter. She wanted to provide Carrie with a happier childhood than she had had. Even during the assessment, Ms. Hartman had begun to link her problems in parenting with her own experiences with her abusive father. Ms. Hartman was bright and insightful; she seemed likely to benefit from an exploration of how current relationship themes of overinvolvement, underinvolvement, anxiety/tension, and anger/hostility paralleled those in her own family of origin.

Recommendations and treatment planning

The team framed recommendations that would both follow its conceptualization of appropriate treatment goals and be responsive to the mother's perceived needs and expectations of intervention. Since Ms. Hartman had called the clinic primarily to get help in managing Carrie's behavior, our recommendations began with Carrie. The team agreed with Ms. Hartman that Carrie was difficult to manage, and suggested that Carrie's out-of-control behavior was related to her feeling out of control. The team thought that Carrie might be: (a) feeling sad and angry when she did not get the attention she wanted from her mother; and (b) feeling out of control when her mother felt out of control. It recognized that the past several months had been especially difficult for Ms. Hartman because of the death of her mother and the birth of the new baby.

Keeping the mother central in the treatment planning, the team affirmed Ms. Hartman's parenting efforts. Team members said that they had seen many strengths in Ms. Hartman's relationship with Carrie and observed that both mother and daughter were motivated, bright, and able to connect with and enjoy each other. The team and Ms. Hartman discussed how Carrie's feelings and behavior reflected her mother's current difficulties, which, in turn, were influenced by Ms. Hartman's own experience of being parented. It reviewed what Ms. Hartman had told us about her early years with her father, who was alcoholic and both physically and emotionally abusive. Ms. Hartman had expressed fear that she would lose control in disciplining Carrie, implying (although not stating explicitly) that she was concerned about repeating her father's abusive behavior. The team also acknowledged Ms. Hartman's statement that she wanted Carrie to look back on her childhood as a happy time and to be happier than she herself had been.

The team mentioned Selma Fraiberg's notion of "ghosts in the nursery" (Fraiberg, 1980) which helped it to understand how important it is to support parents in a family, who are then better able to support the child who is having troubles. Team members said it would be important to continue talking with Ms. Hartman about her own experiences as a child and how she thought these were affecting her current fears and choices, and emphasized the importance of Ms. Hartman getting adequate support for herself. The team expressed concern about her depression and observed that during the previous session she spoke of her "fear of being on Valium" and problems with short-term memory. (During most of the four-week assessment process, Ms. Hartman had been fairly collected, competent, and appropriate, although somewhat tense and blunted in affect. However, during this final session, she seemed increasingly anxious.) The team strongly recommended that, in addition to participating in family therapy, Ms. Hartman begin individual treatment with a psychiatrist, who could help her address her depression and concerns about drug use.

The team described Carrie's developmental needs for independence and closeness as varying with her sense of security. Team members observed that for many parents, a child's first expressions of a need for independence are confusing; the parent may understandably feel less needed and pushed away. Describing Carrie's strengths, the team observed that she was bright, verbal, and engageable. Although she distanced herself from time to time, she could be friendly and wanting to play, especially with her mother. In addition, Carrie wanted to please her mother; when Ms. Hartman felt in control, she could redirect Carrie's behavior.

The team made a number of recommendations for work with Carrie: (a) family therapy to address relationship and limit-setting issues around sleep and disruptive behavior; (b) pediatric follow-up, because of concern about a possible recurrent ear infection, and re-evaluation of her hearing; (c) involvement in the Parents as Teachers home visiting program, to support Carrie's brightness and her mother's involvement in her learning; (d) enrollment in a preschool to enhance Carrie's learning about rules and social interactions (especially with peers), and to foster Carrie's ability to focus; and (e) testing for ADHD and learning problems if Carrie began to experience increased attentional problems when she started first grade.

Ms. Hartman's initial request had been for help with disciplining Carrie. Family therapy provided an opportunity to address this issue and to work closely with the team family therapist, with whom Ms. Hartman was beginning to feel connected. Ms. Hartman agreed to contact her previous psychiatrist for help with her own depression and drug use. She was appreciative of the additional recommendations for Carrie, including medical follow-up for her ear infections and hearing, and enrollment in Parents as Teachers and a preschool to support Carrie's brightness and her learning about rules with peers and teachers.

Intervention (initial phase)

Treatment for Carrie's Adjustment Disorder focused on reduction of stressors in the family. One week after the completion of the comprehensive assessment, Ms. Hartman, Carrie, and Dominic had their first session with the team family therapist. Ms. Hartman said that she was now taking between two and three times her prescribed dose of Valium per day. She said she "had to have something to keep calm." The therapist reinforced the team's recommendation that Ms. Hartman seek psychiatric treatment for her own depression and excessive drug use and offered to help with a referral. Ms. Hartman was given a referral to a female psychiatrist, as requested.

The family therapist shared her deep concern about Carrie and Ms. Hartman herself and warmly, but firmly, confronted Ms. Hartman by pointing out to her that her mental health and substance abuse problems were likely to interfere with her primary goals of improving Carrie's behavior and ensuring Carrie's memories of a happy childhood. The therapist realized that by confronting Ms. Hartman, she risked having her move away from the therapeutic relationship in shame and anger. However, she reasoned that not confronting her would constitute collusion, an acceptance that Ms. Hartman was, in fact, as helpless as she felt when she allowed Carrie to be in control of their relationship. The therapist took the risk, confronted Ms. Hartman, and did not see her for five months.

When Ms. Hartman did not return for her second appointment with the family therapist, the therapist called her home and left a message but did not hear from Ms. Hartman. The therapist continued to make contact, leaving at first weekly and then monthly phone messages, and also wrote two letters in an effort to let Ms. Hartman know that she was supported and that help was available. It was five months before Ms. Hartman felt secure enough to call the therapist and tell her about her hospitalization for detoxification from various drugs, including alcohol. Ms. Hartman thanked the therapist for helping her get treatment for her depression and drug use but did not share the details of her hospitalization or aftercare program. She said she still wanted help with Carrie's temper tantrums and was eager to return to family therapy.

The therapist was pleased that she had been able to help Ms. Hartman get treatment and that Ms Hartman trusted her enough to return to family therapy. The therapist realized that in confronting Ms. Hartman she had underestimated Ms. Hartman's vulnerability. The therapist knew that building on the trust in the therapeutic relationship with Ms. Hartman would be central to the ongoing family therapy.

When the family returned to therapy at the child psychiatry clinic for what would become 10 months of almost weekly family therapy sessions, Ms. Hartman discussed her hospitalization and progress toward mental health only briefly. She focused instead on Carrie. The therapist realized that Ms. Hartman focused on Carrie because it felt safer than discussing her own treatment. Appreciating Ms. Hartman's vulnerability, the therapist kept the focus on Carrie and reinforced Ms. Hartman's efforts to follow through on several of the team's earlier recommendations: A Parents as Teachers home visitor had come to assess Carrie's development, and Carrie was scheduled to begin preschool in the fall. The therapist observed that both Carrie and Dominic were well nourished and making good developmental progress. Ms. Hartman commented that Carrie's increased chubbiness resulted from her replacing her pacifier with food. At 12 months, Dominic was babbling and pulling himself to stand.

Ms. Hartman was still in a precarious financial situation, however, and seemed out of her depth emotionally as well. Despite her efforts, she was still wavering in her sense of control over herself and Carrie. In the session, Carrie, now 31 months old, acted out by throwing toys and refusing to pick them up at her mother's request. When Carrie refused, Ms. Hartman at first did not intervene further. The therapist recalled with Ms. Hartman her ability to redirect Carrie at times during the evaluation. Ms. Hartman was surprised and appreciative of the therapist's recollected details of her success.

Several weeks after returning to therapy, Ms. Hartman reported that she had begun taking Prozac and was attending weekly group and individual therapy sessions in the aftercare program at the psychiatric hospital. Now somewhat more calm, she discussed her plans to get help with job training, transportation, and child care through the local vocational rehabilitation agency.

Three months after family treatment resumed, Ms. Hartman said that she felt more in control and that Carrie, too, was in better control. During most therapy sessions, Carrie and Dominic played separately. When they fought from time to time, Ms. Hartman often intervened authoritatively and was able to redirect their activity. Ms. Hartman said that she had decided to obtain training as either a medical technician or a nurse. Her career choices seemed at least in part related to her identification with the therapist, who had shared with Ms. Hartman that she been first trained as a nurse. Ms. Hartman also began talking more about her childhood, her parents, and her relationships with the fathers of her children. The therapist's suggested that Ms. Hartman come to the next session without Carrie to further discuss these details. Later, as she felt more comfortable, Ms. Hartman herself intermittently chose to leave Carrie at home when she wanted to talk more intimately about her relationships as a child and more recently with men.

Five months after family treatment resumed, Ms. Hartman was once again becoming more anxious and overwhelmed. During family sessions, Carrie was again hitting her mother and throwing things. Ms. Hartman complained that Carrie was also having difficulty sleeping once again.

During one session, she said that she planned to take both children to the crisis nursery for three days, which she did the following day.

At this time, Ms. Hartman said that through her drug treatment she had met a new male friend. The therapist discussed with Ms. Hartman her pattern of choosing men with substance abuse problems, like her father. She also observed that the reappearance of Ms. Hartman's feelings of being overwhelmed and her increasing agitation seemed to be associated with this new relationship, and that the significant increase in Carrie's aggression and sleep problems seemed to parallel her mother's growing difficulties. Ms. Hartman agreed she had a pattern of choosing men like her father. She listened thoughtfully but did not comment on the therapist's observation that Carrie's behavior problems seemed to be worsening as Ms. Hartman's agitation increased.

Ms. Hartman's new male friend moved in with the family. A week later, Carrie played a puppet game with her mother during the family session. Carrie wanted to be "the mother" and chose a female puppet. She wanted Ms. Hartman to be the "friend" and chose a male puppet for her. In the game, Carrie wanted the "friend" puppet (played by her mother) to hit the mother puppet (played by Carrie). Carrie then directed the friend puppet to throw the mother puppet into the trash. In the same session, Ms. Hartman reported that Carrie's behavior had regressed; she was again more aggressive and wetting the bed at night.

As the new boyfriend continued to live in the Hartman home, Carrie's acting out increased. The therapist was concerned about possible physical and/or emotional abuse in the home, but Ms. Hartman denied this.

The therapist invited Ms. Hartman to bring her boyfriend to therapy. He came for one session. Carrie was very agitated and distractible in the presence of the boyfriend, who was critical and did not address her by name but instead called her "the big baby." Two weeks later, in a session that did not include the boyfriend, Carrie appeared very sad and withdrawn when the therapist asked about how things were going at home with the new boyfriend. When the therapist then asked if the children still saw Mr. Roberts, Dominic's father, who continued to help support the family, Carrie lit up as she began to talk about him. The following week, with Carrie at her feet and Dominic in her lap, Ms. Hartman reported that one night while Carrie was asleep, the boyfriend had been arrested for assaulting a neighbor and had moved out. Carrie was more animated in this session and not aggressive.

Ms. Hartman did not retreat with the therapist's confrontation about Ms. Hartman's repetitious choice of alcoholic men. This time, Ms. Hartman's deepened relationship with the therapist helped her feel supported and able to manage her sense of shame about her poor choice of men.

Family therapy continued. Ms. Hartman successfully completed a four-week training course as a medical assistant. Carrie passed her third birthday and was doing well in preschool; Dominic seemed to be developing well. Ms. Hartman demonstrated increasing control and skill in handling her daughter's occasional temper tantrums. Ms. Hartman was also considering becoming engaged to Mr. Roberts. However, 10 months after the therapy had resumed, Ms. Hartman announced that she was pregnant by a man whom she had not previously mentioned. The family did not return to therapy for another five months. Again the therapist left regular messages and wrote letters in an effort to support Ms. Hartman.

When Ms. Hartman was seven months pregnant, the family returned to the clinic. Ms. Hartman again wanted help with setting limits for Carrie, whom she described as continuing to be troublesome—getting up at night, being extremely active, and fighting with Dominic. The therapist observed that Carrie was playing well alone and that her attention span seemed appropriate. Ms. Hartman acknowledged that she herself needed support and promised to return to therapy weekly for the next six weeks, or until delivery. She did come for four visits, and then, after a two-month hiatus, returned with Edward, her fifth child, then four weeks old. The therapist at this time announced her plan to move out of town in three months and began a termination process that included transfer to a new therapist. Weekly visits were planned, but Ms. Hartman missed most of them, returning for just three more visits at approximately one-month intervals. At the time of the family's last visit, Ms. Hartman seemed in control and able to redirect the children's minor differences during play.

Impressions following the initial phase of assessment and treatment

The initial phase of our work with Carrie and her family lasted a total of 23 months, from the time Carrie was 26 months old until she was 4 years, one month old. Ms. Hartman had formed an alliance with the family therapist who had been part of the assessment team, and over a period of 22 months had continued with weekly family therapy sessions, interrupted by two five-month lapses and one two-month lapse. During this time, the goal of treatment had been to reduce the stressors in Ms. Hartman's life, decrease Carrie's disruptive behavior and sleep problems, and explore the impact of the mother's past on the current parent-child relationship. The focus of treatment had alternated among Carrie, her mother, and the family relationships.

Family therapy began with a focus on Ms. Hartman's concerns about Carrie's behavior and her efforts to set limits for Carrie. Ms. Hartman made some progress toward her primary goal, disciplining Carrie appropriately, and had significant success in getting Carrie to sleep in her own bed. In addition, Ms. Hartman provided external supports for Carrie by enrolling her in preschool. Ms. Hartman, also enrolled in the Parents as Teachers home visiting program and in job training. Her successes in parenting and job training were paralleled by Carrie's developmental achievements. However, when Ms. Hartman seemed to lose control or the ability to provide safe limits, Carrie's irritability and aggressive behavior flared. At various points in this phase of treatment, when Ms. Hartman seemed to be losing control or was out of control, the therapist shifted the focus to support the mother, so that she would be better able to support Carrie, provide safe limits, and be a positive object of identification.

The initial focus on reducing stressors in this mother's life required addressing her mental health and substance use problems. Ms. Hartman's positive relationship with the family therapist survived an early confrontation about drug abuse and provided an identification that inspired Ms. Hartman to complete training as a medical technician. Ms. Hartman also continued individual therapy with a psychiatrist. Growing trust in her relationship with the family therapist strengthened Ms. Hartman's fledgling trust in herself as a provider and as a parent. This trust, in turn, facilitated: (a) Ms. Hartman's appropriate regulation of Carrie's moods and behavior; and (b) her initial exploration into themes of anger and hostility in her family of origin.

In the context of the therapeutic relationship, Ms. Hartman could begin to connect her current relationships with those in the past, especially her relationships with males. She had given her first son up for adoption, given primary custody of her second son to his father, and had considered giving Dominic up for adoption. Her relationship with the family therapist increased her ability to trust herself as Dominic's parent and sustain a relationship with him. Ms. Hartman's experience with her abusive father seemed to lead her to choose men like him and to become involved in impulsive relationships, drug use, and pregnancy. However, for at least some periods of time during the two-year initial phase of treatment, Ms. Hartman was able to move toward healthier relationships with men.

Rediagnosis (ages 28 months to 4 years, one month)

When Carrie was first evaluated at age 26 months, her disturbance of mood and behavior was first thought to be an Adjustment Disorder, with Mixed Disorder of Emotional Expressiveness considered as a rule-out. A tendency toward a Relationship Disorder-Mixed was noted, but a diagnosis of Relationship Disorder was not warranted.

Soon after the comprehensive evaluation, when the severity and chronicity of Ms. Hartman's problems with mood and substances became clear, Carrie's Axis I diagnosis solidified as an affective disorder, specifically Mixed Disorder of Emotional Expressiveness. Now, the Axis II diagnosis of Relationship Disorder-Mixed also seemed appropriate. Carrie's maladaptive relationship with her mother seemed more rigidly entrenched. This maladaptive relationship combined features of overinvolvement, underinvolvement, anxiety/tension, and, at times, anger/hostility, and distressed both Carrie and her mother. It was rated as Disordered on the Parent-Infant Relationship Global Assessment Scale (PIR-GAS: 30).

Second Diagnostic Summary

Axis I: Primary Diagnosis
Mixed Disorder of Emotional Expressiveness.

Axis II: Relationship Disorder Classification
Mixed (Overinvolved, Underinvolved,
Anxious/Tense, Angry/Hostile).

Axis III: Medical and Developmental Disorders and Conditions
Decreased oxygen during delivery; recurrent ear infections.

Axis IV: Psychosocial Stressors
Moderate effects.

Axis V: Functional Emotional Developmental Level
Has achieved all six early developmental levels. Shows age appropriate level
of representational differentiation II, but with constrictions, and vulnerable
to stress.

PIR-GAS:30 (Disordered)

Assessment process, second phase

When Carrie was almost six-and-a-half years old, Ms. Hartman again contacted the child psychiatry clinic. She was seeking help for Carrie because of
her attention and behavior at school; Carrie's teacher felt that she had
ADHD and requested "that Carrie get medication." Ms. Hartman asked
specifically for medication and an individual therapist for Carrie, not a family therapist. The child psychiatrist from the original team and a new social
worker/therapist re-evaluated Carrie.

When Ms. Hartman reviewed her earlier experience of assessment and
family therapy, she reported Carrie's difficulties with attention, opposition,
temper tantrums, and manipulative behavior. She expressed appreciation for
the family therapist, who had helped her with discipline and had helped her
identify "not only what was wrong with the children, but what was right
with them." She said that the therapist had helped her go back to school and
get training as a medical assistant, an occupation which she enjoyed, and to
understand better her relationships with men. This new understanding, she
felt, had helped her sustain a relationship for the past year with Mr. Jackson,
who was Edward's father and was employed as a local truck driver.

Ms. Hartman brought four months' worth of weekly summaries from
Carrie's first grade teacher to the interview. The teacher felt that Carrie had
ADHD. The summaries reported consistently that Carrie was doing well
academically but talked excessively, had difficulty listening, was defiant,
acted younger than her age, and had a poor attention span.

Ms. Hartman said that because of the teacher's concerns, a new pediatrician had diagnosed ADHD and prescribed a trial of Ritalin. Ms. Hartman
said that the Ritalin had made Carrie much worse. Her temper tantrums and

threats to hurt her mother and brothers had increased; she was having trouble with sleeping and eating. Ms. Hartman had stopped the Ritalin.

Ms. Hartman told the child psychiatrist that before being given the Ritalin, Carrie had been getting up frequently during the night for at least a month and had been angry when any attention was given to her two younger brothers. In addition, Ms. Hartman worried about Carrie's repeatedly asking her mother, "Are you my friend?"

The evaluating team observed that Carrie was engaging and talkative. She played independently but frequently sought the attention of her mother and the evaluators. Carrie repeatedly tried to change the subject and avoided responding to the evaluators' questions about school and family relationships by saying, "I don't know," or "Let's play."

Rediagnosis (age six-and-a-half years)

By the time Carrie was six and a half, her sleep disturbance, anger, and concern about being loved appeared to be symptoms of mood disorder, in DSM-IV best described as Dysthymic Disorder because chronic low level depressive symptoms had lasted for more than one year. The evaluating team did not diagnose ADHD because the symptoms of high activity, distractibility, and defiance were best explained by the chronic mood disorder and associated difficulties with regulation of emotion (a reflection of the *DC: 0-3* diagnoses, Mixed Disorder of Emotional Expressiveness, and Relationship Disorder—Mixed, which solidified between Carrie's ages 28 months and 4 years, 1 month). It had become clear that the interactive style of mother and child at age two had established the expectations (or "schema-of-being-with," as described by Stern, 1995) of their ongoing relationship and of Carrie's relationships at preschool, and later in elementary school.

Intervention (second phase): Summary

The second phase of treatment began when Carrie was six years, five months old and continued beyond her seventh birthday. As her primary relationship with Mr. Jackson stabilized, Ms. Hartman was able to shift her attention more consistently to Carrie's needs. Following the mother's request, the therapist focused on individual therapy for Carrie, but also attended to Ms. Hartman and family relationships in brief family sessions prior to Carrie's weekly therapy. The therapist scheduled additional sessions, as needed, for the family, Ms. Hartman and Mr. Jackson, or Ms. Hartman alone.

Because of Carrie's ongoing sleep and mood problems, including irritability, anger, and low self-esteem (all characteristic of childhood depression), Carrie was begun on antidepressant medication. The therapist and team psychiatrist explained that improvements in sleep and diminishing irritability would likely facilitate both Carrie's and Ms. Hartman's experience of success in their relationship, and progress in therapy. Five weeks after starting the medication, Carrie was sleeping better and was less moody, but she had been suspended from school because of "lying" and defiant behavior.

With antidepressant treatment, early improvements in sleep and mood are often associated with increased energy and increased acting-out behaviors in children. With ongoing medication and therapy, Carrie's mood-related symptoms, including her irritability and acting out, gradually improved; however, her pattern of seeking attention, learned in her early relationship with her mother, required persistent therapeutic attention.

The therapist saw her relationship with Carrie and the more positive mother-child relationship that the therapist hoped to facilitate as opportunities for Carrie to learn new ways of interacting and to develop new "schemas-of-being-with" others. With the therapist, Carrie established both rules and trust. Over many weekly sessions, the therapist joined Carrie's imaginative school play, during which Carrie set classroom rules similar to rules established by the therapist for the therapy session. Carrie's behavior in school improved over this time. At home, Carrie's temper tantrums persisted until Ms. Hartman realized that Carrie's behavior seemed associated with increased yelling between Mr. Jackson and herself, and modulated her own behavior.

The therapist and Ms. Hartman explored Ms. Hartman's interactive difficulties, which had originated in her own family and had been the template for many of her problems with Carrie. Ms. Hartman clearly identified with her only daughter. She was afraid that Carrie would remember her childhood as unhappy, as she did, and also feared that she might abuse Carrie as her father had abused her. Consequently, Ms. Hartman avoided limit setting, but in her anger she often yelled at Carrie and threatened her, unwittingly repeating her own childhood experience.

Although Ms. Hartman said that "Carrie had been her favorite from the day she was born," she felt that she had often unfairly blamed Carrie for her own troubles when stress had increased with her mother's death, Dominic's birth, and problematic relationships with men. Ms. Hartman felt that as a child she, too, had been unfairly blamed.

Carrie's behavior improved and deteriorated as a reflection of her relationship with her mother, and also as a reflection of her mother's other relationships. Ms. Hartman's feeling of being supported by the family therapist in the initial phase of therapy had helped her establish a stable relationship with Mr. Jackson. During the second phase of treatment, with Ms. Hartman's relationship with Mr. Jackson more stabilized and with the help of Carrie's new therapist, Carrie and her mother spent more time together and began establishing a new style of interaction, characterized by more rules, less blaming, and more trust. This new interactive style was modeled in Carrie's therapy and reinforced at home. It began to generalize to Carrie's relationships at school. Regressions still occurred, however, and Carrie needed continued support in both her family and school relationships.

Prognosis and discussion

A review of five years of intermittent evaluation and treatment of Carrie and her family helps to clarify our understanding of the complexities of Carrie's affective disorder, as a function of the mother-child Relationship Disorder. The therapeutic process that helped stabilize Ms. Hartman's relationships—first with a therapist, then with Mr. Jackson, and finally with Carrie—is typical of the therapeutic process required in treating intergenerational dysfunctional interactive patterns. The improvements in Carrie's ability to regulate her moods depended on Ms. Hartman's ability to regulate her own moods which, in turn, depended on the strength and stability of the therapeutic relationships and her relationship with Mr. Jackson.

It is not surprising that Carrie's first grade teacher and her pediatrician interpreted Carrie's difficulties with attention and behavior at school as symptoms of ADHD, nor that she was given a trial of Ritalin. Symptoms of anxiety and mood disorders are often misdiagnosed as ADHD. The ineffectiveness of Ritalin and the effectiveness of antidepressant treatment in improving Carrie's mood, sleep and behavior and in decreasing her irritability and distractibility provide further support for the affective nature of her symptoms.

The abatement of Carrie's affective symptoms facilitated her improved functioning and increased her mother's hopefulness. The persistence of Carrie's lying and defiance after her affective symptoms decreased suggested problems with trust and issues of control. The team expected that her ongoing experience of a healthy relationship with her therapist and especially with her mother would help Carrie feel more in control of herself and more accepting of limit setting by others.

As the second phase of treatment was well underway, Carrie had become less controlling, less defiant, and more available to learn. She had developed an increased sense of control over her mood and behavior and an increased sense of her social and academic competences. With gradually increasing trust between Carrie and her mother and the ongoing support of her therapist, the prognosis for Carrie's more consistently utilizing her new "schema-of-being" with her mother and others appeared hopeful.

References

American Psychiatric Association (1994). *Diagnostic and Statistical Manual of Mental Disorders, Fourth Edition.* Washington, DC: American Psychiatric Association.

Fraiberg, S. (1980). *Clinical studies in infant mental health.* New York: Basic Books.

Stern, D. N. (1995). *The motherhood constellation: A unified view of parent-infant psychotherapy.* New York: Basic Books.

200. Disorders of Affect

204. Mixed Disorder of Emotional Expressiveness

Sharon Levy, Ph.D.
Karen Frankel, Ph.D.
Robert Harmon, M.D.

The diagnostic category of Mixed Disorder of Emotional Expressiveness should be used for infants and young children who have ongoing difficulty expressing developmentally appropriate emotions. Their difficulties are understood as reflecting problems in their affective development and experiences. The disorder may be manifested by: (a) the absence or near absence of one or more specific types of affects that are developmentally expectable; (b) a range of emotional expression that is constricted in comparison to developmentally appropriate expectations; (c) disturbed intensity of emotional expression, inappropriate to the child's developmental level; and (d) reversal of affect inappropriate to situations.

This diagnosis should not be used if the child is given a diagnosis of Anxiety or Depression. This diagnosis should be used with children with developmental delays only if the disturbance in affective expression is inappropriate to the child's developmental level.

Reason for referral

Anton is a 3-year-old boy who lives with his 26-year-old mother, his maternal grandmother, his 11-year-old brother, and his and 2-month-old sister. Shawna Powell requested treatment for her son because she was concerned about his extreme activity, defiance, and verbal and physical aggression. She said that Anton exhibited some perseverative behaviors: he watched the same video over and over, repeated play sequences, and repeated insults towards his mother. Ms. Powell reported that "time-outs" were unsuccessful in helping Anton modify his behavior and that Anton had considerable difficulty ending or changing activities.

Before coming to our Infant Psychiatry Clinic, which is located in a large teaching hospital, Anton had received an assessment at a center specializing in developmental and genetic evaluations and a screening at the local Child Find agency, part of the state's system of services for infants and toddlers with disabilities. Examiners in both settings experienced difficulty engaging

Anton with tasks. At the development center, Anton would not respond at all to the examiner, who described him as extremely withdrawn, hiding behind his mother. In an attempt to follow him, hospital staff recommended case management and therapeutic day care. Ms. Powell reported, however, that she had not felt comfortable with development center staff, felt unassisted by them and, consequently, did not follow through with their recommendations. During the screening process at the Child Find agency, the Batelle Developmental Inventory was administered. Anton scored at the seventh percentile, with a weakness in receptive language. The second examiner commented on Anton's "disordered" social and adaptive behavior. The examiner noted that throughout the assessment Anton's behavior had been "erratic," sometimes reactive and sometimes withdrawn, and characterized by frequent refusals to do testing items. The second examiner considered it likely that the assessment was not an adequate measure of Anton's cognitive abilities but nevertheless referred him for twice-weekly, half-day special education services. Ms. Powell reported that Anton was currently on a waiting list for enrollment in this publicly funded group program.

Disappointed by her previous two experiences and feeling extremely frustrated by and hopeless about Anton's behavior, Ms. Powell requested assistance from our Infant Psychiatry Clinic. Because the clinic was familiar with one of the agencies she had contacted earlier and felt generally confident in its staff's abilities, the clinic wanted to make sure that it understood what these earlier assessment experiences had been like for Ms. Powell and Anton, and how it could prevent another disappointment. With Ms. Powell's permission, the clinic obtained reports of the earlier assessments and also asked her directly about her perceptions of the assessments and recommendations for intervention. She said that she did not think that Anton would exhibit many of his aggressive behaviors with strangers and therefore was skeptical of their ability to assess him.

Ms. Powell reported that these agencies were not "really doing anything" to help her. When asked what "doing something" would consist of, she said that she believed that Anton had Attention/Deficit Hyperactivity Disorder (ADHD). Ms. Powell had drawn this conclusion from reading magazine articles and watching television programs about ADHD. She hoped the clinic staff would prescribe medication to treat his condition. The staff explained to Ms. Powell its understanding that the behaviors she was observing in Anton could be a reflection of ADHD but could also stem from other causes. The staff explained that in order to understand Anton's strengths and problems, it hoped to observe his behavior in different settings and with people (herself and other members of the family) who were familiar to him. The staff also wanted to learn more about her own experiences, particularly in caring for Anton and her other children.

The team tried to explain clearly our own process at the clinic: Once we felt that we had a sufficient understanding of Anton's situation, we would discuss possible treatment approaches with Ms. Powell. The team said that based on its experience, we believed that with very young children, medication should only be used as part of a plan that involved working directly and closely with the child and family.

Assessment process

Because (as will be described below), the team found it difficult to establish a working alliance with Ms. Powell, the assessment process was considerably longer than usual. The assessment consisted of: (a) a meeting with Ms. Powell alone to discuss the assessment plan; (b) office-based free play evaluations of Anton; (c) an office-based evaluation of Anton's behavior with his mother during free play; and (d) a videotaped separation/reunion task. In all, the assessment consisted of 11 sessions over 18 weeks. During this period, Ms. Powell canceled or failed to keep numerous appointments, which were then rescheduled.

Although in our initial meeting with Ms. Powell the team discussed the benefits of observing Anton in the familiar environment of his home, Ms. Powell would not consent to a home visit. She did not let us know why a home visit would be unacceptable to her. Since Anton was not enrolled in child care or early intervention, the team did not have the opportunity to observe him interacting with children or adults in these settings or the benefit of observations of caregivers who saw him regularly. Ms. Powell responded to inquiries about family history with only general information.

The team's limited success in establishing a working alliance with Ms. Powell was frustrating and disappointing to us and probably so to Ms. Powell, as well. Beginning with the first time that Ms. Powell brought Anton to the office for an observation session, she seemed formal in manner, vigilant, and sensitive to criticism. For example, she watched the therapist closely as she tried to engage Anton. At times, Ms. Powell appeared distressed when the therapist was even mildly successful in engaging Anton in play or coloring. Ms. Powell explained that Anton did not behave that well at home and went on to say that he only behaved well for others in order to embarrass her. The team could appreciate Ms. Powell's dilemma. Here was a mother sufficiently concerned about her three-year-old to make three separate efforts to find appropriate help, despite the demands of caring for a newborn and, as was learned later, her mother's criticism of her attempts to obtain professional assistance. Yet the very nature of her concerns made her vulnerable and placed her in what may have seemed like a "no-win" situation: If Anton appeared competent with the examiner, this could be seen as evidence of Ms. Powell's relative ineptitude; if he were out of control, his mother's inability to regulate his behavior would be vividly apparent.

The team was in something of a bind as well. Aware of the popular media's preoccupation with ADHD, we could understand how Ms. Powell might have arrived at her own diagnosis of Anton and be angry at the team's failure to prescribe the medications recommended by on-the-air experts— especially since our clinic was hospital-based, full of physicians with prescription privileges. Nevertheless, the therapists' general reservations about pharmacological interventions for very young children aside, they needed to understand much more about the situation of Anton and his family before they could develop a shared formulation with Ms. Powell and begin to discuss possible interventions.

The therapist used several strategies to connect with Ms. Powell. As many others have observed, a good assessment is also an intervention. Thus, the therapist's efforts to establish a working alliance were intended not only to facilitate the assessment process but also, it was hoped, to provide some relief to Ms. Powell and, in addition, to suggest the most promising ways to work together over the long term. For example, the therapist watched for any positive interchanges between Anton and his mother. These were subtle, generally consisting of Anton showing toys to his mother for her approval or reaction. Frequently, however, as soon as the therapist drew her attention to these interactions, Ms. Powell would appear self-conscious, disengage from Anton, and begin to discuss his negative behaviors.

The therapist also tried to connect with Ms. Powell by empathizing with her about all she was trying to achieve despite her difficult life circumstances, such as caring for three children and pursuing an education with meager financial resources, limited social supports, and unresolved feelings about Anton's father. Although Ms. Powell's manner was generally formal and emotionally constrained, on two occasions she talked to the therapist with animation, spontaneity, and considerable intensity of feeling about her family conflict and her frustration with her limited resources. Following each of these sessions, however, Ms. Powell missed her next appointment. Instead of coming to the clinic, she would call the therapist and loudly accuse her and the treatment team of withholding assistance (especially medication) from her family. Ms. Powell would then keep her next scheduled appointment and apologize for her outburst. Unfortunately, we were never able fully to explore or resolve her frustration and anger with the assessment process and our preliminary assessment approaches.

Assessment findings

Developmental history

Anton was a slightly overweight biracial boy, whose elongated face, large eyes, and puffy eyelids made him look older than his three years. Although Anton's dysmorphic facial features made the team wonder about potential genetic difficulties, the examiners at the developmental/genetic clinic had noted no concerns. Ms. Powell said that Anton looked like his father (a photograph that she brought in confirmed this) and said that his behavior was also similar to his father's.

Ms. Powell said that pregnancy, labor, and delivery had been normal. She said that she had not used drugs or alcohol during her pregnancy with Anton. Before and during her pregnancy, Ms. Powell had been physically abused by Anton's father, who later abandoned her. She said, however, that she had been happy about her pregnancy, perceiving it as a "gift" after the abuse she had suffered. We noted that Ms. Powell was guarded and expressed little affect during this discussion.

As a young infant, Anton had episodes of wheezing and was diagnosed with asthma, but he was nonsymptomatic during the second and third years of life. Shortly before assessment began, however, Anton experienced a severe asthma attack and was taken to the hospital. He was treated with medication on an outpatient basis. This episode exacerbated Ms. Powell's concerns about Anton's overactivity and noncompliance. She worried that he could "put himself into" an asthma attack, and then not cooperate with treatment.

While Ms. Powell reported that Anton sat independently, walked, and talked within a normal time frame, she said that he had always been difficult to soothe or play with. At about 18 months, he had become more active and defiant. As noted, Anton was screened at 2 1/2 years by the Department of Education and determined to have adaptive and receptive language delays and "severe emotional problems"(the latter conclusion was reached on the basis of Anton's inability to comply with testing procedures).

Family history

Anton lived with his maternal grandmother, mother, 11-year-old brother, and 2-month-old sister. He had no contact with his father. Ms. Powell said that she had no difficulties with her two other children. Although she said initially that her mother was emotionally supportive and helped with child care, as the assessment progressed, she reported that her mother was critical both of her parenting abilities and her attempts to get outside assistance in dealing with Anton's behaviors. It became increasingly apparent that Ms. Powell's support system was extremely limited, and her responsibilities great.

In response to questions, Ms. Powell said that Anton had not experienced physical or sexual abuse or neglect. She said that she had not abused drugs or alcohol. While she reported some experience with counseling, she would not elaborate on why she had been in counseling or what her experiences had been like.

Ms. Powell said that her mother had a diagnosis of bipolar illness for seven years and was stabilized on medication. She had no contact with her natural father but had had a positive relationship with a stepfather, who died while she was in her teens. Ms. Powell seemed reluctant to discuss her relationships with members of her extended families. She said that she had been exposed to severe family violence and that she, her mother, and her children had cut themselves off from their extended family due to this violence. Ms. Powell was reluctant to discuss family violence in more detail. She said that her children had not been exposed to violence themselves, and she did not believe that providing further information about this would be helpful for Anton.

Child functioning

As Ms. Powell had predicted, Anton did not show any of the actively aggressive verbal or physical behaviors in the clinic that she reported occurred at home. At the clinic, Anton did not lash out at his mother or the therapist even when he was angry. Rather, he became passively oppositional, cried, and screamed in a solitary tantrum. For example, when the therapist announced the impending end of a session, Anton curled up in the corner, crying loudly, and refused to interact with the therapist or his mother. Neither his mother nor the therapist was able to soothe him by offering toys, physical contact, vocal soothing, or distraction. Eventually, Anton was carried from the room, still sobbing. On at least one other occasion, Anton exhibited these same behaviors in the middle of the session, for no apparent reason. We were unable to identify anything out of the ordinary that may have triggered this outburst from Anton. On this occasion, however, Ms. Powell was able to soothe Anton with physical affection. There was an anxious and overstimulated quality to Anton's outbursts. His loud cry was difficult to listen to and made his mother visibly tense.

Anton vacillated between appearing sullen, passive, and quiet, and appearing irritable, tearful, and extremely distressed. When presenting as sullen and quiet, Anton appeared especially careful and vigilant about his interactions. He was tense, cautious and unnaturally slow in his movements. He avoided eye contact but appeared to monitor the activities of others with fleeting glances. When he did make direct eye contact, Anton would break this contact quickly and freeze his play. Despite the restrained quality of Anton's play and his apparent lack of enjoyment, he had a tantrum when the end of a session was announced. He would refuse to stop playing, attempt to keep the therapist's toys, cry, scream, and curl up in the corner of the room.

Anton was not aggressive toward his mother or the therapist. Indeed, he rarely sought to interact with either of them. His outbursts seemed to be a form of withdrawal; he would isolate himself and not respond to efforts to soothe through physical touch or verbal contact. When he had a tantrum at the end of sessions, his mother would eventually just pick him up and exit, as he hung limply in her arms.

Anton's avoidance of and vigilance with the therapist made it difficult to assess his language abilities. While his mother reported that Anton frequently verbalized at home and spoke in full sentences, he rarely talked in session. He appeared to understand directions but would only nod in response, or do nothing at all. On the rare occasions that he did speak, Anton used a startlingly low-pitched, almost baritone, voice with poor articulation.

Anton's motor abilities seemed developmentally age-appropriate. He was able to manipulate crayons, small toys, and Legos well. His walking and running appeared coordinated. The quality of Anton's play, however, was worrisome. There was a slow, methodical, and controlled quality to Anton's movements in play. For example, he slowly arranged toys in a circle around himself but did not actively manipulate the toys, produce any themes spontaneously, or seem to enjoy the play. He would not initiate or engage in thematic play even with prompting from the therapist.

Parent-child interaction

It is worth noting that most sessions were conducted with Ms. Powell, Anton, and Tenisa, a chubby, placid baby who was 2 months old at the beginning of the assessment process. Typically, Ms. Powell sat with Tenisa on her lap, facing outward. It looked to us as if Ms. Powell was using Tenisa as a kind of shield or barrier between herself and Anton. She rarely made efforts to touch or engage her son. Although Tenisa slept throughout each session, Ms. Powell did not respond to the therapist's gentle suggestions that she bring in a stroller or a blanket for Tenisa to lie on so that Ms. Powell could involve herself with Anton more easily.

Ms. Powell was seldom affectionate with either Anton or Tenisa. She held the baby in a functional way, never stroked her, and rarely made eye contact. Anton seldom sought interaction with his mother or sister. While he seemed to be careful to remain in close proximity to his mother, he tried to get her attention only infrequently. He never hugged, kissed, or stroked his mother affectionately.

Throughout the assessment period, we observed tension in the interaction between Anton and his mother; the absence of positive or comforting interactions was striking. Typically, Ms. Powell would sit in a chair with Tenisa on her lap while Anton wandered aimlessly around the room. When encouraged to get down on the floor to play with Anton, Ms. Powell commented that Anton rejected her attempts to play with him at home and therefore she did not know how to engage him. Occasionally, Ms. Powell would offer Anton a toy or comment on his play; when he did not respond immediately, she would turn her attention back to the therapist. Occasionally, Anton would show his mother something that he had built with Legos. However, when his mother responded with a comment, Anton would disengage from the interaction. Ms. Powell and Anton could rarely string together more than two or three consecutive turns in an interactive sequence.

During one session, Ms. Powell and Anton were videotaped while playing alone in the clinic playroom. On this occasion, Anton was significantly more active and verbal than he had been when the therapist was in the room, but he still did not seem to be enjoying himself much. Although Ms. Powell got down on the floor and sat close to Anton, she continued to create distance by holding Tenisa between herself and Anton. Her worry that Anton might break the clinic's toys or mix clays of different colors seemed to inhibit her from actively engaging in the play. (Anton, it should be noted, used all play materials appropriately). Anton and his mother made little eye contact and rarely made physical contact with each other.

Although Anton did not respond to verbal commands or expressions of affection, Ms. Powell seemed to use language as her primary means of interacting with her son. At times a comment that might have been intended as a compliment sounded, to our ears at least, negative in content and tone, such as "I don't know why you're behaving so well; I wish you could act like this at home!" In the videotaped play sequence, Ms. Powell frequently scolded Anton for his behavior at home, such as when he played videos over and over.

The third session of the assessment included a separation/reunion sequence. When his mother left the room, Anton noted her departure and appropriately asked where his mother was going. When it was explained that she would return shortly, he did not become distressed. However, when left alone with the therapist, Anton became extremely avoidant, withdrawn, and regressed in his play. He made little eye contact, showed no playful or happy affective expressions, and was careful to take physical distance from the therapist. He accepted toys from the therapist but would not engage in any interactive or symbolic play. He lay on the floor holding a truck and rocking. When his mother returned, she entered the room and called his name. He looked at her for a few seconds from a distance. He began to approach her, but midway he made a "U-turn" and moved sullenly back to his corner. Later, Anton seemed to become anxious and hid behind his mother.

Although several times we observed Anton go into a tantrum without having first sought comfort from his mother and resist her subsequent efforts to soothe him, on one occasion he did make many attempts to obtain comfort from his mother when he was distressed and tearful about the impending end of a session. He asked his mother to play some more; walked around the room crying, but still talking to her; and even pressed against her leg. Ms. Powell, however, continued to sit quietly with Tenisa on her lap, rearranging her daughter's clothing and not responding to her son.

Child-therapist interaction

Anton appeared constantly aware of the therapist's presence but avoided direct interactions with her. When she attempted to engage Anton, he broke eye contact, turned his back to her, and refused to speak. Anton provided few social reinforcements, either verbal or nonverbal, to encourage the therapist to continue her interactions with him. At times, Anton worked hard to distance himself from her. He often would wedge himself between his mother's chair and the wall to shield himself from the therapist. While playing alone with the therapist he constantly maintained a physical distance of several feet. During these sessions, Anton would wedge himself in the corner, lie face down on the floor, or hide under the table.

The therapist maintained a neutral-to-positive, gently encouraging stance. She spoke quietly to Anton or Ms. Powell, describing Anton's behaviors and their possible meanings. When he had less guarded moments, the therapist would make brief eye contact or offer a toy slowly. While he accepted toys from the therapist, sometimes imitated her, occasionally showed her how he could manipulate toys or something he had fashioned from clay, and watched her actions, the interactions between Anton and the therapist were brief and affectless. Anton always ended them by not responding to an overture. The therapist would allow Anton to withdraw and recompose himself, making contact later when he seemed more accepting. The therapist never insisted that Anton interact with her, nor did she set firm limits on his tantrums herself. Rather, she encouraged Ms. Powell to do so. She also supported Ms. Powell in encouraging Anton's interactions and in structuring Anton's behaviors. Although these patterns of interaction were fairly consistent throughout the assessment, Anton appeared somewhat more relaxed and played more with toys in the office during sessions when his mother appeared more relaxed with the therapist.

Reviewing the videotape with Ms. Powell

As part of the therapist's effort to build a working alliance with Ms. Powell, respond to her frustration with Anton's behavior, and explore what might be effective intervention approaches, the therapist reviewed the videotaped play sequence with Ms. Powell. The therapist attempted to direct Ms. Powell's attention to the more positive aspects of her interactions with Anton in hopes that she would be able to build on these at home. Ms. Powell did notice that Anton was most responsive when he initiated a play sequence; she could identify and respond to this pattern at home. However, while watching the videotape she tended to focus more on Anton's avoidance and oppositionality. When the therapist attempted to discuss how Ms. Powell might make the play more child-directed and positive by taking toys offered by Anton, imitating his play, and praising him for good behavior, Ms. Powell responded sharply that she had tried these strategies and "they did not work!"

Diagnosis

The Axis I diagnosis of Mixed Disorder of Emotional Expressiveness captured Anton's difficulty in expressing a wide range of emotions, his inability to modulate his emotional expression, the disproportionate intensity of his emotional outbursts, and the absence of playfulness and happiness. Throughout the assessment, Anton's affect was primarily over-controlled and sullen. He was vigilant without being curious about room, play materials, or the therapist. Team members did not see him smile, laugh, or engage the therapist or his mother in playful interactions. Anton's overcontrolled behavior was interrupted periodically by outbursts of intense, negative affect and tantrums. These episodes were prolonged and resistant to soothing.

While previous assessments indicated that Anton might be delayed in the development of social or language skills, his emotional expressions appeared inappropriate even for a child with delayed language and social development. However, his mother reported that he was able to use language adequately when he was calm. Further, Anton appeared more socially disordered than delayed, although the previous evaluations suggested that both domains were impaired. His social interactions could best be described as odd and erratic rather than age-inappropriate.

The team ruled out a diagnosis of Adjustment Disorder, resulting from the recent birth of his younger sister, because Ms. Powell described Anton's behavioral difficulties as long-standing. While she was concerned about

Anton's aggressive behavior toward his sister, such as pinching and yelling, she did not report any change in Anton's mood or behavior toward her since Tenisa's birth.

The team considered Regulatory Disorder as a possible Axis I diagnosis. During multiple sessions at the clinic, Anton did not demonstrate any sensory, sensory-motor, or organizational difficulties, problems with gross- or fine-motor movements, attentional difficulties, or perseverative behavior. Ms. Powell, however, said that Anton was perseverative in play at home. Anton was neither overreactive nor underreactive to sounds or smells. He was somewhat underreactive to touch, but the team saw this as part of his avoidance of interpersonal interactions and an expression of his sullen affect. Because of Anton's difficulty in regulating his affective states, the team's initial diagnostic formulation included Regulatory Disorder as a rule out diagnosis, pending evidence from additional observations, preferably in other contexts than the clinic. It would have liked the opportunity to develop enough of a rapport with Anton to have directly evaluated his sensory responding through an interactive sensory play assessment, with a referral for more specialized assessment if needed.

The Axis II Relationship Disorder Classification of Mixed, with features of Anxious/Tense and Angry/Hostile interactions reflected the therapists' observations of the tense, constricted nature of the interaction between Anton and his mother as well as Ms. Powell's scolding, negative comments to her son.

Behavioral quality of interaction: Neither mother nor son seemed to enjoy their interaction. While he avoided playful interactions with his mother, Anton's excessive clinginess impaired his ability to explore his surroundings or enjoy play materials. Ms. Powell's overcontrolled, tense demeanor inhibited her ability to interact freely with Anton. She interacted extremely tentatively with Anton and only infrequently made physical contact with him.

Affective tone: Physical affection between Anton and his mother was sadly rare; in 11 sessions we saw only two instances, consisting of Ms. Powell briefly stroking Anton's back. Much more frequent were escalating cycles of negative and anxious affective expressions between Anton and his mother. On numerous occasions, Anton and Ms. Powell left the session with Anton crying and his mother angrily, desperately, and ineffectually trying to quiet him.

Psychological involvement: Ms. Powell personalized Anton's behaviors. She was also highly sensitive to perceived criticism about her parenting abilities.

Axis IV *Psychosocial Stressors:* Stressors that were affecting Anton included the recent birth of a sibling, medical illness (his asthma), poverty, his mother's single-parent status, domestic violence, and intergenerational conflict.

Axis V *Functional Emotional Developmental Level:* Ratings of Anton's Functional Emotional Developmental Level were made with his mother and the evaluator. Anton had achieved age-appropriate levels for mutual attention and mutual engagement, but was constricted and vulnerable to stress. He barely evidenced the capacity for representational/affective communication. With the therapist, he needed structure and sensorimotor support to evidence even mutual attention and mutual engagement. He had not achieved age-expected levels of representational elaboration even with support from either his mother or the therapist.

Diagnostic Summary

Axis I: Primary Diagnosis
Mixed Disturbance of Emotional Expression
Rule out: Regulatory Disorder.

Axis II: Relationship Disorder Classification
Mixed, with features of both Anxious/Tense and Angry/Hostile interaction patterns.

Axis III: Medical and Developmental Disorders and Conditions
Asthma
Rule out: Speech-language disorder(s).

Axis IV: Psychosocial Stressors
Enduring, severe effects.

Axis V: Functional Emotional Developmental Level
Has not achieved age-expected levels of representational elaboration. Has achieved age-appropriate levels for mutual attention and mutual engagement, but is constricted and vulnerable to stress. Capacity for representational/affective communication barely evidenced.

PIR-GAS:30 (Disordered)

Discussion with caregivers and treatment planning

As noted above, despite its length, the assessment process left the team feeling that there were many important questions about Anton and his family that remained unanswered. We had not observed Anton's moods, behavior, or interactions with people outside the clinic setting. We did not know how adults other than his mother perceived him. We had little information about Ms. Powell's relationships with some important people in her past and in her present life. The changing portrait of Ms. Powell's mother that emerged during the assessment process suggested that only over time, and in the course of a trusting relationship, would Ms. Powell be able to articulate, and eventually reflect on, her complex feelings about people and events that were important to her.

As also noted above, from the beginning of the team's work with Ms. Powell and Anton, assessment and intervention were intertwined. In addition to offering the general sense of validation and empowerment that many families gain from the experience of being taken seriously and listened to attentively during an assessment, we made a specific effort to identify strengths in Anton and in the mother/son relationship, and to help Ms. Powell not only see these strengths herself, but also build on them in her daily interactions with Anton. These efforts met with limited success.

After the eleventh session with Ms. Powell and Anton, the team scheduled a meeting to review what we had learned together about Anton and to plan how to proceed. At this meeting, the therapist emphasized Ms. Powell's astuteness in recognizing that Anton's behavior did call for special attention and her persistence in seeking both an explanation and assistance. She recognized Ms. Powell's fortitude in caring for Anton as a difficult infant and toddler, observing that now that he was three he might be able to benefit from a good group experience.

The therapist presented a four-part intervention plan to Ms. Powell to consider, noting that each component of the plan represented an approach that the therapist and Ms. Powell had already begun to explore. The plan included: (a) continuing sessions with Ms. Powell, Anton, and the therapist, with the goal of addressing Anton's behaviors directly, using joint problem solving and therapist modeling; (b) enrolling Anton in a group program such as special education or therapeutic child care; (c) developing a behavioral program for use at home with Anton; and (d) connecting the family with community services.

The therapist told Ms. Powell that after much discussion, treatment team members had decided not to recommend a trial of medication at this time. The therapist had not observed the kinds of behavioral difficulties in Anton that tend to be remedied by medication. If these behaviors were observed in a special education or therapeutic child care setting, the question could be revisited. In addition, the team hoped that increased structure in Anton's environment might result in improved behavior, thus eliminating the source of Ms. Powell's concern. A third factor, raised by team members, was not discussed by the therapist with Ms. Powell. This issue concerned the team's reluctance to prescribe medication when the therapeutic alliance was so shaky and its understanding of Ms. Powell so incomplete. For example, Ms. Powell had said that her pediatrician had told her she could give Anton Benadryl "to calm him down," and she observed that she used it "when at wits' end." The therapists sensed that Ms. Powell was frustrated by the team's decision to postpone any trial of medication; nevertheless, she somewhat grudgingly agreed to continue working with the therapist to implement the four-part plan.

Intervention

The continuing relationship between the therapist, Ms. Powell, and Anton was the vehicle for implementing the agreed-upon four-part intervention approach. The therapist saw Ms. Powell as desperate for help, yet convinced that seeking or accepting assistance constituted an indictment of her own capacities as a parent. The therapist tried to normalize Ms. Powell's experience, noting that all parents of young children need and deserve support and pointing out that Ms. Powell was carrying such an unusually heavy load of responsibilities that feeling stressed or overwhelmed was expectable. Ms. Powell responded positively to this approach.

Ms. Powell and the therapist used some time in session to make phone inquiries together about community services. Through this process, Ms. Powell followed through on a previous recommendation to enroll Anton in a twice-weekly special education program, and also applied for therapeutic child care. However, Anton was placed on waiting lists for both programs. Ms. Powell and Anton were also connected with a community organization that provided family recreation programs and respite care. The therapist was aware that respite care is often perceived as carrying a stigma of association with actual or potential child abuse or neglect. Fortunately, the local respite care agency was staffed by extremely competent and sensitive host families, and the Department of Social Services (DSS) caseworker liaison, whom the therapist contacted before she made the joint call with Ms. Powell, was receptive to encouraging Ms. Powell to use the resource preventively and view it as a normative family support. After the therapist and Ms. Powell called the DSS caseworker, Ms. Powell was authorized to schedule two weekends of respite care for Anton as she felt the need and occasional half-days, also on an as-needed basis.

Making connections with community agencies or, possibly, the experience of working together with the therapist to establish these connections, seemed to enable Ms. Powell to engage more actively with Anton in clinic sessions. For example, immediately after the therapist had helped her to connect with respite services, Ms. Powell came to the next session with a blanket for Tenisa to lie on. (The therapist had suggested this to Ms. Powell weeks earlier, but she had never acted on the suggestion.) This act seemed to signal a willingness on Ms. Powell's part to work directly on her relationship with Anton.

This aspect of the work proceeded slowly. Ms. Powell and Anton stayed close to each other in session, but seemed tense and reluctant to interact with each other. When the therapist, thinking to model appropriate interactions, began to play directly with Anton, Ms. Powell imitated the therapist but in a way that suggested she felt "shown up" and uncomfortable. The therapist then refrained from direct interaction with Anton and concentrated instead on reinforcing and praising Ms. Powell when she either initiated interactions with Anton or responded to his overtures. This approach was more successful. Both Ms. Powell and Anton appeared to become more at ease and spontaneous in their interactions and even made some affectionate gestures toward each other.

To address Anton's behavioral difficulties at home, especially his aggression, Ms. Powell and the therapist attempted to work together to develop a behavioral program. As a first step, Ms. Powell was instructed to record when aggressive behaviors occurred, what had happened prior to the behavior, how she responded to the behavior, and what occurred afterward. Because Ms. Powell had difficulty describing specific behaviors of concern and because the therapist never had the opportunity to observe these behaviors together with Ms. Powell, the behavioral approach reached an impasse. Ms. Powell said that she "restrained" Anton when he tried to do something unsafe, like walking across a glass table or jumping off the furniture, or threatened his brother or sister.

The therapist and other members of the treatment team were concerned about Ms. Powell's increasing frustration with Anton's behavior and her own life circumstances. Ms. Powell said, for example, that she was concerned that Anton "might get hurt" when she physically restrained him. She also complained that her mother seemed to blame her for Anton's behavior but criticized her for seeking outside help. On one occasion, Ms. Powell made arrangements for Anton to be in respite care for three days but canceled these plans when her mother criticized them. Shortly thereafter, Ms. Powell abruptly stopped treatment at the Infant Psychiatry Clinic. She missed several appointments, and the therapist called twice, with no response. The therapist then sent a letter inviting Ms. Powell to call and saying that if she didn't hear from her, the case would be closed for a time. At this point, Anton was still on the waiting lists for special education and therapeutic child care programs.

The treatment team's review of its work with Ms. Powell and Anton yielded several important observations:

1. Although the therapeutic alliance that the therapist had struggled to build with Ms. Powell crumbled very quickly as Anton continued to act out and Ms. Powell's mother weighed in with her disapproval, it was nevertheless true that Ms. Powell had stayed with the therapist longer than she had remained involved with staff at either of the previous agencies she had consulted. She might be able to carry some good from this latest experience into a future helping relationship.

2. Ms. Powell's efforts to get professional help in parenting Anton may have proved too undermining to her self-esteem to continue. A diagnosis of ADHD, a disorder commonly understood as residing "in the child," might have reduced the perceived stigma of not being an appropriate parent. At the same time, it is important to note that Ms. Powell pulled back from any professional effort to get "too close"—for example, by making a home visit. We do not know what Ms. Powell may have felt it necessary to "hide."

3. Ms. Powell did struggle to create an alliance with a therapist who, she thought initially, could not possibly understand her. Ms. Powell's pattern of approach/avoidance with the therapist can be seen as similar to Anton's pattern with her, and not improbably as a template for her interaction with her own mother.

Prognosis and discussion

The team remains uncertain about Anton's prognosis for two reasons. First, it does not feel that its contact with Anton yielded an accurate assessment of his true capacities or potential for healthy development in a structured, consistent, and stimulating environment. Second, it does not know enough about Ms. Powell to predict the likelihood of her return to the Infant Clinic or another agency. Because such uncertainties are far from rare in work with very young children and their families, the policy at the Infant Clinic is to remain available for further work with any child who has ever been involved with it, at whatever age he or she may next appear.

200. Disorders of Affect

205. Childhood Gender Identity Disorder

Susan W. Coates, Ph.D. and
Sabrina M. Wolfe, Ph.D.

The diagnosis of Gender Identity Disorder is a new category in the ZERO TO THREE Diagnostic Classification system. Complete diagnostic criteria are described and explained in *DC: 0-3* (pp. 26-29). It is essential, in making a diagnosis of GID, that great care be taken to differentiate this disorder from age-typical developmental variation and from temperamental variation resulting in preferences that do not conform to gender stereotypes, including tomboyism in girls, and sensitive, aesthetic orientation in boys. The stereotypic cross gender behavior seen in children with GID is characterized by its persistence, its pervasiveness, its rigidity. and its long duration, as illustrated in the two case reports that follow. A discussion of predisposing factors, intervention strategies, and particular considerations in the treatment of GID draws on both case reports for illustrative examples.

COLIN, Age 3¹/₂

Reason for referral

Colin was referred at the age of 3¹/₂ to a mental health practitioner by his nursery school teacher because of his inability to get along with other children. If he did not get his way, he would hit them or else he would scowl, cross his arms, and turn his face to the wall. Moreover, from the perspective of the nursery school his current behavior represented a marked change from the time that he had been evaluated for entrance into the nursery program nearly 8 months earlier. A consultation with a psychiatrist revealed that he also had extensive preoccupations with cross-gender fantasies which included a belief that he was going to grow up to be a girl. He was referred to a center for children with gender identity issues.

Assessment process

The evaluation consisted of meeting first with the parents to get a history of his presenting problems, temperament, and development, then with Colin, who was seen in several sessions that involved play interviews and psychological testing. He was also seen for three sessions with his parents (one with both parents together and one with each of his parents alone) in order to begin to understand their individual styles of interaction with him as well as the family style of interaction. Additional sessions with the parents explored their own childhood histories in an effort to understand whether unresolved issues for either parent might be impinging upon their ability to be emotionally available to Colin as parents. The evaluation took 2 months to complete.

Assessment findings

Presenting behavior

Our initial contact with Colin confirmed the existence of the extensive cross-gender interests and behaviors that were reported to have begun a year earlier. He openly stated that he wished to be a girl and that he hated being a boy. He believed he was born a girl and that if you wore a girl's clothes you could really become a girl and "not just for pretend." Since the age of 2 $\frac{1}{2}$ he had regularly dressed in his mother's clothes and would spend long periods of time cross-dressing while observing himself intently in front of a mirror. He was intensely interested in jewelry and make-up, he repetitively stroked the hair of Barbie dolls, and he had a marked interest in heroines (not heroes) in fairy tales such as Snow White and Rumplestiltskin. He also showed a notable lack of interest in playing with other boys.

According to his parents he did not express anatomic dysphoria, either by saying that he wished that he did not have a penis, or by insisting on urinating in a sitting down position, or by pulling his penis between his legs and pretending to have a vagina as occurs with many boys that have GID. He also had never tried to harm his penis.

In our initial interview Colin's mother seemed highly emotionally invested in Colin and seemed to idealize and overvalue his gentle sweet nature and minimize his more difficult, angry and stubborn side. Although the father was also emotionally invested in Colin, he appeared to be somewhat remote and less involved with Colin.

Interview with Colin

When Colin first came to our center he needed his mother to stay with him throughout the first interviews. He was initially physically clingy, preoccupied with his mother's well-being and very attentive to her affect. He was overly solicitous, asking, for example "Mommy, are you okay?" His attentiveness to her—"That's a pretty dress, Mommy" and "Mommy, I love you"—and her response to that attentiveness were reversed in terms of the ordinary roles of child and parent in that he functioned as the protector of her rather than the reverse.

Despite his initial inhibition Colin was readily engaged by the examiners. Notably, he was uninterested in toys, and appeared to have no interest in playing. In many ways, Colin's initial presentation was that of a precocious, compliant, overattuned adult who responded to meeting with two new adults in a singularly unchildlike way. He exhibited none of the ordinary joyfulness of a child his age and showed no exploratory behavior or curiosity in the new environment, which included a playroom for children. When asked about the details of his favorite stories he recounted them nearly by rote with an exaggerated animation. Apart from this he showed a restricted range of affect.

Throughout the interview he seemed hypervigilant and his gaze was riveted to the eyes of the two interviewers, who were both female; he studied our faces intensely as if he was attempting to understand our every expression. Of particular note was his expressed concern about "ladies with angry eyes." He talked about how afraid he was of a girl in his class who had angry eyes.

He said he did not like himself and wished he was a girl. He felt that it was better to be a girl because you "could wear pretty clothes" and because "boys were too rough." He said he was lonely because other children did not like him, but he could come up with no idea of why this was.

Psychological testing

Colin was given a full battery of psychological tests, including the Rorschach, C.A.T., WISC-R, Sentence Completion, and Draw-A-Person tests. The testing revealed that he was functioning in the intellectually superior range. It further revealed that cross-gender preoccupations were extensive and that his sense of gender stability and constancy was very confused. On projective tests he was preoccupied with themes of annihilation, separation and loss. His representations of females were primitively idealized and representations of males were notably absent.

GID is unique among the psychiatric disorders of childhood in that its primary symptom is organized around a fantasized wish. It is important to explore what the wish means to the child. Why, for example, does he think it's better to be a girl than a boy? A sequence analysis of the child's cross-gender preoccupations as they emerge in play sessions and on projective tests can help inform one about the meaning and the function of the fantasy. For example, does the cross-gender fantasy occur every time the child has an aggressive fantasy or does it occur when he becomes separation anxious? Does it help the child to contain affect that is otherwise very difficult for him to manage? Psychological testing is very helpful in sorting these issues out. In Colin's case, the relation of the cross-gender fantasy to issues of separation anxiety was particularly striking.

Family background, development, and context for the onset of symptoms

Colin was the first born and only child of middle-class parents. His mother had concerns about whether she would be an adequate parent. She was worried that she might be very impatient and had been reluctant to get pregnant. Her husband convinced her to change her mind. Her pregnancy with Colin and his birth were uneventful. Ms. Smith was surprised to discover how much she enjoyed being a mother and how much she enjoyed breast-feeding Colin. She described him as an easy, sensitive baby who would just "drink in" the whole world around him. She called him "Peachy" because he was the "softest thing" she had ever felt. His developmental milestones were within normal limits.

His arrival, however, had significantly altered the dynamics of the family. During the immediate postpartum phase, his father felt unimportant and left out of the mother-child unit and he began to withdraw. This occurred despite the fact that he had eagerly anticipated becoming a father. From his perspective he was disappointed in his relationship with Colin. He felt that Colin was not responsive to him. During the subsequent months, the father found himself withdrawing further and he had a couple of inexplicable rage-ful outbursts that ended up in the destruction of property. He destroyed a waste-paper basket in a sudden burst of anger. He was taken aback and confused by his behavior and had no understanding of what initiated these uncharacteristic episodes.

The family was an extended one. When Colin's maternal grand-mother moved into the apartment next door to assist in caring for Colin, Ms. Smith experienced her mother's assistance as hyper critical, intrusive, and under-mining, and daily there were heated verbal fights between the two women. The history revealed that Ms. Smith's mother had never fully recovered psychologically from a miscarriage she had when Ms. Smith was two years old. When the grandmother was interviewed she became very tearful when recalling the miscarriage that had occurred over four decades ago.

In the year after Colin's birth, Ms. Smith also felt abandoned by her husband as he felt abandoned by her. Both parents had chronic worries about their financial stability. Despite all this stress, Ms. Smith remembers Colin at age 1 as a "laughing baby" with an easygoing temperament who was loving, gentle, and "always happy."

For both parents, the category of gender was highly salient in their own lives and in their perceptions of their growing son. For the father, Colin's gentle temperament brought to mind his own troubled boyhood where his sensitivity and timidity had left him feeling ill-equipped to deal with an angry, inaccessible, and alcoholic mother or to relate to either his father or brother, both bold, aggressive types. His principal concern was that Colin should develop a sense of his own "power"—hence, he encouraged without regard to consequences for Colin, any behavior that he perceived Colin as initiating.

In the mother's family of origin, boys were enormously over-valued compared to girls. Her brother, who was 3 years younger, had many "male privileges" that were very distressing to her. He had the choice of bedrooms in the house and was always offered seconds of food at supper before her. This often resulted in there being no extra food left for her. In addition, he was "sickly with asthma" and Ms. Smith experienced her mother as becoming completely preoccupied with him and emotionally abandoning her. A childhood spent taking care of and catering to her younger, fragile brother was bearable to some degree because she was her father's favorite, but her father withdrew profoundly from her when she reached adolescence. Having a son was thus potentially problematic for her since feelings of loss and deprivation were linked in her own childhood to male privilege.

Shortly after Colin's second birthday, his family planned a five-day trip abroad, but he became ill before their departure. Colin and his mother stayed behind and his father, who was making a business trip, and his grandmother, who was planning to see her son, left for Europe for a week. His mother reported that, during their absence, Colin became inconsolable: "He cried until his father and grandmother returned." During the initial evaluation his mother denied having been upset herself. Later, however, during the course of treatment, she recalled being very angry and disappointed. Since the purpose of the grandmother's trip had been to see the mother's brother, this replicated the painful scenarios frequently experienced in the mother's childhood where the sickly brother received the lion's share of their mother's attention. Colin's mother was hurt and furious at this latest repetition.

Both parents agree that Colin's behavior changed at this point in time. He became anxious, was now markedly clingy, and extremely sensitive to all separations.

Ms. Smith, concerned that Colin "did not have enough companionship," decided to have a second child. She also was eager to repeat her earlier pleasurable experiences with Colin as an infant. However, this time her pregnancy ended in tragedy: amniocentesis led to the fetal diagnosis of Down syndrome. The parents were informed that if the pregnancy was carried to term, the baby would be very likely to suffer from other severe medical complications as well, complications which would necessitate multiple major surgical procedures in the first year of life. In addition to doubting the wisdom of carrying such a pregnancy to term, both parents questioned their capacity to raise a severely disabled child, should the infant survive. They were also deeply concerned about the impact such an experience would have on Colin. Given these considerations, they chose to terminate the pregnancy.

The amniocentesis had also revealed that the fetus was a female, and during the three week waiting period prior to an abortion, Ms. Smith developed elaborate fantasies about this girl child. She named the fetus "Miriam" after a revered teacher and felt grateful for the waiting period prior to the abortion as this allowed her "to get to know Miriam." She had fantasies of sewing dresses for Miriam and of giving her to her mother so that she would "have something to live for." Moreover, though her husband experienced a pronounced grief reaction following the abortion, Ms. Smith did not. Though she felt chronically depressed and anxious thereafter, Ms. Smith did not connect these feelings with the loss of the baby.

Colin's cross-gender behavior began within weeks after the abortion and it rapidly assumed the driven quality characteristic of children with the full syndrome of Childhood Gender Identity Disorder. In the months following the abortion, his mother came to experience Colin's general hypersensitivity and responsiveness as selectively attuned to herself. "He was always tuned in to my feelings," she would recall later, "He always knew how I felt."

At approximately the same time the GID emerged, Colin also began to have temper tantrums at home. These arose when he attempted to intrude on his mother's withdrawn, depressed state. Ms. Smith experienced his tantrums as overwhelming and felt in moments that he was doing her in. It was fully 2 years into her own therapy, however, before she remembered how strongly she would censure his demands that she spend more time with him. She remembered grabbing him about the shoulders and neck and shaking him while screaming at him full face. She recalled that while shaking him she looked into his eyes and realized that he was afraid that she might kill him. At this point, she began to fear that she might in fact harm him and worried that she was going crazy. As therapy proceeded it became clear that his fear of ladies with angry eyes that we heard about in our initial interview was connected to these earlier experiences. It is important to note that we were unable to understand the meaning of this preoccupation at the time of the evaluation.

Diagnosis

Aesthetic interests and sensibility in boys

GID, a rare condition, needs to be distinguished from behaviors that are reflective of variations in temperament, such as artistic interests in boys and an interest in rough-and-tumble play in girls. Where such temperamental variations lead the child in the direction of interests and activities stereotypically associated with the opposite gender, this may become of concern for parents holding to rigid notions of gender roles. However, the behavior in the child is not per se a cause for intervention—and indeed may be an indicator of greater ego-strength and flexibility.

GID, unlike variations in temperament, interests and activities, is defined by its persistence, pervasiveness, rigidity, and long duration and its occurrence in the context of anxious attachment, dislike of the self, and the wish to be someone else. A very verbal three-year-boy old expressed it this way: "I hate myself. I don't want to be me. I want to be somebody else. I want to be a girl."

Boys who have artistic interests, or who avoid rough-and-tumble play, or who prefer solitary intellectual activities like reading or listening to music or who enjoy cooking, do not, based on these behaviors, have gender identity problems. Although Colin was a sensitive, shy boy with aesthetic interests who disliked rough-and-tumble play, his gender atypical behavior took another form: extreme preoccupation with stereotypical female interests, repetitive dressing up in his mother's clothes and jewelry, and preoccupation with make-up and jewelry in the context of disliking himself and disliking being a boy.

Transient disturbances in gender

More difficult to distinguish from GID in very young children are transient disturbances in gender identity secondary to family stress. These can take on many of the hallmarks of GID in terms of the intensity and pervasiveness of the behavior. Ordinarily, however, not only is the precipitating stressor quite clear—the death of a child, an illness to the mother, the birth of a sibling—but the child's reaction is time-limited. Diagnostically speaking, the outside limit for considering such a reaction transient is three to six months. In addition, although the child typically wishes to be the other gender, and although this has psychological meaning and constitutes a defense against trauma, loss, or perceived threat, the child usually does not build up a concomitant degree of loathing and self-hatred for the gender he or she is. A transient reaction can often be worked through by helping the family to find ways to meet the child's needs more effectively. Once such a reaction has persisted for longer than three to six months, as it did in Colin's case, intervention with the child is clearly warranted.

Developmental variations

It is very common for very young children ages 2-3 to dress-up and make believe that they are the other gender as part of an overall interest in trying out roles. This ordinarily will be manifested by children flexibly dressing up as or imitating mommy, daddy, sister, brother, the baby or even the family pet. If the child is compulsively interested only in cross-gender pretend play, and this is very persistent and excludes other interests, as was the case with Colin, this is atypical. The child's continued reliance on this behavior to manage anxiety compromises the child's capacity to develop a flexible range of coping strategies for managing affect. The development of such coping strategies is crucial for the establishment of satisfying peer relationships and for the development of the child's own unique strengths and capacities.

Childhood transvestism

Boys who become obsessed with women's undergarments for the purposes of self-soothing or sensual arousal are distinguished from boys with GID who cross-dress in outer female attire to enhance the illusion of being female. Ordinarily childhood transvestism becomes evident in the latency years, but in rare instances very young children age 2-3 may become obsessively preoccupied with their mothers' panty-hose, bra, or other undergarments. This behavior may be initially motivated by the use of the under garments as transitional objects, but if it becomes a persistent, pervasive preoccupation that begins to interfere with the child's functioning it should be evaluated in the context of issues in the family that may be creating stress and insecure attachment in the child. Colin was only interested in female outer attire that could be used as a prop to support his fantasy that he was a girl. He was not interested in his mother's underwear.

Children with intersex conditions

Children with intersex conditions rarely have a childhood gender identity disorder. However, if a child with an intersex condition is having significant confusion and distress about his or her gender identity he or she should receive psychological help in sorting out this confusion.

There are no known differences in genes or hormones in children with gender identity disorder. A endocrinological work-up is warranted only in the rare case of extreme genital ambiguity or if the boy has a hypospadias. Colin did not have a hypospadias and did not need an endocrine work-up.

Emotional developmental functioning

Colin's capacity for symbolic functioning was underdeveloped for his age. Although Colin had a capacity for symbolic functioning that manifested itself in his advanced language development and in the relatively neutral situation of a cognitive testing session, he was not able to bring this capacity to bear on the more emotionally fraught process of elaborating feelings and experiences via play. His ability to represent conflicts symbolically in play was notably constricted, with concrete and repetitive enactment taking precedence over more flexible, joyful and imaginative symbolic representation. He was unable to develop narrative play themes or participate in reciprocal dramatic play with peers.

Diagnostic Summary

Axis I: Primary Diagnosis
Childhood Gender Identity Disorder.

Axis II: Relationship Disorder Classification
Colin's relationship with both parents was over- and under-involved.

Axis III: Medical and Developmental Disorders and Conditions
None.

Axis IV: Psychosocial Stressors
Moderate effects.

Axis V: Functional Emotional Developmental Level
Has attained age-appropriate levels of mutual attention, mutual engagement, interactive intentionality and reciprocity, representational/affective communication, and representational elaboration. Has not attained age-appropriate levels of representational differentiation.

PIR-GAS:30 (Disordered)

KATHY, Age 4¹/₂

Girls are less commonly referred for GID than boys by a ratio of about 5 to 1. Whether this represents a true difference in the rate of occurrence of GID or is due to other factors is simply not understood at present. Owing to the lower incidence in referred cases, less is known about the etiology of the disorder in girls. In many ways, the clinical presentation in girls is the mirror-image of what is seen with boys. That is to say, one finds the same rigidity and pervasiveness in the cross-gender behaviors, interests, and fantasies. Similarly, one finds the same high degree of dislike for one's own gender. Other factors, however, seem to be present in somewhat different combinations than a strict mirror-image analogy would suggest. In girls, too, there appears to be a high incidence of sensitive, reactive temperaments, though in contrast with boys, who tend also to be behaviorally inhibited, girls with GID are often oppositional and aggressive. The combination of predisposing familial factors that are most often found clinically in girls appears to be somewhat different as well, with the occurrenceof what the child perceives as a life-threatening situation being found in many cases; however, systematic information is currently lacking. The following case of Kathy is in many respects typical of GID in a girl, and makes a useful comparison case for that of Colin. The evaluation process was similar for both children.

Reason for referral

Kathy is a 4¹/₂ year-old girl who was referred by her parents for evaluation for gender identity disorder because of their concern about her persistent wish to be a boy, her extreme unhappiness about being a girl, her intense aversion to anything she perceived as female and her preoccupation with stereotypically male attributes and activities. The immediate precipitant to the referral was a parent-teacher meeting in which Kathy's nursery school teacher indicated that during the past 6 months Kathy had changed her name to Casey, told her peers that she was a boy and that she had a penis, and had become increasingly controlling with her peers. She would not take turns in being "the boss" of a game and when she did not get her way would often have a tantrum. Kathy's marked separation anxiety, her tantrums, and her oppositional and controlling behavior were also apparent at home and were of concern to her parents as well.

Assessment process

The evaluation process was similar to Colin's.

Assessment findings

Interview with Kathy

Upon first meeting Kathy, one could see why she was often mistaken for a boy as her parents reported. She had closely cropped short hair and wore a Power Rangers T-shirt, chunky black sneakers, and a baseball cap, which she consistently wore to each of her sessions, When first meeting the evaluator, she hung her head shyly and clutched her mother's leg. As she and her mother entered the office together she began demanding the soda her mother held in her hand and a brief disagreement occurred that her mother resolved by insisting that she wait until the appointment was over to have her drink. As her mother seated herself, Kathy responded to the examiner's suggestion that they look together at the toys on the toy shelf. Kathy then began rifling through the different boxes of toys, at times holding boxes up high and spilling the toys on the floor. In response to her mother's demand that she be more careful and pick up the fallen toys, Kathy shifted her body so that she sat with her back to her mother and continued to look through the toys, provocatively banging them together. After several minutes she took out the box of action figures and began identifying them by name as she briefly knocked two of them together in animated combat. When she spotted the sports figures, she excitedly exclaimed that she loved football and was going to be a football player when she grows up.

After about 20 minutes the examiner suggested that Kathy's mother go wait outside. Kathy immediately opened her mouth as if to protest, but then, seeming to restrain herself, picked up a Batman figure and began singing the Batman theme song. As her mother left the room, Kathy asked the examiner which of the action figures did she think was the toughest and then without waiting for a response said that Batman was the strongest. Once alone with the examiner, Kathy's speech became somewhat rapid and pressured and her gestures became more agitated. She began posturing as if she was trying to "act bold and tough " in order to manage her anxiety. When asked about her interests and her preferences, she adamantly said she hated girl stuff because "it's stupid" and that boys are better because they are stronger, they know how to fight, and they don't have to have babies. When asked what her favorite color was, she said that she liked all colors, but that she hated pink. Kathy was unable to answer questions about her feelings. Questions about what made her feel angry, sad, and so on appeared to increase her agitation: she said that she didn't know and repeatedly interrupted such questioning to knock together two action figures in mock battle.

Interview with the parents

Kathy's persistent wish to be a boy and her marked aversion to anything she associated with females first emerged at age $2^1/_2$. At that age she asked to be bought boys' clothes, and she began dressing in her brother's clothing. She began saying that she wished she was a boy, and on several occasions insisted that she actually was a boy. Over time her preoccupation with being a boy had become increasingly intense and pervasive. Between ages $2^1/_2$ and 3, she began to refuse to wear dresses even for special occasions. She insisted on having a baseball cap that was identical to one worn by her brother, and she wore it all day long and often insisted that she sleep with it on. When swimming, she would only wear bathing trunks. She only assumed the male role (never the female role) in fantasy play, and refused to play with girls, saying that their games were "stupid and boring." More recently she had begun pretending that she had a penis, and would tuck a large crayon into her panties when she slept at night. She would insist on urinating standing up like boys. During the 6 months preceding the evaluation, she had begun to scream during the course of her tantrums that she wished she were dead.

Kathy's parents described her as always having been a child who experiences significant separation anxiety and who is bossy, oppositional and has to get her way. Since she was quite young, Kathy would have intense tantrums when her demands were not met and her parents felt that at times she would refuse to do something simply because they had asked her to do it. They also indicated that she was extremely perfectionistic and would refuse to try something which she felt she might not be able to do well.

When Kathy was a baby, she did not like to be held by anyone other than her parents. As a toddler, she would cry excessively when left with a baby-sitter, and in response her parents had stopped going out without her. When she began a part-time preschool program at age 2³/₄, she exhibited initially intense separation anxiety, which gradually abated over the first several months of the program. At the time of the referral she continued to be quite clingy when going to new places. She was unable to sleep in her bed alone at night. She insisted on sleeping in her parents' bedroom or in the room with her brother. Despite her marked separation anxiety Kathy's parents noted that once she did "warm up" to a situation she typically became quite talkative and energetically involved in what was happening.

Developmental history

Kathy is the second of two children born to middle-class parents. She was the product of a planned pregnancy which was complicated by extreme nausea. Kathy's mother recalls vomiting several times each day throughout the pregnancy. Kathy was delivered at term by an emergency Cesarean section when her heartbeat inexplicably began to slow. Subsequent to the delivery, Kathy did not exhibit any neurological difficulties and her APGAR was a 9. Kathy was extremely colicky for the first 6 months and both parents recall being both frustrated and exhausted by her, although her father recalled that it was easier for him to soothe her than it was for her mother. Although Kathy's mother had intended to breast feed Kathy, she described Kathy as having difficulty sucking, which resulted in her needing to constantly feed in order to get enough milk over the course of the day. Kathy's mother decided that in order for Kathy to obtain adequate nutrition, she needed to be formula fed. Kathy's developmental milestones for both motor and language skills were achieved within normal limits.

When asked about Kathy's temperament, her parents indicated that she typically sized people up in new situations before becoming engaged with them and she often became very upset when people she cared for left. She also typically became excessively distressed when yelled at and she was quite difficult to soothe when injured. She reacted to even minor injuries with panic. She was easily bothered by bad odors, loud noises and tight clothing.

She insisted that tags be cut out of her shirts and she would "become hysterical" if the seam on her sock was not placed in the precise way that she finds comfortable. She showed timidity, shyness, and fear in many new situations, including most encounters with new children, new adults, and new places. She had always been more active than other girls her age and her parents described her as often being irritable, controlling, and bossy.

Psychological testing

Completing structured tasks was difficult for Kathy and over the course of the several sessions that it took to complete the psychological testing she became increasingly resistant to formal testing. For example, during the third session, she became quite oppositional during a vocabulary subtest as she climbed on top of the testing table and began giving obviously incorrect responses.

Kathy performed within the Average range of intellectual ability. However, her performance was very significantly compromised both by her perfectionism—evident in her refusal to persist on tasks which challenged her abilities—and by her oppositionalism, and it thus appeared likely that her actual aptitude was somewhat higher. Her responses to projective tests indicated that she was preoccupied with aggressive fantasies which overwhelmed and frightened her and defensive fantasies of herself as being extremely strong and powerful. She seemed typically to regard interpersonal relationships between people as characterized either by loss or by threat. Her responses indicated that she was experiencing excessive anxiety about her own basic safety and considerable vulnerability about her body. From a cognitive perspective she knew that she was a girl and that her gender could not change either over the course of development or by assuming the dress or behavior of boys. Nevertheless she was often preoccupied with fantasies of turning into a boy "for real, not just for pretend."

Family background and context for the onset of symptoms

Psychiatric disorders were present in both maternal and paternal family histories. Kathy's mother described herself as struggling with depression "off and on" since college. For several years prior to Kathy's birth she was abusing both drugs and alcohol and only stopped because she wanted to conceive a second child. Kathy's father indicated that he also suffered from depression and that he typically coped with dysphoric feelings by withdrawing from the family and immersing himself in work.

Kathy's mother recalled that as a child she felt crushed by conventional male-female stereotypes. She was the third of four children and always felt that her three brothers were favored by both parents because they were boys. Although she was athletic and enjoyed outdoor activities and regarded herself as a tomboy, she felt that her mother, whom she experienced as cold and remote, was constantly socializing her "to be pretty, nice and a good girl." She was often required to help out at home; in contrast her brothers were encouraged to participate in outside activities. Kathy's mother felt that in response she simply "caved in" to these social pressures and channeled her energy into academic performance. She recalls going away to college as a completely liberating experience and in retrospect thinks that she must have decided that she was going to rebel against every convention which she felt had done her in. During her senior year of college she describes herself as falling in love for the first time. When the man broke off the relationship after about 6 months she recalls feeling devastated and betrayed and becoming quite depressed.

In contrast, Kathy's father described his upbringing as "zany" and unconventional. He was the second of two children and remembers his mother as being "completely uninterested in being a parent" and his father as overly involved in his work. His mother was a writer who was quite involved in pursuing her career, and Kathy's father described himself and his sister as banding together to take care of one another. Although he said that their home was often filled with interesting characters, he felt that he had had to raise himself. During the interview process, he described with considerable contempt how his mother was unable to make even a simple meal without causing some sort of minor disaster in the kitchen. It was difficult for him to acknowledge the impact of his parent's emotional inaccessibility.

Both parents were extremely excited and pleased about the birth of their first child, Kathy's brother Jonathan, but they soon felt overwhelmed and frightened. Jonathan proved to be a challenge to raise because from early age he was, according to his parents' report, excessively active, willful, and demanding. As a toddler, he was "constant destruction." At age 4, at the suggestion of his preschool teacher, Kathy's parents consulted with a psychiatrist, who diagnosed Jonathan as having ADHD and began him on Ritalin. Despite medication being somewhat effective, Jonathan continued to be excessively aggressive towards his parents, his peers and his sister.

In the context of the difficulties involved in raising Jonathan, Kathy's parents began to feel increasingly irritated with each other and blamed each other for Jonathan's difficulties. They often fought bitterly and in time became more and more estranged from one another. In response, Kathy's mother became depressed and began abusing substances and Kathy's father withdrew into his work. The decision to have a second child was, in their minds, made as an attempt to strengthen their relationship and to have a child that did not have so many difficulties.

Kathy's mother recalled being quite excited when a routine sonogram indicated that Kathy was a girl and she remembers thinking that unlike herself, Kathy would be permitted to be whomever she was and do whatever she wanted without being pressured to conform to female stereotypic behavior. She looked forward to having a more loving relationship with her daughter than she had had with her own mother. However, Kathy's parents experienced her, as they had experienced Jonathan, as a difficult child to parent. Although both parents described feeling frustrated by Kathy's difficult temperament, it was Kathy's mother who interpreted Kathy's colic and her difficulty nursing as a reflection on her own competence as a parent. She recalled thinking at the time that she now was a failure to two children. As Kathy grew older, the tension in the mother-child relationship persisted. Kathy's mother found her clingyness to be extremely aggravating and her oppositionalism to be enraging.

In contrast to the strained mother-child relationship during the toddler years, Kathy's father found himself better able to soothe Kathy when she was distressed, better able to avoid engaging her in power struggles, and better able to find a range of play activities that they both enjoyed doing together. He identified with what he regarded as her spirit and spunk. Rather than working to help strengthen the mother-child relationship he often sided with Kathy during her struggles with her mother, calmly maintaining that the mother was "over-reacting." In the evaluation he remarked with considerable contempt that he should be permitted to take over the handling of these conflictual situations with Kathy. He felt that Kathy should simply be permitted to do or to have what she had been asking for. Kathy's father not only sided with her and failed to set limits but also, at other times, directly encouraged what he regarded as her antics. In this context between the ages of 2 and $2^1/_2$, Kathy began openly preferring her father to her mother.

Kathy's preference for her father during this time fueled already existing marital problems and partially in response to his desire to avoid the increased fighting at home, Kathy's father accepted a more demanding position within his company that required his working longer hours.

Jonathan had a particularly negative reaction to Kathy. On the day she was brought home from the hospital, he threw a ball at her and hit her in the face. Kathy's parents said that they tried to be careful never to leave Jonathan alone with Kathy when she was an infant because they were afraid that Jonathan would kill her. However, they felt that once Kathy began walking they were no longer able to watch the children so carefully. With considerable distress they described how they felt unable to protect Kathy from Jonathan's aggression and how she had often ended up scratched or bruised from his assaults on her. In addition to physically abusing Kathy, Jonathan was quite verbally abusive to her as he often taunted her for being a "weakling" and a "baby." Kathy's parents recall responding to Kathy's tears and complaints by encouraging her to fight back.

Kathy's wish to be a boy and her distress about being a girl thus emerged in the following context. Kathy was born with a reactive temperament. Her colic and her difficulty breast feeding undermined her mother's confidence as a parent and generated tension in the early mother-child attachment relationship. This tension was exacerbated by the more chronic temperamental mismatch between Kathy's reactive, difficult temperament and her mother's desire to have an idealized type of relationship with her daughter to make up for what she did not experience with her own mother. The chronic physical abuse at the hands of her brother left Kathy feeling unsafe and unprotected; identifying with males allayed her anxiety about her vulnerability. Her mother's failure to protect her from her brother's aggression, together with her father's derisive comments about her mother's competence at parenting contributed to Kathy's distancing herself from her mother and developing a devalued view of females. The father made no efforts to help Kathy and her mother strengthen their relationship and in fact seemed to enjoy the fact that he was the preferred parent. The decreased availability of Kathy's father as he assumed greater work responsibility was concurrent with the emergence of Kathy's cross-gender behaviors and fantasies; acting like a male in the absence of her father's emotional accessibility may have served to keep alive the father-daughter relationship in Kathy's mind while her father worked longer and longer hours.

Both parents initially reinforced Kathy's wish to be a boy, by purchasing boys' clothing and bathing trunks for her and cutting her hair in a fashion that increased the likelihood that others would mistake her as a boy. Both parents regarded her stereotypical masculine preferences and behaviors as expressions of her individuality and of her bucking the conventions which her mother and father so disdained. They initially did not attend to the multiple manifestations of her distress and self-hatred.

Diagnosis

Transient disturbances in gender

Kathy's rigid and persistent stereotypic cross-gender behavior was not transient. It had lasted for more than six months.

Tomboyism

GID in girls must be differentiated from tomboyism. Girls who have a high energy level, who enjoy athletics, who prefer wearing pants and who shun what they regard as "girlie" or stereotypically feminine behavior, but who do not hate being a girl, and are not preoccupied with the wish to be a boy are referred to as "tomboys." In general, tomboys are not significantly distressed about being females, and they will respond to parental demands for stereotypical feminine behaviors, such as wearing a dress to a formal party when their parents feel the occasion calls for it. Tomboyism is not a pathological phenomenon and indeed may be associated with a greater degree of behavioral flexibility and health.

In Kathy's case, the rigid, persistent and driven quality of the stereotypical cross-gender behavior which emerged in the context of intense self-dislike distinguished her from girls who are considered tomboys. Unlike tomboys however, many of the girls who develop GID, though they are typically described as having high activity levels, actually have shy, inhibited temperaments.

Childhood transvestism

Childhood transvestism has only very rarely been reported in girls, and, as in boys, this condition involves girls who dress in male underwear for purposes of self-soothing or self-simulation. There was no evidence of any transvestitic interests in Kathy's behavior.

Intersex conditions

Kathy did not have any genital ambiguity and did not have an intersex condition.

Emotional developmental functioning

Kathy's capacity for symbolic functioning was notably underdeveloped for her age. Although Kathy had a capacity for symbolic functioning that manifested itself in the relatively neutral situation of a cognitive testing session, she was not able to bring this capacity to bear on the more emotionally fraught process of elaborating feelings and experiences via play. Her ability to represent conflicts symbolically in play was notably constricted, with concrete and repetitive enactment taking precedence over more flexible, joyful and imaginative symbolic representations. She was unable to develop narrative play themes or participate in reciprocal dramatic play with peers.

Diagnostic Summary

Axis I: Primary Diagnosis
Childhood Gender Identity Disorder.

Axis II: Relationship Disorder Classification
Kathy's relationship with both parents was over- and under-involved.

Axis III: Medical and Developmental Disorders and Conditions
None.

Axis IV: Psychosocial Stressors
Moderate effects.

Axis V: Functional Emotional Developmental Level
Has attained age-appropriate levels of mutual attention, mutual engagement, interactive intentionality and reciprocity, representational/affective communication, and representational elaboration. Has not attained age-appropriate levels of representational differentiation.

PIR-GAS:30 (Disordered)

Discussion of GID in boys and girls

Predisposing factors

There are a number of factors that are regularly associated with GID in children that are also regularly associated with a variety of other childhood anxiety disorders. These involve a sensitive, highly reactive temperament, particularly in the boy, and severe stress and psychopathology in the family. The specific risk factor for GID is parental reinforcement, either overt or covert, of the child's wish to be the other gender, often coupled with a restriction in the child's access to same sexed peers.

1. *Temperament*—Boys with GID are most often sensitive, shy, and behaviorally inhibited children who are avoidant of rough-and-tumble play. Once they are over their initial shy reaction boys with GID often make very intense emotional connections to people. The majority of boys with GID have heightened sensory sensitivities especially to colors and odors.

   Colin was shy in new situations but once he felt comfortable he made very intense connections to people. He was very sensitive to color and sound. He loved music and had artistic interests. As an infant he had been particularly sensitive to sound and would cry whenever the door-bell rang. He like to draw and was unusually competent at it. He was fearful of getting physically hurt and very avoidant of rough-and-tumble play.

   Girls with GID typically show greater temperamental variability than boys, but a significant number of them also have sensitive, highly reactive temperaments. In contrast to many of the boys, however, the girls often have high activity levels as well. Kathy was typical of many girls in her combination of heightened sensitivity and high activity level.

2. *Concurrent psychopathology*—Both boys and girls with GID have overall levels of psychopathology comparable to other clinic-referred children. Concurrent separation anxiety, symptoms of depression, and difficulties in managing aggression are typical in children with GID. Both Colin and Kathy were separation anxious. Colin worried about his own and his parents' safety whenever they were separated and had a tendency to be physically clingy at times. Kathy alternated between being clingy and needy and acting out counter-phobic fantasies of being all-powerful. Some parents refer to children with GID as behaving as if they were human Velcro. Both Colin and Kathy had significant problems with self-esteem. Neither child liked who he or she was and both wanted to be someone else. Both children also had difficulty regulating other negative affects. Colin was very prone to temper tantrums when he did not get his way and once during the evaluation when he became angry at his father, he took a train and hit his father in the face with it. Kathy, too, was prone to tantrums, and her over-controlling and over-perfectionistic stances were in the service of preventing her from experiencing negative affects.

3. *Parental psychopathology*—Significant parental psychopathology occurs in most families that have a child with GID. In mothers, depression and anxiety are typically manifest; in fathers, difficulties in regulating affect and problems with substance abuse are predominant.

   Colin's mother had been depressed for a year. She was alternately emotionally withdrawn and rageful. She had screaming outbursts at Colin when she felt that he was making unreasonable demands on her. His father handled his disappointment and anger by withdrawal. He had rare but intense explosive reactions. Colin found the rageful reactions of both of his parents very frightening.

   Kathy's parents also had significant problems with depression, with the mother medicating herself with drugs and alcohol prior to Kathy's birth, and the father coping by immersing himself in his work. Depression in the mother during the child's infancy is extremely common in the history of girls with GID and appears to be an important, though non-specific risk factor.

In many instances, parental difficulties stem from unresolved mourning and/or unresolved trauma dating back to their own childhood that have become coded—consciously or unconsciously—in gender constructions. That is to say, the trauma will have been experienced as contingently related to gender, for example as in Colin's mother's belief that her relative neglect by her mother and her emotional abandonment by her father were because of her gender. These issues pertaining to the parents' own traumas and unresolved grief often have lain dormant until reactivated in the process of parenting their child.

4. *Severe family stress*—Events that parents experience as traumatic occurring during the child's first 3 years when gender is first developing have been documented in almost 75 percent of the families with boys with GID. Common stressors are the death of a child or other loved one, a life-threatening illness or accident occurring to a significant family member, a move to a new city or home that the parents experience as disorganizing, the birth of a new sibling, particularly one that is ill and causing severe anxiety in the parents. In addition, chronic severe marital conflict occurs in the majority of families. These stressors often lead directly to parents becoming anxious, depressed and emotionally unavailable to the child. This in turn leads to derailment of a sense of secure attachment often leading to separation anxiety in the child.

In families of girls with GID, the prevalence of significant trauma to the mother has not been documented to the same extent. Clinically, one often sees trauma in these families (paternal or fraternal physical abuse directly against the child and/or medical problems or severe emotional stress in the mother), whose net impact on the child is to convince her that it is not safe to be a girl. In several cases, a mother experienced a pregnancy as life-threatening and communicated to her daughter that it was not safe to be a girl. Also in many cases where a mother had been sexually abused in her own childhood, she communicated to her own daughter that it was not safe to be a girl.

5. *Strong parental encouragement of stereotypical cross-gender behaviors*—This specific factor, which appears to be the sine qua non for a GID to develop, can be very direct, taking such forms as cross-dressing a child, or very indirect such as occurs when a mother or father becomes more affectively attuned or vitalized when their son or daughter is pretending to be the opposite gender. In families of girls, one often sees that the mother colludes with the father's denigration of women, either by masochistically succumbing to it or else through her own denigration of the female gender.

6. *Isolation from peers*—Children with GID, for a variety of reasons including temperament, maternal and paternal attitudes, and lack of opportunity, often have not developed relationships with same sex peers. It is particularly common for parents of boys with GID to not play an active role in helping their child to develop social skills with same-sex peers.

Intervention strategies

Treatment should always be undertaken within the context of a contract to work with the family as a unit following a thorough assessment. We stress to the child that the whole family has been in difficulty and that we will be working not just with the child but with his or her parents as well. Only such an arrangement, in our view, provides the child with sufficient security that his or her parents are being taken care of to allow him or her to experiment with alternative modes of coping with anxiety. Moreover, without significant parental involvement in the treatment, familial factors that are contributing to perpetuating the GID and its associated psychopathology will continue to undermine the progress the child is making.

Successful treatment of gender identity disorder thus requires intensive clinical intervention with both the child and the parents, and most typically entails seeing the child twice a week and the parents once a week. It is important that the same therapist work with both the child and the parents in order to maintain the necessary high level of integration between the two facets of the treatment. The earlier treatment is begun the easier it is to help the child to develop a wide range of strategies for regulating affect and managing conflict rather than relying predominantly on rigid, stereotypic cross-gender enactments.

The length of treatment can vary between one and three years, or sometimes longer depending on the complexity of the family's emotional difficulties and the presence and severity of co-morbid psychopathology in the child. Since it is common for parents of children with GID to have serious marital difficulties as well as notable psychopathology and unresolved traumatic experiences in their own histories, it is essential that a therapist taking on this work be well-trained in both individual child therapy and family therapy.

Goals of treatment with the child

Treatment of children with GID needs to focus not on the cross-gender behavior but rather on the underlying emotional problems that the child and his family are experiencing and not directly on the cross-gender behavior. The following are the goals of therapy:

1. To restore (or sometimes to create for the first time) a secure attachment relationship between the child and each parent.

2. To enable the child to develop an authentic sense of self and to experience himself or herself as having a stable identity which can also evolve over time. An authentic sense of self can provide the child with an important and flexible means of integrating his or her experience. Fostering the development of a child's sense of self in treatment entails helping the child to develop a sense of stability and continuity of the self over time, and then, as treatment proceeds, helping the child to integrate feelings, especially conflictual feelings, with her or his self-experience. An authentic sense of self can only be achieved when the child can hold self and other in mind, while simultaneously experiencing himself or herself as being reliably known by the other.

3. To help the child develop strategies for regulating affect particularly around separation anxiety, depressive affect, and anxiety about the management of aggression. Beyond helping the child develop particular skills, this entails helping the child to develop symbolic and creative capacities so that a range of options can be employed not only for managing anxiety but also for self expression.

4. To help the child to value and enjoy her or his temperament in a way that helps to restore self-esteem. Where treatment is successful, these children come to appreciate themselves in their atypical preferences , while becoming less preoccupied with gender.. In this latter respect, they begin to catch up to their peers, who after initially adopting a high degree of gender stereotypy typically become less stereotyped and less concerned with gender as they mature.

5. To help the child to resolve the difficulties that have been interfering with his or her capacity to make age-appropriate friendships.

Goals of treatment with the parents

Help the parents to become affectively attuned to the child's internal experience, temperament, and developmental needs.

Help the parents to become able to help the child develop effective coping strategies for managing affect.

Help the parents to work through the unresolved trauma or "ghosts in the nursery" that are impinging upon and compromising their ability to function effectively as parents. In Colin's case we discovered that for three generations there had been losses of very young girls in the family. Issues both of inter-generational transfer of unresolved traumatic loss and inter-generational transfer of a need for reparation need to be sensitively addressed in the treatment of the family.

Particular considerations in the treatment of GID

In addition to using individual play therapy sessions to work toward the above-outlined treatment goals, the therapist must carefully address difficult and long-standing family dynamics which frequently coincide with this diagnosis in a child. Issues of parental depression, substance abuse, and anxiety, as well as overt or subtle emotional and physical abuse of the child need to be addressed directly, promptly and sensitively in the treatment of parents. A critical piece of the work, with the parents as well as the child, needs to be helping the family members to develop strategies for regulating affect, and this may at times include psychopharmacological consultation. In tandem with this work, parents also generally need to be helped to become better attuned to the child's internal experience and to learn to hold this experience in mind. A necessary adjunct to the more dynamically based aspects of the treatment is working to help parents to provide more sensitive and active support for their child's social development. As we have stated, most children with gender identity disorder have limited social skills in interacting with other children, and this is often most dramatically manifest in their difficulty playing with same-sex peers. Not only does this difficulty impair further social development, but it often leads the child to become quite isolated, and frequently to be painfully ostracized at school. It is therefore critical that the child be helped to develop social skills that enable him or her to feel confident and to enjoy playing with peers of both sexes. This generally entails encouraging the parents to arrange frequent play dates with same-sex peers.

It is important to recognize that, although in some cases much of the child's rigid and stereotypical cross-gender symptomatology may greatly diminish relatively early in the treatment—and the child's behavior may thus no longer warrant a diagnosis of Gender Identity Disorder—it may take considerably more time to help the child and the family to resolve associated difficulties with separation anxiety, affect regulation, and regulation of self-esteem.

Prognosis

The prognosis for achieving the above outlined treatment goals is positive especially when parents seek treatment at an early age and when families are able to participate fully in the treatment process described above.

200. Disorders of Affect

206. Reactive Attachment Deprivation/Maltreatment Disorder of Infancy and Early Childhood

Alicia F. Lieberman, Ph.D.

This disorder is observed in the context of persistent parental abuse or neglect, frequent changes in primary caregiver, or other environmental circumstances which seriously interfere with the child's ability to form a specific and enduring emotional connection with a primary parent figure. The case of Reggie presents a variety of such environmental etiologic factors, compounded by biological risk factors that complicated the diagnostic picture upon referral.

Reason for referral

Reggie was 22 months old when he was referred for a mental health evaluation by Child Protective Services when his pediatrician discovered that he had consistently failed to gain weight for the previous six months. Reggie was below the 5th percentile in weight and in head circumference, although he was at the 20th percentile for height. His foster mother described him as an apathetic child who did not like to eat and showed little interest in toys or people. The pediatrician alerted Reggie's social worker at Child Protective Services about this picture, informing her of the need for a diagnostic evaluation to determine whether Reggie was autistic, mentally retarded, or suffering from the effects of environmental deprivation.

Assessment process

The assessment period comprised seven weekly sessions, each lasting approximately one hour. The first meeting involved an individual session with Reggie's foster mother to inform her of the assessment plan, gain her cooperation, and solicit her perceptions of Reggie's functioning. The next meeting involved an office-based free play evaluation of Reggie's behavior with his foster mother and with the assessor. The third session consisted of administering the Bayley Scales of Mental Development to assess Reggie's level of cognitive functioning. This testing was followed by a free play period as well. The fourth session involved a home visit to observe Reggie's behavior in his family context. The last three sessions involved feedback and treatment planning with the foster mother and with the social worker. In addition to these face-to-face meetings, the assessor discussed Reggie's history with the social worker over the telephone and reviewed his medical and Child Protective Services charts as an integral part of the assessment. In addition, Reggie was referred for hearing tests and a neurological evaluation, which yielded no abnormal findings.

Assessment findings

Developmental history

Reggie's medical charts revealed that he had a history of a positive toxicology screen for crack cocaine at birth, was small for gestational age, and had intracranial bleeding. He was also cyanotic, hypotonic, and jittery. He was treated for methadone withdrawal and discharged from the hospital to his parents at 23 days of age. One week later, he was brought to the emergency room with diarrhea and pneumonia, and was rehospitalized for one week. When his parents failed to visit or to respond to telephone calls, Reggie was discharged to Child Protective Services. He stayed in a temporary shelter home for one month, and was transferred to a long-term foster home at 2 months of age when efforts to locate his parents and reunify Reggie with them ended in failure.

The plans to provide Reggie with a stable foster family were disrupted 6 months later when his foster mother acquired a medical condition that forced her to relinquish the two children in her care. By the social worker's report, Reggie had formed a solid attachment to this foster mother and responded to her loss at eight months of age with prolonged crying, disruption of sleep-wake cycles, loss of appetite, and overall behavioral disorganization. When not crying, he seemed listless, confused, and withdrawn. His new foster mother, Ms. Brown, complained that he was difficult to soothe, stiff, jittery, and that his need signals were difficult to interpret because her interventions did not seem effective in calming him down. The social worker reported that Reggie's previous foster mother had not voiced similar complaints in spite of his having been a more fragile and ill infant when he came to her care at one month of age.

At the time of the assessment, Reggie had been living in Ms. Brown's home for 13 months. In the individual interview at the beginning of the assessment, she described Reggie as a withdrawn and solitary child who did not participate in the life of the family and kept mainly to himself. She reiterated her previous statements to the social worker that Reggie had little interest in food, toys, or people. She reported that he only brightened when Ms. Brown's 2-year-old granddaughter was visiting. The assessor observed that Ms. Brown's own affect brightened only when speaking about this child. Except for this brief interval, she appeared to be somber, depressed and withdrawn—the very qualities she attributed to Reggie. This observation raised the question of whether Ms. Brown had been unable because of her own psychological state to help Reggie recover from his grief reaction upon losing his first foster mother, setting up mutually reinforcing transactions of negatively tinged emotional experiences that interfered with Reggie's ability to rely on Ms. Brown as a source of comfort and protection and prevented him from forming a new attachment with her.

Observational findings

Throughout the assessment period, Reggie's demeanor was that of a sad, withdrawn, and listless child. In the office-based free play sessions with his foster mother, Reggie was consistently apathetic and unresponsive. When she showed him toys, he moved away from her rather than towards her, looking at her from a distance with a vacant expression and making no effort to reach out for the toys or to engage in play with her. Ms. Brown, in turn, did not change her strategies in an effort to entice Reggie to come closer to her. She sat on a chair at some distance from Reggie and simply resorted to showing him one toy after another, saying "Look, Reggie" and pretending to play with the toy. When this did not work, she neither approached Reggie nor waited for him to show spontaneous interest in a toy. Her affect in interacting with him seemed like that of a teacher resigned to having an unsatisfying and hopeless student in her charge. Reggie's affect, in turn, was simultaneously vigilant and subdued. Neither of them smiled or showed any sign of mutual pleasure or affection in the course of a 30-minute free play session which was recorded behind a one-way mirror.

In order to assess how characteristic this affective picture was of Reggie, Ms. Brown was asked to go out of the room for about 15 minutes, leaving Reggie alone with the assessor. Ms. Brown did not say good-bye to Reggie when she left nor did she explain that she would come back. Reggie, for his part, did not respond to Ms. Brown's departure in any visible manner. He looked briefly in the direction of the door as it closed behind her but did not search for her or protest her departure.

In Ms. Brown's absence, the assessor sat on the floor rather close to Reggie and started a game where she pretended to drink with great pleasure from a cup, talking to Reggie about how delicious her juice was. After looking at her briefly with a rather neutral expression, Reggie approached her and stood very close to her, looking on with increased interest. The assessor pretended to stir the juice in the cup with a spoon and then offered the cup to Reggie, who leaned over and pretended to drink from it. When the assessor encouraged Reggie to hold the cup and offered him the spoon as well, Reggie took the cup, stirred it with a spoon, drank from it, and smiled. The assessor asked if she could have some juice, and Reggie readily complied by putting the cup to the assessor's lips. After that she pretended to drink and thanked Reggie, the child proceeded to "feed" the assessor by dipping the spoon into the cup and putting it to the assessor's lips. This game revealed that Reggie was quite capable of understanding simple commands and of emerging reciprocal symbolic play. His affect during this game, although always rather subdued, became increasingly more pleasurable. Moreover, his willingness to engage in an eating-feeding game with the assessor revealed that he was more interested in food than the foster mother had reported.

The observations made during the home visit replicated the initial impressions gathered during the playroom sessions. The assessor encouraged Ms. Brown to go about her daily routine as she would if the assessor were not there. Ms. Brown went about tidying up the house while talking with the assessor in a casual manner. She made no efforts to structure Reggie's experience. The child stood by looking at the assessor with a sober expression, and then sat on the floor fingering a couple of toy trucks in a desultory fashion, without actually looking at them. He showed none of the vitality and interest in motor exploration that are characteristic of well developing toddlers. He moved tentatively, as if afraid of losing his balance, and seemed to be a stranger in his own home. As had been the case in the office playroom, he kept considerable physical distance from Ms. Brown. She spoke to him briefly and at long intervals, always to tell him to play with something in a matter of fact, rather discouraged tone of voice. Reggie looked at her when she spoke to him and sometimes started to comply, but he did not follow through with any kind of rich or elaborated play theme.

Reggie's affect changed when his foster father arrived. A large and jovial man, he immediately took Reggie in his arms and said: "Hi, big boy, what did you do today?"

Reggie smiled broadly and spoke for the first time, saying quietly: "Played." Mr. Brown sat next to Reggie on the floor and engaged him in playing with the trucks, banging them against each other and laughing when Reggie laughed. Mr. Brown then turned to the assessor and said: "He's a good boy, a little shy." After a few minutes of play, Mr. Brown excused himself and said he was going to take a shower after a long day's work. Reggie did not follow him, but he looked sadly after Mr. Brown as he left the room and his affect again became quite constricted during the rest of the home visit.

These observations indicated that Reggie had not formed an attachment with Ms. Brown, and that he relied primarily on Mr. Brown as a source of emotional nourishment. Since he spent most of the day with Ms. Brown, this situation left him in a state of considerable emotional deprivation. The lively exchanges with Mr. Brown were merely islands of pleasurable reciprocity in the course of a long and empty day in Ms. Brown's care. At the same time, it was likely that these positive experiences with his foster father allowed Reggie to preserve the ability to engage in age-appropriate social interactions when given the opportunity to do so, as had been the case during the free-play situation with the assessor.

Testing results

During the administration of the Bayley Scales of Mental Development, Reggie was initially quite tentative, touching the items in a gingerly fashion after a long period of visual inspection. However, he became increasingly more interested in the items in response to the assessor's warm encouragement and enthusiastic praise. In contrast to the regular pattern of performance, where children initially succeed in solving items designed for younger ages but gradually begin to fail items that are designed for older children, Reggie actually improved in his performance as the testing proceeded. This suggested that Reggie thrived on the assessor's encouragement as he became more familiar and comfortable with her. Reggie never turned to Ms. Brown to show her a toy or to share his pleasure over a successful performance with her, a stance that was consistent with his behavior during the free-play sessions and the home visit. Ms. Brown for her part took no initiative in praising Reggie or commenting on the materials he was working with. She looked on with an impassive facial expression and responded with monosyllables to the assessor's efforts to engage her in Reggie's experience. In spite of Reggie's increasing interest in the testing, his performance was markedly below his age level. His average developmental age was 15 months at a chronological age of 22 months. This placed his developmental quotient at MDI=55. His earliest failure was at the 11-month level (putting 3 or more cubes in a cup). He also failed to place even a single peg in the pegboard (13 months), to build a tower of two blocks (14 months), and to close the round box (14 months). His lack of success in these items indicated substantial delay in the area of fine motor coordination.

In contrast, language was an area of relative strength. Reggie did not put two words together, but he engaged in long bouts of expressive jabbering and said several single words, including "baby," "cup," "drink," "nose," and "thank you." He imitated the assessor with pleasure when she said "zip" during the paper and crayon tasks. His two highest performances involved language: using words to make wants known and following directions with the doll, both 18-month items. However, he repeatedly failed to show his shoes in response to the examiner's request, a 15-month item, suggesting some unevenness in his language development.

Reggie's low developmental index made it easy to feel pessimistic about his future cognitive development. In the context of the biological insults he had suffered through intrauterine drug exposure, the possibility of mental retardation could not be ruled out, although the neurological exam had found no hard signs of neurological damage. At the same time, there were reasons for a more optimistic prognosis. Reggie was clearly able to concentrate on the performance of the tasks, and his attention seldom wavered. He also showed low-keyed but unmistakable delight in the materials presented to him, and began to eagerly engage the assessor as the testing proceeded and he became more comfortable with the situation. These strengths suggested that Reggie was capable of improving his cognitive performance under the appropriate social and emotional circumstances. In the context of Reggie's emotionally impoverished relationship with his foster mother, it was possible that his cognitive deficits were inextricably associated with the lack of appropriate social and cognitive stimulation and the absence of an attachment to a cherished mother figure.

Diagnostic Summary

Axis I: Primary Diagnosis
Reactive Attachment Deprivation/Maltreatment Disorder of Infancy and Early Childhood.

Axis II: Relationship Disorder Classification
Underinvolved relationship with the foster mother.

Axis III: Medical and Developmental Disorders and Conditions
Failure to thrive.
Rule out mild mental retardation.

Axis IV: Psychosocial Stressors
Overall effects severe and enduring. Foster placement, repeated changes in caregiver, early loss of attachment figure, neglect in current home, early hospitalization, in-utero drug exposure.

Axis V: Functional Emotional Developmental Level
Has achieved age-appropriate levels of mutual attention, mutual engagement, and interactive intentionality and reciprocity, with constrictions; needs some structure to evidence capacity for representational/affectivecommunication.

PIR-GAS:10 (Grossly impaired)

Discussion with caregivers and treatment planning

Feedback to the social worker

The feedback to Reggie's social worker involved a frank discussion of the findings outlined above. The assessor also sought the social worker's input about the likelihood that Ms. Brown would be willing to engage in infant-parent psychotherapy and developmental guidance geared at enhancing the quality of the relationship between Reggie and herself. The rationale was that Mr. and Ms. Brown had made a long-term commitment to provide a home for Reggie, and they were the primary caregivers in his life. Working to improve the quality of the relationship was considered to be a less potentially damaging alternative than subjecting Reggie to yet another change in caregivers, particularly in the context of his close connection with Mr. Brown and with the couple's little granddaughter.

With the social worker's agreement, the feedback to Ms. Brown was planned to involve a discussion of Reggie's special needs for focused social and emotional stimulation. The underlying hope and expectation were that such a discussion would mobilize Ms. Brown's unexpressed affection for Reggie, allowing for a freer exchange of views about his needs and the best way of addressing them.

Feedback to the foster mother

The feedback to Ms. Brown involved two sessions. Mr. Brown was invited to attend, but he declined on the grounds that he could not leave work and that his wife's views represented his own as well. In both sessions, the assessor was careful to avoid placing any blame on Ms. Brown for Reggie's predicament. She was aware of the foster mother's own depression and her defensiveness about the extended evaluation that Reggie was undergoing, and sought to gain her cooperation by highlighting the difficult circumstances surrounding Reggie's birth and first year of life, and by empathizing with Ms. Brown's complaints about his lethargy and lack of appetite. As the discussion proceeded, however, it became increasingly clear that Ms. Brown held firmly to the belief that "Reggie was born that way and will never change." She found him an unrewarding child and was convinced that the drug exposure in utero had caused irreparable damage to his intelligence and his capacity to enjoy life. When the assessor tried to gently present a more hopeful view, Ms. Brown sighed and said in a hopeless tone of voice: "You might be right, but I don't have the energy to try to turn him around." She then revealed, with tears in her eyes, that a few months before Reggie's arrival in her home she had been on the verge of adopting a 2-year-old foster child she had raised from birth. However, the Juvenile Court had decided to return this child to the biological parents, and Ms. Brown had no recourse but to give the child up. She was still depressed over that loss, she said, and had made the decision to never again become attached to a foster child in order to spare herself the pain of another loss.

The assessor tried to persuade Ms. Brown that talking about this loss could help her manage it at less cost to herself and her family, but Ms. Brown stated firmly that her Church and her family were all she needed to help her with her grief. She denied that her refusal to become attached to Reggie had any negative repercussions for the child, but acknowledged that if indeed he needed special care, it would be better for him to move to another home. The assessor surmised that Reggie's sad affect mirrored and exacerbated Ms. Brown's own sense of loss, making it harder for her to become close to him. Foster mother and child were each locked in their respective depressions, perpetuating each other's hopelessness and unable to reach out to the other. It became clear that an adoptive home represented Reggie's best hope for recovery. Indirectly, Reggie's departure might also relieve Ms. Brown from the emotional pressure of caring for a child whose depressed affect mirrored and reinforced her own.

The assessor explained to Ms. Brown that the best alternative for Reggie would be to find him an adoptive home that could keep him forever. Ms. Brown agreed readily, saying that she did not feel she could offer such a home for Reggie and that it weighed on her to know that sooner or later she would run out of energy to care for him. She said she preferred to have older foster children who knew who their parents were and hoped to go back to them. She agreed to cooperate with efforts to find a home where Reggie could really feel that he belonged.

Intervention

The assessor informed the social worker of the outcome of her conversation with Ms. Brown, and recommended that Reggie be placed in an adoptive home where the parents were made aware of Reggie's cognitive and emotional problems and had the motivation and the personal resources to help him.

Until such a home could be located, it was important to expose Reggie to the age-appropriate social and cognitive stimulation he was so clearly missing in his interactions with Ms. Brown. The social worker tried to find an opening in a nursery school where the quality of care could meet Reggie's needs. Unfortunately, the waiting lists for such placements are very long indeed, and Reggie's needs were not more urgent than those of the many children who preceded him in the waiting lists. As an interim measure, an intern was assigned to visit Reggie in the home twice a week to play with him, talk to him, and, in the process, also establish a friendly relationship with Ms. Brown that might lighten her mood and offer her some adult companionship. The underlying expectation was that Ms. Brown's exposure to the intern's way of interacting with Reggie and his positive response might encourage her to become more involved with him.

The social worker's earnest efforts to locate an adoptive home were met with success in record time. Six weeks after beginning the search, she found a husband and wife with special interest in helping drug-exposed infants and told them about Reggie's background. They then met with the assessor, who showed them a videotape of Reggie interacting with her during the office-based free play session in which they helped each other to drink from the toy cup. These potentially adoptive parents were charmed by the videotape of Reggie and expressed an interest in learning more about him. The assessor then discussed with them the results of the developmental testing, including the strengths and limitations of Reggie's performance and discussing the type of assistance he would need with fine and gross motor coordination and language.

The assessor and Reggie's social worker worked closely together in developing and implementing a program for introducing Reggie to his potential new parents. It was agreed that the least stressful way of arranging the first meeting would be for Mr. and Ms. Logan to visit Reggie in his home and to establish a cordial connection with Mr. and Ms. Brown. The Browns were amenable to this plan and welcomed the Logans into their home. The social worker later reported that the mood was somewhat strained but characterized by good will and by an effort to put Reggie's interests above the adults' understandably mixed feelings. The Logans tried to restrain their impulse to become Reggie's instant saviors; the Browns tried to contain their sense that, their ambivalence about Reggie notwithstanding, the Logans were there to take "their" child away.

Reggie seemed to sense from the beginning that he was the reason for the visitors' arrival. The child was entranced by their vitality and enthusiasm as Mr. Logan brought small toys out of his pocket and Ms. Logan vied with him for showing them to Reggie. By the social worker's report, Reggie's head kept turning from Mr. Logan to Ms. Logan and back again, as if unable to decide who to pay attention to. They stayed for one hour, and Reggie cried when they left.

Mr. and Ms. Logan expressed a wish to be considered as adoptive parents for Reggie after this first visit. This led to a schedule of increasingly more frequent and longer visits, first in Reggie's foster home, later on outings to the playground, and, finally, to the Logan home, initially for day visits which later culminated on a couple of overnights.

After 5 weeks of ever-increasing visitation, it became clear that Reggie, the Logans, and the Browns were all ready for the final move to take place. Reggie's face lit up when Mr. Logan told him he would now live with them. To their credit, Mr. and Ms. Brown gave him a photo album which included pictures of Reggie, the Browns and the Logans all together in addition to pictures of Reggie's life while he lived with them. Reggie was allowed to take with him his favorite toys, his pillow and his blanket to help him in the transition to his new home. For the month after the move, the Logans made a point of going over the album with him and referring often to Mr. and Ms. Brown and to their granddaughter using the names that Reggie had for them. The Browns also called on the telephone a few times, but preferred not to visit.

The assessor made herself available to the Logans for any questions they might have during this transition time, but it was clear that they needed to claim their baby as their own and that they felt well equipped to take care of whatever problems might arise. They also declined to enroll Reggie in a nursery school, arguing that he was too young for group care, that Ms. Logan was able to care for him full time, and that Reggie needed adoring parents more than anything else. Their decisions seemed very appropriate and understandable given the circumstances and met with no objections from any of the professionals involved.

Follow-up assessments

Reggie was assessed using the Bayley Scales as well as free play observations 2 months after placement in his new home, when he was 27 months old. At this time, the pediatrician reported that he had grown one inch and gained one pound since the last pediatric check-up—the first growth spurt observed since he was 8 months.

Although still developmentally delayed, his performance in the Bayley Scales showed considerable improvement: he gained 12 points in his developmental index, which increased from MDI=55 at 22 months to MDI=67 at 27 months. Reggie continued to show an unusual capacity to engage with the assessor during the testing. He approached each task with interest, and he tended to persist at each task until he had mastered it or until he was certain that it was beyond his capacity. He experimented with the test materials and learned as he went along, clearly benefiting from the experience. He derived much pleasure from his successes, and turned with a smile to his adoptive parents when they clapped in response to a completed task. He showed a new interest in repeating a successful task again and again, turning repeatedly to his parents as they celebrated his achievement.

During the free play session, Reggie displayed a new capacity to put together two- and three- word sentences. Although his articulation was often unclear, he clearly enjoyed talking and repeated what he said again and again until his parents understood him. His affect continued to be low-keyed but now had a much greater predominance of pleasure and interest. There were only fleeting glimpses of the worried, withdrawn look that had been so characteristic of him during the initial assessment. He responded readily to his parents' initiatives, kept track of them, and stayed close to them. Ms. Logan reported that he was beginning to show separation protest, crying when she needed to go out and left him with a babysitter. This protest, however, was short-lived and he quickly accepted the babysitter's attention, an indication perhaps of his precocious resignation to having to "do without," as he had during such a major portion of his life. On the other hand, his reunion behavior clearly indicated that he was forming a preferential relationship with Ms. Logan. He approached her with a shy smile when she returned and stayed close to her until she picked him up or otherwise made contact with him. In comparison, he did not approach Mr. Logan after a separation, although he greeted him from a distance and showed him a toy if he happened to be playing at the time. This discriminated response suggested that Reggie was singling Ms. Logan out as his preferred attachment figure. This preference notwithstanding, Reggie readily accepted Mr. Logan as a substitute when his adoptive mother was not available to him.

Differential diagnosis

Reggie's rapid improvement in cognitive and socioemotional functioning after he was placed with loving and responsive parents confirmed the appropriateness of the choice of Reactive Attachment Disorder as the primary diagnosis. A diagnosis of Regulatory Disorder had been ruled out because, although clearly suffering from early regulatory difficulties in the form of stiffness, jitteriness, and behavioral disorganization, these problems were not the primary cause of Reggie's hypervigilance, withdrawn mood, and failure to form an attachment with his foster mother. In fact, the social worker reported that Reggie's first foster mother had not complained about these symptoms, which seemed to subside in the first few months of Reggie's life and only re-emerged in the context of a global grief bereavement reaction when Reggie was separated from this foster mother.

A possible diagnosis of Multisystem Developmental Disorder was ruled out when Reggie was observed to engage in age-appropriate social interaction and symbolic play with the assessor during the free play situation. Finally, a diagnosis of Mental Retardation was ruled out as a primary diagnosis following the rapid improvement in cognitive functioning following placement in the adoptive home. Although clearly still in the borderline range and needing appropriate intervention, Reggie's cognitive functioning was not the cause of his mental health difficulties.

Long-term follow-up

Reggie's adoptive parents were apprised of Reggie's marked improvement as a result of their devoted care. As is often the case with emotionally invested parents, they had noted this improvement themselves and were pleased but not surprised by it. They were also quite cognizant of Reggie's cognitive limitations, but declined neurophysiological testing to pinpoint with greater accuracy the sources of his difficulties. They believed that Reggie needed time to adjust to his new home and worried that extensive developmental testing would only serve to "label" Reggie in ways that might be damaging to him when he entered preschool. The parents readily accepted the suggestion of bringing Reggie back should they want a consultation about Reggie's functioning in the years to come.

When Reggie was 3 years 9 months, Mr. and Ms. Logan requested another cognitive assessment to plan for Reggie's preschool. They explained that although Reggie had become very attached to them and he was a sweet and affectionate little boy, his overall functioning seemed to be at about the 30-month age level. They found him rather limited in his curiosity and sense of purpose and direction, although he liked to follow their directives and was helpful with small tasks. He showed very little negativism, had only short bouts of protest in response to frustration, and was easily persuaded to accept substitute objects or activities when he could not do what he wanted. His play with peers was simple, consisting mainly of physical games and parallel play, with little elaboration of symbolic themes. He had a favorite friend, a little girl 6 months younger than himself who might have served as a substitute for Mr. and Ms. Brown's granddaughter and whose developmental status was closer to his than other children his age. He was friendly and sociable, although he continued to have the quiet, low-keyed style that had characterized him as a toddler.

The adoptive parents' report was confirmed by the results of the cognitive testing and free-play observation. In the Stanford-Binet Intelligence Scale, Reggie received an IQ=66, with a mental age of 2.11 years at a chronological age of 3.9 years. He was quite compliant and willing to work on the tasks, showing sparks of enthusiasm when he succeeded at solving a task, but he often seemed confused by what was requested of him. His best skills were at basic visual perceptual tasks, such as solving simple puzzles. His visual-motor skills for pencil and-paper work appeared limited to imitating the drawing of basic forms. He could not copy a printed circle, a skill that is average for 3-year-olds.

Reggie's language was quite simple for his age. His vocabulary was limited and he had difficulty putting his thoughts in fluid sentences. He often repeated what was said to him, as if trying to understand it. His articulation was below age level as well.

During the free-play session, Reggie played with quiet pleasure with trucks and building blocks, often asking for his parents to join him in play. In contrast with his first assessment, he clearly preferred to interact with his parents and was quite free and comfortable with them. He established physical contact with them in a casual and affectionate manner, which contrasted with the physical distance he kept from his previous foster mother. Although friendly with the examiner, he was noticeably more formal and self-contained in his interactions with her.

Mr. and Ms. Logan were able to maintain a growth-promoting balance between being available to help Reggie when he encountered difficulties in his negotiations with the environment and encouraging him to find ways of managing by himself. They fostered autonomy but were ready to recognize (with some pain) that Reggie could not be as autonomous as they would expect for his age. Sometimes, in their wish to encourage Reggie, they became a little overly enthusiastic in their praise and at other times they overestimated what he was capable of achieving, but they managed their sadness about Reggie's cognitive limitations with remarkable grace.

The parents reported no symptoms of emotional distress in Reggie, with one possible exception: he ate voraciously, and often had to be told when he had had enough. The pediatrician had found no organic basis for this behavior, which could well indicate a residual insecurity and need to compensate for his early deprivation. Although still small for his age, Reggie was now in the 20th percentile for height and weight.

Updated diagnostic summary (3 years, 9 months)

Axis I: **Primary Diagnosis**
No diagnosis.

Axis II: **Relationship Disorder Classification**
Rule out mild mental retardation.

Axis III: **Medical and Developmental Disorders and Conditions**
No diagnosis.

Axis IV: **Psychosocial Stressors**
Ongoing influence of psychosocial stressors noted in initial evaluation.

Axis V: **Functional Emotional Developmental Level**
Has not reached capacity for representational differentiation I or II; needs some structure to engage in representational elaboration.

PIR-GAS:90 (Well adapted)

Feedback to adoptive parents

The assessor confirmed the parents' impressions about Reggie's performance, and discussed the different areas of difficulty that became apparent in his cognitive testing performance. They were referred to a neurodevelopmental psychologist for more detailed evaluation of Reggie's strengths and vulnerabilities and more specific advice about appropriate intervention. The parents followed through with this evaluation and felt cautiously optimistic about the chances that their child would adjust reasonably well to a preschool environment with appropriate developmental supports.

Prognosis and discussion

Reggie's prognosis for long-term functioning are reasonably good. He showed remarkable resiliency and capacity for quick improvement in social, emotional, and cognitive functioning when he was given the chance to form a deep and lasting attachment to his adoptive parents. He liked people, was liked by them, and, in his own low-keyed style, was able to engage in satisfying relationships with adults and peers. He had no symptoms of emotional disturbance when last assessed. His cognitive functioning might well remain in the low range, but his pleasure in learning and his willingness to persist at tasks bode well for his ability to make use of specialized intervention geared at helping him to find appropriate strategies to cope with his limitations.

Reggie's case illustrates the importance of follow-up in cases of early and severe deprivation, particularly when environmental deficiencies are compounded by biological risk factors. Given the pronounced improvement in Reggie's emotional and cognitive picture following his move to the adoptive parents' home, it would be easy to anticipate a steady continuation of this pattern of improvement. The fact that following the initial improvement, Reggie's cognitive functioning did not come closer to age expectations after approximately two years in his new home indicates that, whatever the etiologic factors at work, the cognitive limitations are likely to have become long-lasting, unrelated to present emotional factors, and calling for specialized intervention.

At the same time, Reggie's emotional recovery is an essential ingredient in enabling him to profit from such intervention.

300. Adjustment Disorder

J. Martín Maldonado-Durán, M.D.*

The diagnosis of Adjustment Disorder should be considered for mild, transient situational disturbances that cannot be explained by or do not meet the criteria of the other proposed diagnoses. The onset of the difficulties must be tied to a clear environmental event or change. As a result of the child's developmental age, unique constitutional characteristics, and family circumstances, the infant or toddler experiences a temporary reaction, lasting days or weeks but no longer than four months. To make this diagnosis, the clinician should be able to identify both the clear environmental event and the transient nature of the affective or behavioral symptoms.

Reason for referral

Jalil was nine months old at the time of his evaluation. He was the only child born to his parents, Mr. and Ms. Marzuk, who lived in a small midwestern city. Jalil was healthy physically and was thought to be developing normally from the physical and behavioral-emotional points of view. Ms. Marzuk, a 20-year-old housewife, was originally from Jordan. Mr. Marzuk, also from Jordan, was 34 years old; he worked as a mechanical engineer for a state organization. They were both Moslem and Ms. Marzuk wore the traditional costume for women, including a headpiece, but did not cover her face. Both parents were in good health. They had no extended family in the city, although they had a somewhat close relationship with a neighboring family, an older Anglo Saxon couple without children at home. Mr. Marzuk had lived in the United States. for 10 years, but Ms. Marzuk had for only two years.

---

* The work described here was conducted while the author was sponsored by a grant from the Jessie Ball Dupont Foundation at the Child and Family Center, The Menninger Clinic. The author wishes to thank Ms. Anita Epps, M.S.W., of the Maternal Infant Care Project, Topeka, and Shawnee County Health Department, for her collaboration in working with this child and family.

Jalil was referred for consultation by a social worker at a maternal infant care project in the family's neighborhood; she was close to the parents and trusted by them. For about three weeks, they had been struggling with a sleep problem in Jalil. They were concerned about the advice they had obtained from their pediatrician on how to deal with the problem, and believed that they needed some other ideas about how to try to solve it.

Jalil had developed a remarkable inability to stay asleep and to remain in his crib. He had been sleeping well there before, but, about three weeks prior to the initial consultation, he began waking up in the night and crying intensely, apparently wanting to be picked up by his parents and taken to their bed. Whenever he woke up, he would cry and scream. His parents had tried various maneuvers to help him stay in the crib rather than bring him to their bed, as they had read that this was a better child-rearing practice.

Jalil's sleep problem had appeared shortly after the parents struggled with a marital difficulty about Mr. Marzuk's family of origin. His mother had announced that she was coming to visit them and stay in their home for a couple of weeks. Her forthcoming visit had exacerbated the couple's disagreements about how to deal with their respective families. It also coincided with a disagreement about how to deal with Jalil's sleeping problem, and how to treat him in general. The father wanted to follow the pediatrician's advice as much as possible, at least a little bit longer, while Ms. Marzuk wanted to follow her intuition and soothe Jalil at night, rather than let him cry. When the parents had consulted their pediatrician about Jalil's sleep problem and explained that he would cry intensely at night until he was picked up and taken to their bed, the doctor advised them to just "let him cry it out" and assured them that the problem would soon disappear. Mr. Marzuk was eager to try this strategy, but Ms. Marzuk was more hesitant about letting her son just cry.

The first night that they tried this approach, Jalil "cried and cried" for almost three hours until his parents could not tolerate it any more. Finally, they picked him up and took him to their bed, at which time he went to sleep almost immediately. When Mr. Marzuk. called the pediatrician to tell him that his suggestion had not worked well, the doctor insisted that they just needed to lock their door, "put a pillow over their heads, and go to sleep," no matter how long the baby cried. The second night they tried to do this, Mr. and Ms. Marzuk reported that they let Jalil cry until he was almost hoarse and had "turned blue" from such intense crying. They could not bring themselves to let him cry any longer, so they put him in their bed again. Once there, he calmed quickly and went to sleep.

Jalil's parents were also concerned because he slept very restlessly after he was in their bed. He would move around and kick them, not letting them get a good night's sleep. After such a night, Mr. Marzuk found it difficult to wake up the next morning and go to work.

At this point, the couple had visited a social worker at the maternal infant care project, where they sought help. This clinician, in turn, suggested an infant psychiatry consultation to evaluate the situation, hoping that further suggestions could be made to resolve the problem. One point that alarmed the social worker was that Ms. Marzuk said that she felt over-whelmed by her child's sleeping problems, his suffering, and his constant crying. She said that she was not enjoying her life now, and she reported feel-ing that she did not want to go on "living like this."

Assessment process

Jalil and his parents were seen for a total of only seven sessions, as the situa-tion that brought them in for consultation with the child psychiatrist improved quickly. The first four sessions mostly involved assessment. During the gathering of data, however, some interventions were quickly implemented, such as having the parents keep a "sleep diary" of Jalil's nights between one session and the next. The first four sessions took place over the course of four weeks, and the remaining ones were scheduled several weeks apart. Both parents came with Jalil to all the sessions, which required Mr. Marzuk to miss a few hours of work. On all occasions, the social worker whom they knew was present and participated. Developmental testing was not considered essential, as it was clear there were no questions about prob-lems in these areas, either from the parents or the consultant.

Each session lasted about fifty minutes. The consultation took place at a Maternal Infant Care Project, a local county health department program. This setting is one where obstetricians and nurses render services mostly to clientele of low socio-economic status or who are on some form of public assistance. The mental health consultations in this clinic are readily accept-ed by clients, in part because they do not have the social stigma of taking place in a psychiatric setting. Mr. and Ms. Marzuk were not on public assis-tance, but trusted the social worker's judgment because they had a relation-ship with her that went back a year and a half. The consultations were to be covered by their health insurance. The evaluation sessions focused on the assessment of the infant along the various developmental lines and observa-tion of the interaction between him and each of his parents. The situation of each parent was also taken into account, and, as it turned out, marital issues took prominence as the consultation unfolded.

Assessment findings

History of presenting problems

Mr. and Ms. Marzuk were quite eager to talk about their son's sleeping dif-ficulties. Both expressed feelings of guilt about having attempted to use the method of letting Jalil cry through the night, because they felt it was some-what cruel to let him cry when he seemed frightened and was calling for them. Mr. Marzuk tearfully said that his son "put a lot of energy into his cry" and seemed very intense in expressing his desperation and fear at night when he found himself alone in his darkened room.

On being questioned about the customs in their native country of Jordan, Ms. Marzuk confirmed that most parents there sleep with their infants during the first few years of life. But she and her husband had decided early on, when their baby was a just few months old, to adopt the American custom of putting the child to sleep in his own bed in another room, which had worked well until now.

When Jalil initially started waking up at night and crying intensely, they had tried to distract him and put him back in his crib, but he would immediately resume his crying. Mr. Marzuk had also tried to put Jalil to sleep with a recently worn T-shirt at his side, hoping that the smell of his father's body would be reassuring, but this had failed as well. The infant had no interest or attachment to any cuddly objects or stuffed animals.

Ms. Marzuk, in particular, felt rather overwhelmed with the situation, which kept her from enjoying her own life. She commented tearfully that she had thought getting married and having a child would be more enjoyable, and that this was not what she had expected at all. Since her son did not sleep well, he was quite irritable, fussy, and demanding during the day. He seemed to want to be with his mother almost all the time.

Both parents said that they had been quite disappointed with the advice of their pediatrician, who seemed very mechanical in his approach. He had not seemed concerned about their hesitation to use his approach, on which he insisted without listening to their concerns. At the same time, they also felt at a loss about what else to do.

A crucial issue in their seeking further help was the announced visit of Mr. Marzuk's mother. Ms. Marzuk had previous disagreements with her mother-in-law, whom she described as intrusive and dictatorial about cooking, housework, clothing, and child rearing. When there had been disagreements in the past, over the telephone or personally, Ms. Marzuk's own mother had eventually heard of those confrontations and had called her daughter from Jordan. Ms. Marzuk's mother would chastise her for disregarding the elder woman's advice and for confronting her mother-in-law openly, which according to their tradition should not be done. Ms. Marzuk was feeling quite unsupported, lonely, sad, and angry about her situation. She felt that no one understood her feelings or her position, and she longed for her father, to whom she felt the closest, who lived in Jordan with her mother.

Mr. Marzuk, for his part, explained that he was "between a rock and a hard place." On the one hand, he did not wish to offend his mother by agreeing with his wife on such issues as how something should be cooked or where the family members should sit in the car. But on the other hand, he loved his wife and realized that his mother was intrusive. He hoped that his wife would just tolerate her "once again," since the stay would be a short one of only two weeks or so. Ms. Marzuk felt very angry about her husband's attitude, because it made her feel unsupported and misunderstood. She mentioned that her mother-in-law, if not confronted, would continue her practice of calling frequently to ask abut the baby, and of giving instructions about how to rear him.

This line of discussion had led to open altercations at home between the spouses, in which they shouted at each other and said negative things about their respective families of origin. After such fights, they particularly noticed Jalil's sleep and crying problems. When he witnessed these encounters, he would cry and cling to his father.

After these yelling episodes, Ms. Marzuk would feel depressed and burdened. She also experienced Jalil as extremely demanding and needy, and felt that he interfered with her daily chores because he wanted constant attention. She not only felt disappointed in her son, but she also began to feel that she did not want to go on with this "kind of life," to the extent that she even had fleeting wishes to die.

Developmental history

Jalil had been born two weeks premature. He had developed pneumonia and had to remain in the neonatal intensive care unit for about two weeks, a time that his parents experienced as very difficult and traumatic. He weighed seven pounds at birth and was considered entirely normal except for the infection, which resolved with appropriate treatment.

Jalil ate and slept well. He was breast-fed for one month, at which time his mother switched him to the bottle. She felt that her son was too impatient to extract milk from the breast because he would start fussing if enough milk did not come quickly. With the bottle, the process seemed easier, so she stopped breast-feeding altogether.

Jalil had reached developmental milestones at normal times. He had good eye contact with his parents at one month of age, smiled socially, and seemed quite curious and content. He was thought by them to be a very intelligent and exploratory child who wanted to look at everything around him. He was very sociable and would make contact with people readily when someone approached him. His language development proceeded normally, and he was saying syllables like "pa," "ma," and "ba" repeatedly. He had mild stranger anxiety, staying close to his parents whenever a new person approached.

Jalil's parents felt that he had a short attention span or that perhaps he was somewhat hyperactive. They noted that he had little patience and could not concentrate for long periods of time, which led him to interfere with Ms. Marzuk's cooking and other housework.

Observations of the child

During the initial consultation sessions, Jalil appeared to be a well-developed, strong, attractive infant. He was good-humored and very sociable. He made good eye contact, and was quite curious about everything in his surroundings. He explored new toys by playing with each for several minutes before going on to a new one. His behavior alternated between sitting on the floor to play with toys, and lifting his arms toward his parents so that they would pick him up. After being held awhile, he would want down to resume his explorations.

While on his mother's or father's lap, Jalil would typically go back and forth between them as they sat side by side. If he was with his mother, after a short time he would want to sit on his father's lap, and vice versa, repeating this action many times.

Jalil appeared to be very alert and vigorous, with a lot of energy and a relatively short attention span. However, when interested, he would explore a toy for longer periods of time. He had excellent gross motor skills. His fine motor skills were a bit immature, with a very mild intentional tremor in his fingers when conducting a delicate or small movement. Nevertheless, he exhibited good pincer grasp. He had excellent capacity for joint attention and was able to point with his right index finger to indicate when he wanted something.

Jalil smiled readily at the interviewing clinicians, and he would show them toys or ask them for toys. He would make physical contact with the interviewer briefly, then go quickly back to his mother and father in a show of "secure base behavior." His mother and father spontaneously played "peek-a-boo" with him, which he enjoyed very much. He exhibited object permanence, as he would look for a toy when it was covered with a piece of paper or handkerchief.

Jalil had good motor planning skills, and there was no indication either from questioning of parents or from direct observation of any remarkably diminished or exacerbated sensitivities in any sensory channel (visual, auditory, tactile). He had normal perception of pain and reactions to vestibular stimulation.

He exhibited a range of emotions, but was mostly content or even joyous. After a while, if he became frustrated with a toy, he would start fussing and want to be picked up. He showed initial cautiousness toward strangers, but quickly warmed up when his parents were around.

Jalil would pay attention when his mother or father showed baby books to him, and occasionally he would point to a character in the book. He would socially reference both parents, seeking visual contact with them so that he could share with them what he had discovered in the book. He was physically quite active, but would not go more than a very short radius away from his parents.

Observations of parent-child interaction

When his mother or father cried as they spoke of the problematic situations they had faced with their son, Jalil looked at their faces, appeared puzzled, sobered up and ceased his explorations. This reaction indicated his sensitivity to the emotional expressions of others. Both parents showed a great deal of warmth and tenderness toward their son. Mr. Marzuk, for instance, became tearful when discussing his baby's cries during the night, and described them as sounding as if Jalil "really meant it," (i.e., he really was very upset and scared). He regretted now that they had followed the pediatrician's suggestion to let him cry.

Ms. Marzuk, on her part, appeared very close to her son, touching him from time to time while he was playing on the floor. She would put her hand behind his back when he leaned back, or she would cover the edge of a chair with her hand whenever it looked as if he would bump into it while moving around. She clearly predicted his moves and seemed very responsive to his needs, despite her verbalizations that she was not enjoying the interaction with her son.

Both parents seemed very close to Jalil. They appeared patient and accepting of his projects and explorations. Even when they were upset or crying, they kept a close eye on him, following his movements, and assisting him whenever he needed help. For Jalil's part, he was mostly cheerful, although a bit anxious, particularly when moving from one parent to the other.

The parents as individuals

During the consultation sessions, Ms. Marzuk spoke briefly about her life history and the circumstances of her move to the United States. She was the youngest of six children, all of whom lived in Jordan. She had always felt very close to her father but less so to her mother, who was the family disciplinarian and more critical. Ms. Marzuk felt that she was her father's closest daughter, and she greatly regretted not being about to talk to him regularly or spend time with him. She also regretted that he was missing out on getting to know her son.

When talking about her father, Ms. Marzuk cried intensely, as if mourning her country, her culture, and her family. She spoke about her sense of isolation in the small city where they lived, which has little cultural diversity. She missed her family, and had few people to rely on, except for neighbors and the staff at the infant clinic. When her husband went to work, she felt lonely and somewhat scared. She was studying English at a local school, but could not really communicate her thoughts well to anyone except her husband, with whom she could speak Arabic.

The Marzuk's marriage had been arranged by their respective families. Mr. Marzuk had gone back to his home country to get married after his mother advised him she had found a wife. Ms. Marzuk said many times that she loved her husband and was happy living with him, except that she felt lonely and she disliked the way her husband's mother interfered in their lives.

Mr. Marzuk was an outgoing and personable man who spoke good English and conveyed his ideas well. He had been a resident in the United States longer than his wife, and had adopted American cultural practices. He felt very close to his wife, whom he loved, and he was very happy with his son, in whom he saw many features of himself when he was a child (such as high level of activity and great curiosity). He was also interested in his career, but not to the exclusion of his family. He had several brothers who also had emigrated to the United States whom they saw occasionally. Mr. Marzak had been very close to his family when he was young, but, curious about other cultures, he had studied in England and then decided to move to the United States. He was a fairly self-reliant individual who quickly felt at home in diverse settings, and although he worried about his son and wife, overall he was happy.

During the family's sessions with the consultant, Mr. Marzuk would translate questions to his wife. There was obvious closeness and intimacy between them, as evidenced by their gestures and other nonverbal communication.

Diagnosis

Jalil's circumstances fit the *D.C: 0-3* criteria for Adjustment Disorder because the child had a clear onset of symptoms after a stressor (a major argument between parents and depressive status of his mother). The alteration was quite brief, and there were no modifications in other areas of functioning. Despite the impact of sleep disturbance and crying on the parents, the sleep disturbance itself was not severe. Jalil would wake up one time and cry, but he was quite consolable when he could interact with his parents. This relatively mild disturbance caused a great deal of parental concern, partly because of the pediatrician's advice not to soothe the baby.

The problem seemed to occur as a result of the baby's anxiety and his need to have his parents with him during the night. This same anxiety was more evident also during the daytime, resulting in Jalil's wanting to be close to his mother and father. During the sessions, Jalil would go from one parent to the other repeatedly, as if to reassure himself that he could be close to both of them.

This diagnosis is more apt than the diagnosis of Sleep Behavior Disorder, because of the brief duration of the symptoms that affected the sleep, and its onset after a stressor, plus the fact that it was relatively mild and of very short duration, indicating not a pervasive disturbance in the function of sleep but a transient affectation in the face of difficult circumstances.

Another differential diagnosis considered was that of Regulatory Disorder. The child had relatively speaking, a short attention span, high level of motor activity, and little patience if things did not go his way. This diagnosis is ruled out because the patient was content most of the time and could be calm for extended periods. Additionally, he did not exhibit abnormalities in sensory integration, like tactile defensiveness or motor planning problems, or abnormalities in the perception, reaction to, or processing of visual or auditory stimuli. Jalil could be said to have had challenging emotional and behavioral features. He needed more entertaining, because he was easily bored, and had less tolerance of frustration than other children his age, yet without exceeding the behaviors expectable in the continuum of typically developing children (i.e., his behavior was not in the pathological range).

His relatedness and eagerness to engage in reciprocal interactions rule out the diagnosis of a Multisystem Developmental Disorder, as well as his language functioning, which was developing along normal lines, as were his playfulness and imagination. The relationship between Jalil and his parents was perturbed only briefly, mostly centering in the areas of sleep and the strong need for attention and interaction perceived by his mother. After the intervention and behavioral changes occurred in the child, the relationship became mutually satisfying and enjoyable again.

There is no indication of any medical condition or other emotional or behavioral disturbances in the infant. The stressor was the emotional disturbance in Ms. Marzuk, her depressive feelings, and the intense arguments between the parents; all these clearly had an impact on the child's behavior. When these issues were resolved (see below), the disturbance in behavior improved in short order. As noted in the examination data, Jalil was functioning at appropriate levels in all of the areas assessed.

Diagnostic summary

Axis I: **Primary Diagnosis**
Adjustment Disorder.

Axis II: **Relationship Disorder Classification**
No diagnosis. Relationship transiently perturbed with both parents.

Axis III: **Medical and Developmental Disorders and Conditions**
No diagnosis.

Axis IV: **Psychosocial Stressors**
Moderate. Acute. Arguments between parents in presence of child. Depressive feelings in mother. Overall impact on child. Moderate.

Axis V: **Functional Emotional Developmental Level**
Has fully reached expected levels for mutual attention, mutual engagement, and interactive intentionality and reciprocity.

PIR-GAS:70 (Perturbed)

Discussion with caregivers and treatment planning

This case illustrates the technical model of "therapeutic consultation," in which the process of evaluating and consulting about a child's and family's problems becomes itself a theraputic response to the distress evidenced by the child and the parents. As the consutation sessions unfolded, Mr. and Ms. Marzuk reported a great improvement in their son's sleeping pattern, and in Ms. Marzuk's mood, which led to the conclusion of the therapeutic work. The consultation/intervention areas can be conceptualized as exploring and affecting three areas: the infant's sleep disturbance, the mother's depressive mood, and the couple's marital conflict.

Intervention

Sleep disturbance

From the first interview, given the level of frustration and concern that both parents had about their son's problem of waking up in the middle of the night, a behavioral model of intervention was undertaken. The first intervention consisted of having the parents merely record the problem in a "sleep diary." The parents were asked to record the time they put Jalil to sleep, how they achieved this, and how long it took him to go to sleep. They were also to keep track of what time he awakened and what he did or how he behaved on awakening, as well as what his parents did, including the outcome of their actions.

At the second consultation session, Mr. Marzuk brought a printed report with all these details that he had compiled in his computer. It also included whether there had been any additional stresses or concerns during the day-time that might have disrupted Jalil's sleep. This latter point was added by the parents themselves as part of the sleep diary.

Their report noted only one night, the night of the first consultation, when Jalil had not awakened during the night but had instead slept in his crib, which had reassured the parents. The next night, he woke up crying at around 2 a.m. Instead of letting him cry, they followed the consultant's sug-gestion of "giving up" quickly and taking Jalil into their own bed, after which he soon went to sleep. Having him in their bed, however, resulted in the undesirable effect of disrupting Mr. Marzuk's sleep, because Jalil kicked and moved about most of the night as he slept.

The sleep diary noted that the next day they had another argument, not as heated as before, about the impending visit of Mr. Marzuk's mother and how Ms. Marzuk should interact with her. Their altercation was intense, and witnessed by Jalil again. The spouses disagreed on whether they should go along with Mr. Marzuk's mother and placate her, or whether Ms. Marzuk should openly ask her not to tell her how to run their home. At this point, the parents wondered if their arguments might not be upsetting Jalil. The consultant quickly agreed with them, suggesting that perhaps they were frightening, or at least very stressful for him. They decided to refrain from exposing him to these scenes.

At this point, the consultant asked the parents how they would feel most comfortable in handling Jalil's sleep problem. They clearly did not want to let him to cry, which the consultant also discouraged. Mr. and Ms. Marzuk suggested a compromise with their son's nighttime demands for attention, a "middle-of-the-road" solution: to move Jalil's crib to their bedside. If he awakened, then they would try not to pick him up or take him into their own bed, but would instead just reach out and touch him from the bed and see whether this would suffice to reassure him. The consultant agreed that this was an excellent idea. Over the next week, Mr. and Ms. Marzuk tried this approach and it quickly became clear that it was effective. The first cou-ple of nights, Jalil would wake up and cry, but then be reassured when his mother touched him, and soon went back to sleep.

As other issues took precedence over the course of the following sessions, Mr. and Ms. Marzuk still kept the sleep diary. They reported that gradually Jalil would wake up, sit up, look for his parents, and upon seeing them, lie back down and go to sleep without needing to be touched anymore. We dis-cussed an approach of gradually moving the crib a bit further and further away from them, which they did. Finally, they reported that Jalil did not seem to be waking up at night any more, at which time they moved the crib back to his room, and he was able to sleep through the night.

Mother's depressive feelings

It was no surprise that Ms. Marzuk felt depressed. The discussions and arguments with her husband, the impending visit of the mother-in-law, and the fact that Jalil developed sleep problems, together with the unhelpful advice to let him cry, which led to feelings of guilt, were all added stressors in Ms. Marzuk's already stressed life. These problems precipitated her sense of failure as a mother and her occasional thoughts of wanting to disappear altogether.

As these feelings were explored, the Marzuks were able to express a number of concerns that they had not been able to discuss earlier. As their discussion was facilitated through the consultations about Jalil, a great burden appeared to be lifted from their shoulders.

Both Mr. and Ms. Marzuk had looked forward to their son's birth with great anticipation and joy, hoping that having a child would be a wonderful experience. In great detail, they gave a rich narrative of the birth and subsequent events.

They explained that in their country it is common to have a family doctor, someone who looks after the health of the family for years or even a lifetime, who often comes to the home to see the patient. They had talked to a female obstetrician with whom Ms. Marzuk felt comfortable about being the one to deliver their baby. She promised to be there for the birth, so they felt reassured. But when the time of the birth came, the female obstetrician was on vacation and a male obstetrician was covering for her. Ms. Marzuk felt very disappointed at the broken promise, even more so because the new doctor was male. She did not feel comfortable with him, which had much to do with her cultural traditions concerning childbirth. In addition, she was disappointed by subsequent events, because the baby was immediately diagnosed with pneumonia from having aspirated meconium. Instead of having the baby at her bedside as she had expected, she was left alone while he was taken to the neonatal intensive care unit (NICU) of the hospital.

During Jalil's two-week NICU stay, both parents felt traumatized. A major reason for their reaction was the way they were treated there. Mr. Marzuk explained with much emotion that during the baby's stay, the NICU staff seemed to treat them as if he, and Ms. Marzuk especially, were "dumb." He explained that since he spoke with a foreign accent, some of the nurses treated him as if he could not understand their explanations. But they would not even bother to provide explanations to Ms. Marzuk, assuming she could not understand anything anyway. So she spent many mornings in the hospital, without getting any information about the status of her son. Only when her husband came to the NICU from work was there some information available.

Mr. Marzuk recalled that one nurse told him openly several times that she thought he did not understand, and he resented very much what he perceived as her impatient and angry demeanor. During their explanations of these and other negative experiences at the hospital, both parents oscillated between expressing anger and a sense of having been hurt and offended.

Mr. and Ms. Marzuk recalled that one time, close to the baby's discharge, they had wanted to hold him. Instead, the nurse on duty told them impatiently that they did not understand that the baby was "very, very sick" and should not be touched all the time. They felt that they were being treated as an unwelcome nuisance at the NICU and that the baby was treated as if he belonged to the nursing staff.

After this incident, they went home for a while, but just one hour later, they received a call telling them the baby was being discharged from NICU to a regular pediatric bed. When Mr. Marzuk questioned this decision, based on what he had been told before, the nursing staff explained that they had reevaluated the situation and decided that the baby was much better now, which was indeed the case. He felt that the nurse who had prevented them from touching the baby had not taken their needs into account, and was not aware of the true status of the baby's health, which they knew had improved a great deal.

Both Mr. and Ms. Marzuk seemed very much to need to talk about these experiences around Jalil's birth. It may have been that they perceived the consultant as a secure person to talk with about these things, because he himself was an immigrant who spoke with an accent. The consultant empathized with them and legitimized their feelings of sadness and anger. After some weeks, they seemed to be much less sad, tense, or stressed and appeared much relieved, particularly Ms. Marzuk. She reported feeling much happier and content again, which indicated that she had suffered from an adjustment disorder with depressed mood.

The issue of the baby's frequent demands was framed as a perception that Jalil was very intelligent, curious, and wishing to explore everything. The consultant encouraged both parents not to worry so much about the house being clean and to spend more time with Jalil in playful interactions. A few weeks later, Ms. Marzuk reported that she was now truly enjoying the relationship with her son, who also seemed much more relaxed, content, and able to focus his attention on things. This development coincided with the time that he was also sleeping through the night and with the resolution of their marital conflict.

Marital conflict

During the consultation sessions, the issue of how to deal with their extended family came up several times. Both spouses were invited to discuss their point of view, and they both finally agreed that it should be Mr. Marzuk who would talk with his mother when she visited. His approach would be to advise her that there were several ways of thinking about children, household organization, cooking, and other matters, and that they wanted to relieve her from having to give advice, so instead she could just enjoy her visit and her grandson. Mr. Marzuk agreed that he would tell his mother that he liked very much the way his wife was doing things, which did not mean that he did not appreciate how his mother would have done them. When Ms. Marzuk's mother-in-law came, Mr. Marzuk had to make only two or three comments of this nature before his mother apparently decided not to make further critical remarks to Ms. Marzuk. The two-week visit went relatively well, and Ms. Marzuk felt reassured that her husband had stood by her. This is a different way of handling family conflicts from what would have been common in Jordan. In the traditional system, the husband is expected always to be more faithful to his family of origin, even if it creates disagreements with his wife. But Mr. and Ms. Marzuk had opted to protect their marital relationship, even if doing so caused some degree of distance from their families of origin. Ms. Marzuk repeatedly said that she realized that her husband loved her.

This case also touches on issues commonly seen in immigrant families and couples. Mr. Marzuk was more "acculturated" and his character style was more accepting of the new and the different; he was more willing to accept American values and practices. Ms. Marzuk was more tied to her country, and was perhaps more genuine in expressing her disagreement with some practices. Mr. Marzuk tended to smooth over the differences in beliefs and practices, while she was able to voice more clearly her disagreement with some of them, and her wish to preserve some of her traditions and practices. As Mr. Marzuk felt more comfortable with the consultant, he expressed his own conflicts about this problem of living in two cultures at the same time.

The situation also points to the issue of culturally dissonant advice. The pediatrician, using a common approach for dealing with sleep problems, recommended letting the infant cry. His recommendation was tried reluctantly by Ms. Marzuk and more eagerly by Mr. Marzuk, although both felt quite uncomfortable and guilty in using an approach that ran counter to their cultural practice of soothing a crying infant. Furthermore, it was worsened by the fact that, as often happens, that advice did not produce the desired result, because infants can cry inconsolably for long periods of time when they feel frightened and desolate. The advice to "let infants cry" offers an apparently pragmatic solution to a problem that has to do with anxiety and neediness on the part of the infant. To recommend just ignoring the child seems contrary to the idea of promoting parental responsiveness and concern about the child's emotional state. It seems far more acceptable to try to soothe the child and to use a gradual approach to help the infant feel secure enough to tolerate separations. Unfortunately, it is still common in some circles to recommend ignoring the baby, rather than to promote a more empathic response.

As Mr. and Ms. Marzuk began to see improvement not only in Jalil's behavior and sleeping patterns but also in their own interactions, they decided to discontinue the consultation process. The consultant encouraged them to contact him again in the future if there were new problems.

Prognosis and discussion

The prognosis is optimistic, given the parents' engagement with their child, their emotional closeness, and their concern and responsiveness toward him. The parents also are mutually supportive and have a satisfying relationship. Both were encouraged to develop further social contacts locally, and to establish connections with a Moslem community in a nearby city. Given their degree of involvement in treatment, their cooperation, their creativity in trying to find solutions, and their flexibility, it is likely that their family life will continue to improve and that Jalil will continue to do well behaviorally and emotionally.

The case of Jalil illustrates the vulnerability of young children to stressful circumstances involving emotional turmoil in their parents and their environment. This infant's behavioral changes appeared in response to specific difficult circumstances, were of brief duration, and disappeared quickly when the stressors were alleviated. This clinical situation highlights the importance of early mental health intervention and its efficacy in addressing problems in the emotional life of infants and their families.

400. Regulatory Disorders

401. Type I: Hypersensitive. Fearful and Cautious

Lois M. Black, Ph.D.

Regulatory Disorders characterize a broad range of children all of whom show emotional or behavioral problems along with some form of constitutional or maturational challenge. Other diagnostic classifications, such as DSM-IV, have treated emotional conditions as separate from developmental disabilities, which, nevertheless, when present can fuel those very emotional issues. The new *DC: 0-3* classification of Regulatory Disorder finally captures the concomitance of these conditions and speaks to the complex psychological vicissitudes of the child who has sensory, motor, or other brain-based difficulties. In what follows, assessment of whether a child evidences some form of neuropsychological dysfunction, and its possible interweaving with psychological conflict, also within a family system, will be treated as the critical diagnostic path for differential diagnosis and treatment recommendations of a child with a Regulatory Disorder.

A note on terminology: "neuropsychological dysfunction" is used here synonymously with "maturational and constitutional issues." It refers to any neurogenic, that is, brain-based, difficulty or pattern of difficulties that can affect the way a child moves, understands, speaks, thinks, reasons, sees, senses, relates to others—that is, that affects motor, language, cognitive, visual, or sensory functions—, and, as the approach taken here will show, inevitably affects how the child relates to others and thinks of himself.

Regulatory Disorders provide, then, not merely a long-awaited conceptualization but, at times, a real diagnostic challenge because of the need to evaluate whether a neurogenic disability is involved and what role it plays in the overall picture. Although the mental health professional may receive a referral from another professional who has already diagnosed a sensory, motor, language, or neurological condition, often the mental health professional is the first person the family approaches because of concerns over the child's emotional well-being or hard-to-handle behavior. In evaluating for a Regulatory Disorder, it becomes necessary to understand whether those presenting emotional or behavioral symptoms are possibly tied up with, exacerbated by, or intertwined with an underlying neuropsychological disability, even a subtle or hidden one. A history of a child's sensory over- or underreactivity, for example, or poor muscle stability and coordination, may be overt enough to discern a constitutional vulnerability. However, here the question may become what does this constitutional vulnerability have to do with any of the presenting emotional issues, or do the emotional problems have separate psychogenic or environmental stresses as causes. When assessment aims at differential diagnosis with treatment recommendations, a comprehensive approach, which includes a broader and more complete understanding of the child's neuropsychological profile of strengths and weaknesses and how these may impact on the child's sense of self, interactions with others, and defensive coping, may be preferred.

In what follows, the case of 2^{1}/$_{2}$-year-old Sara will be presented to highlight one form of Regulatory Disorder, the "hypersensitive" type, where the dominant behavioral pattern is "fearful and cautious" and the emphasized constitutional difficulty is a sensory pattern of hypersensitivity to sounds, sights, or touch. Although diagnosis of type of Regulatory Disorder depends on how closely a child may approach these dominant patterns, individual children can show varied emotional and behavioral issues and quite complicated neuropsychological profiles. This was the case with Sara.

In what follows, too, an integrated approach to assessment will be described, one that combines neuropsychological assessment procedures with clinical understanding of psychodynamic and family systems issues. Several themes run through this approach to evaluation and treatment. First, it considers neurogenic disabilities to be subjectively experienced by any child who has them (even though they may be hidden to others) and taken up into the child's sense of self. They are given meaning and "explanation" by the child, elaborated upon in fantasies, and played out in behavior. This takes place alongside, and in response to, interpretations and reactions to such behaviors, conscious and unconscious, that have been made by family and others. Second, there may be enmeshment of the behaviors in such an interpretive framework so that underlying roots of the difficulties are hidden. The interpretative framework—the meaning given by both the child and others to the child's behavior—can become itself a perpetuating factor in the child's emotional and behavioral problems. Disabilities become overlaid with many issues. Third, the task of assessment thus becomes one of "unbuilding"—to find the disability in the child and how it has been exacerbated by, or implicated in, psychological conflict, also within a family system. This is done while simultaneously finding the child's key strengths, both to compensate for brain-based difficulties and to build the child's self-esteem. Fourth, and a key point, is that to accurately diagnose a Regulatory Disorder through such an integrated, combined approach can result in: (a) circumscribing the neuropsychological weaknesses; (b) damming the spill onto personality structure and family dynamics; and (c) identifying avenues for therapeutic intervention, remediation, and growth.

Assessment process

The combined emphasis on neuropsychological assessment with clinical understanding of defensive dynamics in child and family can take the following general format.

Before the initial session, the parents complete a comprehensive developmental history questionnaire. This information, along with any previous evaluations, orients the first interview with the parents (without the child present) to areas of their concern and raises initial hypotheses about what is going on psychodynamically with the child, couple, and family. Some clinically revealing questions ask, for example, about parental fantasies and hopes about the child before the child was born, parental "theories" about what is wrong with the child and why this is so, what the parents' worst fears for the child are, and how each of them sees the child as like or unlike the other parent. These types of questions begin to elicit some of the deeper fantasies and fears as well as possible projections and defenses that may be orienting, even if not consciously, for each of the parent's interactions with the child. They start to bring into focus, as well, what the child may be experiencing and responding to in the family. In the case of Sara, because of her parents' complicated family backgrounds and personal histories, the parents were seen, both individually and together, a number of times without Sara present.

Assessment of the child begins with observation of the family during a free play session in the office, where each of the parents are encouraged to interact and play with the child as usual. An observational visit to the child's school may also be useful, to get a picture of the school's view of the child as well as to see the child in another situation and in interaction with other children as well as other adults. If necessary, a home visit is also made. This is followed by a series of more formal neuropsychological evaluation sessions, each about one hour long, where neuropsychological evaluation proper is carried out with one or both of the parents present, along with continuing clinical observations of interactions between child and family. The number of these sessions varies for toddler-age children from about two to five or more times depending on the questions raised and how much testing is required to answer them. In Sara's case, neuropsychological assessment was carried out over five sessions. Following this, findings are discussed with the parents, usually over one or two sessions, and picked up thematically in the course of treatment.

Reason for referral

Sara was 29 months old when her parents requested an evaluation because of anxious and, for the parents, confusing and sometimes bizarre behavior. Ms. Hart, Sara's mother, described her daughter as extremely irritable, anxious, and unhappy, 24 hours a day. She threw sustained temper tantrums daily, with her mother's efforts to console and control her were fruitless. Ms. Hart said that Sara had a better relationship with her father and with strangers than with her, and that she behaved very differently in public than she did at home. Sara's mother thought of her as having up/down swings: cheerful, active, engaging with others; clingy, dependent, and miserable at home. She always awoke from sleep crying. Ms. Hart was also worried that Sara was "unusually repetitive," in play and in focus. Once concerned about something, such as her father going to work, she would repeat insistently, imploringly, and seemingly unendingly, "Daddy work? Daddy work? Daddy work?" Also, on occasion, she would interrupt an activity and carry on a conversation by herself as if she were talking to someone; and sometimes while doing so she would become very anxious and start to cry. Ms. Hart also described some peculiar habits: for example, she would try to soothe herself by stroking an adult's arm or by putting an adult's "elbow in her eye socket."

Sara had a younger sister 6 months old, who, by contrast, was described as easygoing and happy. It was, in fact, the difference noted between her and her sibling that, in part, was responsible for the parents seeking an evaluation.

Assessment findings

School report and observation

At her preschool, Sara's teachers thought of her as shy, passive, and in her own world. She never had tantrums at school, but neither was she outgoing and engaging. She would, however, tune out and daydream a lot. Although she was said to show a desire to play with other children, she had a hard time with turn-taking and extended interactions. She appeared overly involved in her own play, so that if someone said something to her, it was at times like talking to a blank wall. Although symbolic and imaginative, Sara's play lacked elaborate or extended play schemas and could appear disjointed and repetitive. She particularly disliked playing on any playground equipment and did not participate in singing songs at circle time.

Sara could be very verbal, even loquacious, and had an extensive vocabulary, especially for a 29-month-old. She could repeat many things that had been said to her and remember them for quite some time—complicated expressions such as, "Mommy is a wife, Daddy is a husband" or ask "Had a good time skiing in Colorado?" to her teacher after a vacation, with her mother's prompting. Often, however, Sara would insert expressions into verbal exchanges at inappropriate times. She could appear internally preoccupied while talking to herself in extended "monologues," using language almost like a transitional object to play with by herself. She showed inconsistent eye contact and limited attention span, and her teacher was very concerned about her peculiar and withdrawn behaviors.

Remarks: So, what's going on with Sara? Given such descriptions by her parents and school, it is not yet clear that Sara has a Regulatory Disorder. Constitutional/ neuropsychological weaknesses are not obvious (although later on, many features of her classroom and home behavior will be seen as very much related to her particular neuropsychological profile). In fact, the first diagnosis that poses itself as a possibility is an anxiety or mood disorder. In school, she appears excessively constricted, withdrawn, shy, and nonparticipating, possibly due to anxiety. Her mother is overtly concerned about her anxious reactions and describes perseverative worries that may be an early form of obsessive-like preoccupations. Her mother also raises questions about mood regulation and poor development of ego functions that could be related to excessive anxiety. In addition, especially because of Sara's tantrums as well as because of the extreme disparity noted by her mother in her behaviors at home and, with others, one could also begin to question whether stresses at home and in parental care and management techniques may be essentially contributing to Sara's problems.

Developmental and medical history

The developmental history revealed that pregnancy course was complicated by a kidney infection with vomiting during the first trimester which required hospitalization. Delivery was at term after a prolonged 24-hour labor. Apgar scores were 8, then 9. As an infant, Sara was colicky and extremely difficult to soothe, with fussiness continuing till 14 months of age. Sleep routine was irregular with frequent awakenings during the night and little sleep during the day. Sara, in fact, had a history of hyperreactivity to sounds (e.g., to sirens, radio music, and her overhead mobile) with tantrums and anxious crying occurring. During infancy, she was said to gag a lot during feeding. Motor milestones were within normal limits: Sara sat at 6 months and walked at 13 months. Language milestones were delayed, although the parents were unaware of this fact: They stated that she started to respond to simple directions at about 17 months, to her name at about 2 years. Single words and simple phrases appeared at around 18 months. Medically, she was vulnerable to frequent illnesses, allergies, and chronic ear infections. Myringotomy tubes were placed in her ears at 26 months, with infections continuing. Hearing was normal.

Remarks: By history, one already clearly sees the constitutional vulnerability in Sara's reported early colic and fussiness, overreactivity to sounds, and delayed language. But what do these difficulties have to do with her emotional symptoms? Do they explain them? What else is going on with Sara?

Background/ family history

In the series of interviews with Sara's parents it became apparent that Sara's mother, in particular, had a complicated story which also fed into her immediate concerns about Sara, and several individual sessions were scheduled with Ms. Hart.

Both parents appeared to be sensitive, educated, and articulate, but each had a loaded family history and more than slight leanings to illogical thinking. Sara's father had an aunt with schizophrenia and a grandmother who had manic-depressive illness. Sara's mother came from what she described as a chaotic, dysfunctional family. She had four younger brothers, all of whom had learning disabilities; one suffered from a sleep seizure disorder. In addition, one of the brothers had a substance abuse problem and another had abused a child.

Ms. Hart is the only one in her family who completed college and "made something of herself." She has a degree in literature and fine arts and teaches music at a top Ivy League college. She is a highly verbal woman who, in fact, talks excessively. Before marrying Mr. Hart, she had several relationships with men, all of whom she saw as being "diametrically different from her" because they came from "good family backgrounds." One was a diplomat in the foreign service. Mr. Hart "shares more of her background" than these others.

Like Sara, Ms. Hart has a history of heightened susceptibility to physical illness, and presently has allergies, ulcers, and a hiatal hernia. She feels that her illnesses are exaggerated by stress. She said that she developed ulcers after Sara's birth and after having had an argument with her mother. (Her mother, too, was quite sickly, and as a 14-month-old was given by her own mother to a relative because of this sickliness.) Ms. Hart complains that her mother was never able to meet her needs but constantly required Ms. Hart to cater to her, to listen to her problems, and to take charge of her four younger brothers for her.

Although Ms. Hart felt she had never been listened to, encouraged, or understood, and that everything she has since obtained for herself was in contradistinction to her family and her family's expectations of her, she says she is not angry. She doesn't want to be angry. She feels, instead, sorry for her mother and speaks to her often on the phone. Her mother continues to be unsupportive and even resentful of Ms. Hart's new values and her moving away from their small southern town. If Ms. Hart comments on her brothers' behaviors or on any of the family's "irrational" doings to her mother, she is told that she is selfish and judgmental and that she should be ashamed to talk about her own family like that.

Since adolescence, Ms. Hart has had repeated bouts of depression. She also describes a serious postpartum depression after Sara was born that lasted for almost a year. She describes Sara as "not bonding with her," "straining away from her" and averting her gaze. "In the beginning," Ms.Hart said, "she stared at me constantly, but I would always fall asleep and she would avoid eye contact after that." She openly interpreted Sara's behavior as angry and rejecting of her from the beginning.

When I asked Mr. and Ms. Hart about their "theories" of what was the matter with Sara, both saw in her the threatened resurgence of bad genes. They feared that she might develop schizophrenia or manic-depressive illness, like Mr. Hart's side of the family. And, indeed, in their initial descriptions of Sara, she seemed on the way. Ms.Hart was also frightened by Sara's possible resemblance to her dysfunctional brothers. She wondered if Sara was brain-damaged? Or had a sleep seizure disorder? What was neurologically the matter with her? Ms. Hart, in particular, appeared alienated from her daughter.

Ms. Hart also felt responsible for the way Sara was: If it wasn't her genes and her postpartum depression that were to blame, it was what she had done prenatally. When hospitalized during the first trimester for kidney problems, she had wanted to abort the fetus. She feared that she had already caused it damage from her constant vomiting and medical treatment.

Ms. Hart' fantasy about having a child was of a baby who would amuse herself in a playpen while she played music. Her second child was that kind of baby, but not Sara. Her fantasy, in other words, was of a baby who would "let her be." Instead Sara became the clinging, needy, dependent child — just as Ms. Hart had experienced her mother to be. The anger toward her mother, which Ms. Hart denied, seemed to be displaced onto Sara. Ms. Hart wanted to distance herself and turn away from this child, who was a reminder to her of all the dysfunctional aspects of her family (and possibly of herself) that she was so ardently striving to disidentify from. So she focused on the mismatch between herself and her daughter, and on Sara's preference for others.

Remarks: How much do Ms. Hart issues and fears color parent-child interactions and contribute to Sara's emotional symptoms? Do they dominate the picture, is there a relationship disorder here, or is the child's neurogenic disability the primary source of difficulty? In other words, is the disability the critical underpinning for both the child's emotional and behavioral symptoms as well as an important complicating factor in the quality of the parent-child relationship? Combining an understanding of the individual family member's psychological difficulties with observations of interactions and neuropsychological assessment of the child may be the best way of answering these questions.

Neuropsychological assessment

Sara's evaluation can best be understood in the context of a brief overview of a neuropsychological approach to assessment of the very young child.

The targeted skills listed on Table 1 (p 203) stem from neuropsychological assessment of brain functions that are known to be affected in developmental disabilities of various kinds as well as in neurological conditions. They are skill areas that refer to different systems and subsystems in the brain with a neuropsychological evaluation seeking to find out whether consistent, known clusters or patterns of functioning within these different areas are conjointly affected. This list gives examples of functions assessed; it is not exhaustive.

Neuropsychological assessment is necessarily comprehensive in the breadth of functions assessed. It is inherently developmental, incorporating knowledge of brain development as well as developmental expectations across all functions. It is also inherently transdisciplinary, with understanding necessary, for example, of language disorders, movement disorders, and neurological syndromes. Its procedures include both formal and informal methods that are intended to tap into targeted skill areas, whether or not a normed test is available. An important advantage, however, to using formal, normed measures (individually normed subtests, not IQ or other composite scores) is the ability to generate a more precise picture of intra-individual differences in the child, which can be crucial for disclosing patterns of relative inefficiencies and a characteristic neuropsychological profile known to be reflective of a disability. The most desirable subtest is one from which a percentile ranking can be derived, measures a circumscribed skill area, and whose input and output demands are so defined that they can be easily weighted in performance outcome.[1]

Also critical to a neuropsychological evaluation is analysis of the component skills necessary to perform any given task. Most formal tests do not tap into one skill but rather demand use of multiple functions; in everyday life activities are inherently complex. Thus, it is vital to ask not merely what a child scores or does but, importantly, how he achieved that score or performance. It is the how that reveals what component skills are making him fall down, or what avenues of compensation he may naturally bring to bear or can be taught to use. Every assessment importantly includes task analysis of how a child achieved, or failed to achieve, a performance. It thus also essentially involves modifications of tests and standardized procedures in order to elicit the child's optimal performance potential and adjust for any handicapping condition. It is, in fact, through reiterated testing of hypotheses about what skill areas are affected that intervention strategies can be discovered and hidden strengths found.

---

1. There are few normed subtests for 2-year-olds available. More measures are available from 2.6 years on and especially after 3.0. Many have norms for individual subtests, others for "scales" that assess broad domains such as "motor skills" or "visual reception." It is important to remember that with any score, it is detailed task analysis of the specific demands required to perform a test that is essential for interpretation, and so for using a score in a meaningful way. Such a score could then be considered representative of the child's abilities in the neuropsychological area that the test was considered to essentially measure (e.g. visual-spatial skills). With this caveat, some of the measures available where subtests can be used to obtain information in a neuropsychological evaluaation include: The Stanford-Binet, 4th edition (ages 2.0 to adult), the McCarthy Scales (ages 2.6 to 8.6), the Leiter (ages 2.0 to adult), the Illinois Test of Psycholinguistic Abilities (ages 2.4 to 10.3), the Bayley Scales, 2nd edition (birth to 42 months), the Mullen Scales (birth to 69 months), the Differential Ability Scales (ages 2.6 to 17.11), the Purdue Pegboard (ages 2.6 to 16), the Miller Assessment for Preschoolers (ages 2.9 to 5.8), the Reynell Scales (ages 1 to 6.11), the Zimmerman PLS (ages ages birth to 6.11), the Peabody Picture Vocabulary Test (ages 1.9 to 18.0). After age 3.0, add the WPPSI-R (ages 3 to 7.3), the Hiskey-Nebraska (ages 3.0 to 16.0), the K-ABC (ages 2.6/3.0 to 12.6), the Pictorial Test of Intelligence (ages 3.0 to 9.0), the TACL-R (ages 3.0 to 9.11), the Token Test (ages 3.0 to 12.5), the CELF Preschool (ages 3.0 to 6.11).

Table 1: Neuropsychological functions

Organizational and executive functions:
Vigilance and selective attention
Mental tracking and flexibility
Dynamic motor coordination

Language-related functions:
Auditory processing
Phonological production and speech
Auditory cognitive functions
Language comprehension and expression

Memory functions:
Verbal memory and word retrieval
Visual memory

Visual-related functions:
Visual-perceptual processing
Visual cognitive functions
Visual spatial functions

Sensory-perceptual functions:
Auditory/visual/tactile perception
Finger gnosis and stereognosis

Motor functions:
Fine and gross motor coordination
Graphomotor functions
Oromotor functions
Motor tone, motor planning and praxis

Sara's neuropsychological evaluation

Observations

Sara appeared during the evaluation, contrary to expectations, to be highly curious and to take pleasure in interactions with others, with each of her parents as well as with the therapist. Play with Ms. Hart appeared less focused than with Mr. Hart, but then, especially during the free play session, Ms. Hart was either talking incessantly to Sara, or, as was yet more often the case, to the therapist; she could hardly focus on Sara. When she did turn to Sara, it appeared difficult for her to follow Sara's lead. Rather, she became overly verbose in suggesting what to do with the toys, and would frequently end up playing out her own scenarios. Mr. Hart seemed to concede initiative to his wife. When he came alone with Sara, he was more attuned and supportive of Sara's interests in a quiet way.

Although cooperative, with no negativistic behaviors, Sara did show a tendency to be self-directed and had considerable difficulty responding to verbal requests. She also appeared easily distracted by noises or objects in the room as well as by what appeared to be internal thoughts or preoccupations. Thus, seemingly out of the blue, she would start talking about something that was hard to follow. Her activity level seemed to increase when more materials were presented or when task demands were multimodal. Also, when gross motor activities were tested she seemed less able to modulate herself or be redirected, especially by verbal means.

Sara appeared skillful in figuring out how many of the new toys in the office worked and showed good nonverbal skills, especially memory skills. She remembered and seemed to take comfort in repeating activities done on previous sessions. For example, once the therapist showed her a closet in which she put a puppet figure. In the next session she initiated the shared background context with the question "Hiding?" and pointed to the closet. She also showed a creative bent in her symbolic play, which she enjoyed all the more when it was interactive and when affect was intensified. For example, after a peek-a-boo game that she initiated, she gleefully initiated another such game with a tent-like test booklet (from the Stanford-Binet) which she called a "tunnel." After the therapist admired her action with joyful laughter, she then put an empty box on her head and smiled broadly, calling it a "hat."

Neuropsychological assessment findings

The results of the neuropsyhological evaluation showed that Sara was a child of at least average intelligence who had organizational and attentional weaknesses, a developmental language disorder, motor planning difficulties, and affect processing problems. Thus, over and beyond her history of sensory integration problems, manifested especially by her hypersensitivity to noises, Sara had a more involved neuropsychological profile that was complicating her life. (It is possible that sensory issues could be considered makers of more extended neuropsychological involvement in the young child. They could thus be seen as flags signaling the need for further evaluation.)

The following is a description of Sara's performances that led to these conclusions along with some brief explanations of some of the relevant skill areas assessed.

Overall cognitive functioning: Overall cognitive level as measured by both the Stanford-Binet, 4th edition (IQ 101, 52nd percentile) and the Bayley Scales (MDI 104, 60th percentile) was in the average range. Generally, composite scores are far less informative than the pattern of strengths and weaknesses seen from the differing performances that make them up. At Sara's age, moreover, such IQ-type scores are considered nonpredictive of future performance. Also, when there is neuropsychological involvement, composite scores are, without doubt, adversely impacted and reveal only what the current overall cognitive level may be considered at least to be. The important question, of course, is what component skills are affected and in what way are they interfering with the child consistently demonstrating cognitive potential. On the Stanford-Binet, individual subtests can be looked at and analyzed; on the Bayley, individual performances that reflect different skill areas can be interpreted.

Organizational and executive functions: These skills are concerned with the regulation and organization of behavior and thinking at all levels, automatic and reflective—from automatic regulation of motor movements to being able to reflectively step back and critically evaluate what you're doing. Called "executive" and, in fact, comparable to "upper management" of a large organization, these functions correspond in the brain to the frontal lobe, that part of the brain that is most characteristic of humans, and that takes the lead, is on "top of" many other functions. It is also called the "brain's brain" and is "supramodal." The frontal lobe is connected to many other parts of the brain through complicated fiber networks, so if other areas of the brain are affected, in many cases the frontal lobe will be, as well. These connections explain, in part, why attentional difficulties, which are involved in executive functions and are part of frontal lobe and related brain systems, are so often copresent with many other forms of disabilities.

Organizational and executive functions include:

• functioning in an organized, systematic fashion;

• keeping track simultaneously of different trains of thought as well as input from different modalities;

• initiating, shifting, sustaining attention;

• planning/anticipating vs. acting impulsively;

• inhibiting distractions, whether internal or external;

• monitoring and checking one's own activities; and

• using past and future to guide behavior.

Organized, systematic functioning can affect different and multiple levels, spanning motor functions, visual functions, auditory functions as well as higher order processes such as play, problem solving, and even cognitive style. There are no normed tests for organizational functions per se at Sara's age; rather, one has to analyze performances, whether on tests or in life, to see if any of the above features are affected.

One could thus look at how systematic and organized Sara's approach to completing tasks was and do this across all modalities—visual, motor, and auditory. For example, Sara's fine motor coordination was good, but when asked to place pegs in a pegboard (on the Bayley), she showed a scattered, nonsystematic approach, putting pegs in randomly and taking them out again (with her otherwise agile performance now equivalent to only a 20-month level). If you looked at how organized her visual search was and whether she could find things easily, select the relevant, essential details easily, she had problems. For example, when asked to quickly find a hidden figure (on the ITPA Visual Closure Test), she couldn't do it. Her difficulties were not related to visual problems, but to disorganized, haphazard scanning. When asked to tell what she remembered of a story (e.g., McCarthy

Verbal Memory II), she could not put into words her understanding and memory of the information. Here difficulties were related to an inability to organize expressive output.

Sara also showed problems in simultaneously keeping track of two different trains of thought or commands, and in integrating input from different modalities. This is called mental tracking and makes use of working memory as well as the ability to flexibly shift attention and integrate information. Sara, in fact, had notable problems here. She had a very hard time if too much input from different modalities was given to her at the same time. Sara was hypersensitive not only to noises but also across both auditory and visual input and, especially, in the integration of input simultaneously from both modalities. For example, (on the Bayley) if given a number of objects to discriminate ("Show me a plate," "cup," "box"), she could identify the first item asked for (a plate) but then, instead of responding to repeated directives to identify the other objects, she proceeded to play a feeding game with them. Thus, distracted by the toys, she appeared self-directed and unable to simultaneously cue into any verbal input, although the particular verbal commands were ones she could comprehend and respond to if delivered without so many visual manipulatives. Sara's activity level and mood appeared to change during testing depending on the amount and kinds of materials used. The more multisensory, verbal, or numerous the materials were, the more she reacted with increased activity, unfocused regard, or a tendency to tune out. In interactions with Ms. Hart, this was more typical than not, but again, Ms.Hart was constantly verbal with Sara.

Sara also had problems in other features related to attention, such as shifting, inhibiting, and sustaining attention. On formal tasks that had no great dynamic or emotional import, Sara showed real difficulties in shifting attention: For example, she could not shift to draw a vertical line after drawing a horizontal one (Bayley), but just repeated the same horizontal strokes. Or, on another task (McCarthy Draw-a-Design), she could draw the first design asked for, a much harder-to-draw circle, but then could not shift to draw the simpler horizontal line, which of course she was able to do. This inability to easily shift may also be an essential brain-based characteristic which contributes to her perseverative tendencies—her inability to shift out of an activity, a thought, or a mood state.

Sara's play, although symbolic, lacked in elaborate sequences, which strongly suggested that it, too, was affected by her organizational weaknesses. Although her play could appear age appropriate because she could use one object as a substitute for another, (a box for a hat; a doll for herself) (expected 27-30 months) and group objects meaningfully together while narrating what she was doing (also expected 27-30 months), she could not sequentially elaborate or sustain the play in logically organized serial steps (bathes doll, puts clothes on, then feeds it). When Sara was left on her own to play, as she often was, her play became more random. Such a child needs the structured support from others to organize and sequence her play until she can internalize and appropriate the structure for herself.

Her problem-solving also appeared wanting because of a sometimes weak ability to use an intended result to guide and plan her actions, or to use cause and effect reasoning to organize her approach to a task. This was also manifested in a weak ability to use past and future to regulate behavior. Sara was unable to tell herself when her father left for work in the morning that he would come back later. Was this anxiety based on a lack of libidinal object constancy or assurance that a significant other would be lovingly available; or, was it, possibly in addition, the lack of a sure temporal, sequential organization to her experience which did not allow her to automatically use past experiences to give herself the needed reassurance?

Sara's cognitive style, more generally, seemed affected. She could be, on the one hand, overly absorbed or perseveratively stuck in something, or, on the other hand, highly disorganized, with loss of attentional focus. Children with organizational weaknesses, like Sara's, are known to fluctuate in style between an approach that is disorganized, impulsive, or easily side-tracked and one at the opposite extreme of being rigid, compulsive, perseverative. Children with frontal lobe dysfunction can show both these extremes. It seems that the very problems (in frontal lobe dysfunction) that underlie organizational and attentional difficulties may also codetermine defensive style and personality. The child who is highly distractible and unable to plan and guide actions in accord with rules or anticipated consequences can show a propensity to be impulsive and anxious in dealing with emotionally laden issues. A child sensitive to experienced disorganization and loss of attentional focus as beyond her control, in an ego-dystonic way, may well opt for overcontrol and a rigid, obsessive style. Children who have difficulty shifting attention and show a perseverative focus may exhibit a cognitive inflexibility that appears to be an obsessive preoccupation with things. Sara's obsessively anxious quality, seen in her repeated questionings and repetitive behavior at home, may be an offshoot of these brain-based problems as they impact on personality style.

According to her parents' report, Sara had had hypersensitivities, especially to sounds, and fussiness until she was about 14 months old. Not only was she hypersensitive to the sirens outside, but also to her mother's music playing and to the lullabies of her overhead mobile. Consistent with Sara's early history of hyperreactivity were her organizational and executive function difficulties and her consequent problems with self-regulation. Sara showed a continuing pattern of disorganizing and withdrawing from too much stimulation, especially excessive verbal and multimodal stimulation. Unable to integrate and keep track of different input simultaneously, she was easily overstimulated and found regulation and modulation of behavior and mood states difficult. It is not unusual for a child with these types of problems to "learn" to close some access channels—in Sara's case this was primarily the auditory channel—as well as to become less reactive to others, or even avoidant of others, as a form of coping.

Language-related functions: On tasks requiring listening and comprehension, Sara did relatively poorly. Verbal commands had to be repeated frequently.

Attentional issues, as previously described, seemed to interfere, especially when materials were numerous. For example, the Reynell Scales of Language development, which uses many small toys presented together, could not be administered because she appeared overwhelmed by the presentation and totally unable to cue into verbal directions to manipulate them in certain ways. Yet, beyond attentional and organizational difficulties, receptive issues were also present and interfering with responsivity, especially to more syntactically and semantically complex commands. On a formal language measure, such as the Zimmerman Preschool Language Scale, Sara had a receptive language score at the 12th percentile, in the low average range (age equivalent 19 months). Her expressive language abilities, by contrast, were much better. On the Stanford-Binet Vocabulary test, which at Sara's age is simply a picture-naming task, she scored at the 60th percentile. Her Expressive Communication Score on the Zimmerman Preschool Language Scale was also solidly average, at the 61st percentile.

The significant discrepancy between receptive and expressive skills in favor of expressive is somewhat unusual but, nevertheless, typical of one neuropsychological subtype of developmental language disorders (DLD), that of a semantic pragmatic language disorder. [The heterogeneity of developmental language disorders and the fact that distinct neuropsychological subtypes can be detected was shown by Wilson and Risucci (1986). Rapin and Allen (1983, 1987, 1992) have also described clinical subtypes of language disorders found among children with DLD as well as children with autism. The "semantic pragmatic" subtype that Sara showed was described by Rapin and Allen (1983, 1987). In my research (Black, 1988,1993,1994), an overlap was found between this "semantic pragmatic" subtype and Wilson & Risucci's (1986) neuropsychological subtype "C."] Characteristic of this kind of DLD, and part of Sara's profile, is also excellent rote verbal memory—that is, the ability to repeat long strings of words without necessarily processing their content (e.g., such as seen on McCarthy Verbal Memory I; Stanford-Binet Sentence Memory). These features—good expressive language, large vocabulary, and good rote verbal memory—give others the misleading impression that the child can understand much more than she can, eliciting from others more complex language than the child can possibly process. This adds to the likelihood that the child will be nonresponsive to verbal input. (Receptive difficulties, in addition to the organizational/attentional problems previously noted, make more understandable Sara's closing off the auditory channel since it is an unreliable channel to begin with.) In this type of semantic pragmatic disorder, moreover, pragmatics — that is, the ability to maintain a verbal topic or nonverbal interaction, or to be appropriately responsive (and so be able to close numerous circles of communication), is also characteristically weak. The inept pragmatics that is typically part of this DLD picture usually has at its source both receptive language difficulties and serious organizational/attentional problems, so the child easily gets sidetracked and goes off on tangents. This was the case with Sara.

The conclusion that Sara has a language disorder of the semantic pragmatic type was crucially based on disclosing intra-individual differences and a characteristic profile of relative inefficiencies and strengths. Also associated with this neuropsychological subtype of DLD are relative strengths in visual cognitive and visual memory skills, which Sara also demonstrated. (See especially Wilson & Risucci [1986] and Black [1988].)

Motor planning: Sara also showed low motor tone and a motor planning weakness (dyspraxia). Dyspraxias affect whether a child can use her body in accord with an idea or intent, whether her own or someone else's. A child with a dyspraxia has difficulty automatically doing or imitating complex, sequenced movements or responding to verbal requests to move in a certain way. For example, Sara could not automatically plan and execute a fluid series of movements necessary to climb a jungle gym. When asked to show how she would use a hammer or a toothbrush and toothpaste, given pictures, she could not use gestures to demonstrate her understanding (ITPA Manual Expression). Sara's nonparticipation at circle time, when expected to gesture her way through songs, as well as her difficulties on the playground, may be related to these motor praxis difficulties. Motor praxis difficulties can often be inhibiting for the young child whose behavior can easily be interpreted as oppositional or seen as timid withdrawal.

Affect sensitivity: Finally, Sara showed affect sensitivity problems, that is, difficulty reading affective cues, whether presented visually or vocally. This was assessed informally by a series of tests that require the child to identify facial affect expressions or to identify whether things are said in an a happy, sad, or angry tone of voice.[2]

Given the importance of affect sensitivity to early reciprocal social interactions between parent and child, this is one more reason why it is not surprising that Sara's mother found her daughter unresponsive and difficult to regulate. Affect processing is known to be important for the development of affect tolerance and affect modulation. For example, mothers are known to modulate and transform their babies' negative affect, as well as increase optimal levels of positive arousal, through their own exaggerated facial and vocal displays. In order for this to work, however, the child must be able to pick up the affective signals communicated to it vocally, facially, through gestures, or cross-modally. If not, the child is likely to experience increased negative affect and tension, with poor coping and poor modulation. In addition, the development of healthy self-esteem and narcissism, typically fostered as the infant feels admired by mother and responds in turn, is likely to go awry. Being able to read another's affective expression is also important for "disambiguating" the world—for understanding when a situation is really frightening, and also for alleviating confusion and anxieties.

---

2. Facial affect tests, normed for children aged 3 to 8, were developed by Fein, Waterhouse, Lucci, & Braverman [1985]. The vocal affect test was developed by Berk, Doehring & Bryans [1983]. All measures were validated and re-normed for 3-5 year olds by Black [1988, 1994].

Diagnosis

Given this neuropsychological profile, many of Sara's emotional difficulties as well as the concerns and relationship problems shown by Ms. Hart could be better understood. What Ms.Hart had not known about her daughter was, importantly, that Sara had a hard time receptively processing her verbal input to her and that, more generally, she had a difficult time organizing and regulating different kinds of sensory input and was so easily overstimulated. Although Ms. Hart was aware, for example, of Sara's sound sensitivities and, of course, of her early fussiness, she had not understood her hypersensitivity to too much stimulation. Thus, in an effort to be a better mother than her own, and feeling guilty about her depressive withdrawal, she tried to provide her daughter with the cognitive stimulation she never got. So, besides talking to her a lot, she surrounded her with "infant-stimulation" paraphernalia—lots of black-and-white-striped objects and toys—which she dumped in her crib. The effects on Sara were to catapult her into disorganization and heightened periods of negative tension. This state of being so easily overwhelmed can adversely affect the development of signal anxiety (e.g., anxiety that warns and elicits coping defenses) which in turn can make the child yet more prone to disorganizing diffuse anxiety states.

What Ms. Hart also had not known was how difficult it is for hyperreactive children like Sara, who also have difficulty in reading affect, to be regulated by their parents or to self-calm, and that they typically tend to avert eye gaze and resist being held. These are typical early forms of coping with too much stimulation, not rejection. But such behaviors can make a mother, especially one vulnerable to depression as was Ms. Hart, feel rejected, and can lead her to project onto the child negative motives so that she ends up believing the baby actively dislikes her. The already poor quality of mutual regulation is then likely to become even worse.

In Sara's case, the behavioral manifestations of as-yet-unrecognized neuropsychological difficulties became interpreted and enmeshed in the fantasies and fears of the parents and caused problems in the parent-child interactive system very early on. Here vulnerabilities and challenges in the child escalated psychic conflict in the parent and rebounded back again to affect the child's cognitive growth and personality development. The neuropsychologically vulnerable child puts a hard developmental task onto any parent; for a parent with her own baggage, it is that much more difficult. The results, in Sara, were a compounding and exacerbation of those behaviors that had a neurogenic basis, such as perseveration, distractibility, and disorganization, with a concomitant increase in anxieties and poor coping skills.

Diagnostic summary

Axis I: **Primary Diagnosis**
Regulatory Disorder—Type I—Hypersensitive.

Axis II: **Relationship Disorder Classification**
Overinvolved/underinvolved tendencies.

Axis III: **Medical and Developmental Disorders and Conditions**
Mixed receptive-expressive language disorder, chronic otitis media, allergies.

Axis IV: **Psychosocial Stressors**
Mild enduring effects of psychiatric illness in parent.

Axis V: **Functional Emotional Developmental Level**
Has attained mutual attention, mutual engagement, interactive intentionality and reciprocity, and representational/affective communication, with constrictions related to her regulatory difficulties.

PIR-GAS: 40 (Disturbed)

Making the differential diagnosis: Neuropsychological underpinnings to Sara's fearful, cautious, and bizarre behavior

This case illustrates that making a differential diagnosis of a Regulatory Disorder entails not only assessing that there are constitutional challenges in the child along with behavioral symptoms but also understanding how these constitutional or neuropsychological difficulties are coupled with or interwoven with psychological conflict. In Sara's case, diagnosis of an Axis I Anxiety Disorder can be ruled out with a Regulatory Disorder clearly taking precedence because her fearful, cautious, withdrawn, and even bizarre behaviors had primary underpinnings in her particular areas of neuropsychological compromise. Moreover, while parental difficulties contributed to the problem and a disturbance in the parent-child relationship was a source of Sara's problematic emotional development, these environmental stresses were themselves exacerbated by the unrecognized Regulatory Disorder. The neurogenic disability could be seen as the critical underpinning for both the child's emotional and behavioral symptoms as well as an important complicating factor in the quality of the parent-child relationship. Here, then, the Regulatory Disorder diagnosis takes precedence and the caregiving-interaction patterns are expressed in Axis II.

One could, then, ask the following questions explicitly about Sara's presenting symptoms. Was it anxiety that was principally responsible for Sara's withdrawn behavior on the playground and in the classroom during singing time? Or was her behavior in part due to her dyspraxias? Was she withdrawn and noninteractive with others, at least in part, because of her receptive language problems, because of her sensed inadequacy in being able to reliably understand the meaning of what was being said to her? Was her isolation from others fueled also by her organizational difficulties, which so clearly infected her play and her responsivity to others? Sara would go off on tangents and easily "lose set" or focus, as well as the established connection to another. This made her pragmatics look poor, and her interactions lack extended, reciprocal turn-taking volleys.

Many of Sara's emotional preoccupations and "anxious worries" seemed to be engendered, if not exacerbated, by a cognitive inability to readily shift focus or mood. This "being stuck," overwhelmed by negative affect and tension, and tendency to diffuse anxiety states also had a long history in her sensory integration problems and poor affect processing, as these were overlooked or misinterpreted by others.

Even some of Sara's "bizarre" behaviors seemed very much a part of her particular neuropsychological profile, which featured a semantic pragmatic developmental language disorder in which expressive skills are better than receptive, excellent rote verbal memory is combined with weak semantic processing of content, and organizational problems are prominent. Such children, as was the case with Sara, may develop "scripts" that they often rehearse over and over again and either insert at inappropriate times into conversations because they do not fully understand the content of what they are saying, or use in seeming monologues with themselves. This, above all, gives others the sense that these children are "bizarre." But if, instead of interpreting this behavior as evidence of social problems and unrelatedness, one listens closely to such rehearsed scripts, one often hears messages from remembered significant interactions. In other words, sometimes the scripts are not evidence of social unconnectedness but, on the contrary, are used by the child as transitional phenomena, to mediate connectedness to others.[3]

---

3. It is important to clarify that some children with semantic pragmatic disorders may have a pervasive developmental disorder, or MSDD. Bishop (1989), for example, discusses the overlap with Asperger's syndrome and autism. Rapin and Allen (1987) reported that 28 percent of preschool children with autistic spectrum disorders had a semantic pragmatic type of language disorder. These children also use "scripts," but with more bizarre and interpersonally irrelevant topics. Important to note, however, is that, according to Rapin and Allen, language disorder subtype does not differentiate between children with autistic spectrum disorders and children with DLD. Both groups show the same types of language disorders (except that children with autistic spectrum disorders do not have pure expressive disorders). In their study, 7 percent of children with DLD had a semantic pragmatic type of disorder. In my research 15 percent of children with DLD had semantic pragmatic types of profiles (the neuropsychological "C" subtype). The presence of a particular type of language disorder is, therefore, not a sufficient condition for diagnosing MSDD, PDD NOS, or Autistic Disorder. Since children with semantic pragmatic disorders usually do have social interaction difficulties, it can sometimes, however, make differential diagnosis more problematic. (In years past, in fact, some of these children were among those too often misdiagnosed as having a "thought disorder" rather than a linguistic-cognitive deficit.) In Sara's case, her emotional relatedness and engagement, symbolic play, and level of verbal and nonverbal communicativeness all made a diagnosis of MSDD or PDD NOS unlikely. For children who are lower functioning, have less language, less symbolic play, and whose relatedness may be more compromised, the boundaries become more blurred and diagnosis more challenging.

Discussion with caregivers and treatment planning

Mr. and Ms. Hart appeared relieved to hear that there were identifiable reasons for so many of Sara's behaviors. Accurate diagnostic formulation had the effect of demystifying the difficulties and tempering the anxieties that had taken a stranglehold on their understanding and interactions. Also, because the evaluation of Sara's strengths and problematic areas, as well as the family's, was so detailed, specific recommendations addressing core issues could be made. The family was glad to be given a diagnostic formulation that was adjoined to a plan of action.

The feedback information, however, was too much to process actively and use after just one or two informing sessions. Long-adhered to ways of understanding and dealing with Sara led to the need for ongoing supportive sessions. In this way, discussion and appropriation of the findings, along with constructive change, were facilitated at a pace and in a way that the parents felt comfortable with.

Critical to the treatment plan was understanding the ways neuropsychological weakness had been involved and had interfaced with others' reactions so as to affect interaction patterns, Sara's coping style, and personality development. The need presented itself, on the one hand, to work therapeutically on Sara's heightened anxieties, disorganization, and difficulties in mood and self-regulation while actively incorporating an understanding of the neuropsychological weaknesses underlying them and how to address them: Therapy with the child would be modified then to incorporate remedial-type strategies. On the other hand, what also had to be addressed were the parent-child interaction patterns and family issues that were affected by and, in turn, affecting Sara. Thus, the family and therapist decided that treatment should include twice weekly psychotherapy sessions with Sara together with her mother. These joint sessions would attempt to address both aspects of the child-parent system that needed support to facilitate change: They would focus on strengthening Sara's coping and regulatory capacities while facilitating more adaptive engagement between mother and child.

Mr. and Ms. Hart understanding of Sara's weaknesses and sensitivities, and of how to compensate for them, also at home, would be taken up in a more focused way in separate once-a-week parental guidance sessions without Sara. These meetings would also be used to further discuss the parents feelings or, more generally, the impact that caring for Sara was having on them individually and as a couple.

The therapist recommended that individual therapy sessions with Ms. Hart might be valuable in helping her come to terms with her own complicated reactions to her past which, rekindled by her concerns and reactions to her daughter, were spilling over into her present relationships. (Although sometimes, a parent may benefit from her own private therapist, in this instance, issues related to the mother were bound to surface in the joint sessions with Sara, which could then be brought up again and productively used in the mother's own sessions.)

In addition, the therapist recommended that Sara enter a structured half-day intervention program. Given the extent of her organizational, language, and motor planning difficulties, such a program could provide her with a small peer group environment where predictable routine and structure could foster learning, cooperation, and a sense of well-being. It could also give on-site language and occupational therapy to address directly her language, sensory, and motor planning difficulties, and so obviate the organizational stress that would befall Ms. Hart were she to have to arrange and coordinate this herself. In a small school classroom, moreover, there would be many adult-enhanced opportunities for free play and more focused attempts to mediate interactive peer play for Sara.

The therapist suggested that Sara consult a pediatric allergist, for evaluation and control of her oft-occurring allergies, and that the family consult an audiologist trained in auditory integration training for possible treatment of Sara's hypersensitivities to sound.

Intervention

The therapist helped the family in finding out how to obtain funding for an intervention program as well as in selecting the best program for Sara. An important consideration in program choice was the extent to which sensory input would be regulated, and how calm and nurturing an atmosphere would be available. Given Sara's hypersensitivities, a classroom was sought where toys and materials were stored neatly and presented in simple and uncluttered ways, distractions were kept to a minimum, sounds and noise regulated, transitions through busy areas avoided. The therapist and family sought a program with a multidisciplinary approach, where the teacher would incorporate into the classroom curriculum some of the goals and strategies of the other professionals working with Sara, and where coordination with the outside therapist and the family would also be routinely embraced. Fortunately, such a program was found. The teacher was very sensitive to Sara's receptive language and organizational-attentional difficulties and was able to reduce verbal comprehension demands, help Sara with shifts in her everyday routine, and help her participate in activities (e.g., to motor plan during circle time singing or on the playground) through simple verbal rehearsal of what was expected along with nonpressured practice over time. An occupational therapist trained in sensory integration also advised on brushing and other self-calming and focusing techniques, which became part of Sara's everyday school routine.

Therapy sessions with Sara and Ms. Hart fostered mother-daughter engagement and connectedness through floor-time-type principles (Greenspan, 1992) where the child's lead is followed and elaborated upon, attentional focus is enhanced, and symbolic play is extended and made more interactive. In order for this to work, Ms. Hart needed to apply much of what she had been unaware of about Sara. This included reducing her language input to Sara; adding drama to the play, which would build on Sara's own focus while using more exaggerated affect, in face and voice; helping Sara engage in longer sequences of play through, for example, helping her to understand cause and effect and by modeling such sequences for her ("If baby doesn't see daddy, then she will be sad, and then she will cry"); and reducing Sara's distractibility by presenting a minimum of toys and by punctuating Sara's abrupt attentional shifts with gently spoken statements like "If you want to stop playing with ____, let's put it away first." This had the impact of reminding Sara of what she had just forgotten, and made any shift more willful and conscious. Sara's poor modulation of affect was addressed by helping her elaborate and recognize in more representational ways, such as through play and language, those times when she would fall apart, feel anxious, and lose control. This was important for helping to develop signal anxiety—for helping Sara, and Ms. Hart as well, understand and anticipate situations and feelings that could lead to intense experiences of disorganization. More effective calming and coping strategies could then also be played out in the therapy hour as well as at home.

The therapeutic process was particularly beneficial for Ms. Hart because she came to see how she could gain Sara's positive responsivity to her. The joyful gleam in Sara's eye, seen during the evaluation as something she was so capable of, finally became directed to and joined by her mother. Ms. Hart began to feel admired by her daughter, and positive interactions began increasingly more to characterize their relationship.

The approach of following the child's lead was of particular value for Sara because it helped raise her subjective sense of control, accomplishment, and mastery, and so provided an important antidote to her tendency to anxiously withdraw, tune out, and be self-directed in her play. Ms. Hart' attunement to her sensitivities and weaknesses, in particular her being overwhelmed by too much stimulation, her problems integrating input from different modalities at the same time, and her limited semantic comprehension and closing down when spoken to incessantly, began to lessen Sara's tendency to disorganize and subjectively feel out of control. For Sara, it thus also added to increasingly more positive experiences of the self as capable of feeling affectively well-modulated, especially while being with a significant other. This went a long way in helping Sara's regulatory difficulties.

The parental guidance sessions were instrumental for reviewing impressions of therapy sessions, for problem-solving issues that were recurrent at home, and for helping integrate the school's goals and strategies with those of the family and therapy. Issues that came up included how to manage Sara's negative behaviors, her crying, tantrums, and perseverative tendencies, which were more prevalent at home. Specific strategies were discussed, for example, to make the home routine also more predictable and structured for Sara, especially the parents comings and goings; to arrange her bedroom and play areas in a simple way free of clutter; for her toys to be put away in an organized way; and for soft, calming places to be made available to retreat to. Firm but kind limit-setting was practiced to deal with tantrums, whining, and negative behaviors. Although the auditory integration training, which was carried out, appeared to help some of Sara's hypersensitivities to sounds, she continued to be sensitive to her mother's music and other sounds at home. One strategy that appeared to work was to get Sara her own musical instruments to play, and allow her to control other noise-making things, such as a taped recording of her mother's music, making it louder and softer, and turning it on and off. Calming strategies were also developed, always keeping in mind Sara's hypersensitivities.

Individual therapy sessions with Ms. Hart became quite important to Sara's treatment. For example, an obstacle presented itself early on: Ms. Hart started to doubt that Sara had any problems understanding language, and began anew to talk constantly and in an overly verbose way to her. This occurred at a point when Ms. Hart felt the therapy was not making adequate progress, and that Sara's behaviors weren't changing fast enough. At this time, in individual sessions Ms. Hart started to describe herself as having been a verbally precocious child who spoke in full sentences at age one. Thus, Ms. Hart, who had originally seen little similarity between herself and her daughter, and who didn't want to see any similarity, began to see Sara's expressive language abilities—her loquacious vocabulary and her ability to repeat long strings of words her mother said to her—as being the one area in which she could identify with Sara. Her hopes for things normalizing had been shaken by a period of what she perceived as little movement in Sara's therapy. Denial of Sara's language issues in some way helped her, during this period of uncertainty, to remain connected to Sara and connected to the hope of things being normal for Sara, and for Sara and herself. In sessions, she became more aware of this wish, also as it reflected on hopes, repeatedly threatened, for herself and her larger family. In individual sessions she was also able to explore the anger she felt especially toward her mother, and the ambivalence she felt toward her own success. Most importantly, individual sessions allowed Ms. Hart to obtain the needed attention and recognition that she felt she had never gotten. In turn, she was able to give that much more to Sara.

Discussion

In sum, this case of a Regulatory Disorder illustrates how constitutional and maturational challenges in the child are taken up actively and psychodynamically and affect the child's emotional well-being and behavior. Neuropsychological dysfunction plays a role in how self-image, personality, defenses, and relations to others develop. Comprehensive neuropsychological assessments that pay heed to psychological dynamics and family systems considerations are thought to be a vital tool for differential diagnosis and for providing guidelines for appropriate intervention. The medium for intervention becomes, in part, the education of the parent to who the child is and what the fantasies and misreadings are that the parent, because of his or her own history, may bring to the exchange. Intervention with the child and the parent is guided directly by knowledge of the constitutional make-up of the child. Accurate diagnostic assessment of a Regulatory Disorder can thus be critical in outlining a therapeutic course of action. Understanding the child's strengths as well as weaknesses can be used to support more effective coping strategies as well as compensatory strategies, and so enhance overall development. Disclosing positive avenues of access to the child, through the child's open channels or strengths, while, at the same time, keeping in mind the dysfunctional channels and their impact on both the child and others, can be used as an important instrument of intervention in the service of adaptive relatedness.

References:

Bishop, D.V.M. (1989). Autism, Asperger's syndrome and semantic-pragmatic disorder: Where are the boundaries? *British Journal of Disorders of Communication*, 24, 107-121.

Black, L.M. (1988)..Subtypes of language disordered children at risk for social-emotional problems. *Dissertation Abstracts International 1989*, 50-3B (University Microfilms, No. 8910782.

Black, L. M. (1993, April). *Neuropsychological subtypes of developmentally language disordered children: Problems in affect discrimination and emotional adjustment.* Paper presented at the meeting of the New York Neuropsychology Group, New York, N.Y.

Black, L. M. (1994, February). *Affect processing problems of preschool-aged language disordered children.* Paper presented at the meeting of the International Neuropsychological Society, Cincinnati, Ohio.

Greenspan, S.I. (1992). *Infancy and early childhood: The practice of clinical assessment and intervention with emotional and developmental challenges.* Madison, CT.: International Universities Press.

Rapin, I. & Allen, D. (1983). Developmental language disorders: Nosologic considerations (pp. 154-184). In U. Kirk (Ed.), *Neuropsychology of language, reading, and spelling.* NY: Academic Press.

Rapin, I. & Allen, D. (1987). Developmental Dysphasia and Autism in Preschool Children: Characteristics and Subtypes. (pp. 20-35). *In Proceedings of the first International Symposium on Specific Speech and Lang-age Disorders in Children.* London: Association For All Speech Impaired Children (AFASIC).

Rapin, I., Allen, D. , & Dunn, M. (1992). Developmental language disorders. In S. E. Galowitz & I. Rapin (Eds.), *Handbook of neuropsychology,* Volume 7: Child Neuropsychology (pp.111-137). Amsterdam: Elsevier.

Wilson, B.C. & Risucci, D. (1986). A model for clinical-quantitative classification. Generation I: Application to language disordered preschool children. *Brain and Language,* 27, 281-309.

ZERO TO THREE. (1994). *Diagnostic classification of mental health and developmental disorders of infancy and early childhood.* Arlington, VA: ZERO TO THREE: National Center for Clinical Infant Programs.

400. Regulatory Disorders

401. Type I: Hypersensitive. Fearful and Cautious

G. Gordon Williamson, Ph.D., OTR
Gambi White-Tennant, M. S., Ed.

It is understandable why parents and practitioners tend to focus on the motor challenges of a child with a physical disability. Children with cerebral palsy, spina bifida, and other developmental disabilities have neurological and orthopedic requirements that demand attention. However, this case study is presented to illustrate that the *DC: 0-3* diagnostic classification system is also applicable to these children. As part of a comprehensive assessment, it is important to consider the presence of these other diagnostic conditions that may be independent of the physical disability or associated with it. In this instance, Nathan was a toddler with cerebral palsy and spastic quadriplegia (total body involvement). The key to the assessment process and his eventual intervention was realizing the profound impact of a regulatory disorder on his behavior and development.

Reason for referral

Ms. Moore contacted the nearest early intervention program that served children with developmental disabilities. The program was located at a regional rehabilitation center. She and her husband had recently relocated to the area to pursue employment opportunities. Ms. Moore stated that her only child, Nathan, was 16 months of age and had cerebral palsy with spastic quadriplegia. She was interested in obtaining physical therapy because of her son's poor motor development. It was apparent from this initial contact that the family was eligible for state-supported early intervention services due to the diagnosis of cerebral palsy. The assessment process needed to generate an Individualized Family Service Plan (IFSP).

Assessment process

Since one purpose of the assessment was to develop an IFSP, a multidisciplinary team was involved. It included the parents, an educator, social worker, physical therapist, occupational therapist, and speech pathologist. This team composition was larger than typically used by the early intervention program because of the complex needs of Nathan and his family. Following state guidelines, the assessment addressed the child's unique strengths and vulnerabilities related to physical, cognitive, communicative, and social/emotional and adaptive development. Likewise, a family-directed assessment needed to include the parents' concerns, priorities, and resources. The resulting IFSP identified specific services necessary to support the family and enhance the child's developmental and coping competence.

The intake phone call was the beginning of the assessment-intervention process. Based upon mutual agreement by the team and the parents, the assessment period involved four components over the following month. The social worker conducted the initial home visit to develop a relationship with the family, gather background information, observe the child and family in the home, and to discuss the early intervention program and the anticipated assessment procedure. This session was followed by a team assessment conducted by the interdisciplinary staff and parents at the center. As a result of the team assessment, the occupational therapist conducted a second home visit. The fourth component of the assessment was a meeting with the parents and practitioners to design the IFSP and discuss Nathan's classification.

Assessment findings

Intake phone call

The initial contact by the family with the service provider is considered not only the beginning of the assessment process but also the initiation of intervention. Often the parent's initial phone call to an early intervention program is associated with an array of mixed emotions, such as worry about the child, fear of the unknown, and relief that one is finally pursuing a course of action. Because of these complex dynamics, the program has a social worker receiving the intake calls. The social worker's major concern is to be responsive to the family and begin the process of establishing communication and trust. Extensive data collection by the social worker is not the focus of the intake call.

During the initial phone call Ms. Moore repeatedly expressed concern about Nathan's poor motor development and her interest in his receiving physical therapy. She stated that his sitting balance was poor, and he used rolling and limited crawling for mobility. Nathan had received physical therapy prior to moving to this community. Ms. Moore stated that he was highly resistant and uncooperative during these weekly sessions. She felt that the therapy had not been very beneficial given his slow progress and that he needed more intensive physical therapy in order to make up for his delay. Ms. Moore was not particularly concerned with the other aspects of Nathan's development because "if we improve his coordination, everything else will fall into place." The social worker suggested that a home visit by her might be beneficial, and Ms. Moore readily agreed. They discussed the nature and purpose of the visit and made specific arrangements.

The social worker's clinical impression after the intake call was that Ms.

Moore was very articulate and deeply concerned about her son's well-being. The mother gave the impression of being quite anxious by her rapid speech and repetition of thoughts during the conversation.

Initial home visit

When the social worker arrived, Nathan was unexpectedly having a nap. Ms. Moore took this opportunity to talk intensely about Nathan and her family. She shared that she and her husband had been married for ten years with a history of unsuccessful pregnancies. Despite a troublesome prenatal course, they remained excited about the prospect of having a child.

Ms. Moore shared copies of Nathan's medical reports and stated that her pregnancy was significant. There was spotting in the first trimester with bed rest required for two weeks. Nathan was born two months premature with a single umbilical artery and collapsed lung. He was in the intensive care unit for six weeks where he was treated for a number of medical problems, including hyaline membrane disease. During this period he had several incidences of respiratory distress and was eventually discharged with an apnea monitor. At this time the parents assumed that Nathan was essentially healthy except for his prematurity. The apnea monitor was discontinued after one month. Due to his medical history, he was enrolled in the high risk follow-up clinic at the medical center.

Nathan was periodically seen in the follow-up clinic until eight months of age when he was diagnosed with cerebral palsy. Up to this time, Mr. and Ms. Moore had no concerns about their son except that their relationship with him was "not easy." Their comfort with caregiving was strained due to problems with eating, sleeping, and general behavior. From the beginning, Nathan was difficult to feed with a poor suck, frequent gagging, and bouts of reflux. He had erratic sleeping patterns with particular difficulty staying asleep for any period of time. Since the parents felt that his cranky, demanding behavior was due to "prematurity and chronic colic," they were not prepared for the diagnosis of cerebral palsy. Ms. Moore stated that there was a period of shock and grieving in which she and her husband basically withdrew from outside activities and used each other for support. They focused on "figuring out ways to help Nathan get stronger." At this time they enrolled him in an early intervention program which provided physical therapy. He received this service until the time of the family's relocation.

Mr. Moore worked in construction as a site supervisor, and Ms. Moore was a part-time lab technician. They arranged their schedules so that the father worked during the day and the mother worked at night. This arrangement assured that one parent was always with Nathan. Ms. Moore reported that they had a strong marriage with their occasional disagreements related to the best way to raise their son. Since they were new to the community, their social network was limited, with the greatest support derived from friends at their church.

The discussion between Ms. Moore and the social worker was interrupted by the waking of Nathan. Although the mother greeted him with a welcoming smile, he was fussy. When he saw the social worker, however, he became hysterical. The mother reported that he had a low tolerance for strangers and, indeed, was upset whenever anyone except close relatives came to visit. Nathan seldom was left with a baby sitter due to his anxious reaction. Ms. Moore attempted to calm him with a bottle and rocking. The boy responded with increased agitation and stiffening of his body into extension. Eventually, he fell into a restless sleep.

The mother stated that this behavioral pattern was typical in the home. Nathan had poor self-comforting skills and could not bounce back after stressful events. Commonly after becoming upset, he would cry excessively while she tried to soothe him. When he became composed, he would fall asleep from exhaustion and the mother would feel alone and inadequate. Ms. Moore was teary when she shared this information and said, "He's so hard to understand. . . to know what he really wants." This statement led to a discussion of the mother's feelings of disappointment, confusion, and frustration.

Before leaving, the social worker spent time describing the early intervention services and the parents' active role in determining the program components best suited for their family. Particular attention was given to the preferred way to implement the assessment process. The social worker helped Ms. Moore to understand that early intervention was concerned with all developmental areas of the child and the well being of the family. From this discussion, Ms. Moore concurred that an interdisciplinary view of Nathan would be most profitable but was worried that so many people in the home would be "too much for him to handle." The social worker suggested that the assessment could be conducted at the center since an observation booth would be available for the interdisciplinary team. They planned specific details of the assessment experience, such as the best time for the appointment, the format of the session, the role the parents wished to play, and which of Nathan's favorite toys and activities would promote his adjustment.

Clinical impressions

From the home visit it was clear to the social worker that Nathan had multiple developmental delays. He appeared to have a minimally effective coping style, with great difficulty in managing changes in everyday living. The social worker speculated that Nathan's fear was secondary to a poor ability to self-regulate. She hypothesized that his rigid and controlling behaviors were attempts to cope with routine and novel situations that he considered threatening. His physical limitations and low sensory threshold caused him to react with alarm. Ms. Moore was overwhelmed by his lack of self-comforting ability, his slow developmental progress, and the physical and emotional demands of daily caregiving. The social worker wondered if a classification of a relationship disorder was indicated since there was such stress in the mother-child interaction. Another concern was identifying more clearly the reasons for Nathan's marked cautiousness and irritability.

Team assessment

The social worker greeted Mr. and Ms. Moore when they arrived at the early intervention program. She introduced them to the team members and previewed the assessment procedure with them. As had been previously determined, the occupational therapist would conduct the developmental assessment in a play format with the parents and Nathan. The occupational therapist had been chosen because of her combined skills in motor development and sensory processing. The rest of the interdisciplinary team—the physical therapist, speech pathologist and teacher— would stay in the observation booth The social worker would remain in the assessment room to support the parents and facilitate communication. Only the parents would physically handle Nathan due to the poor tolerance and irritability that he demonstrated during the home visit.

The session began with a request for the parents to play freely with Nathan in whatever way they felt comfortable. A variety of toys were provided, and they could choose to play on the floor, at a child-size table and chair, or on adult-size furniture. Ms. Moore took the lead by placing Nathan on the floor and introducing a series of toys at a rather brisk pace. Nathan was very particular about the types of toys that he preferred. He was restricted in the sensory properties that he would tolerate. In the tactile arena, he avoided light touch and disliked many textures. Visually, Nathan was overly sensitive to bright light and distracted by high contrast, colorful toys. Auditorially, he had a startle reaction to high frequency sounds and would cover his ears to decrease the stimulation. The child also had a strange tolerance to physical movement. He craved rough-house play with his father and yet feared being moved in space. All of these signs of hypersensitivity were apparent in Nathan's play with objects and his interactions with his parents as well as the practitioners. In general, he was leery of the professionals and preferred to have them sit at a distance.

Nathan's motor disability limited many of his experiences. His sitting position was somewhat precarious, and his ability to reach and grasp objects was labored and slow. A long period of time was required for him to determine and execute a plan of action. The mother often failed to take into account this prolonged latency in movement. As a result, she did not give Nathan time to play with toys before introducing a new one. This fast pace often resulted in his forcefully pushing the novel toy away or throwing it. A couple of times the father intervened to change the direction of the play. Once he softly sang a lullaby to Nathan and at another time he "chased" Nathan as they both crawled on all fours. During this game of "I'm going to catch you," Nathan showed the most enjoyment of the entire session.

At one point, rather unexpectedly, Nathan began to cry vigorously. Ms. Moore picked him up, held him against her shoulder, patted him on the back, and repeatedly asked him to quiet down. She then walked him around the room, sat down on the couch, turned Nathan upside-down while picking up a towel from the floor to wipe his mouth. She then introduced his bottle while bouncing him on her lap and, after his refusal to drink, she stood up and started swaying back and forth. The result of these actions was an increasing escalation of Nathan's hysteria and the mother's associated frustration. At this time, she handed Nathan to the father who was able to gradually calm him with a limited number of consoling gestures.

After this incident, the social worker suggested that it was a good time for Nathan to have a snack. This break provided an opportunity to observe Nathan's feeding skills and more interactions with his parents. At this time, team members in the observation booth requested some additional "testing" to be conducted in order to address unanswered questions, such as degree of unsolicited vocalization, purposeful problem solving, and joint range of motion. They also asked for more information about Nathan's coping in the home environment and how representative was his present performance to his behavior in daily living. After the snack, the occupational therapist tried to engage Nathan in additional activities in order to respond to the team's questions. He fussed and was uncooperative despite the parents becoming active in getting his involvement. It soon became apparent that Nathan was tired and overloaded from the accumulated sensory stimulation. Nathan was then placed in his stroller and given his favorite blanket while the Moores and the practitioners met for a brief discussion.

The conversation initially focused on general impressions of Nathan's developmental status. His expressive and receptive language skills were discussed as areas of relative strength. Nathan was able to communicate with his parents through simple words and gestures when the tempo of the conversation was unhurried. At these times he could show interest, express his wants, and demonstrate pleasure in social interaction. Motor development was the area of greatest deficit. The team also identified delays in the cognitive and adaptive domain. The parents said they were surprisingly relieved by the discussion since it allowed unstated worries to be addressed openly.

A team member observed that a possible source of Nathan's irritability and misbehavior could be related to his sensory intolerance. The parents immediately responded to this possibility by sharing examples of his "picky and demanding" behavior that seemed to be associated with sensory experiences. Consequently, it was decided that the occupational therapist would make a home visit to address the critical area of sensory processing and how it influenced Nathan's functioning and family life. The mother reported a host of difficulties in such areas as feeding, dressing, bathing and play. At the same time, the therapist would attempt to finish parts of the developmental assessment that had not been completed. The therapist scheduled an appointment for the visit with the Moores.

Clinical impressions

The practitioners were pleased with the emerging comfort and trust that the Moores were establishing with the early intervention program. Already the parents had a broader developmental picture of their son and realized that cerebral palsy is more than a physical disability. A particular concern was

Nathan's general cautious, inhibited behavior with episodic periods of fearful crying and tantrums. It appeared that he had a very narrow zone of sensory tolerance. His irritability and frequent outbursts seemed related to hypersensitivity. From a generally flat, rather disconnected, behavioral state, it seemed to take a minimal amount of sensory input to throw him into overload. This coupling of a distinct behavioral pattern to sensory processing dysfunction indicated the very real possibility of a regulatory disorder. His hyperreactivity was too significant to be merely an associated condition of the cerebral palsy diagnosis. The home visit by the occupational therapist would allow careful scrutiny of his sensory status and its relationship to his presenting behaviors.

Formal testing of Nathan was limited due to his negativity, physical disability, and resistance to anyone handling him but his parents. Data were gathered through clinical observation and parental interview with sections of the following instruments informally administered: Hawaii Early Learning Profile (Parks, 1992), Ordinal Scales of Psychological Development (Uzgiris & Hunt, 1975) and the Erhardt Developmental Prehension Assessment (Erhardt, 1982). At a corrected age of 14 months, his receptive and expressive language were approximately at the 10-to-14 month age level. Nathan understood simple sentences and communicated through gestures and a limited functional vocabulary (e.g., juice, momma, all gone, mine, eat). His cognitive skills were approximately at a 12-month level (e.g., cause-effect relationships, object permanence). His repertoire of play schemes was limited to such actions as banging, shaking, and patting. However, Nathan showed interest in favorite toys and was persistent in his play with them.

In the social-emotional arena, he had difficulty separating from his parents and adjusting to babysitters. He cried when approached by unfamiliar adults, until a parent picked him up and tried to comfort him. He tended to withdraw in new situations by lying on his back and sucking his thumb, even when given a warm-up period to adjust. Nathan was not responsive to limit setting, and there was a minimal ability to delay gratification. He tended to be most comfortable when left alone. At these times, the parents reported that he occasionally "spaces out."

Skills in motor development varied from 5-to-8 months of age typified by a poor quality of movement. Muscle tone in the trunk was low but spastic in the arms and legs. As a result, gross motor skills were restricted, and balance was poor. He was able to roll with effort and move into a sitting position. In sitting, reach and grasp patterns were uncoordinated so that he had difficulty exploring objects manually. His primary means of mobility was crawling on all fours at a slow, effortful speed. The parents presently pushed him in a stroller and were ambivalent about purchasing a wheelchair which was increasingly needed. He also required adaptive equipment to provide postural stability while sitting on a chair or on the floor.

The mother-child relationship seemed strained due to a poor fit between the partners. Ms. Moore had a very active, intense personality which was not in easy synchrony with Nathan's passive and cautious demeanor. As a result, she had difficulty reading his cues and tended to do too much too fast. His response was to overload, cry, and reject her consoling efforts. This pattern seemed to make activities of daily living stressful for all concerned. Mr. Moore appeared to be rather quiet and reserved. In order to be helpful, he would decrease tension by assisting in caregiving and playing with Nathan.

The team used a coping frame of reference for integrating assessment findings and planning intervention (Zeitlin & Williamson, 1994). The practitioners completed an Early Coping Inventory (Zeitlin, Williamson & Szczepanski, 1988) on Nathan in order to assess his coping style. This instrument evaluates the behavioral characteristics of infants and toddlers that are most relevant for successful coping. These attributes are clustered into three descriptive categories—sensorimotor organization, reactive behavior, and self-initiated behavior. Nathan scored in the minimally effective range in each area, due in large part to his rigidly repetitious behavior.

Of greatest clinical use, however, was the identification of his most and least adaptive behaviors. These two lists of coping behaviors were helpful in planning intervention. The list of vulnerabilities provided guidance in setting goals to be addressed. The list of strengths suggested intervention strategies for addressing the designated goals. Nathan's most adaptive behaviors on the Early Coping Inventory were the ability to: complete self-initiated activity, anticipate events, demonstrate persistence, maintain visual attention, exhibit pleasure after successfully accomplishing activities, and display awareness that one's behavior has an effect on others. His least adaptive behaviors were a tendency for sensory overload, poor adaptability to daily routines and changes in the environment, excessive caution in entering new situations, failure to self-comfort, minimally coordinated movements, and problems in accepting substitute people and objects.

During their deliberations using a coping intervention frame of reference, the practitioners identified the demands (stressors) experienced by Nathan, the adequacy of his coping resources that determined his coping efforts, and the environmental feedback he received in response to these efforts. Through parental report and observation of Nathan, the team felt that they had a growing understanding of Nathan's coping transactions and his critical coping resources—emerging beliefs, physical and affective states, developmental skills, human relationships, and material and environmental supports.

Follow-up home visit

When the occupational therapist arrived, Ms. Moore was about to bathe Nathan. The therapist observed the mother struggling with the activity because of Nathan's physical condition. He was fearful of the splashing water, and his body remained stiff throughout the task. The mother did all the work and Nathan showed little interest in social interaction. He seemed to prefer deep pressure when being dried with the towel and clearly found wiping the face, feet, and hands noxious. Nathan became irritable when being dressed as the mother quickly moved him in all directions in order to

put on the diaper and clothing. Ms. Moore slowed the tempo when requested by the therapist, and Nathan seemed to relax with the slower pace.

Nathan was next placed in his high chair and given milk in a two-handle
cup. He drank it independently with great satisfaction and the mother was
clearly pleased. Next, she gave him a bowl of cereal with slices of apple.
Nathan immediately spit it out and refused another bite when being coaxed
by the mother. The therapist shared that the contrasting textures may be difficult for him to manage and suggested that the apples be removed. To the
mother's surprise, Nathan was willing to eat most of his cereal with the
spoon. It was clear that the sharp texture of the apples was adversive to his
oral hypersensitivity.

Nathan was left to play on the floor with some of his favorite toys while
Ms. Moore and the therapist talked about a typical day. They discussed the
daily routine and how Nathan managed each task. They were looking for
patterns of arousal, attention, and affect that would help to explain his
behavior. For example, they looked for characteristic times of fussiness,
cycles of low and high energy, and the types of toys and interactions that he
favored. They identified some reasons that Nathan had temper tantrums
such as anger, frustration, fear of new situations, sudden interruptions, and
sensory overload. This discussion was facilitated by reviewing the Infant and
Toddler Symptoms Checklist (DeGangi & Poisson, 1995) which the parents
had completed prior to the home visit. It provided information regarding
Nathan's sensory-based self-regulation, attention, movement, language, and
activities of daily living.

Since Nathan was cooperative at this time, the occupational therapist
played with him directly on the floor to gain additional information regarding his physical and developmental status. The mother joined them and participated in some action songs at the suggestion of the practitioner. This
interaction led to a game of hide-and-seek which they played with pleasure.
The therapist noted spontaneous expressions of affection between them such
as eye contact, smiling, vocalizing, and gesturing.

At the end of the home visit, the therapist talked with Ms. Moore about
the purpose of the IFSP meeting, making it clear that the specific structure
and format of the meeting would be tailored to their preferences. After discussion, it was determined that the meeting would be held at their home in
the early evening. The parents had previously decided that it would be overwhelming for all of the team members to be present. They wished that the
team's deliberations be represented by the social worker, occupational therapist, and the physical therapist. The disciplinary perspectives of the teacher
and speech pathologist would be shared in the meeting. Ms. Moore said that
she would have one of her friends from church attend Nathan during the
meeting so they would not be interrupted. There was discussion regarding
what role the Moores would like to have in the meeting so that it would be
most comfortable and helpful. The mother said that both of them would
like to play an active role in the development of the IFSP.

Diagnosis

The occupational therapist discussed her findings with the other team members. It appeared that Nathan's poor self-regulation was due to his neurological deficit. The challenge to the team was whether to classify Nathan as having a Regulatory Disorder or merely hyperreactivity associated with his cerebral palsy. Secondary sensory problems are common in this condition. A distinct regulatory disorder was eventually established due to the following factors: (a) the severity of his hypersensitivity was greater than typically seen in cerebral palsy; (b) the sensory dysfunction was linked to a behavioral pattern characterized as excessive irritability, cautiousness and fearfulness; (c) he was globally hypersensitive to touch, sight, sound, and movement; and (d) his minimally effective coping style was intricately connected with his poor self-regulation. To avoid sensory overload, Nathan became rigid and resistant to change. He had a very narrow range for modulating his sensory threshold, arousal, and affect. Consequently, he became easily upset and found it difficult to self-comfort and recover from distress. His classification was a Regulatory Disorder; Type I: Hypersensitive; Pattern: Fearful and Cautious.

As noted, the mother-child relationship was under ongoing strain. However, two observations suggested an underlying health in the relationship. Nathan and his mother were observed playing with delight during part of the second home visit. Each partner clearly expressed affection and warmth when they interacted reciprocally. The other significant observation was that Ms. Moore could adapt her caregiving based on the therapist's suggestions. When asked to slow her tempo and follow the child's lead, the mother adjusted her pace and recognized that Nathan was performing more effectively. As a result of these observations, the team decided that a relationship disorder classification was not indicated. The stress in the parent-child relationship was due primarily to difficulties in social reciprocity and communication.

Nathan experienced significant stress when interacting with people and managing his daily activities. The stress appeared to be heightened by the mother's anxiety regarding caregiving and the child's rigid, minimally effective coping style. Nathan seemed frustrated by the motor limitations caused by his cerebral palsy. Likewise, his irritability and inflexibility were related to his hypersensitivity and arousal level. All of these stressors contributed to derailing Nathan's adaptation.

Nathan functioned at expected levels in mutual attention and engagement but with constrictions. He did not perform at these levels when under stress, and he lacked a full range of affect (e.g., cautiousness and fear tended to override spontaneous expressions of intimacy and closeness). Likewise, there was a discrepancy between parents in his attention and engagement, with an easier fit demonstrated with the father. The best engagement occurred when the environment was free of distractions and took into account Nathan's hypersensitivity, when interactions were paced slowly to allow time for him to respond, and when sensory support was available to elicit pleasure and curiosity. The capacity to attend and stay engaged was undermined when Nathan became overwhelmed and could not regulate his emotions.

Interactive intentionality and reciprocity were most evident when Nathan moved on his own and could be self-initiating and in control, such as the joy experienced when playing chase with his father and hide-and-seek with his mother. Reciprocal interactions also occurred when Ms. Moore was less tense, and Nathan's physiological status was stable. He seemed to connect best with others when he had an opportunity to choose, explore, and relate at his own pace. The number of circles of communication were not, however, at age expectation. In general, Nathan's ability to initiate and respond reciprocally during interactions was restricted and depended on supportive conditions to achieve a good fit.

Diagnostic summary

Axis I: Primary Diagnosis
Regulatory Disorder—Type I Hypersensitive; Pattern: Fearful and Cautious.

Axis II: Relationship Disorder Classification
No diagnosis.

Axis III: Medical and Developmental Disorders and Conditions
Cerebral Palsy, Spastic Quadriplegia.

Axis IV: Psychosocial Stressors
Moderate effects.

Axis V: Functional Emotional Developmental Level
Capable of mutual attention and mutual engagement, with constrictions under stress, and within constricted range of affects. Below age-appropriate level for interactive intentionality and reciprocity, with similar constrictions.

Discussion with caregivers and treatment planning (IFSP meeting)

The social worker, occupational therapist, and physical therapist met with the Moores in their home the following week. They had a wide ranging discussion that addressed Nathan's status in all developmental domains, the nature of his cerebral palsy, and his coping style. His developmental strengths were accentuated to counterbalance the honest discussion of his delays. The parents were helped to understand his problems in movement and posture as well as ways to facilitate his motor development. His ineffective coping was related to a hypersensitive regulatory disorder. The parents found it extremely useful when the occupational therapist discussed how his hypersensitivity was linked to his difficult behavior and their challenges in caregiving. They had never realized that his fearful and cautious behavioral pattern was associated with his problems in sensory processing. The classification of Regulatory Disorder clarified their understanding of Nathan's condition and therefore brought relief. It finally became apparent why "rushing" him generally lead to temper tantrums. Ms. Moore was emotional when she said, "It seems clear now, but it wasn't back then. Finally, an opportunity to get past the frustration."

At a certain point in the discussion, the social worker started writing down some of the developmental, coping, and family outcomes that the parents wished to pursue. Using a coping frame of reference, the intervention outcomes were designed to encourage a good fit between Nathan's coping resources versus environmental demands and expectations so that he could manage daily living with a positive sense of self. In this process he could modify previously learned coping strategies and develop new ones. Intervention was targeted to modify demands so that they were congruent with Nathan's capabilities, enhance his coping resources, and provide appropriate, contingent feedback to his efforts.

The outcomes emphasized improving Nathan's sensory, communicative, motor, and coping competence. For example, Nathan's activities of daily living would be adapted to be more compatible with his sensory tolerances (e.g., accommodate for and eventually diminish hypersensitivity related to feeding, dressing, and sleeping). Nathan would be encouraged to express his thoughts through gestures, signing, and vocalization. Improvements in expressive language should foster a sense of personal control and opportunities for self-initiation. Intervention in the motor domain would be geared to improving sitting balance, functional use of the arms, transitions between positions, and standing.

The Moores were not only intimately involved in developing outcomes but in voicing their commitment to putting the IFSP into practice. Ms. Moore wished to improve her relationship with Nathan and address her confused feelings regarding her functioning as a mother. It was agreed that time would be spent on improving communication and interactions between mother and son. Both parents wished to modify their handling skills so that Nathan could be physically managed with comfort. For example, they wanted to have a variety of ways to lift and carry the child. Mr. Moore requested greater information regarding his son's condition and prognosis. The father stated that he initially felt that "nothing could be done. But now I see that small changes by us can cause big changes in Nathan."

In designing the IFSP, the parents and practitioners agreed that it would be a mistake to do too much too soon. Nathan's program needed to be phased in gradually due to his minimally effective coping style. For the first two months, the occupational therapist would function in a transdisciplinary manner and provide home visits twice a week. The other team members would not work directly with Nathan because of his fearful, defensive behavior. Instead, the other practitioners would temporarily work through the occupational therapist who would incorporate their input within her therapy sessions. At this point, she would be working with the physical therapist in the construction of adaptive equipment, such as chair adaptations and an insert for the stroller. The speech pathologist would provide input regarding management of the child's oral hypersensitivity during feeding, and the teacher offered suggestions for enhancing cognitive development. It was understood that these practitioners would gradually have a more direct involvement as Nathan and his parents adjusted to the early intervention program. During this time, the social worker would meet twice a month with the mother in the home to address some of her social and emotional concerns.

Intervention

After two months, Ms. Moore requested that she participate in a parent discussion group at the center. She said that she felt socially isolated and wanted to be with other families who were "in the same boat." She was able to join a group that was facilitated by her current social worker. Since the sessions were going well with Nathan and the occupational therapist, weekly intervention by the physical therapist was introduced at the center. It was hoped that center-based physical therapy would prepare him to attend a toddler group conducted by the early intervention program. In addition, Mr. Moore joined a six-session educational series that was co-sponsored by the center and other community agencies in the evening. The meetings were designed to gain information related to the management of cerebral palsy and to encourage informal sharing.

Over time, Nathan demonstrated gains in his coping and sensory status. The improvement in his sensory integration seemed to reduce his cautious rigidity. The parents' new skills in handling their son also contributed to his progress. As Nathan developed confidence and a better fit with his environment, the degree of his spasticity lessened and he had greater motor control than originally believed. In other words, his interpretation of the world as a less threatening place freed him to be more physically and psychologically secure and thus more interactive.

As a result of these gains, Nathan was able to be enrolled in a toddler group which was led by the teacher and speech pathologist. This group offered rich experiences in social, adaptive, and language development. His physical and occupational therapists played a supportive role in the group but continued to work with him and his parents during individual sessions. Eventually, Nathan was adequately prepared to participate in a child care program at the local "Y." Nathan received therapy in the context of the program's activities. In addition, the child care staff received consultation regarding his special needs. The early intervention team provided rather substantial support because of the complexity of the cerebral palsy and Regulatory Disorder. Nathan's ability to tolerate a community placement liberated both parents from excessive child care requirements. Ms. Moore was particularly delighted to be free to explore other dimensions of her life. She stated, "I can now see myself as more than a mother of a child with a disability."

Prognosis and discussion

Intervention with children who have a regulatory disorder needs to be targeted at three different dimensions: (a) helping parents understand their child's behavior and fostering nurturing relationships; (b) modification of the environment to facilitate a good fit; and (c) direct intervention strategies designed to remedy identified problems. It is critical to determine the sensory profile or "sensory diet" of the child. This profile reflects the impact of sensory input on the child's arousal and activity levels throughout the day. In Nathan's case there was a major effort to prevent or decrease sensory overload while simultaneously achieving an optimal degree of arousal and engagement. Since his response to sensation built up over time and was cumulative, it was essential that any changes in the amount or type of sensory input be provided slowly and conservatively.

It was also important that Nathan have opportunities to be self-initiating and not always function in a reactive mode. A particularly effective intervention was the provision of a child-size, battery-operated jeep that had been adapted to provide him with postural support. When in the jeep, he was able to practice separation from adults in a more self-generated manner. For example, he would gleefully drive away from his mother in order to explore his surroundings independently. At a certain emotional point, he would return to his mother and drive in circles around her. It was a moment for attachment, refueling and belonging.

A key to working with Nathan and his parents was to realize that his physical disability was not the primary issue of concern. The Regulatory Disorder was a major factor influencing his fearful, irritable behavior and contributed to difficulties in parent-child interaction, motor control, and coping. His initial resistance to physical therapy was due in large part to his hypersensitivity. As long as Nathan felt threatened by environmental demands, he had increased spasticity and decreased balance and coordination. He was not a candidate for motor-oriented therapy without simultaneously addressing his sensory and coping skills. His poor self-regulation was more influential than his physical disability on his behavioral and developmental competence. As he learned to modulate his sensory-based arousal and affect within the context of relationships, Nathan was able to engage the world with greater confidence and success.

References

DeGangi, G. A., & Poisson, S. (1995). *Infant and Toddler Symptom Checklist*. Tucson, AZ: Therapy Skill Builders.

Erhardt, R. P. (1982). *Erhardt Developmental Prehension Assessment* (revised). Tucson, AZ: Therapy Skill Builders.

Parks, S. (1992). *Inside HELP*. Palo Alto, CA: VORT Corporation.

Uzgiris, I. C., & Hunt, J. McV. (1975). *Assessment in infancy: Ordinal Scales of Psychological Development*. Urbana, IL: University of Illinois Press.

Zeitlin, S., & Williamson, G.G. (1994). *Coping in young children: Early intervention practices to enhance adaptive behavior and resilience*. Baltimore, MD: Paul H. Brookes.

Zeitlin, S., Williamson, G.G., & Szczepanski, M. (1988). *Early Coping Inventory*. Bensenville, IL: Scholastic Testing Service.

400. Regulatory Disorders

402. Type II: Under-reactive. Self-absorbed

Barbara Kalmanson, Ph.D.

Regulatory disorders are characterized by the infant or young child's difficulties in regulating behavior and physiological, sensory, attentional, motor, and affective processes. The child has trouble organizing a calm, alert, affectively positive state. These difficulties affect the child's daily adaptation and interpersonal relationships. Infants and young children who are underreactive to various stimuli may show a pattern of self-absorption, seeming to "march to the beat of their own drummer." The case of Jerry presents a variety of behavioral and physiological processes that led to this diagnosis.

Reason for referral

Jerry, 32 months old, was referred by a developmental pediatrician. She initially diagnosed the problems Jerry was having as stemming from the mother's difficulties. She had been treating the mother for anxiety and seeing Jerry intermittently. After a few months, she felt she was not seeing any change in the situation and agreed with the mother to refer the child for a speech and language evaluation. She also referred the family for infant-parent psychotherapy. The pediatrician described Jerry as aloof, in his own world, and awkward. She felt he had sufficient speech when he was motivated to talk. She found the mother anxious and alternately intrusive and withdrawn from the child.

Assessment process

The assessment process involved one-hour meetings at the therapist's office over a six-week period. Sessions were scheduled with both parents, both parents with Jerry, each parent with Jerry, mother alone, and a home visit. The therapist also observed Jerry at his preschool and talked with teachers. After collection and review of all the relevant medical charts and school reports, the therapist referred Jerry for an evaluation with an occupational therapist who specializes in sensory-motor integration. The speech and language therapist the family had been referred to assessed Jerry over the same several weeks period, and shared information with the therapist throughout this process.

Assessment findings

Developmental history

Ms. Green reported that her pregnancy and Jerry's birth were healthy and without complications. She had problems nursing him during his first three weeks until she had help from a nurse who taught her how to feed a baby with a weak sucking reflex. His parents described Jerry in his first year as an "easy baby—the kind you could take to a restaurant and have a nice meal." The only concern they recalled, though noting it in retrospect, was a sensitivity to sound. He would cover his ears and respond fearfully to ordinary household noises. He also had a powerful response to quiet background sounds. On the other hand, he was a limp, floppy baby who didn't seem to notice or tune in to much in his environment. Difficulties began to emerge in Jerry's second year. He developed pollen and dust allergies. He had difficulty eating a variety of textures of solid foods. From age 12 to 16 months he was seen by an occupational therapist who specializes in eating problems. Jerry had repeated otitis media between ages 12 months and two years, which was finally treated with the insertion of tubes. Accurate articulation was slow to develop though Jerry was clearly trying to talk. His articulation did improve without further intervention, so that he was age appropriately intelligible by 30 months. Mr. and Ms. Green described Jerry as a quiet infant and toddler, happy to lie on a blanket and watch the ceiling. Ms. Green felt that as Jerry became more active, he had a rich fantasy world he played in and entertained himself well. He was rarely upset and even when he fell, which he did often, he seemed unmoved by it and carried on self-sufficiently. Jerry began to attend a toddler playgroup at a local community center at age two. His teachers soon alerted the Greens about their concern regarding Jerry's lack of social engagement, his unusual use of pragmatic language, his physical awkwardness, and difficulties organizing his attention in a group setting.

Observational findings

Jerry was content to play on the floor at the therapist's office. He was only interested in cars and trucks, which his parents encouraged as "boy toys." Most of his "play" seemed to go on inside his head so that to the casual observer he appeared to be lying on the floor, repetitively pushing a car back and forth, mumbling to himself in hushed tones. By joining his activity the therapist was able to discover that he personified the vehicles and imagined them living in a house and sleeping in beds. Jerry did touch base with his mother through mutual gaze throughout the sessions. He was affectionate toward both parents. Some of his affection seemed to satisfy a craving for tactile stimulation as he stroked his mother's hair, her soft sweater, or her nylons in a manner that suggested more pleasure in the sensory experience than in the interpersonal qualities of the moment. Jerry engaged in appropriate social referencing toward his parents, looking over to them with a glint in his eyes and a smile as he declined to follow through on a task, or to share in their pleasure over his accomplishments. He was too readily affectionate with near strangers. For example, he hugged the occupational therapist on first meeting her.

In the more structured context of the occupational therapist's evaluation, Jerry refused directed activities by commenting "Not now," but he initiated manipulation of objects on a shelf across the room. Jerry seemed to have an awareness that certain tasks were hard for him, and he resisted any efforts to have him try those. His cooperation improved significantly whenever visual or auditory tasks were presented without motor demands. In general, Jerry's interactions were characterized by a processing lag time of about 30 seconds, and up to one minute if there was a motor component to the activity. Jerry had a hard time organizing his attention to stay focused on any task introduced by someone else, and he was easily distracted by any peripheral sound, even the ticking of a clock.

Jerry had better expressive than receptive language. While he had a uniquely advanced vocabulary for mechanically related words, such as pendulum or elevated highway, his comprehension of language tested at the twentieth percentile. Jerry was easily sidetracked by minute details on objects or in pictures, and these details often had a mechanical component, such as the windshield wipers on a car. The speech and language therapist found he had to join fully with Jerry in his off-target interest until he was willing to let it go, if the therapist was to have any chance at steering him toward the task at hand.

There was never a sense that Jerry was avoiding people or defiant, but rather that what was typically relegated to the background for most of us was in the foreground for Jerry, and vice versa. One could think of him as attentive to the parts of objects or ideas without curiosity or perhaps capacity to synthesize those parts into a coherent whole. This made it particularly difficult for Jerry to respond to questions or prompts. He frequently ignored other peoples' comments or questions, or he attempted to respond with highly personalized associations. Talking with Jerry, one needed a parent available to interpret the connections he was making.

Observations during the home visit revealed Jerry at his most comfortable. His affect was lively and he moved about the house freely. Left to his own devices, he was most likely to engage in self-isolating play in his room. Although he was clearly familiar with routines in his household, he seemed to easily forget where he was going. This appeared more as a function of attention than memory, because he readily recalled facts and near-time events cued by his mother. The quality of his affect and interaction was very similar with his mother and father. He seemed more affected by unfamiliar places than people. He performed more for his mother, but she was more insistent and spent a great deal of time with him. During the home visit the therapist learned that Jerry was very cooperative regarding toilet training, but that he was often constipated and withheld bowel movements. His parents felt he was unable to read the cues from his body and often interpreted his need to relieve himself as a nervous feeling in his stomach.

At school, Jerry isolated himself in the "quiet corner" as often as possible. He spent much of the group activity with his hands cupped over his ears. He was not able to focus on the activities available at the tables or on the rug, and drifted from one to another aimlessly whenever he was ushered out of the quiet corner. Jerry made no attempts to engage the other children, nor did he respond interpersonally when other children initiated contact with him. He would, on the other hand, stroke another child on the arm or back if they were wearing a particularly soft or appealing fabric. Jerry actively avoided the gross motor toys in the room and on the yard.

Parents' psychiatric status, marital functioning, and current circumstances

This was the second marriage for both parents. Mr. Green had a grown son from his first marriage. Jerry was Ms. Green's first child. Ms. Green suffered from anxiety and depression, and both conditions were exacerbated as Jerry's difficulties became apparent. She had adverse reactions to several medications and had given up trying to use medication to alleviate her symptoms. At a follow-up meeting with the therapist, she refused offers to assist her in finding an individual therapist. There had been a dramatic change in her life following Jerry's birth. Prior to his birth, she had assisted her husband in his computer business and spent a great deal of time traveling and entertaining with him. Once Jerry was born, she became a fulltime homemaker and curtailed all travel and entertaining. However, Mr. Green's travel and entertainment schedule did not change with the birth of children, and he was much less available than she had wished. Shortly after Jerry's birth, Ms. Green became pregnant again, and had a healthy baby girl when Jerry was only 15 months old. Ms. Green felt guilty about the two children being so close in age, and worried that she hadn't been sufficiently available to Jerry with a newborn to care for. Ms. Green is an intelligent woman capable of genuine warmth and affection. She would appear to understand a great deal about the complexities of Jerry's developmental needs, and then go through periods of panic, imagining she didn't understand what was wrong with him. She thought she could be doing something more to help him or that she was missing some crucial diagnosis or intervention that would lead to his recovery. During these periods, she would contact a wide variety of health professionals in her local community and beyond, make many phone calls and take Jerry to be tested or interviewed in many new settings. This exacerbated her anxiety, strained her generally nurturant relationship with her son, and added stress Jerry was ill-equipped to manage.

Ms. Green's relationship with Jerry was always warm and supportive. She complained that she had to "ride him" to keep him going, but much of her monitoring of Jerry was actually helpful to him in organizing his world, and was typically achieved with good humor and warmheartedness. Because Ms. Green spent so much time with Jerry and was well-attuned to his idiosyncrasies, she was able to engage in and maintain interaction and conversation with him much longer than other people.

Mr. Green's warmth was expressed in a joking manner, often making himself the object of humor. He was very supportive and understanding toward Jerry. Mr. Green reported that his mother and other relatives remembered him as being just like Jerry as a child. Mr. Green worked for himself, though he courted clients. His work involved meticulous computations and intimate involvement in his world of computers. Ms. Green reported that she often felt Mr. Green could not connect with her affective experiences, and that he usually headed for the computer when she wanted to have an emotional talk. Although Mr. Green functioned well in his work, he could be seen as in his own world and not available for emotional intimacy. This, and the termination of Ms. Green's participation in the fun-loving aspects of Mr. Green's work life, caused a marital disharmony that was not able to be resolved despite considerable marital therapy.

The marital issues exacerbated Ms. Green's feelings of depression, which had a significant impact on the degree of animation and energy she had available for Jerry. Mr. Green often experienced himself as an outsider to the family system due to his own escape to work and to his wife's sense of control by being in charge of the household and children. Culturally, this family valued academic achievement and was conscious of economic status. It was very difficult for them to resign themselves to the limited school options for Jerry, and to face the reality that he could not attend an elite private boys' school.

Diagnosis

Although Jerry was at times aloof and unavailable interpersonally, he was most reliably reciprocal and interactive with his parents. Despite his mother's anxiety and her tendency to become overzealous, even intrusive in her interactions with him, he was clearly most related and animated with her. His caregiving arrangements had been stable since birth and his home environment supportive and nurturant. Therefore, his social atypicality did not suggest a Reactive Attachment Disorder. Although Jerry may have poor motor skills and uneven cognitive development, his good memory, unusual advanced vocabulary, and facility with letters and numbers rule out Mental Retardation. Attention Deficit/ Predominantly Inattentive type was considered because Jerry met many of the language-related criteria, and ruled out because the diagnosis failed to capture the sensory organizational issues and interpersonal issues Jerry was struggling with. Although Jerry avoided other children and seemed to have an awareness that certain activities were difficult for him, Avoidant Personality Disorder was ruled out because his social difficulties did not reflect a fear of being ridiculed or shamed. Jerry did not quite meet the criteria for Asperger's Disorder as he was able to regulate social interaction with nonverbal gestures and facial expressions, albeit, not reliably and not with peers. He was capable of social and emotional reciprocity and able to spontaneously seek shared pleasure, especially with family members. There was a diagnostic fit in Jerry's preoccupation and restricted pattern of interest in cars and mechanical devices, and parts of objects; an inflexibility in routines, (his mother could not drive a new route without upsetting him); repetitive motor mannerisms (a shaking of the hands Jerry reported to be the flashing lights of an emergency response vehicle); his disturbance caused clinically significant impairment in social functioning; there was no clinically significant language or cognitive delay; and criteria were not met for another Pervasive Developmental Disorder or Schizophrenia. At the functional emotional developmental level, Jerry showed good capacities for mutual attention, mutual engagement, and interactive intentionality and reciprocity when he was provided with some structure or sensorimotor support. He did not fully reach expected age levels for representational/affective communication, but was beginning to elaborate his ideas and feelings in pretend play.

Jerry showed both sensory-motor and organizational processing difficulties. His physiological organization was compromised by early weak sucking responses, oral-tactile hypersensitivity, and later by poorly differentiated signals for elimination leading to constipation and withholding of bowel movements. His low motor tone and poor motor planning and coordination led to significant delays in gross and fine motor development and avoidance of motor tasks, a primary field for social interaction in early childhood. His sensory systems were either overreactive or underreactive. He was hypersensitive to sound, craved soft tactile experiences, and barely took note of many visual or kinesthetic experiences. Jerry appeared inattentive and preoccupied with his own thoughts, sensations, and emotions. Considerable effort was needed to pull him into interaction. He readily escaped into his own fantasy world rather than seek or respond to interaction with his family or peers. Jerry's subtle receptive language difficulties coupled with his internal preoccupations made it more comfortable for him to live in his own world rather than join the unpredictable, spontaneous interpersonal world.

Diagnostic summary

Axis I: **Primary Diagnosis**
Regulatory Disorder: Type II: Underreactive; self-absorbed.

Axis II: **Relationship Disorder Classification**
Tendency toward Anxious/Tense Relationship.

Axis III: **Medical and Developmental Disorders and Conditions**
Receptive Language Disorder
Sensory-Motor Integration Disorder
Allergies
Oral-Motor Disorder
Sensitive Bowel.

Axis IV: Psychosocial Stressors
Birth of a sibling
School entry
Overall effects: predominantly acute and mild.

Axis V: Functional Emotional Developmental Level
Needs structure and sensorimotor support to evidence capacity for representational/affective communication; otherwise manifests capacity inconsistently. Has attained mutual attention, mutual engagement, and interactive intentionality and reciprocity, with constrictions related to inconsistent processing, requiring sensorimotor support.

PIR-GAS: 55 (Between Significantly Perturbed and Distressed)

Discussion with caregivers and treatment planning

The treatment plan included interventions focused on several aspects of Jerry's development. The Greens were enthusiastic about continuing a relationship-based interactive, developmentally oriented psychotherapy. The therapist planned weekly office meetings to develop Jerry's capacity to maintain genuine interpersonal interactions, expand interactive play, improve spontaneous pragmatic language, develop flexibility, and provide opportunities for sensory motor experiences to be spontaneously integrated. The work also included development of higher executive functions requiring complex sequential thought, planning, organizational skills, activation and modulation of arousal, and focus of attention. These goals were best met in a developmentally oriented, highly interactive psychotherapy that included Jerry's parents and sister in a flexible arrangement. Designing the treatment to include Jerry's family gave the therapist an opportunity to have the parents learn how to extend the style of interaction most beneficial to Jerry into their daily lives. In the context of these treatment goals, a behavioral approach focused on targeting discrete behaviors for modification may have expanded Jerry's repertoire of splinter skills but would not have focused on the meaning of relationships and on expanding flexibility and abstract conceptualization; nor would it have made spontaneous interaction a fulltime family affair. Since integration and generalization were central to Jerry's needs, the interpersonal approach to treatment was expected to be most useful.

The therapist agreed as well to consult with teachers as needed and to coordinate with the speech and language therapist and the occupational therapist. Ongoing consultation from each specialist was arranged for the preschool teachers. With the Greens' approval, the members of the therapeutic team talked frequently, mostly on an informal basis. More organized meetings with the team, parents, and teachers were arranged approximately quarterly.

Intervention

Psychotherapy

The initial objective of the relationship-based interactive therapy was to help Jerry incorporate multiple objects in his play, enact representational scenarios, and include other people. His mother's task was to learn to join his play without attempting to direct it. Early sessions focused on the cars and trucks. Ms. Green initially preferred to talk to Jerry from the couch. She asked many questions Jerry didn't answer, clarified the meaning of his language, restated paragraphs that often began in the middle of an idea, and affectionately directed him, trying to keep him "on task." She felt her job was to make him goal-directed. Jerry worked valiantly to shut us out. His "play" went on inside his own head, with very little movement of toys or combining of objects, and no interpersonal interaction. I suggested a new way to play with Jerry, down on the floor, heads at mutual eye level, joining his activity, anticipating his needs. Ms. Green learned quickly to follow Jerry's lead without attempting to direct him. I had her lying on the floor, offering cars she knew Jerry wanted. She added blocks to the game creating tunnels and overpasses that intrigued her son and motivated him to combine toys and even try to build with blocks, a motor task he had always avoided. If he made an interesting engine noise, she laughed and made a different one for her truck. With the therapist's encouragement and willingness to be playful and silly, Ms. Green began to enjoy playing and became increasingly reciprocal rather than directive with her son. Jerry laughed more, included us in his ideas and even requested that we take part in the play. Soon he allowed small dolls to drive the cars and built a doll house for them to live in. Gradually the action shifted from mechanical interests to interest in human interaction.

In one breakthrough session, Jerry enacted scenes of coping with separation. He instructed the therapist to be the baby doll and he was the mother doll. As mother drove away to do some errands, he told his own mother to be the babysitter doll. When I asked how the baby felt about being with the sitter, he told me, "not so good." So as he drove his mother doll away, I pretended to wail in my role as the baby, and complained about not liking it when her mother left her. Jerry was enthralled. For several weeks he instructed me to cry as we played out this scene over and over. Ms. Green was amazed by Jerry's interest in the affective nature of the game, and surprised, because she recalled he hardly took note when she left him with the sitter as an infant or toddler.

This example illustrates how a child with regulatory issues and underreactivity can appear unaffected by emotional events such as separation, though these events may have been internalized and taken on meaning. Jerry's interest in cars was certainly in part determined by his interest in mechanical things and his parents' encouragement, but it was also true that he represented the loss of his mother and separation themes by repeatedly having her drive away. In this approach to treatment the therapist looks for representational themes and their emotional meaning, though the initial representations may be quite skeletal and seemingly remote. Simultaneously, the therapist assists parents in learning to play in a new way, while consciously working at opportunities to develop motor, language and conceptual abilities as well as focusing attention.

After several weeks, the therapist brought in a life-size baby doll and sat her on the floor with us. Jerry was quick to incorporate this doll and shifted our play to role-playing family interaction, using the doll as a baby sister. Jerry began to enact scenes that offered a window into events that upset him at home, such as spilled milk or a missing T-shirt. The therapist could now help him understand these events as representing things that were hard for him, such as making his hands do things he wanted and organizing the things that were important to him, rather than his idea that he was being a bad boy. The therapist took this information to the occupational therapist, who worked on the skills related to these issues, and within a few months, Jerry successfully made it through a meal with his milk on the table.

In his play, Jerry began to assign himself the role of devoted father who cares for the children and doesn't need to go to work. This shift in his play brought the therapist and parents to talk about the meaning of wishes and yearnings. Jerry was now able to play out wished-for emotional experiences. He became interested in differentiating reality and fantasy, and in discovering that thoughts don't make things happen. Simultaneously, we arranged a series of sessions with Jerry and his father. During these sessions, Jerry played enthusiastically, reversing roles with his dad. The therapist was able to help Mr. Green understand Jerry's desire to spend more time with him. One outcome of these sessions was that Mr. Green began taking Jerry swimming several times a week, an activity recommended by the occupational therapist to develop strength and bilateral coordination.

Treatment proceeded over several years, with themes of play advancing at new developmental levels. Jerry worked on the complexities of gaining autonomy from a mother he depended on more than most children for assistance with motor tasks, organizing him and being his interpreter in the outside world. Ms. Green was appreciative of the therapist's assistance in helping her understand and maintain empathy for Jerry's shifts from dependence to anger. From this time forward, Jerry chose whether or not he wanted his mother included in the sessions. Other stages of treatment focused on Jerry enacting events from school, which gave the therapist a chance to help him understand the other children's expectations of relationships with him. During this stage, speech therapy focused on topic initiation, topic maintenance, and how to use language to terminate interaction or shift attention to another game. Through consultation with the team, Jerry's teachers were able to help Jerry practice what he was learning in his therapies at school. During this time, many sessions included Jerry's sister as a playmate. With the therapist's facilitation, Jerry's sister was able to teach her brother many of the basics of peer play.

Jerry's diagnostic picture remained similar throughout early childhood, though there were significant improvements in every area of functioning. As he entered elementary school, and the demands for independent task completion and organized sustained attention increased, questions about attention deficit-disorder resurfaced. Jerry's inflexibility, though greatly improved in general, got him into more trouble in school, as he would only walk one route to the cafeteria, or only use one special pencil. Sensory-motor integration issues took a back seat to issues of fine motor development as Jerry now had to complete written assignments within a classroom time limit. Subtle difficulties with language comprehension led to an investigation of a central auditory processing disorder. Socially, Jerry interacted appropriately and charmingly with adults. Although he played well with peers and was able to be involved in complex representational play, he'd also drift away from a friend who stayed too long to play at his house, or turn his back on a board game in progress and focus on his internal thoughts. Generally, his social interaction was somewhat immature, and he played better with his younger sister's friends than with his classmates. Academically, Jerry was functioning at and above grade level in his reading, spelling and math skills, though his classroom performance didn't reliably match his ability.

Collaboration

Coordinating family, school, and therapeutic efforts was a time-consuming but worthwhile task. In many ways, Ms. Green served as the logistical coordinator. But she also felt overwhelmed by the many demands on her and frequently looked to the therapist to assume the role of case manager. Beyond the evident needs to coordinate the school program and the three therapies, the therapist also needed to provide supervision for teachers and specialists about their feelings about this little boy and his sometimes-perceived anxious and demanding mother. And the therapist had to help the teachers realize the value of many of the mother's suggestions, in part, because they created extra work demands the teachers were not accustomed to. Through these efforts, Jerry was able to remain in a typical educational setting, receiving his special services outside of school. The team and the Greens agreed this was the most beneficial arrangement for Jerry because he was able to learn social skills from his peer experts, and, as he developed, he saw himself as a "regular guy."

Prognosis and discussion

Jerry's prognosis over the span of development is good. He made steady progress in all the developmentally challenged domains. He is cognitively capable, reading above his grade level, with excellent comprehension skills. He is able to accomplish pencil and paper tasks that are clear and legible. His capacity to make connections between emotions, ideas, and actions bodes well for his future capacity to develop the critical-thinking skills necessary for report writing or analysis of literature. It is uncertain whether Jerry's organization of attention will improve adequately through maturation or require medical assistance in the future. Socially, Jerry enjoys being with people and actively seeks out companionship. He is especially appealing to adults and well-liked by peers. Questions remain about how much intimacy he will be able to manage as he matures, whether he will prefer more solitary work, and to what extent his social facility will become formulaic. Although he made significant progress in becoming more flexible, his need for rigid routines may appear compulsive as he grows up. Jerry's continuous improvement in sensory integration, social and emotional development, and information processing are good signs. He is also fortunate enough to have the continued benefit from his parents' commitment to assisting his development as well as from their capacity for sustained warmth and empathy.

400. Regulatory Disorders

403. Type III: Motorically Disorganized

Judith Ahrano, M. D.

Regulatory Disorders are characterized by difficulties in the regulation of physiological, sensory, attentional, motor and affective processes. These difficulties affect the child's daily adaptation and interpersonal relationships because the child has trouble organizing a calm, alert, affectively positive state. Infants and young children who are motorically disorganized show a pattern of mixed sensory reactivity and motor processing difficulties. They crave sensory input and have poor behavior control. They are impulsive and may appear aggressive and fearless. The case of Amanda Black presents a variety of disordered behavioral, sensory, and motor processes, complicated by relationship and situational issues that confounded the diagnosis on referral.

Reason for referral

Amanda was first taken by her parents to a child psychologist at around two years of age. The initial impression was that she demonstrated autistic-like tendencies—poor eye contact, inconsistent response, and language delay. This impression was withdrawn after subsequent visits; however, the parents were not satisfied and Amanda was referred by her pediatrician to an early intervention program for evaluation at 27 months of age. The pediatrician was concerned about her delayed expressive language development, short attention span, and high level of motor activity. The evaluation by a speech pathologist and an early childhood specialist revealed that Amanda's receptive and expressive language and socialization skills were moderately delayed. Amanda was reported to have motor sensory-seeking behavior, and she clearly performed better with external guidance.

For five months Amanda received individual speech/language therapy twice weekly. Her parents met weekly with the early childhood specialist to work on developmentally oriented relationship issues. The therapist made a home visit during the course of treatment to offer specific suggestions to the parents about enhancing Amanda's play organization and language development in the home. Because of ongoing concerns and an impending move by the family, Amanda was referred to a multidisciplinary developmental clinic for further evaluation subsequent to the move.

One month after the family moved into a new area, the parents brought Amanda into the clinic. She had been placed in a Montessori school soon after moving, but after only two weeks her parents were asked to remove her. Staff cited Amanda's lack of bowel and bladder control, and the need for one-to-one supervision to manage her continually difficult behavior. Amanda's parents were also concerned about her behavior at home. She was aggressive and reckless, didn't listen to or follow instructions, and seemed either irritable, perseverative, or stubbornly oppositional most of the time. The parents felt clueless about how to set limits on or discipline Amanda. The moments of mutual shared pleasure and joy were dwindling in frequency.

Assessment process

Amanda came to the clinic with her parents when she was 35 months old. A multidisciplinary team saw her on three occasions over a two-month period. The visits included individual evaluations by a developmental pediatrician, an early childhood developmental diagnostician, an audiologist, and a speech language pathologist. The evaluation sessions were from $1^1/_2$ to 2 hours duration. The first visit included interviews with the parents together and individually, with and without Amanda's presence. The team obtained comprehensive medical and developmental histories and performed a complete physical exam, including evaluation of neurological function. The team made free-play observations of each parent with Amanda and of Amanda with the assessors. During the second visit, the early childhood specialist administered the Bayley Scales of Infant Development and observed free play with the parents present. The third session was devoted to a reevaluation of speech and language skills using the Preschool Language Scale-3 (PLS-3).

Medical information about Amanda's biological parents was limited because of Amanda's adoption at birth. The team obtained reports of behavioral observations from the preschool/daycare setting and from each of the parents via the Child Behavior Checklist, and it reviewed reports of the prior evaluation and treatment notes from age 27 months to 33 months. The team obtained limited medical laboratory tests, including thyroid function and blood lead screening, to eliminate a couple of possible treatable causes of high-level motor activity and disorganization. Audiometry was repeated to reconfirm normal hearing. An Auditory Scan was obtained later to determine if there were definable auditory processing problems. The parents were given verbal reports of results, impressions, and recommendations at the end of each session and received written reports detailing findings and recommendations subsequently. The developmental pediatrician and a psychology intern made home visits independently during the course of treatment.

Assessment findings

Developmental history

Amanda was adopted at birth by Mr. and Ms. Black, who were 35 and 40 years of age, respectively, at the time. She was their first and only child. She was delivered by Cesarean section two weeks postterm, healthy and with an average birth weight. She was exposed in utero to regular small amounts of nicotine. There were no intranatal or neonatal complications. The pediatrician reported a history of attention deficit disorder in an eight-year-old female biological sibling and undefined learning and emotional problems in the biological father.

The parents described Amanda at birth as appearing healthy and "wide awake." She continued to be a very alert, active, reactive, and interactive baby. They felt she was somewhat hard to hold as an infant. She had no feeding problems and thrived in infancy, with excellent continued growth. Gross motor milestones were precocious, with crawling at 7 months and independent walking at 10 months. Expressive language milestones were delayed, with single words appearing at 2 years of age and two-word combinations at 30 to 32 months. Amanda did not babble much as an infant nor vocalize much as a toddler during play. Much of her communication was gestural, showing clear intent but without words. During play she often made loud noises and laughed loudly. She had achieved almost complete bowel and bladder control prior to the family's move. Amanda remained healthy with no serious medical problems and no hospitalizations. She did have four ear infections in the first year of life, which were treated with antibiotics. There were no residual middle ear problems and audiometry was normal at 27 months. She had suffered two minor accidents requiring stitches. Amanda was beginning to help dress herself and was capable of using a cup independently. She fed herself with the spoon and fork without spilling, but she preferred the bottle and her fingers.

Amanda was cared for in the home by her parents and by one or the other of two nannies, all of whom took a keen interest in her progress and participated in her early intervention program. She and her mother participated in play groups and gymnastics groups together in their community. As a toddler Amanda was described by her parents as a "gentle, sweet" child who was "constantly on the go," "squirmy," difficult to calm for naps, and unable to sit still. She was reported to not like her hands or clothing to be "dirty." She would not share toys readily with other children and was not willing to take turns.

The parents reported that after the move, Amanda had reverted to her bottle and had regressed in bowel and bladder control, preferring "pull-ups" to the toilet. She had also become more aggressive, hitting her mother, and pulling her mother's hair when she was angry or frustrated. She was hitting the ailing family pet, a small dog, and expressed jealousy of the dog, who was receiving special care because of its illness. She was climbing recklessly, running down the street, and running about the house carrying sharp knives.

Although she was able to verbalize the danger of some of her activities, she fearlessly continued them. The parents reported that she had never learned to modify her behavior based on safety concerns or anticipation of harmful or painful consequences, and said that she had a high pain threshold. The parents felt that Amanda continued to require monitoring as if she were still a 2-year-old. She was not listening to or following instructions. She was having more intense, prolonged tantrums with screaming, kicking, and hitting at bedtime, mealtime, and bathtime. Her former "bubbly" demeanor was being replaced by irritability and stubborn opposition. Because she would not sit for meals, her mother would follow her around the house with a bowl and spoon, feeding her bites on the run. The parents were very worried that she would lose weight because she was not eating properly. Amanda would undo and get out of her seat belt on a regular basis when traveling in the car. She had begun hiding toys and food.

Mr. and Ms. Black reported that Amanda talked in a loud voice most of the time and would persist in the pursuit of something she wanted, to the point of perseveration, with ceaseless verbal repetition. She "would not listen" except at a quiet time at home when books were read to her. She was "easily distracted" and was unable to sit or play with other children. Her father described her as a "darling little angel that needs her wings clipped." Her mother described her as a "very sweet, affectionate, loving" child who was "very smart and very inquisitive" who would not listen when told "No," and who seemed "anxious" but not fearful.

Initial observations

During the initial early intervention speech/language evaluation, Amanda at 27 months was observed to be highly visually alert to her environment. Most interpersonal visual contact occurred during intentional communication interactions. She had fleeting eye contact at other times. Whole-body movements were entrained in communication efforts. Amanda imitated motor actions relatively easily, but unstructured motor activity appeared disorganized and clumsy. There was response delay in imitating oral motor movements. Amanda imitated words infrequently. She initially demonstrated good oral motor skills, with an ability to produce most expected phonemes. Her jargon consisted of simple patterns. She was interested in the activities of others and was able to imitate complex adult tasks. She liked to be in charge and said "No" if the assessor tried to change the activity. She expressed pleasure at praise and demonstrated a desire to please. Auditory response seemed variable. At times, she was overly sensitive, responding to extraneous noise in the environment and, at other times, she seemed insensitive, variably responsive to auditory verbal stimuli. Receptive skills were variable. She tended to seek visual cues to aid in comprehension.

Amanda's play involved primarily sensory-motor and perceptual exploration. She sought proprioceptive and some vestibular stimulation, climbing to dangerous heights and jumping fearlessly. She expressed frustration using affectively intense facial expressions, gestures, and vocalization without words. She demonstrated appropriate functional use of a variety of objects and toys. She enjoyed cause and effect, spatial, and part-whole relationships. She did not consistently use eye contact, gestures, or language to clearly initiate or terminate interactions with others. It was possible to achieve brief eye contact but difficult to sustain it with Amanda during interactions. She was willing to engage in limited turn-taking during play in the form of vocal nonverbal imitation and motor imitation. She displayed brief symbolic episodes in play with representational objects but without affective themes. She showed a need (and the ability) to self-calm, retreating to a confined place or isolating herself with a comforting object for brief periods. When left to play freely alone, she would begin and discontinue activities rapidly with poor organization to her play, without beginnings and endings to sequences. At times she sought to be confined, and at other times she resisted being restricted or structured by others. Interpersonally, she vacillated between periods of intensely and intrusively seeking involvement with others and periods of physically distancing herself, withdrawing to play alone without attention to others. Her affect was intense but was reported to be predominantly pleasant. She was more attentive when in a highly structured setting, such as sitting with an adult who continued to help structure her play. She would match her pace to that of the adult. She clearly responded with improved performance in all areas when she was given more environmental structure, clear boundaries, and a slowed pace of interpersonal interaction.

Reevaluation in her early intervention program at 33 months of age, after five months of intervention, found her auditory comprehension at a 34-month-age equivalent and expressive communication at a 19-month level on the PLS-3. Her receptive vocabulary was at a 32-month level on the Peabody Picture Vocabulary Test-Revised Form L (PPVT-L). Amanda showed resistance to performance on tests of expressive language and achieved an age equivalent of <two years on the Expressive One-Word Picture Vocabulary Test-R. However, no basal level was achieved, and only one half of the items were completed. She continued to have difficulty imitating new single words and during testing would use gestures to represent a picture rather than saying the word. She seemed now to show some oral motor difficulties with blowing. She enjoyed oral stimulation games. Her phonologic repertoire was now noted to be mildly restricted relative to age. There was concern about an apraxic or word retrieval component in her expressive language difficulties.

Amanda's play at this time reflected some increase in organization and sensory regulation. She was less reactive and more willing to engage in and maintain social interaction including, with prompts, sustaining eye contact during initiation and termination of social interactions. She was using non-realistic objects for pretend play. Her play themes consisted mostly of reenactments of small daily units of experience. Sequencing reenactment of related events and elaborating with affective themes still required assistance from adult modeling. She was imitating vocally more frequently and had added verbal as well as gestural responses to frustration. In her problem-solving, she was showing brief forethought.

Observation of Amanda at 35 months

During free play, Amanda was observed to be disorganized much of the time. Many of the observations of the quality of her play made at the 27-month evaluation continued to be characteristic of her current play. She engaged primarily in sensory-motor play (predominantly large motor activities), seeking proprioceptive stimulation. At times she was fairly agile, but at other times she appeared clumsy, turning over chairs on arising and bumping into objects, furniture, and people. She proceeded forward pell-mell, often physically overshooting her intended goal. Her vocalizations during play included different intonations, but she spoke seldom and used only single words. When she did talk or vocalize during play, her voice was loud, with little modulation.

Amanda demonstrated creativity by devising physical problems for herself to solve. She would first ask for help, attempting to draw others into her play, but would then proceed to solve the problem herself, not waiting for a response. For example, on one occasion, she climbed over the back of the couch down into a tight space where, once in, she could not turn her body around. She remained there for a while as if it felt safe and calm to her. Her affect became calm and positive. She then attempted to wiggle out by an alternate route from the way she had gotten herself inside and worked at it until she was successful. She showed delight in her own success.

Amanda sought limits when her parents were present, at times engaging in activities with increasing risk until the limit was held. For example, she climbed on the top of the back of the couch where her father was sitting and walked along the back of the couch behind her father, coming closer each time to a heating element behind the couch, visually referencing to him indirectly with sidewise glances along the way. He stopped her and physically helped her down, requesting calmly that she not climb up there. She repeatedly tested this limit but gave up when the father persisted in his response without escalation. This activity seemed also to have as a goal entraining her father in her play. It did not, however, develop into a shared, pleasurable playful interaction.

Amanda created contained spaces for her play to help organize herself. She also manipulated her environment, physical and interpersonal, to obtain support for calming herself. On occasion she would lie down briefly on the floor to comfort and calm herself, holding a soft, stuffed animal against her. She also would climb onto her mother's lap and relax momentarily with her back against her mother or climb in her father's lap and ask him to read her a story, which he did. She was able to cease physical activity briefly at these times.

Amanda did not demonstrate focused representational play on her own but went from one activity to another in a disjointed fashion. Play with toys centered around movement, function, perceptual (spatial or part-whole relations), and sensory experience—visual, auditory, proprioceptive, and some tactile, including oral motor. She tended to ignore observational comments (especially if at all directive) from parents and assessor during free play, unless they were expressing obvious delight with something she had accomplished. Then she smiled and made warm, brief eye contact. Her facial expressions changed infrequently during her play, usually only at times of intense pleasure, joy or frustration. There were, however, no representational affective themes observed and little sequencing, other than some trial-and-error effort at sequencing in solving motor challenges. Amanda was visually aware of others in the room during much of her play, watching them indirectly through a mirror and/or when they were not looking at her.

Observing Amanda's individual play with her parents, the team noted that Amanda's mother was able to facilitate her organization and modulation of activity and voice, using a soft tone and a slow pace and establishing eye contact with her before an interaction. She attempted to follow Amanda's lead but tended to be anxious and tense, seeming concerned about appearances and performance. She commented on minute details that were inconsequential, adding distraction to the interaction. Interactions with Amanda were often sudden and jerky.

In general, Amanda's father had great difficulty attending to the interaction between himself and Amanda. Occasionally their interactions were focused and positive, but these instances were brief. He was concerned with controlling Amanda's behavior, but was unable consistently to provide her with calm organization to assist her in controlling her own behavior. When she approached him physically with an invitation to play, he was unable to refocus to attend to her and would look around past her, fending her off by putting his arms up in front of himself. He would turn to the assessor/observer and revert back to discussing his difficulties with Amanda and his own problems. Resisting Amanda's intrusions and then being intrusive with her seemed to have become a pattern with the father. Her response to his resistance was to persist—loudly repeating herself, leaning into him, and invading his personal space in an attempt to get him to respond. If she failed to obtain reengagement with him, she would abandon the attempt and become motorically more active and disorganized. Sometimes she would attempt to leave the room. Their play escalated to a state of frustration, anger, and dissatisfaction for both.

In play with the assessor, Amanda responded to ongoing assistance with organization in such a way that she was able to engage in symbolic representational play, incorporating some simple affective themes. Because it took some effort to achieve intermittent eye contact with her during play, it was helpful to obtain eye contact at the beginning of an interaction; this was true whether Amanda or the assessor initiated the interaction. It was hard to sustain a natural pattern of reciprocal eye contact during a sequence of play. The adult had to remain focused on Amanda and undistracted.

Amanda's language consisted primarily of one- or two-word utterances, and she most frequently responded to questions with one word. The assessor found that Amanda gave cues when she needed help with organization. It was at these times that she requested input from her partner in play. If these cues were responded to, play could continue in a reciprocal manner. If they were ignored, play would deteriorate or be abandoned, and she would jump to a new unrelated agenda, such as retrieving a toy she remembered from the waiting room.

During the physical exam, Amanda was inquisitive in her approach to novel objects and activities, even with the changing of tasks. She showed delight in reciprocal exam play. She did attempt to control the process but was amenable to negotiation when offered an opportunity to do something she wanted (such as, use the exam instruments) in exchange for allowing the examiner to examine her first. She would then imitate the process, using a doll or a parent as her subject. She tended to grab things impulsively without asking and would invade the space of another person, impulsively overshooting boundaries, but without apparent aggressive intent. She seemed to understand what she had done if it was brought to her attention, but she was unable to make the adjustment before acting impulsively. Impulsivity characterized her interpersonal interactions with everyone in the clinic, including the nurse, the secretary, and other children in the waiting room. Amanda abruptly initiated and terminated interactions with others without warning, and would only explain the shifts, if requested, over her shoulder as she was proceeding impulsively along her way. Her comment would most often consist of one word to inform the other of her next interest or agenda, requiring a translation of intent.

Amanda did not have any openly aggressive behavior or tantrums during the evaluations. She was compliant with a few limits that were set by the assessor, such as staying in the playroom. She needed help with putting away one toy before getting out another. She would not respond to a verbal prompt alone but required the involvement of an adult in the activity to comply. She enjoyed making cleanup a motorically active game.

Physical findings

Amanda was an exceptionally attractive little girl with blue eyes and sandy-blonde curly hair pulled back, exposing a broad forehead. Her facial expression at rest appeared sober to sad. She had no genetic or neurocutaneous markers. She was at the upper end of normal size for her age. Weight was commensurate with height and head circumference. Her physical exam was normal. She had normal oral and palatal anatomy and oral motor function. Her thyroid was normal size. Her neurologic exam was positive for impulsivity and distractibility. She had poor motor organization, characterized by disorganized motor planning in gross motor activity, producing clumsiness without ataxia. Fine motor skills were close to expectable for chronological age. She had no motor tics and had no fine motor tremor. A few brief staring episodes were observed but did not contain autonomic or motor components suggestive of seizures. The episodes appeared to function as moments of calm or rest. Expressive language function was delayed. Sensory responsivity was variable as described, with strengths in visual integration, and variable hyperreactive and hyporeactive auditory responsiveness. She seemed to have tactile hyposensitivity. Medical lab tests were normal, as expected.

Findings from developmental testing

Amanda's performance on the Bayley Scales of Infant Development revealed age-appropriate skills in all domains except social/emotional and expressive language categories, which were 5 to 6 months below her chronological age. Amanda exhibited difficulty attending, oppositional behavior, and manipulative control during testing. Her average developmental age was 33 months at 37 months with a Mental Developmental Index (MDI) of 83. This score was considered to be an inaccurate representation of Amanda's capability but an accurate reflection of current functioning.

Speech and language evaluation on the PLS-3 at 39 months, after two months of intensive intervention, placed auditory comprehension at a 36-month level and expressive communication at a 37-month level, showing continued gains. Articulation proficiency was normal, with a notation that some sound errors were made in continuous speech. Audiometry confirmed normal peripheral hearing.

Parents' psychiatric status, marital relationship, and current circumstances

Amanda's parents came to the clinic in crisis. Describing themselves as "high-strung," they said that they were at the point of exhaustion. There had been multiple stressors in their lives during the previous year. The father had been hospitalized for a major depressive illness. Amanda's maternal grandfather had died and her maternal grandmother had become ill. The family moved a considerable distance to be near the mother's family, but Amanda's mother did not consider the move home as particularly supportive to her own needs. Just after the move, she suffered a back injury and had been confined to bed for a week, unable to lift or hold Amanda. The move coincided with Amanda's father making a significant job change into self-employment as a sales representative. There was little income from this undertaking as yet, and the family was seriously in debt. Nevertheless, they had rented an expensive house in an upscale suburban neighborhood. The father had set up his office in the basement of the house and now that Amanda was no longer in pre-school he was close to her and her mother all day, every day.

The parents' stress was intensified by the constant vigilance needed to ensure Amanda's safety and deal with her worsening behavior. They were concerned about their ability to continue to cope with the demands of caring for her. The father expressed fear that he could hurt her in the heat of his own anger at her noncompliance, failure to listen, aggressiveness, tantrums, and incessant badgering.

Mr. and Ms. Black, who came from quite dissimilar family and religious backgrounds, had been married for 16 years. They were unable to have their own biological children but both wanted a family and had hoped to adopt at least two children. Both parents had experienced fantasies of having a large, happy, bustling, warm, and loving family with several children. Amanda was adopted after the parents had been married for 13 years; they considered her, in the father's words, "a miracle child, a dream come true." After experiencing the demands of raising Amanda, however, they were unsure of their ability to add another child to their family

Ms. Black was a middle-group child in a large family. Most of her siblings had remained in the area where they were raised. With respect to religious and philosophical beliefs, she saw herself as somewhat different from the rest of her family, whose members, she felt, criticized her mothering ability, especially as reflected in Amanda's behavior. Ms. Black had completed two years of college. She wanted to be a mother and homemaker, and also wanted a life of affluence and social prominence. She had become very concerned that Mr. Black's ability to provide for the family was compromised by his depression and dependency needs. She had observed that he seemed to be slipping back into a serious depression, characterized by difficulty getting mobilized to work, starting late, and taking long naps during the work day. She felt that his family was too intrusive in their affairs and that he was too dependent on them financially.

Ms. Black said that there was much conflict between herself and her husband in the home and that they often disagreed over management of Amanda's behavior. Ms. Black described herself as "nervous, high strung, and uptight." She was feeling tense, unhappy, overwhelmed, exhausted and thought she was disengaging from the marriage. She felt that Amanda's increasing difficulties were primarily because of stresses at home but wondered about how much her own intrinsic nature contributed. She and Mr. Black had both wondered whether Amanda had hyperactive attention deficit disorder and if so how severe it was. They had discussed medication for her but Mrs. Black was opposed, feeling that if they could resolve the major stresses and adjust to the changes they could help her in other ways.

Mr. Black had grown up as an only child. His mother had schizophrenia and was hospitalized multiple times during his childhood. He experienced his father as preoccupied with business and unavailable to him. He felt that his life as a child and adolescent had been painfully lonely and that he had essentially raised himself. His family had supported him financially, however, and Mr. Black's uncle continued to be a source of financial rescue. Mr. Black felt that he had overcome great odds to complete college and half of the work toward a master's degree in psychology, marry, have a family, and now start his own business.

Although, like his wife, he aspired to an affluent lifestyle, his confidence in himself was at a low point. He was under the care of a psychiatrist and was being treated with antianxiety and antidepressant medication. He was also in individual psychotherapy. He had difficulty making decisions without consulting his therapist first. He felt that Amanda's problems were largely intrinsic to her, but did feel that the stresses of the last year had added to the difficulties. He observed that both parents had difficulty setting and holding behavioral limits for Amanda. He wondered if medication might be helpful to her and wanted to try that route. He also had concerns about the long-term outlook for her emotional health and feared that she might later manifest a disturbance similar to his mother's.

Seen together, the parents had difficulty agreeing on anything except that they were stressed and that Amanda's behavior had brought them to the point of despair. During the joint interview, they responded to each question posed by arguing between themselves, contradicting and sharply criticizing each other. When they were not arguing, they seemed disengaged from each other. In the presence of her parents, Amanda's activity level became noticeably increased and her behavior more intense and disorganized, reflecting the tension between her parents. Both parents had been reassured by Amanda's clear progress in language during her earlier treatment and were deeply concerned about the deterioration in behavioral organization, responsiveness to requests, and compliance. Daily life had become extremely stressful for all.

Mr. Black was experienced as capable of warmth and, if anything, overly intensely involved with his family. However, he seemed unable to express his affection because of a preoccupation with his own problems and needs and an overriding feeling of hopelessness. Mrs. Black also appeared capable of nurturing and warm affection but at the same time overwrought and easily irritated by her husband. Both parents were intrusive with Amanda. They seemed at times overly vigilant about what she might do, wanting to prevent her from crossing boundaries that they presumed would be of concern to the assessors during the evaluation sessions. Yet, as they realized themselves, they both had problems with limit setting and were unable to find ways to carry through with consequences for Amanda's lack of response to defined limits. They experienced Amanda as hyperactive, uncontrolled, manipulative, persistent, willful, and independent, wanting to do things herself and at the same time not able to make judgments about safety—creating a dichotomy of agendas.

Diagnosis

Amanda and her parents presented a complicated composite of symptoms, including relationship problems, poor sensory integration, disorganized motor activity, verbal communication difficulties, a history of significant interpersonal and physical environmental changes, a pervasive change in Amanda's mood, and deterioration of behaviors and of previously acquired developmental skills. It was difficult to initially sort out the diagnostic hierarchy. There were elements suggestive of Traumatic Stress Disorder, Regulatory Disorder, disorders of affect, disorders of relating and communicating, relationship disorders, and Adjustment Disorder. It was possible to substantiate, from the earlier history and through developmental observations reported over time, a consistent underlying constitutional-maturational component presented by Amanda. Her increased basal level of alertness, motor activity, and reactive nature, observed from birth, with difficulties calming for sleep and attending to eating, variations in sensory integration and sensory-motor-seeking behavior (particularly noticeable after she became ambulatory) were suggestive of a primary regulatory disorder. The following additional clues from her early history helped eliminate other primary diagnoses.

1. She was experienced as interpersonally interactive as an infant; and intentional affective communication, though predominantly nonverbal, was usually clear through gestures. Although Amanda did engage in some specific perseverative behavior, was delayed in functional language, and engaged in primarily sensory-motor play, she did not show a restriction in range of interests. She also demonstrated the capacity for reciprocal interpersonal affective interaction and expression of multiple emotions including joy, pleasure, anger, jealousy, excitement, pride, and empathy. These characteristics served to eliminate a primary disorder of relating and communicating.

2. An acute environmental change (the family move) correlated with acute changes in behavior in the two months prior to the evaluation, suggesting superficially the possibility of an adjustment disorder. However, Amanda's symptoms were not mild and turned out to be persistent rather than transient, with subsequent periods of improvements and exacerbation. A primary diagnosis of Adjustment Disorder would not explain previous concerns and difficulties.

3. There was chronic enduring stress in the family with several definable events during the preceding year. Amanda showed symptoms under every category of Traumatic Stress Disorder, with the exception of reexperiencing the trauma. However, most of these symptoms—attentional difficulties, strong protest at bedtime, manipulativeness to gain control, aggression, and some restriction of range of affect—had existed before the period of chronic enduring stress. Thus we reasoned that the chronic enduring stress of the preceding year had intensified previously existing symptoms and stimulated new symptoms, but was not the overriding cause of Amanda's underlying difficulty.

4. Symptoms suggestive of Anxiety Disorder with poor development of basic ego functions included poor impulse control, difficulties with mood regulation, sleeping and eating disturbance, and recklessness. However, the presence of clear sensory reactivity, auditory processing, visual-spatial processing, and variable motor planning difficulties require that the regulatory disorder categorization take precedence.

5. The diagnosis of Attention Deficit Disorder, Hyperactivity-Impulsive type was considered but was confounded by issues of sensory integration, relationship issues, and chronic enduring stress. It, therefore, could not be applied to fully explain the composite picture of developmental and emotional findings.

Once it was clear that the primary, Axis I diagnosis was a regulatory disorder, it became necessary to distinguish between the negative and defiant hypersensitive, type I and the type III, motorically disorganized, impulsive. The child with a hypersensitive type regulatory disorder tends to avoid or be slow to engage in new experiences, rather than craving new experiences. The motorically disorganized child seeks and appears to crave new experiences. The latter is definitely more descriptive of Amanda. Also, Amanda's sense of self was not organized around negative defiant patterns. Her sense of self seemed to be organized around seeking satisfaction of sensory-motor cravings, which frequently resulted in negative or aggressive responses from others. These external responses did not match the internal pleasure she experienced in the satisfaction of her own sensory-motor cravings and consequently provoked an aggressive, controlling, manipulative reaction from Amanda.

In summary, Amanda's composite of symptoms included basic constitutional-maturational characteristics of variable degrees of sensory reactivity and integration, a high level of arousal, and motor activity that was impulsive and disorganized. These difficulties negatively impacted language development, reciprocal interpersonal interaction, and representational affective communication and elaboration. Interacting with Amanda's difficulties were the disordered primary caretaker relationships (one intrusive parent and the other anxious and tense). These interactive styles of the parents were intensified by the acute and chronic enduring stresses from parental illness, the family move, and marital discord. These multiple factors produced a complicated behavioral picture at the time of presentation with acute functional deterioration.

Diagnostic summary

Axis I: Primary Diagnosis
Regulatory Disorder Type III: Motorically Disorganized, Impulsive.

Axis II: Relationship Disorder Classification
Tendency toward Anxious/Tense Relationship: Mother
Tendency toward Overinvolved Relationship: Father.

Axis III: Medical and Developmental Disorders and Conditions
Expressive Language Disorder
Sensory-Motor Integration Disorder.

Axis IV: Psychosocial Stressors
Chronic and acute parental illness-psychiatric
Family move-major
Marital discord
Acute parental illness-physical
Overall effects: moderate and enduring with acute exacerbation.

Axis V: Functional Emotional Developmental Level
Needs structure and sensorimotor support to evidence capacity for representational/affective communication; otherwise manifests capacity inconsistent-

ly. Does not yet demonstrate capability of elaboration of affective themes in representational play, even with support. Has capacity for mutual attention, mutual engagement, and interactive intentionality and reciprocity, with constrictions under stress.

PIRGAS:50 (Distressed)

Discussion with caregivers and treatment planning

We saw Amanda's dangerously impulsive reactive and aggressive behaviors as a reflection of the desperation and increasing lack of control that she and her parents were experiencing. In our judgment, the family needed immediate intervention to help them deal with confusing and overwhelming feelings. Amanda needed monitoring to insure her safety, consistent structure to lessen her anxiety, and an interpersonal environment supportive of function at a more integrated level. The best setting available for her was a full-time, five-days-a-week, therapeutic day treatment program for toddlers and young children with emotional and behavioral disturbance. This also offered the parents immediate relief from the daily monitoring of Amanda, which had become exhausting to them.

Because of her distractibility, impulsive disorganization of play and behavior, and high motor activity, a trial of stimulant medication was recommended. This was initially considered as a temporizing measure to take the edge off Amanda's lack of attention, impulsivity and activity; provide a pause in the negative cycles of interaction at home; and provide an immediate opportunity for reestablishing some sense of control. Though the parents had basic differing philosophical attitudes toward giving medication to Amanda, they agreed to allow a trial, understanding that the medication would be discontinued if it did not help or had objectionable side effects.

The third and simultaneous step in intervention was to begin joint parent therapy with a psychologist involved in Amanda's day treatment program so there could be close coordination and interpretation of the parents' issues as they impacted Amanda's development in the light of her special developmental needs. The intervention was begun within 10 days, starting with parent sessions. Amanda started the day treatment program one month from the date of presentation at the clinic.

Intervention

After a one-week trial of stimulant medication, during which Amanda showed some improvement in hyperactivity and impulsivity, the medication was discontinued because of unacceptable rebound irritability and aggressiveness each day when the positive dose effect lapsed. A mild sleep medication was somewhat beneficial in decreasing the time required for Amanda to cool down for bedtime and fall asleep.

In the day treatment program Amanda had difficulty remaining focused during structured activities, even with continuous adult supervision. She was oppositional to supervisional intervention, prompts and redirects, and would not make eye contact with the therapists. After Amanda had been observed for two months in the day treatment group program, the consulting child psychiatrist prescribed Imipramine at night, replacing the milder sedative. She responded well, falling asleep more easily at night and participating more easily with the group in the daytime. She was still taking her bottle to bed at night. The parents had earlier acknowledged having conflicting feelings about their daughter becoming older.

In the therapy group setting, Amanda was observed initially to have inconsistent relationships with peers. She alternated between eagerly approaching them, physically and verbally, and aggressively taking toys away and taunting them. Most of her play with peers was parallel. Interactive play required continuous adult input to be successful. Amanda did not seek out relationships with adults, and she ignored or refused outreach from the adult therapists. Therapeutic goals in the day treatment program were to develop a trusting relationship with Amanda, and then, from within that relationship, to improve eye contact, verbal expression of emotion, and organization of behavior, and to facilitate interactive play with peers.

During seven months in this program, Amanda made modest progress. She began toileting herself. She was less aggressive and provocative with peers. She responded to adult requests but continued to need reinforcement. Attention to tasks at hand improved. Eye contact with adults and peers improved. She remained somewhat oppositional and manipulative. Progress was reported by her therapists to be supported by establishing "firm limits, consistent reinforcement of appropriate skills, and regular praise." At home Amanda began expressing her feelings verbally. Much of what she was reported to say consisted of negative statements directed toward her father—"You don't love me," "Stupid daddy," "Bad daddy," "Don't look at me," "I won't," and "I don't want to". Mr. Black was still fairly easily manipulated by these statements. At the same time, Amanda was becoming more demonstrative in her affection toward her parents.

The parents' therapist encouraged Mr. Black to pursue better medication regulation of his depression through his psychiatrist. Marital conflicts and difficulties with communication were addressed, particularly as they affected establishing clear boundaries with Amanda and defining who was responsible for her at a particular time. The therapist encouraged the Blacks to negotiate their differing ideas of parenting to a consensus, in order to promote consistency. The therapist advised them to avoid responding impulsively and intensely to Amanda's behavior, and using extreme descriptors of her behavior.

Although Amanda was observed to respond to Imipramine with improvement in getting to sleep, ability to focus and better behavioral organization, Ms. Black felt guilty using medication and wanted to stop it because of perceived side effects—Amanda's pulling at her eyelashes and eyebrows. (These behaviors continued when Amanda was taken off medication and seemed to be related to anxiety rather than the medication.) Mr. Black believed that the medication was quite helpful and did not want it discontinued. He anticipated deterioration in sleep patterns and behavior and feared a return to the family's former desperate state. The mother's concerns prevailed, and Amanda was taken off medication by the parents.

There was definite progress in the parents' management of behavior at home. However, marital, financial, and family stresses continued to undermine the day-to-day energy required for making lasting changes in patterns of relating. Significant difficulties remained.

Amanda's parents removed her from the day treatment program in order to involve her in community-based summer activities. The Blacks also stopped coming to their therapy sessions. At the end of the summer, the parents reported regression. Amanda would not listen. Her impulsivity persisted. Eye contact was still sporadic. She continued to be aggressive with peers. She had lost the gains she had previously made with bowel and bladder control and began playing in and smearing feces. Her father was having difficulty controlling his anger when she would not listen to him.

Because of Amanda's regression, a psychological reevaluation was performed by the psychologist who had been seeing Amanda and her parents. The Stanford Binet (4th Ed) was administered. During testing Amanda was observed to be "very wiggly in her seat," to fidget with her clothing, and to sit directly on her hands, attempting self-restraint. She was observed to attend well if frequently praised for successes. She was willing to try the more difficult items and did not become easily frustrated. Results placed her overall at the 50th percentile. Verbal reasoning subtest scores were highest at the 75th percentile. The results were judged to be an underestimate of her potential because of her activity level and distractibility. A test of visual motor functioning showed an age equivalent of 3 years, 6 months at her chronological age of 4 years, 1 month. She was noted to have a palmar grip and to have difficulty crossing the midline. Her Draw a Person, Draw a Family responses suggested avoidance. Amanda drew figures from television shows rather than herself and family members. The Plenk Storytelling Test elicited descriptive responses only, without emotional themes, suggesting anxiety about family and relationship issues. The Conner's parent questionnaire, completed separately by her parents, placed her in the clinical range of symptoms of attention problems, distractibility, and hyperactivity. The therapists recommended continued placement in a highly structured child care program to continue work on play skills and relationships, as was re-evaluation of the possible utility of medication for her continued distractibility and impulsivity. The therapists urged continued parent treatment to provide them with coping skills and energy necessary to manage constructively Amanda's challenging behaviors at home. Amanda was referred back to the developmental pediatrician to reconsider medication treatment. The parents were referred to another psychologist, since Amanda was no longer attending the day treatment program, for continued conjoint therapy.

The family was again at a point of crisis. The developmental pediatrician reinstituted medication therapy with a different stimulant, since the parents did not want to resume the Imipramine. The dosage was slowly increased to avoid side effects, to provide coverage during waking hours. It was also recommended that Amanda be enrolled in swimming and dancing activities to provide proprioceptive stimulation and work on sensory motor integration. The developmental pediatrician began seeing Amanda and her parents together every one to two months in consultation to follow up with medication and to provide hands-on supportive reflective work in play sessions designed to change interaction styles. The developmental pediatrician also functioned as the pivotal person for the parents, coordinating with other professionals. The duration of involvement was determined by the parents' perception of need and benefit.

At this point, there was a definitive change in the way Mr. and Ms. Black reflected on the family's problems. They had given up impatiently wanting the problems "to just go away." They now soberly acknowledged that their daughter needed their help and that this would involve time and hard work.

Within two months, Amanda was able to play independently in the clinic playroom for periods of 10 minutes without requiring adult direction. For example, she would put three puzzles together in sequence, then return to the most difficult one and put it together again. She still needed help with structure over longer periods of time. She had begun modulating voice intensity, with more periods of normal speaking tone. Her eye contact improved. She appeared less driven physiologically, and her facial appearance became less anxious and tense. She displayed more varied facial expression of emotion. Her preschool reported an increased ability to focus and ability to participate in groups with her peers. Amanda began to take in and integrate new information in a meaningful way. Her play became more elaborate, although emotional content remained sparse.

Despite the progress observed by others, the Child Behavior Checklists (CBCLs) completed independently by each parent ranked Amanda in the clinically significant range in aggressive behavior and attention problems, borderline in delinquent behavior, and borderline to clinically significant in thought problems. The only differences between the parent reports were more somatic complaints observed by Ms. Black and more social problems observed by Mr. Black. A simultaneously obtained preschool teacher's CBCL reported normal scores in all behavior categories, with the exception of a modestly elevated aggressive behavior score. The teacher's perspective provided helpful information about the similarities and differences in each parent's perceptions of Amanda, and the differences in behavior and/or perception of behavior outside the family.

The Blacks' work with the developmental pediatrician focused on helping the parents identify and respond to the cues expressed by Amanda's behaviors. They learned to recognize when she needed to reconnect with them, needed active proprioceptive stimulation to help her focus, needed help with organization (finding a contained quiet place to play), or needed calming and comforting (being read to and held). Validating Amanda's feelings by verbalizing and meeting her expressed needs became their goal, rather than simply reacting to the behavior. Amanda responded to this approach beautifully. Once her immediate need was met she proceeded along her way, maintaining a positive affective state and a greater level of behavioral organization.

When possible, the parents' needs were addressed in the same way by the developmental pediatrician. The parents were positively supported by pointing out to them what they did well and how well Amanda responded. The developmental pediatrician was readily available to them days, nights, and weekends by phone. The Blacks availed themselves of this support without ever abusing the service, and they recognized the boundaries of the relationship. For example, in one family session with Amanda present, Mr. Black remarked to the developmental pediatrician with humor, "I could be telling you that I am going to have my leg cut off in surgery tomorrow and you would respond to her before you responded to me." He recognized at that point that it was only through meeting Amanda's immediate need that a response to him was afforded. He also understood that he was better equipped to wait to have his need met than his 4-year-old daughter. It was a moment of recognition and differentiation for him.

Amanda regained bowel and bladder control within two months. Other areas continued to be problems at home including transitions, difficulty listening, and Amanda's need to be in control.

One month later Amanda returned, having been left off medication after it was discontinued during an illness. There was continued ambivalence about medication treatment because of appetite suppression, though Amanda's weight was maintained in an acceptable range. The loss of appetite was reported to aggravate the difficulty of trying to have Amanda sit at the dinner table for meals. Off medication, Amanda again showed a gradual deterioration of integration and a reappearance of behavioral symptoms. For example, Amanda began pretending she was a dog. She defecated on the front lawn and urinated in different parts of the home. The family dog had been hit by a car, required extensive surgery, and was home recuperating; her behavior was interpreted to reflect a need to receive the care that the family dog was receiving.

The parents sought a consultation with all professionals who had been involved with Amanda, and there was a consensus to recommend reinstitution of medication. The parents were agreeable to following the recommendation although the mother continued to feel ambivalent. This time a serotonin reuptake inhibitor was prescribed along with a lower dose of the stimulant Amanda had taken previously, with good effects. She again showed observable improvement.

During a home visit, while she was on medication, Amanda proudly showed the developmental pediatrician what she had helped plant in the yard and the bugs she had collected. She was observed playing interactively with a neighborhood friend, relinquishing control if necessary to keep the play going. The two children were observed exchanging ideas and negotiating successfully how they were going to accomplish something. Amanda was content to play with her friend and did not need adult assistance. In contrast, Mr. Black intrusively asked her to perform or answer questions that were not relevant to her play but were relevant to his agenda. Amanda's verbal response time continued to be delayed. An auditory scan obtained later revealed average to above average auditory processing in all subtests, suggesting that the delay in verbal response had another etiology.

Along with the above interventions, a psychology intern, working under the supervision of the parents' new therapist, began working with the school and with the parents in the home on three areas of difficulty common to both settings: complying with requests; persistent interrupting with repetitive questions, demands, and gestures; and difficulty with transitions. A coordinated positive feedback-based program of behavior management was put in place between the preschool and home, with reciprocal information exchanged daily. The parents began putting into action, with this support, what they had learned in the "Love and Logic" and "1-2-3- Magic" parenting classes they had recently taken. Amanda also began a daily morning program to prepare her for the upcoming kindergarten schedule.

The parents began seeing some positive impact from the changes in their approach. They decided again to try Amanda off medication It was reported that on medication she seemed to be more rigid in her thinking, more perseverative, aggravating the difficulty with transitions. She also was reported to be more emotionally labile. This time she continued to make progress off medication, although she did return to her more impulsive mode of action and interaction.

Over the ensuing few months the father's business began to show some financial return, and old debts were resolved, completely alleviating the financial stresses that had dogged this family for several years. The relief of this major stress resolved a significant area of marital conflict. The parents established new patterns of respectful, open, and direct communication with each other and with Amanda. The family members began to respect each other's boundaries and were able to make boundaries clear to one another in a constructive manner. The father's depression was resolving, and he was gaining a new sense of self-respect. He became less intrusive with Amanda. He was able to see Amanda less as a reflection of his own ego and more as an independent person with her own needs and privileges. Amanda's mother became less anxious and tense and became fully able to participate with warmth, joy, and pleasure in her daughter's successes and creativity, and was thrilled with Amanda's unique ways of expressing herself and her feelings.

As plans were being made for Amanda's fifth birthday party, Amanda requested that it be a "Stay Four" party. Her parents completely went along with her wishes, placing just four candles on her cake, and making no apologetic explanations to friends or other parents. This said that Amanda had a clear sense of where she was and what she yet needed to work through. The parents' joining with her spoke to their intuitive understanding and acceptance of her being where she needed to be. When Amanda was asked by the developmental pediatrician how long she wanted to remain four years old, Amanda answered, "Forever!"

Amanda did not remain four forever. Upon her return to the clinic a few months later, when asked how old she was, she stated emphatically, "Five!" She had grown into being five and was functioning well academically and socially in her Kindergarten. She occasionally had conflicts with peers in play because of her desire to control. She was responsive to verbal cues from peers, however, and would relinquish control. She had friends and regular playmates in school and in her neighborhood. Her home had become a hub for neighborhood children, filling the home with a happy, bustling warmth, akin to the family described in her parents' early fantasies.

At her last session with the developmental pediatrician, Amanda was happy. The anxious intense look that had been present in her face so often before was gone. It was replaced with emotional expressiveness. She came into the playroom and for the first time sat down at the table to play with the doll house. She arranged the furniture and the family figures and said proudly, "I'm making a house." Indeed she was, at home and in play. The pediatrician noted that Amanda was self reflective. She verbally observed aloud to herself how she had dropped the string as she tripped while pulling the pull xylophone, as if it was an expectable event, before reaching down and picking it up again. It was also notable that she continued moving the xylophone, creating a distracting noise, while she was talking about something her mother asked her to describe. Neither parent commented to her and she stopped on her own. When their patience and restraint was pointed out to them, her father smiled and said, "Well, I thought about saying something because it was bothering me." He enjoyed being praised for withholding interference, letting Amanda discover for herself that the noise of the xylophone was distracting to her, and changing her behavior on her own.

Amanda's mother reported recent questions raised by Amanda regarding her origins. Amanda knows that "babies come out of their mother's tummies." She asked if she came out of her mother's tummy. When her mother explained that she had not been able to have a baby that way, but instead chose Amanda from the babies in the hospital, Amanda adamantly denied that she did not come out of her mother's tummy and did not want to hear otherwise. The parents are for the first time considering adopting a second child.

Prognosis and discussion

Mr. Black asked toward the end what would be in the report from this last session. When asked if he wanted to know "if there were residual problems" and "what was Amanda's prognosis," he nodded. The therapist explained to him and Ms. Black that Amanda was continuing to show some regulatory and sensory integration difficulties with impulsive motor disorganization. However, she also was making progress through her own neurophysiological maturation in these areas. The significant changes that her parents have made in their interpersonal relationships and interaction, the therapist said, will continue to foster Amanda's growth and mastery of these difficulties in the future. They were told that it had been gratifying to witness the process and the results of their dedication and difficult personal work, bringing them to a blossoming sense of pleasure and enjoyment of each other and an appreciation of one another's contributions to the family

Amanda continues to have problems with motor planning, tending to jump up and head rapidly toward her intended destination, heedless of people or objects in her path, and often overshooting. At home and at school she is helped to reform the action in a slower, more organized manner. Amanda continues to delay verbal response to verbal input and requires time and encouragement to elaborate verbal expression. She is more fluent when she initiates spontaneous verbal expression than when she responds to verbal input from others. She is verbally expressive of her agenda, wishes, and needs, and more frequently talks before she acts. Standardized testing places receptive vocabulary five months ahead of her chronological age. Performance on the Oral Language Sentence Imitation Screening Test suggested normal morphological and syntactic development of expressive language.

Her parents experience daily delight in Amanda's initiative, creativity, and spontaneity. There are still intermittent struggles with her father over bedtime and her dawdling in the mornings, doing other things rather than eating and dressing. Mr. Black verges on losing his patience to anger but is able most of the time to recognize his feelings and stop himself.

Amanda's primary (Axis I) diagnosis remains the same with significant changes in all other parameters (Axes). It is not clear yet whether these problems will cause significant interference with functioning and relationships in the future. At this time it does not seem likely, but problems may recur during times of stress. It is likely that a question of Attention Deficit Disorder will be raised again.

500: Sleep Disorders in Infants and Toddlers

Klaus Minde, M.D., FRCP(C)

Sleep difficulties in infants and toddlers may involve problems in settling into sleep in the evening and/or episodes of waking during the night. Parents who bring their children to a mental health professional because of the child's distressing night behavior have often lived with disturbed nights for many months. They are, therefore, frequently exhausted, irritable, and frustrated. Some also feel guilty or afraid that they are "bad parents" when they do not want their children in their bed or do not cuddle or give them drinks in the middle of the night. For this reason, parents should be told that up to 15 percent of young children develop sleep problems, and that the great majority of such children can be helped by a few treatment sessions.

Sleep problems may have a number of causes. In some children with sleep disorders (10 percent), they may be related to birth difficulties or early temperamental irritability. A second group of young children (about 40 percent), in addition to their sleep problems, show symptoms compatible with Regulatory Disorders, Hypersensitive Subtype (see Black, this volume). These children may have difficulties in modulating their affect or in coping with sudden changes of their internal state or external surroundings. For example, they may wake up crying as if they cannot tolerate the transition from sleeping to waking. Their parents also often report that these children have great difficulty falling asleep in the evening and that they have virtually never slept through the night in their lives. A third group of children (about 20 percent) develop trouble settling in the evening or sleeping through the night after an illness or a visit away from home. A fourth group of youngsters with sleep problems (about 30 percent) have parents who have never allowed them to learn how to settle into sleep alone; as a consequence, whenever these children awaken, they require a parent's presence in order to fall asleep again.

While it is important to try to understand the original cause of an infant's disturbed night behavior, it is also crucial to recognize that different factors may be responsible for maintaining the behavior at present. Consider, for example, an infant with biologically determined difficulties settling into sleep. This baby's mother may be so distressed by the problem that she becomes angry at the youngster. By the time he is a toddler, this child may be oppositional and anxious, his sleep compromised by his emotional state. Management of a young child's sleep problems, therefore must take into account: (a) the biology of the child; (b) the parents' past and present emotional and social history; and (c) the parents' current assessment of their child's intentions. The two case reports below illustrate how one can assess these aspects of a child and family situation and use the information gained to plan and implement treatment.

JAMES COREY, Age 15 months

Reason for referral

Jamie's mother brought him to the infant clinic because she did not know "how to cope with James' sleep pattern any more." Since his birth 15 months ago, Jamie had awakened 6 to 8 times per night to demand the breast. His mother's sleep was severely curtailed; she felt that sleep deprivation was causing her to react angrily to Jamie's brother, 33-month-old Matthew.

Assessment process

The assessment consisted of three interviews at the clinic—one with the mother, one with both parents, and one with mother and child (although this had been scheduled for the whole family, including mother, father, and two children). After this third interview, the Bayley Scales of Infant Development were administered to Jamie.

Assessment findings

History of sleep disorder

Ms. Bryant (she continued to use her own name after marriage) began to describe Jamie's sleep pattern by comparing it to that of Matthew. As newborns, both boys had awakened every four hours. Jamie, however, had never slept longer than four hours at a stretch. In fact, at 15 months Jamie would sleep for a single four-hour period at night and awaken every hour thereafter.

The family's evening routine usually involved Ms. Bryant bathing the two boys together. Then she read a story to Matthew at his bedside, with James present. After tucking Matthew in, she would carry Jamie and the humidifier into his room, give him a teddy bear and his special blanket, lie down with him, and nurse him until he fell asleep. This routine took between 15 and 20 minutes. At about 11 p.m., Jamie could be expected to awaken crying on the first of up to 8 occasions during the night. Ms. Bryant would then leave her own bed and move to Jamie's, where she would spend the rest of the night. (Until Jamie was six or seven months old, he had slept in his parents' bed. This arrangement had disrupted Mr. Corey's sleep, so a mattress was placed on the floor for Jamie in another room.)

Ms. Bryant felt that if she did not respond to Jamie immediately, he would become distraught. Consequently, she had never allowed him to cry for any length of time but had always quieted him by nursing. This pattern of interaction was observable on one occasion during the initial interview when Jamie approached his mother and gave a little knock on her breast. Although Jamie did not seem to be making an urgent request, Ms. Bryant nursed him immediately. Jamie then dozed, one hand fiddling with his hair and once putting his finger in his mother's mouth.

Ms. Bryant reported that Jamie napped between noon and 2 p.m. each day. Often part of Jamie's nap took place in the car while Ms. Bryant picked up Matthew from a play group. Occasionally, Jamie would also sleep in the late afternoon. None of these naps seemed to affect his sleep at night.

Ms. Bryant recalled that as a child she had had great difficulty falling asleep. Now she reads herself to sleep. She interpreted Jamie's awakenings as an attachment to the particular comfort of nursing at the breast; she commented that he had always refused bottles, fingers, or pacifiers. She also recognized, however, that nursing had become a habit for Jamie rather than an intense need.

Jamie's developmental history

Ms. Bryant reported that her pregnancy with Jamie had been more tiring than her first pregnancy. She did not sleep well and wondered whether, at 40, she was too old to have another child and should have been content with Matthew. Jamie's delivery was easy, however. He was born alert and healthy, weighing 8 pounds 10 ounces, with Apgar ratings of 8 and 10. He and Ms. Bryant were discharged after one day in the hospital. Unfortunately, Jamie's father was not at home at the time, and Matthew began to throw bean bags at the new arrival. Ms. Bryant responded by calling a teenager to come to the house to take Matthew out for a walk.

Ms. Bryant recalled that as infants both her sons were very strong, wanting to be lifted, and stood very early. Jamie was more cuddly than Matthew but also needed to be held and entertained a lot, in contrast to Matthew, a "low-maintenance baby." Ms. Bryant added that Matthew was able to amuse his brother and had become increasingly comfortable in doing so.

Although Jamie showed some evening fussiness between 8 and 16 weeks, he did not have colic. He was sitting at about 6 months, crawled at $7\frac{1}{2}$ months, and walked at $9\frac{1}{2}$ months. At 15 months (the time of the first interview), Jamie could say about 5 words. He had never had any allergies or feeding problems, had never been hospitalized, and had never been away from his mother for more than 4 or 5 hours. He tended to fuss and cry whenever an unknown visitor came or his mother left him to go out on her own, but in general he coped well with day-to-day changes in family life. Jamie attended a weekly play group with his mother; there he related better to two older children than to an 18-month-old girl.

Jamie is disciplined by being spoken to. He clearly understands the word "no." If he persists in a forbidden activity, he is usually removed from the situation; very occasionally Ms. Bryant gives his hand a slight slap. When this occurs, Jamie seems outraged, and his mother usually apologizes.

Family history

Ms. Bryant, now 42 years old, was born and raised in the midwestern United States. She described her family as "very Catholic." Ms. Bryant was the oldest of six children. She was 17 years old when her youngest sibling was born and said she often felt more like one of the parents than like a child. Ms. Bryant's father, now retired, was the vice-president of an insurance company. She described her mother as "exceptionally bright," earning a B.A. at age 16 and an M.A. at 17, and working briefly as a research chemist before staying home to raise her family. In the family, "schoolwork always came first," although the children were also encouraged to do other things. Mr. Bryant talked to the family a lot, but mainly about business. Emotional issues were rarely discussed. Of Ms. Bryant's five siblings, three have MBAs and one is a chartered accountant. They are all involved in active and successful business enterprises.

Ms. Bryant earned a B.A. in economics and went on to study for an MBA but did not complete it. She met and married a man who shortly after their marriage moved to Canada with her to avoid being sent to Vietnam. The marriage lasted for two years. Ms. Bryant recalled, "We were expecting the revolution . . . but then we just quit." She remembers her mother's comment: "You people think about how to be happy. Your father and I thought about what was the right thing to do."

Ms. Bryant began to work at a major bank and became the manager of its international money market operation. At the same time she was involved with a "therapeutic community" of people with whom she could "share her feelings." She lived with Mr. Corey for $5^1/2$ years before marrying him; one year after the marriage, Matthew was born. When Matthew was four months old, Ms. Bryant enrolled in a doctoral program in economics but soon quit as the course of study seemed "too theoretical."

Mr. Corey, also 42 years old, was born and raised in Canada. His father was a farmer who, in middle age, had taken over and rescued a failing business, an achievement of which he was very proud. Mr. Corey's father had been a pilot in World War II and, for a time, had operated a flying school after the war. Mr. Corey's mother was the daughter of a minister and a nurse.

Mr. Corey was the youngest of three children and the only son. He is not close to his sisters. He claimed that his family would have meals together without ever exchanging a word. He recalled that his mother had "doted on him" because he had asthma and said that "the house ran around me." Mr. Corey described his father as quite traditional; he would not pay university tuition for his daughters.

Mr. Corey earned a B.S. degree and an MBA. After graduation he developed a computer consulting business. He was always very involved in sports, still plays hockey four evenings each week in the winter, and engages in other sports during the summer. He also plays the piano and takes flying lessons, referring to himself a s "a workaholic and a playaholic."

Ms. Bryant and Mr. Corey say that they are close and can confide in each other. However, Ms. Bryant also mentioned that she "keeps a lot of things to herself" because her husband's active lifestyle does not give him much time to listen to her "emotional thoughts."

Subsequent interview

Both of Jamie's parents had been asked to attend a subsequent interview, as described above, so that the examiner could obtain a sense of the range of their concerns and learn something about their individual backgrounds. The contrast between Ms. Bryant and Mr. Corey, in both appearance and manner, was striking. Ms. Bryant looked very tired. She wore an old parka and boots that were covered with mud because she had been on a picnic in the park with the children during the day, even though the weather had been rainy and cold. Mr. Corey, dressed neatly in a dark business suit, looked clean, crisp, and alert.

The couple reviewed the sleep problem and noted its link with nursing. Mr. Corey described his concern for Matthew, who was becoming increasingly angry at his mother's chronic fatigue and preoccupation with Jamie. Mr. Corey also stressed his own need to be involved with sports. He seemed rather judgmental concerning his wife's ability to cope with their children. During the whole discussion, he seemed distant toward his wife.

The therapist suggested that the parents keep a detailed record of Jamie's sleep behavior for the next two weeks and then return with both children for an assessment of the family's overall relationships.

Third interview

On the day of the interview scheduled for the whole family, only Ms. Bryant and Jamie arrived. Ms. Bryant returned the sleep diary; she said that her husband would be unable to come and that Matthew had developed a cold and was at home with a babysitter.

The interview took place in a special playroom for infants and toddlers within the hospital's department of psychiatry. Ms. Bryant carried Jamie on her back from the lobby to the playroom. Once they had settled, she encouraged him to explore the room. Initially, Jamie was reluctant to relate to the examiner and remained standing close to his mother, who caressed him and obviously enjoyed the physical closeness. After about five minutes, Jamie moved toward some of the available toys, concentrating on one that featured Sesame Street characters who popped up as different mechanisms were manipulated. Jamie was only able to manipulate the simpler mechanisms. His mother tried eagerly to show him how to get additional figures to pop up, but Jamie showed little interest in her teaching and soon turned his attention to other toys. Again, his mother explained their functions in great detail rather than allowing him to explore the toys on his own.

After about 12 minutes, the examiner began talking to Jamie as he explored a toy nearby. He commented on what the boy was doing, his apparent intentions, and his exploratory strategies. Ms. Bryant watched for about three minutes and then tried to distract Jamie away from the therapist with another toy. Jamie did not respond to this new toy but went to his mother, looked her in the eyes, and tapped her right breast as he had done during the first interview. Ms. Bryant immediately began to nurse Jamie, who became drowsy and rested on her lap. Some six minutes later, Jamie was up again, exploring different toys. Now Ms. Bryant seemed less inclined to act as teacher. She appeared happy that Jamie had connected with her and talked at length about her wish to continue to breastfeed for "many more months to come."

When Ms. Bryant began to talk about her breastfeeding, Jamie went back to the toy he had explored with the therapist, repeating his actions with it and frequently looking at the therapist, almost as if he expected to hear the therapist repeat his comments on his activities. When this did not happen immediately, Jamie stood up and moved into the visual field between his mother and the therapist, looking directly at him until he turned his attention to Jamie and commented on the child's apparent wish to have him participate in his games. The therapist then began to talk to Ms. Bryant about the possibility of Jamie's father's taking over a good deal of the evening routine with his son. Ms. Bryant was not sure that her husband would be willing to do this, but said she would consider the suggestion and return with Mr. Corey three days hence to discuss the issue further with the therapist.

After their session with the therapist, Ms. Bryant and Jamie spent time with a psychologist who administered the Bayley Scales to Jamie. He had an MDI score of 145 and a PDI score of 132, putting him at the superior level.

Diagnosis

Jamie seemed to have had difficulties getting to sleep since birth. He needed his mother to help him, either by nursing him or providing him with the monotonous movements of a car ride. Jamie had no history of organic trauma that would have explained his sleep difficulty. No severe psychosocial stresses had been part of Jamie's life, nor did he show any signs of undue anxiety or depression. Jamie seemed able to relate well to the examiner and be capable of playing and learning in an age-appropriate way.

Observation of the interaction between Ms. Bryant and Jamie suggested that she was excessively preoccupied with her son. She had a hard time letting him play with the examiner and almost seemed to need Jamie's constant attention and devotion. This suggested the possibility of a relationship disorder, overinvolved type. However, the patterns typical of an established relationship disorder were not present: Although his mother behaved in a somewhat dominating and overcontrolling fashion, Jamie appeared neither fuzzy nor unfocused, he did not display overcomplying behaviors, and his motor skills were good overall.

The provisional formulation was that Jamie's sleep problems had their origins in his mother's conflicted feelings about her professional and caregiving roles—if she were not going to be chief of the international money market operations of a national bank, then she would breastfeed all day and all night for 15 months. This conflict, probably originating in Ms. Bryant's relationship with her own mother, seemed to be preventing Ms. Bryant from developing the resolve necessary to have Jamie fall asleep alone.

Diagnostic summary

Axis I: Primary Diagnosis
Sleep Behavior Disorder.

Axis II: Relationship Disorder Classification
No diagnosis.

Axis III: Medical and Developmental Disorders and Conditions
No diagnosis.

Axis IV: Psychosocial Stressors
Mild effects.

Axis V: Functional Emotional Developmental Level
Has fully achieved mutual attention, mutual engagement, and interactive intentionality and reciprocity, at age appropriate levels.

PIR-GAS:62 (Between Perturbed and Significantly Perturbed)

Discussion with caregivers and treatment planning

Second interview with both parents

During this interview, Mr. Corey expressed his willingness to be part of Jamie's treatment, and both parents also agreed on a plan. They decided to buy Jamie a crib. Ms. Bryant would nurse Jamie in the rocker beside the crib at about 7:30 p.m. and again at 11:00 p.m. If Jamie cried during the night thereafter, his father would go into his room to reassure him, as often as every 15 minutes if crying continued, but would not allow him out of the crib.

Toward the end of this session, talk returned to Mr. Corey's activities. He mentioned that he had told Matthew that he wanted him to come jogging with him next summer. The parents laughed together at Matthew's assertive response to his father's proposition—he announced firmly, "I go to play group." The couple then filled out the Fullard Toddler Temperament Scale; their assessment of Jamie suggested that he had an intermediate low temperament, indicating that he showed no difficult temperamental characteristics.

Intervention

Third interview with both parents

When they returned after two weeks, both parents were sick with the flu and coughing. They said that they had put up a crib for Jamie and were following their program consistently despite sickness in the family. Ms. Bryant would breastfeed Jamie and put him in the crib between 7:30 and 8:00 p.m. He usually slept then until 11:00 p.m., when his mother would feed him again. Then his father took over, going in 10 minutes after the 11 p.m. feeding to put Jamie down if he was not asleep already. Mr. Corey would also get up for Jamie's other wakenings during the night. Each time Jamie cried, Mr. Corey would wait for 5 minutes before responding. Jamie was able to fall back to sleep on his own about 25 percent of the time. At the other times, Mr. Corey would pick Jamie up, wipe his nose, give him a sip of water, put him back down, and rub his back. When Jamie stopped crying, his father would leave.

The sleep diary indicated that Jamie's wakenings had decreased from eight to four per night; the night preceding this interview, he had awakened only twice, at 12:30 a.m. and at 4:30 a.m. Mr. Corey was very encouraged by this success. He pointed out that the frequency of awakenings was decreasing; settling Jamie was becoming easier; Jamie had occasionally gone back to sleep on his own, something he had never done before; and he had accepted his father attending to him at night. During this account of her husband's successes, Ms. Bryant seemed somewhat wistful. She reported that Jamie had become more demanding of the breast during the day, that he was not happy, and that he would not sleep in his crib during the day. In fact, she concluded, "both kids had been pretty obnoxious lately."

The parents then discussed their children's eating patterns and recent difficulties in getting Matthew to the table at supper time. Ms. Bryant said, rather helplessly, that "regular scheduling was not her strong suit." Her husband contradicted her, pointing out that the children ate both breakfast and lunch with her. Ms. Bryant seemed somewhat defeated and defensive throughout the session. As the discussion returned to the issue of sleep, she said to her husband, "If I had known last year that you were willing to help."

Diagnostic update

The two joint interviews with Jamie's parents suggested that things were improving after the father took over some of the bedtime routines. These sessions also revealed Ms. Bryant's ambivalence about the effectiveness of this process, despite her admission that "regular scheduling was not her strong suit." These observations supported the initial diagnostic impression that Jamie's sleep disorder was related to difficulties within the mother-child relationship.

Fourth interview

Both parents attended the session. Ms. Bryant described the previous two weeks as "kind of mixed." Mr. Corey attributed setbacks to his wife's deviating from the agreed-upon plan of putting James down awake. He also felt that the 5:30 a.m. breastfeeding led Jamie to calculate, when he awoke during the night, that "one of these times Mom will come and feed me." Mr. Corey thought that the hall light should be out at night. As this light had been left on for Matthew's benefit, both parents agreed that the older boy could be given a flashlight to use if he had to go to the bathroom during the night.

Ms. Bryant then described how very difficult it was to get Jamie to nap during the day. In fact, he would nap only in the car; after driving Matthew home from nursery school, she would leave Jamie sleeping in the car and watch him through the window. When Mr. Corey suggested at this point that Jamie could be put down for a nap with a bottle, Ms. Bryant replied that "kids get their teeth rotted out with bottles" and that this was "a serious worry." She then said, warningly, to her husband, that Jamie would be weaned only very gradually.

Fifth interview, three weeks later

The parents reported that Jamie was more and more frequently sleeping through the night—that is, from approximately 11 p.m. to 5:30 a.m. or 6:30 a.m. Mr. Corey now thought it was better to go in immediately to Jamie when he awakened during the night, before he became fully aroused. He was continuing to do this whenever necessary.

Ms. Bryant said she was generally getting much more sleep now and was very pleased about this. She looked better and smiled several times during the session. Toward the end of the session, both parents observed that they had gone as far in settling James as they could right now. They decided to end treatment at this point; both said that they were very pleased with the result.

Six weeks later, Ms. Bryant telephoned. Ostensibly she called simply to report that Jamie's sleep problems had totally abated. However, she seemed needy and appeared to want some validation of her role as housewife and mother at this time. She declined the therapist's invitation to come and talk further.

Follow-up interview, six months later

James and his mother were seen six months after the final interview for follow-up, a standard part of the treatment approach. At this time, Ms. Bryant revealed that the treatment process had been tremendously difficult for her. She said that during the first weeks her husband "had three children in the family," since he had to comfort her during her crying spells as much as he had to teach Jamie the new rules of the house.

Interestingly, Jamie had learned these rules quite well. He now regularly slept through the night. When he did awaken, he could usually get back to sleep without calling for his mother or father. However, a stressor—getting a cold or an unpleasant incident during the day—could send Jamie back immediately to waking up at night and calling for his mother. Ms. Bryant had not quite given up some of her old habits. For example, she still breast-fed Jamie before he went to sleep at night (he was now 25 months old) and when he woke up at 6 a.m., although she realized that Jamie did not mind doing without the early morning feeding.

Some other interesting developments had occurred in Jamie's family in the six months since the last session. On two occasions, the bank where Ms. Bryant had been employed had called to probe her interest in rejoining them. Ms. Bryant was very happy about this, although she thought she was not ready for this at present and thought that in the future she would probably prefer to work in a different field. There was little talk about the marital relationship. Ms. Bryant seemed very pleased with the present state of affairs and was even trying to have another baby. This was a somewhat problematic endeavor: she had had a miscarriage four months earlier, and she worried that her advancing age (she was now 43) made it less likely that she would have the daughter she so very much wished for.

Ms. Bryant was still overly responsive to Jamie's every whim. She described him as "a very sensitive little boy right now who needed a lot of her attention." In fact, Jamie was quite demanding during the interview. He had trouble tolerating his mother talking to the therapist. When this was directly pointed out to him, he smiled and then looked at his mother, who put him on her lap and hugged him, saying "We are a very special team."

Prognosis and discussion

The therapist's experience with Jamie and his family illustrates a number of important issues seen frequently in families whose children have sleep disorders. Jamie's mother appears to have struggled all her life against her desire and need to be nurtured by others. She had used two coping strategies: becoming a nurturer of others (her first husband and James); and identifying with her mother's high achievements (in her job at the bank and as spouse of a highly competent husband). Ms. Bryant obviously hoped to be appreciated and valued by those she nurtured; she must have been saddened by the failure of her first marriage. Jamie seemed to be insatiable; her initial request for a consultation constituted a kind of admission of failure—she was unable to give this child what he needed.

The therapist's first goal was to reassure Ms. Bryant about her mothering abilities. The issue of weaning was sidestepped for the moment. At the same time, the therapist validated Ms. Bryant's wish to be fairly treated. Since during her childhood she had functioned as a second mother to her siblings, without recognition, it seemed important that in her present family she be able to let others know about her contributions and demand appropriate support from them. Mr. Corey had come from a rather constricted family and one, moreover, in which men were considered superior to women. He needed to recognize the mutuality of his and his wife's roles and functions in their life together. Taking over the care of James during the night was presented as a chance to be a good father and to become more aware of his own somewhat neglected nurturing capacities.

The difficulty with this approach lay in the possibility that the sleep disorder reflected a tendency on Ms. Bryant's part to deprive Jamie of an autonomous existence. Yet an attempt to explore the full extent of what seemed to be a rather enmeshed mother-son relationship before a solid therapeutic relationship had been established would have led to failure. Ms. Bryant's agreement to make changes in Jamie's sleep routine and her husband's willingness to be involved boded well for a focused approach. Ms. Bryant's apparently less overinvolved relationship with Matthew also suggested strengths and flexibility in her mothering capacities.

Jamie's own capacities, revealed in the assessment, also guided the intervention approach. He seemed to be a well-developed boy who had neither experienced overt biological insults nor exhibited early temperamental difficulties that might have explained his poor sleep habits. Presumably, then, he could and would learn to modulate his own patterns of sleeping and waking.

The parents' positive response to Matthew's comment that he was not, at age four, willing to join his father in jogging but preferred to continue with his play group suggested that both parents were able to back off when their children gave them direct, firm messages. The therapist directed the treatment to encouraging this process.

This case illustrates two other aspects of the assessment and treatment of sleep disorders in young children. First, Ms. Bryant's suffering during the initial weeks of treatment, when she was forced to give up her total care of James, is a common phenomenon. Therapists should be aware of this possibility so that they can support parents consistently; regrettably, Ms. Bryant did not tell us about her suffering until the six-month follow-up interview. Second, this family, like many who come to a sleep clinic, did not choose to deal with many underlying issues that were complicating their lives together. Ms. Bryant and Mr. Corey never took advantage of opportunities to discuss the quality of their marriage or the relationships they had with their own families. The therapist refrained from commenting on the possible connection between Jamie's demandingness of attention during the follow-up interview and his wish to be breastfed hourly during his infancy. There was reason to believe that exposure to peers in the nursery school would support Jamie's individuation and that further positive experiences, in addition to the real strengths in Jamie and his family, would help him become a solid young man.

Diagnostically, this sleeping problem was clearly related to the conflicting needs of Ms. Bryant and Jamie. The boy needed to learn to soothe himself and regulate his state of arousal in a more autonomous fashion. His mother, however, wanted somebody she "could be everything for." Since Jamie never showed most of the behavior considered symptomatic of a full-blown relationship disorder, it seems most appropriate to think of his sleep problem as a reflection of a perturbation in his relationship with his mother.

DEBORAH ROSS, Age 6 months

Reason for referral

The physician who cared for six-month-old Debbie Ross's maternal grandmother called the infant clinic after his patient had mentioned to him how exasperated her daughter had become with Debbie's sleep pattern. In fact, the young mother had voiced fears of physically harming the baby. The grandmother's physician felt the case was an emergency and asked us to arrange an initial interview with Debbie's parents within 72 hours. The therapist immediately called Mrs. Ross, who seemed elated by the call; an appointment was made for an initial interview with Mrs. Ross and her husband.

Assessment process

Instead of coming to the interview alone, the couple brought Debbie along. They had never once left her with a substitute caregiver with the exception of one trusted babysitter, and could not conceive of doing so now. As Debbie slept for more than half of the interview (the parents attributed this behavior to the rather long car ride), the therapist could obtain a good deal of information from the Rosses. The parents also completed an Infant Temperament Scale on this occasion.

Assessment findings

Both parents claimed that during her entire life Debbie had never slept more than 2 to 3 hours in one stretch. Her mother usually nursed her after she woke up, but Debbie would cry even after the feeding and could only be comforted by being carried around continuously. She seldom slept in her crib because she seemed to "dislike it." Being placed in a bassinet or car seat seemed to calm her. She often wore a snowsuit, seeming to like the containment it provided, but hated blankets and being tucked in tightly. Even with a snowsuit on, Debbie would at times cry for up to two hours, despite her parents' willingness to carry her around.

While both parents voiced their frustration over Debbie, it became clear that they had never developed any kind of routine with the baby. There were no routines for bedtime or naps; the parents' ministrations to their daughter seemed to have a hectic, improvised quality.

Developmental history

Debbie was the couple's first child. Ms. Ross observed that her pregnancy had been quite easy initially but that from the fifth month onward she would wake up three to four times each night. She then became worried that she would not manage to deliver Debbie in a "totally natural way." Some of her doubts reflected comments from friends and family members who thought that her small body size (she weighed only 100 pounds before her pregnancy) would not allow her to go to term with her baby.

In fact, the pregnancy lasted 40 weeks; Ms. Ross went into labor three days after her due date. Her first contractions were diagnosed as false labor; she was discharged from the hospital labor room three times on three consecutive days. Ms. Ross became increasingly desperate. When she developed a fever and the baby's heart rate increased precipitously, an emergency cesarean section was performed. Debbie was born weighing 7 pounds, 10 ounces, with Apgar ratings of 5 and 8 at 1 and 5 minutes.

Ms. Ross recalled being "shattered" by the cesarean. She had dreamt of a delivery without anesthesia, placing the newborn on her stomach, and feeding it right away. Instead, she found herself with "a big scar and a baby who did not even want the breast." Ms. Ross became quite depressed. She said that during the five nights immediately postpartum she had slept only about 10 hours in total. Debbie was the first grandchild on both her father's and mother's side. The innumerable visitors to the hospital made it, according to Ms. Ross, "hard for her to bond with Debbie." Ms. Ross also observed that this baby had "come out of her with a frown on her face."

After Debbie came home, she "began her yelling routine"—crying for three hours a day and leaving her mother increasingly exhausted. Ms. Ross nevertheless remained determined to breastfeed. She called in a lactation consultant, who reassured her that mothers often do not have enough milk in the beginning and encouraged Ms. Ross to substitute an occasional bottle for the breast if Debbie seemed to need additional food.

At four weeks of age, Deborah suddenly began to show projectile vomiting. The first day this occurred, she vomited some 20 times, according to her mother, requiring a visit to the hospital. There the doctor tried to put an IV in and ordered an ultrasound examination. However, following a big bowel movement Debbie stopped vomiting and was discharged home.

The next three months saw little change. Debbie appeared stiff when she was carried and would cry, in a colicky fashion, for up to two hours a day. No routines for sleeping and eating were established. At night, Ms. Ross usually had Debbie in bed with her.

Ms. Ross noticed changes in Debbie beginning at three months. She now seemed to "hate missing anything" and, while she appeared very tired at 9 p.m., would refuse to close her eyes and actively fight sleep. Both parents tried to deal with this new behavior by playing with Debbie for long periods. They learned, however, that she was very sensitive to sounds and could easily become overexcited. The father, who sang to Debbie more than her mother did, was the first to notice this sensitivity, which he tried to use to calm Debbie at night. For example, he would sing softly to her from 2 a.m. to 4 a.m., hoping that she would go back to sleep once more during the night. However, this strategy never worked; Debbie remained an extremely vigilant, poorly modulated infant.

When Debbie was four months old, Ms. Ross decided that she did not sleep because she got "too much milk." Ms. Ross stopped breastfeeding Debbie during the day, a change that Debbie seemed to accept quite well. However, breastfeeding on demand continued during the night, and, since Debbie awoke almost every 90 minutes, her mother still got little sleep.

Family history

Ms. Ross was 28 years old. She was the second of three children and the only girl. Her father was an engineer and her mother an art therapist. Ms. Ross said that her early life was "quite wonderful" because her father spoiled her. Although Ms. Ross's mother had had depressive periods, Ms. Ross had always confided in her and felt that she had been a great help in understanding Debbie. Her overall "good life" notwithstanding, Ms. Ross remembered that as a child she had always been afraid to sleep alone; she recalled pacing her room tearfully as other family members watched TV. She used to imagine that there might be bugs in her bed and would persuade babysitters to stay with her in her room for many hours if her parents were out.

Ms. Ross met her husband in high school; they married when Ms. Ross was 25. She described her marriage as a very good one, saying that she and her husband helped each other and compensated for each other's weaknesses. Ms. Ross observed, for example, that she was a very sensitive person who could at times be taken advantage of, but her husband was much tougher and could get things done quickly.

Ms. Ross had trained as a lawyer and worked in a firm owned by a relative. Since Debbie's birth, however, she had spent only 5 to 10 hours per week in the office; she hoped to continue this pattern for the next year.

Mr. Ross, age 29, had three older sisters. He said that things had been difficult in his home at times since his mother was a "real powerhouse" who tried to dominate her children's lives and careers. Mr. Ross coped by "being a wild boy," especially during adolescence, when he was "too preoccupied with other things to study very much." His mother had decided that after high school he would study engineering. However, he failed most of his courses, switched to a major in commerce, and now worked as a real estate agent.

Mr. Ross observed that he was very much like his daughter Debbie. He described himself as "very unregulated," without any real routines in his life. Even though he was always awake by 6 a.m. or 7 a.m., he might go to bed any time between 11 p.m. and 2 a.m.; he thought nothing about dropping in on friends at 10 p.m.

Mr. Ross said that at times he went into Debbie's room when she cried at night and gave her a bottle, which she accepted. He acknowledged, however, that there were no regular caretaking patterns at night and that both parents wondered whether Debbie needed more routines.

The initial interview

When Debbie arrived with her parents, she was dressed in a big snowsuit. She had fallen asleep in the car on the way to the hospital; some 30 minutes into the interview, she awoke and immediately began to whimper. Ms. Ross instantly turned to Debbie, took her out of her snowsuit, and prepared a cold bottle for her (claiming that Debbie preferred cold milk to warm). Debbie did not calm after her feeding but remained restless and whimpered from time to time. She looked at the therapist curiously and smiled occasionally but did not engage in any finger play and had little use for age-appropriate toys. Mr. and Ms. Ross shifted her back and forth between their laps and her car seat, but Debbie never seemed truly content.

The therapist suggested that both parents keep a detailed sleep diary and think about establishing some sort of routine for Debbie's daily activities. He also gave them an Infant Temperament Scale to complete; Debbie scored in the "difficult" cluster, with high ratings on scales of negative mood, intensity, and activity, and with low ratings on the adaptive scale.

Diagnosis

Debbie's history revealed biologic vulnerability and suggested that she had been a difficult youngster since birth. Her birth followed a somewhat problematic prenatal course, and her Apgar ratings of 5 and 8 were low (a normal score would be at least 7 at one minute and 9 at five minutes after birth.) Mrs. Ross reported characteristics compatible with a difficult temperament beginning at birth and a range of behaviors demonstrating her unhappiness: failure to sleep through a single night, poor feedings, and frequent colicky episodes. This pattern was confirmed by the temperamental assessment at seven months, in which Debbie scored in the "difficult" cluster."

Debbie's more recent symptoms were consistent with a regulatory disorder. Her parents reported an apparent difficulty in shifting her attention from something in which she had become interested. Investigators of regulatory disorders sometimes describe this phenomenon as a problem of "attentional organization" among children who have a hard time focusing their attention but once they have done so have equal difficulty "letting go." Debbie's parents described her as "being cranky and unfocused," but they also reported that she "refused to close her eyes" or "fought sleep." Debbie's sensitivity to all noises and especially to loud sounds was also typical of children with regulatory disorders.

Interestingly, both of Debbie's parents had histories of struggling with some aspects of their own behavioral regulation. Ms. Ross reported that she had always been somewhat anxious, reacting to external stresses, such as separations and pregnancy, with disturbed sleep. Mr. Ross, for his part, described himself as "poorly regulated," without solid routines.

Diagnostic summary

   Axis I: Primary Diagnosis
   Regulatory disorder: Type I: Hypersensitive.

   Axis II: Relationship Disorder Classification
   No diagnosis.

   Axis III: Medical and Developmental Disorders and Conditions
   No diagnosis.

   Axis IV: Psychosocial Stressors
   No obvious effects.

   Axis V: Functional Emotional Developmental Level
   Has not reached expected levels for mutual attention and mutual engagement, but shows some capacity with wooing.

PIR-GAS:75 (Between Adapted and Perturbed)

Discussion with caregivers and treatment planning

The overriding diagnostic impression at this point was that Debbie showed many signs of a regulatory disorder. However, since the Rosses had come to the clinic primarily because of Debbie's sleep problem, the staff felt that treatment should be directed initially to this symptom. At the same time, the staff framed its suggestions to the family as a discussion of ways to handle Debbie's more general difficulties in regulating her mood and attention, not only her sleep.

Ten days later, Ms. Ross returned to the clinic with Debbie. She said that things had been difficult. Most nights, she and her husband had managed to get Debbie to bed by about 8 p.m. They thought she might be more comfortable sleeping on her stomach and had tried to wrap her gently in a blanket. Although Debbie had resisted this initially, she now seemed to like the routine and settled fairly easily.

On most of the nights since our first interview, Debbie had slept for some three hours and then had been fed by her mother. Thereafter, she would wake frequently and by 4 a.m. would end up in her mother's bed, where she would suckle almost continuously without seeming to take any milk. Debbie's parents were tired. They felt it was time to "do something."

Naps were not much better. Debbie would often sleep in the stroller or the car for about half an hour in the late morning, and again between 4 p.m. and 5 p.m., but seldom in her bed.

Discussion with Ms. Ross centered primarily around the need to give Debbie a predictable daily routine and allow her a chance to regulate herself. The therapist pointed out that some of Debbie's sounds (responded to by her parents as signals of distress) were not really cries, but rather attempts to soothe herself. The therapist suggested trying new routines around afternoon naps, since a very competent babysitter was in the house and eager to help in settling Debbie.

Intervention

Third interview, three weeks later

Both parents came to the interview and reported feeling "rather optimistic." Debbie was now willing to be put in her crib and sleep there, falling asleep on her own without a lengthy fuss. Ms. Ross had decided to give Debbie a big feed at around midnight and let her husband deal with any later wakings, since she had, in her words, "soft heart disease." Mr. Ross had taken on this charge, refusing to pick Debbie up when she awakened at 2 a.m. and 4 a.m. Debbie would protest quite loudly for about 10 minutes, but following a gentle back rub by her father would usually calm and fall back to sleep.

In this interview, Mr. and Ms. Ross noted that Debbie liked a pacifier but would lose it at night and therefore couldn't turn to it when she awoke. They wondered what they could do about this. They also wondered why they had not been able to be more consistent on their own and what had made them think that "babies always knew what was best for them." The Rosses had bought a book on sleep problems and had been relieved to read that routines "were a good thing" and that some babies had a hard time establishing routines. Ms. Ross ended the session by asking the therapist to "let her try things out for four weeks, to give them more time to establish their new ways with their daughter."

Diagnostic update

The active and sensitive attempts of both parents to join the therapist in discovering ways to help Debbie establish better control over her behavior supported the initial notion that Mr. and Ms. Ross were not significantly conflicted about supporting Debbie's autonomy. Similarly, Debbie's apparent positive response to a more predictable regime of eating, sleeping, and bathing supported the initial diagnosis of Regulatory Disorder. She needed more structure to help her develop, and now she was getting this support.

Fourth interview, four weeks later

Mrs. Ross came to the interview with Debbie and said that things had improved. Debbie now went to bed routinely between 8 p.m. and 9 p.m., after being fed downstairs in the living room. At around 11:30 p.m., she would wake up and be fed in her bedroom. Then she was placed back in her bed. She would wake up once or twice during the night, but both parents felt comfortable allowing her to cry or whimper for up to five minutes. Ninety percent of the time she would be able to get back to sleep on her own. At 6 a.m., Debbie would awaken for her feed; Mrs. Ross would often take her into her own bed "to reward her for her good behavior."

The Rosses reported another milestone—they had gone to a movie without Debbie and had enjoyed it. They felt that they needed no further appointments and said that they would call if further problems arose.

Follow-up

In a follow-up call four weeks after the fourth interview, the Rosses reported that things were well with Debbie. She now slept through most nights without crying or needing support. She was also sitting up on her own, had become more interested in playing games, including peek-a-boo, and was eager to let her parents know what foods and games she enjoyed. She was still sensitive to sounds and liable to becoming overexcited. In general, however, Debbie was "much more fun to be with." Both parents were actively considering the prospect of providing Debbie with a sibling some time within the next year.

Prognosis and discussion

Illustrating a number of issues common to families whose infants and toddlers experience sleep disturbances, the story of Debbie and her parents may be most usefully discussed in comparison to that of Jamie.

Ms. Bryant, it will be recalled, had established a regular daily routine in her home, while Debbie's mother took things "one day at a time." The therapist's task, therefore, was to work with the parents to develop structures in the Ross family that would be offered to Deborah. This took some time to accomplish, as the family had never functioned in this way and Deborah resisted routines at first. However, Ms. Ross, her mother, and the babysitter did establish a daily routine for general caregiving as well as sleep.

Ms. Ross was much less hesitant than Ms. Bryant to give up her night-time involvement with her baby. In fact, Mr. Ross had already stepped in before our initial consultation. Because Ms. Ross was much less possessive of Debbie than Ms. Bryant was of Jamie, change in Debbie's parents behavior was less conflicted and therefore easier.

In summary, Debbie's sleep disorder seemed to reflect a biologically driven difficult temperament and poor behavioral regulation. Lacking supportive structures provided by her parents, Debbie could not organize her own behavior. Change in parental management modified Debbie's sleep within seven weeks.

Differential diagnosis of sleep disorders

The descriptions of Jamie and Debbie and their families provide two scenarios that can lead to a Disorder of Initiating and Maintaining Sleep (DIMS), or Dyssomnia. It should be stressed that dyssomnia can result from a number of other conditions, including epilepsy, mental retardation, and the effect of medications such as barbiturates or benzodiazepines.

It should also be noted that infants and young children may experience types of sleep disorders not discussed in this chapter. Most commonly seen are infants who sleep too much (Disorder of Excessive Sleep [DOES] or Hypersomnia). This condition may be associated with mental retardation, the presence of obstructive sleep apnea (a distinct medical condition), or general deprivation and loss. Children of the latter group, who often qualify for the diagnosis of Reactive Attachment Deprivation/Maltreatment Disorder of Infancy and Early Childhood, seem to attempt to shield themselves from a hostile outside world by disconnecting from it through sleep. Other children are more appropriately diagnosed as having a mood disorder.

Among toddlers, night terrors are not uncommon. Symptoms here reflect an incomplete arousal from the deepest stages of sleep. Children often cry out in a high-pitched and agitated voice, appear confused, and talk incoherently. Breathing is usually very quick and shallow, the pulse is quite fast, and the child may sweat profusely. An attack may last for 10 to 15 minutes, after which the child falls asleep again. Night terrors may have a familiar base and require a neurological evaluation and possible pharmacological treatment.

Sleep problems in young children, then, usually reflect complex interactions between a child's specific vulnerabilities and a compromised relationship with his or her primary caregivers. Assessing and treating such conditions require expert knowledge about and sensitivity to the developmental needs of the infant and his or her family. Treatment will not only benefit the child's sleep but also help the child's emotional and social development and the overall family cohesion.

600. Eating Behavior Disorder

Irene Chatoor, M.D.

The diagnosis of eating behavior disorder, which may become evident at different stages of infancy and early childhood, should be considered when an infant or young child shows difficulties in establishing regular feeding patterns resulting in inadequate food intake and growth deficiency. The child does not regulate his or her eating in accordance with physiologic feelings of hunger or fullness. In the absence of general regulatory difficulties or particular precipitants such as separation or trauma, one should consider a primary eating disorder.

Specific feeding disorders of infancy and early childhood such as pica and rumination can be found in DSM IV.

Reason for referral

Mary was 17 months old when she was referred by a gastroenterologist because of food refusal and failure to thrive. A recent physical examination had shown that Mary had "outgrown" the gastroesophageal reflux which had caused her to vomit and to be irritable during the first six months of life. When the reflux was diagnosed at three months of life, she was treated with medication. Her mother was instructed to thicken the formula and position Mary after feedings in an almost upright position. Symptoms gradually subsided, and Mary fed well and thrived until she was around nine months of age. At this time, she started to refuse to be fed baby food, although she continued to drink her bottles of milk and juice. By the time of referral, Mary lived almost completely on bottles and only occasionally ate a few spoonfuls of baby food. The more her parents tried to distract her, cajole her, or force food into her mouth, the more adamant her refusals became. Interestingly, the parents reported, although Mary refused to be fed by them, she liked to pick food from their plates and eat it.

Assessment process

Three sessions, lasting two hours each, were scheduled for the diagnostic evaluation. These sessions were planned to take place within a two-to-three week period to facilitate an intense therapeutic alliance between the therapist and the parents.

A two-hour session was scheduled to interview the parents in regard to Mary's developmental, medical, and feeding history, and to observe Mary with her mother from behind a one-way mirror during 20 minutes of feeding and 10 minutes of free play.

Another two-hour session was scheduled to meet with the mother alone in order to explore her background and childhood experiences with her own parents, and to discuss the mother's eating patterns from infancy to the present. The assessor explained to the mother that the more she understood the mother's thinking about child rearing and her own attitudes towards eating, the better they would be able to work together to help Mary develop better eating patterns.

A third two-hour session was scheduled to share diagnostic impressions with the parents and to discuss the treatment plan.

Assessment findings

Developmental, medical, and feeding history

Mary was the first child of highly educated professional parents. The parents had planned on having a child for several years and were delighted when Ms. Smith finally became pregnant. The pregnancy was complicated by vaginal spotting in the third trimester. Ms. Smith had a cesarean section because of placenta previa at 38 weeks gestation. Mr. Smith was present during the delivery and remarked that Mary had her eyes open as soon as she was born. He commented that she kept looking at him and around the room, watching everything going on for the next half an hour. To observe this in a newborn surprised him. The mother added that Mary's eyes were so intense that she felt "eerie" when they first looked at each other. Mary weighed 6 lbs. and 5 ounces, her postnatal course was uncomplicated, and mother and baby were discharged from the hospital four days after birth. Ms. Smith had planned to breastfeed Mary. However, Mary would suckle only for short periods of time, look around, and would frequently show no interest in resuming feeding. Ms. Smith started feeding Mary every two hours, day and night, but in spite of her intense efforts, Mary showed no weight gain when she was examined by her pediatrician at two weeks of age. The pediatrician recommended that the mother introduce supplemental bottle feedings to increase Mary's intake. The mother followed this advice, and Mary seemed to drink better from the bottle, one with a large opening in the nipple. However, Mary started vomiting at the end of her feedings, or sometimes up to one hour thereafter. In addition, she became increasingly irritable during and after feedings. Frequently, she would cry and arch herself during feedings and refuse to drink any more. After several formula changes, which did not seem to improve Mary's feeding problems, the pediatrician referred Mary to a gastroenterologist. Mary was diagnosed as suffering from gastroesophageal reflux. She was treated with medication, thickening of the formula, and positioning after feeding, and her feeding behavior and food intake improved remarkably. She stopped vomiting and gained weight steadily, reaching the 25th percentile for height and the 10th percentile for weight for babies her age.

Mary progressed well developmentally. She sat independently at 7 months, crawled at 8 months, took her first steps at 10 months, and walked independently at 11 months of age. Her parents described her as a curious baby who enjoyed exploring things and looking at books. At the age of 17 months, Mary used about 30 words.

However, in spite of good progress in her motor and language development, Mary seemed to have no interest in feeding. Occasionally, she took food from her parents' plates, but when the parents tried to feed her, she was unusually resistant. This behavior started when Mary was around nine months of age. She began refusing to open her mouth when her mother presented the spoon. If Ms. Smith persisted, Mary would turn her head and sometimes arch her back and cry. The mother explained that she had tried "everything." She had distracted Mary with toys, played games, and turned on the television at mealtimes. She had sung to Mary, coaxed her, and offered her different types of food and different tastes, but the harder she tried, the less interested Mary seemed to be in food. The mother stated: " All Mary wants are her bottles, which keep her alive." Ms. Smith said that she gave Mary 8 to 10 bottles during the day and one or two bottles at night. She explained that Mary would usually drink only a few ounces at a time and said that she drank a lot of juice and not enough milk. A recent pediatric checkup revealed that Mary's weight had fallen below the 5th percentile on the growth chart. Both parents expressed fear that they would lose Mary if she did not increase her food intake.

Mother's history

Ms. Smith was the oldest of three children. She grew up in a small city and moved away from home as soon as she graduated from high school. She described her father as an alcoholic who demanded performance, was harsh in his punishment, and was unavailable emotionally. The only pleasant experiences she remembered sharing with him were occasional trips to the ice-cream parlor. Ms. Smith described her mother as caring, but timid and unable to stand up to her father. She described resenting her mother for staying in the marriage and for not protecting her from her father.

Ms. Smith's mother said that she had been a "picky eater" from the time she was a toddler. Ms. Smith remembered that her father would sometimes "yell" at her during meals and that she would force her food down out of fear of punishment. Ms. Smith remembered "food battles" with her parents throughout her childhood and adolescence. She reported that she had always been a thin, small child until she went to college. Then she went through a period of overeating and dieting. Ms. Smith admitted that food and weight had always been and continued to be an issue in her life. She stated that she did not like her body and that she felt overweight and unattractive, although her husband kept telling her that she looked fine. She admitted that she liked to eat ice cream or sweets when she watched television or when she tried to relax herself, but that she could not eat when she felt upset or angry.

Father's history

In the third session, Mr. Smith discussed his upbringing and eating patterns, although in less depth than had been done by Ms. Smith. He grew up in a small town in a stable, middle-class family, and continued to have close ties with his parents and two sisters. Mr. Smith reported that he had always had a good appetite and that he enjoyed food. He exercised regularly, had always been slim, and never worried about his weight.

Observational findings

The initial two-hour session included observing mother-infant interactions during 20 minutes of feeding and 10 minutes of play from behind a one-way mirror. When Ms. Smith stopped Mary from exploring the room and put her in the highchair, Mary protested by kicking and screaming. She also resisted having a bib put around her neck. The mother strapped her in the highchair, but settled to feed Mary without a bib. She put some toys on the tray for Mary to play with while she prepared the food and positioned herself to feed Mary. Initially, Mary seemed engrossed in manipulating the toys and opened her mouth a few times without resistance. However, as soon as Mary became aware of being fed, she turned her head and pushed the spoon away. When the mother persisted in her attempts to feed Mary, Mary arched her back and cried. The mother gave up and waited until Mary calmed herself and returned to playing with her toys. After a few minutes the mother tried again to slip some food into Mary's mouth, but was met with the same resistance. This time, she tried to force the spoon into Mary's mouth. Mary protested angrily, spat out every little piece of food, and screamed until her mother took her out of the highchair and let her run around the room. Once left alone, Mary recovered from the angry outburst and tried to engage her mother by looking and pointing at the pictures on the wall. Ms. Smith appeared sad and defeated, but tried to respond to Mary's curiosity by explaining the pictures to her.

When given a basket full of toys, Mary was eager to take out the toys and show them to her mother. However, if her mother took the initiative and tried to get Mary interested in a toy the mother had picked, Mary ignored her. Mary clearly wanted to be in charge, and Ms. Smith responded to Mary's bids for attention with warmth and interest. Mary seemed to enjoy playing with her mother, appearing cheerful and excited about the new toys, whereas Ms. Smith continued to look sad in spite of her efforts to be responsive and share Mary's excitement.

After the formal observations from behind the one-way mirror, the assessor came back to the playroom to take some additional history from Ms. Smith and to set up future appointments. After a few minutes, Mary began to make increasingly forceful bids for mother's attention, finally pulling on her, crying, and generally making it very difficult for the mother to continue with the interview. Mary seemed unable to play by herself with the toys available and unwilling to share her mother's attention with the assessor, who decided to have Mary join her father in the waiting room in order to complete the interview.

Diagnosis

From the time she was born, Mary was a very curious and observant baby whose interest in her surroundings and the people therein took priority over her interest in feeding. Her poor weight gain led to early concerns about breastfeeding and forced the mother to switch to bottle feedings. The mother's anxiety about Mary's poor food intake was further heightened by Mary's vomiting and irritability secondary to gastroesophageal reflux. The reflux was not diagnosed until Mary was three months old—a long time for a first-time mother to doubt herself and to feel insecure about her ability to feed her baby. Although Mary responded well to treatment of her reflux and although she grew and developed age-appropriately for the next six months, the mother's anxiety about Mary's growth was reawakened when Mary, at nine months, began to refuse to open her mouth during feedings.

On specific questioning, the mother remembered that Mary at nine months would grab the spoon or grab her arm, but Ms. Smith had been too anxious to interpret these behaviors as Mary's attempts at autonomy and as bids for more control in the feeding situation. Consequently, instead of offering Mary a second spoon or finger food, she had responded by distracting Mary with toys or by playing games. In fact, because she wanted to avoid messiness during feedings, Ms. Smith deliberately kept the food out of Mary's reach and offered her toys to handle. Mary had always been a curious baby, and initially she was so entertained by her mother's distractions that she opened her mouth unwittingly. However, as Mary became older, it became increasingly more difficult for the mother to distract Mary, and feeding became a battleground for control between mother and infant. Mary yelled a forceful "no" and averted her face when her mother tried to give her solid food.

Increasingly, Mary refused to accept food from her mother and relied on getting her nutrition from bottles, which were offered to her throughout the day and also at night. Frequently, Ms. Smith would arrange special pillows on the sofa so that Mary could drink from her bottles while watching television. Thus, Mary enjoyed special attention from her mother while having full control over her bottles.

The observation of Mary and her mother during feeding, play, and the interview revealed that Mary was not only a very curious and observing toddler, but that she was also very strong-willed and demanding of attention. She reacted intensely and negatively if her wishes were not met, and her mother seemed unable to set limits on Mary's behaviors. During play, when she allowed Mary to be in full control, Ms. Smith seemed to find it easy to respond to her daughter in an affectionate, caring manner. However, during feeding and the interview, Ms. Smith appeared unable to deal with Mary's tyrannical behavior. She appeared worried and helpless, as Mary arched herself, kicked, and screamed in protest in an effort to assert herself.

These observations and the parents' report that Mary liked to grab food from their plates to feed herself, led to the diagnosis of Eating Behavior Disorder. Mother and infant were embroiled in a battle over control and dependency, with food being the major battleground.

A continued, underlying organic cause for Mary's food refusal was ruled out by the feeding history and by the gastroenterologist's examination. A feeding disorder characterized by hypersensitivities to certain tastes or textures or by the fear of swallowing textured food was ruled out by a negative history. The parents reported that Mary seemed to be able to eat all types of food if she chose to do so.

The relationship between Mary and her mother appeared characterized by intense battles over issues of control and dependency. On the one hand, the mother appeared overly anxious to care for and to please Mary; on the other hand, she seemed unable to provide and foster appropriate autonomy during feeding or to set limits to Mary's inappropriate behaviors.

It appeared that the mother's own upbringing by a harsh and tyrannical father and a caring but ineffective mother had left her without appropriate internalized role models for dealing effectively with issues of care and control. In addition, the mother's insecurity in regulating her own eating, including her tendency to experience emotional inhibition of eating when upset, and her use of food for pleasure and relaxation, left her insecure in interpreting her infant's signals of hunger and satiety.

In addition, this vulnerable mother was faced with a temperamentally very difficult infant. From birth, Mary seemed prone to respond with intense curiosity to the world around her and appeared more interested in attending to external stimuli than in responding to internal signals of hunger. Her mother's insecurity in interpreting Mary's behavior was further heightened when Mary became very irritable and started vomiting secondary to gastroesophageal reflux. These experiences during Mary's first three months of life were very frightening for the mother and left her vulnerable, so that she reacted with intense anxiety when Mary, at nine months of age, began to refuse to accept food from her. Mary's intense drive for control and autonomy, on the one hand, and her strong need for her mother's attention, on the other, rendered the mother confused and helpless to deal with this strong-willed and demanding toddler during the transition to self-feeding. Mother and child became increasingly embroiled in battles of will which interfered with Mary's development of appropriate feeding behaviors and left the mother feeling ineffective and frightened about her child's health and future development.

Diagnostic summary

Axis I: **Primary Diagnosis**
Eating Behavior Disorder.

Axis II: **Relationship Disorder Classification**
No diagnosis.
Tendency toward Anxious/Tense relationship.

Axis III: **Medical and Developmental Disorders and Conditions**
Failure to Thrive (Growth Deficiency).

Axis IV: **Psychosocial Stressors**
Moderate effects of medical illness in first six months of life.

Axis V: **Functional Emotional Developmental Level**
Has fully reached mutual attention, mutual engagement, and interactive intentionality and reciprocity.

PIR-GAS:50 (Distressed)

Discussion with caregivers and treatment planning

Both parents were invited to meet with the assessor for a two-hour session in order to discuss the diagnostic findings and to develop a treatment plan.

The assessor explained three points that seemed to have contributed to Mary's eating behavior disorder:

1. Mary's intense interest in the world around her and her tendency to seek and respond to external stimulation, instead of attending to her internal signals of hunger, seemed to have interfered with her learning to internally regulate eating. This characteristic seemed to have been present from birth.

2. Mary's early feeding difficulties, and irritability and vomiting secondary to gastroesophageal reflux, sensitized the parents to experience anxiety when Mary refused to be fed at nine months of age.

3. Mary's strong drive for autonomy and control and her intense interpersonal sensitivity and demands for attention made her a challenging child to deal with, particularly during this developmental period of separation and individuation, which included the transition to self-feeding.

The therapist explained that the overriding goal of treatment was to facilitate Mary's internal regulation of eating in response to sensations of hunger and fullness. In order to accomplish this goal, she suggested focusing on three areas:

1. In order to help Mary become more aware of hunger cues, the parents could offer her food at 3 to 4 hour intervals only, instead of allowing her bottles whenever she wanted them, currently 8 to 10 times daily.

2. In order to make Mary more aware of her internal signals, it would be important to minimize external distractions during mealtime, such as play-

ing with toys, watching television, or playing games with her.

3. In order to foster Mary's transition to self-feeding, it would be helpful to structure mealtime in a way that would reward her for self-feeding but not for the amount of food eaten, and put her in "time out" for inappropriate behaviors, such as throwing food or feeding utensils.

Intervention

The parents were comfortable with the overall goals of treatment and eager to discuss details of how to implement them. At this point, the therapist handed each of the parents a list of 11 specific "food rules, " which addressed in detail the three major points outlined above. One rule, for example, was "Compliment the child for self-feeding by saying, 'Great job—you got the spoon into your mouth!' but do not comment on how much or how little the child eats by saying, 'Good girl, you ate a lot today' or 'You ate only two bites today.'" The therapist explained that these rules were just meant as an outline and asked the parents to read the rules, so she could discuss with them how they wanted to individualize and modify them for their use with Mary.

After the parents read the whole set of rules, the mother looked distressed. To a question from the therapist, she responded that she felt overwhelmed and did not think that she could handle all the rules at one time. The therapist replied by telling the mother that she appreciated the mother's openness. She explained that this was exactly what she meant when she met with the mother before and told her that she wanted to get to know her better in order to be able to help her pace herself in making changes in her interactions with Mary. Ms. Smith appeared relieved. She said that all she could handle at this point in time was the first rule ("Feed your child at regular intervals of three to four hours"). She would give Mary her bottles every 3 to 4 hours instead of any time Mary wanted a bottle.

At this point, the therapist engaged both parents in a discussion of how to deal with Mary when she demanded "her bottle" and was told that she had to wait until later. The therapist suggested explaining the new schedule to Mary in simple words before implementing it. The mother said she expected Mary to protest, scream, and carry on when she could not get her way. The father was very understanding of the mother's difficulty in dealing with Mary's temper tantrums. He offered to deal with Mary in the morning before going to work and to spend time with her in the evening before her bedtime. The mother said she would need three weeks to work on Mary's new schedule, and the parents decided to set up another appointment to discuss the remaining "food rules."

When the parents returned after three weeks, they were eager to tell the therapist that Mary had accepted the schedule of regular "bottle times" quite well. She had asked for her bottle a few times during the first few days, but then did not seem to think about it any more. Instead of drinking only 2 to 3 ounces, she had started to drink 6 to 8 ounces at a time. However, during the first week, Mary appeared extremely irritable and provoked her mother into constant power struggles over putting on her diaper, holding her mother's hand when crossing the street, or anything else the mother asked her to do. She was less difficult with her father who, all along, had been more comfortable with setting limits for Mary. The mother said that it seemed to her that Mary had used the bottles to exercise control and to calm herself. Ms. Smith observed that it had been relatively easy to be firm with Mary about holding her hand while crossing the street. However, she still felt apprehensive about dealing with Mary during mealtime. On further exploration, Ms. Smith said that she was worried that Mary would not eat if she got angry at her mother. She still struggled with the fear that Mary would starve for days if she tried to wean her from the bottle. The therapist reminded the mother that Mary had adjusted to drinking larger amounts of milk once she got her bottles only every 3 to 4 hours; she felt confident that Mary would recognize hunger once she did not have her bottles any more. After this discussion, the mother decided to omit the bottles during the day in order to make Mary hungry for lunch and dinner.

The therapist discussed with the parents the importance of allowing Mary to decide "how much" she was going to eat. She encouraged them to praise Mary for using the spoon and learning to feed herself but to stay emotionally neutral concerning how much or how little Mary ate. The therapist explained that Mary's eating should not be a performance for the parents: Mary would only learn to appreciate her physiological signals of hunger and satiety if the parents did not interfere.

Finally, the therapist discussed with the parents in detail how to use "time out" for Mary if she behaved inappropriately during meals or at any other time. The parents were helped to understand that "time out" was meant to help Mary to calm herself when upset and to learn to deal with the frustration of not getting her way. The therapist suggested putting Mary on a small chair facing the corner for time out, and using a timer with an alarm, setting the timer for only one minute. This would allow Mary to return to the high chair in a calm state and give her a chance to correct her behavior. The therapist stressed that it was important to explain the time out procedure to Mary ahead of time when she was calm and could understand it. Once they were ready to implement time out, it was important to give Mary only one warning before putting her in time out and to return her to the highchair after the time out. The therapist emphasized that particularly at first it would be important to put Mary in time out as often as necessary until she was ready to behave in the expected way.

The therapist explained that other parents had reported that their toddlers went into time out up to seven times in a row until they decided to comply. The therapist asked the parents to think about which of Mary's behaviors were truly unacceptable to them—once they had decided to pick a fight, they had to be sure they would win it. She reassured the parents that most young children learn very quickly when their parents are serious about something, and that they usually become less anxious and feel more secure when they know what limits to expect. The parents felt that they needed another three weeks to implement these changes and scheduled a follow-up appointment accordingly.

When the parents returned, they were very pleased with Mary's progress. The mother was glad the therapist had warned them that Mary might need repeated time outs the first time they implemented the procedure —indeed, she had gone to time out five times until she decided to sit in the highchair without throwing food or feeding utensils. The first few days had been try-ing also because Mary had insisted that she wanted her bottle, and would push food or throw the cup away. However, after a few very tumultuous meals, Mary settled in and started to eat her food. She still enjoyed her bot-tles at night and first thing in the morning, and Ms. Smith said that she was not quite ready to take them away from Mary. The mother wanted to give Mary a few more weeks to consolidate her eating pattern during the day before she felt "safe" stopping the bottles altogether. The parents felt confi-dent that they could manage that last step but said that they would call for another appointment if they ran into any difficulties.

Follow-up

When Mary was 27 months old, the Smiths returned to discuss ways to help Mary to sleep in her own room. They reported that Mary had progressed well. She had learned to verbalize when she was hungry and when she was full. Her food intake had markedly improved. She had gained weight and was back on the 10th percentile for weight and the 25th percentile for height. There was no more conflict during mealtime. The parents reported that they had observed that on special occasions, like birthday parties or when the family had houseguests or went visiting themselves, Mary tended to eat very little. However, they had noticed that when the excitement was over and Mary had calmed herself, she would ask for food and seemed to make up for her poor intake. The mother noted that Mary was just like her, but Mary had learned to recognize when she was hungry and when she was full, while, she added sadly, "I still don't know." Ms. Smith said that she con-tinued to find it difficult to leave food on her plate when she went to a restaurant, and that she was grateful that she had been able to help Mary to regulate her eating internally so that she would not have to struggle with food issues all her life.

Prognosis and discussion

Ms. Smith's emerging ability to differentiate her own experiences from those of her daughter bode well for this child's continuing capacity to recognize and regulate her internal states. The father's role in supporting both his wife and his daughter during their struggles suggests that he will continue to play a constructive role as mother and daughter negotiate future developmental issues.

700. Disorders of Relating and Communicating

701. 702. 703. Multisystem Developmental Disorder

Serena Wieder, Ph.D.

Multisystem Developmental Disorder (MSDD) has the potential to derail a child's development, including the child's abilities to relate, communicate, play, and learn. As conceptualized in *DC: 0-3*, however, the relationship difficulty in MSDD is not viewed as a relatively fixed, permanent deficit, as autistic spectrum disorders have traditionally been, but as open to change and growth. While all three proposed patterns of MSDD (701, 702, 703) involve severe difficulties in relating and communicating, combined with difficulties in the regulation of physiological, sensory, attentional, motor, cognitive, and affective processes, each child will present with a unique profile. It is the assessment and interpretation of this unique profile that will allow parents and clinicians to understand the child's difficulties and adaptations, as well as point to the necessary interventions.

When first defined by Kanner as infantile autism, difficulties in relating and communicating were considered a primary or basic disorder—that is, present from the start of life, ". . . from the beginning, an extreme aloneness that disregards, ignores, shuts out . . . anything from the outside" (1943 p. 247). The original definition, later expanded in succeeding versions of the Diagnostic and Statistical Manuals (DSM) to include pervasive developmental and autistic spectrum disorders, continued to consider it a primary disorder—i.e., involving a primary deficit in relating and communicating—but also recognized that children with these disorders may have some capacities to relate and communicate.

DC: 0-3 proposes an alternative diagnosis for infants and young children who present such deficits in relating and communicating. The diagnosis of MSDD suggests that these difficulties are **secondary** to other processing difficulties and are therefore more flexible and responsive to intensive early intervention. As clinicians have become more interactive and more experienced working with children who have these developmental disorders, capacities for relating and communicating have become more evident and many children now respond well to intensive intervention.

Although the original and subsequent descriptions of pervasive developmental or autistic spectrum disorders referred to numerous behaviors related to sensory processing, these were neither well understood nor necessarily treated. Yet the ways in which children process information through their various senses account for important individual differences in all infants, affecting regulation, interaction with the environment, and the responses of caregivers. A growing understanding of young children's variations and difficulties in sensory processing has suggested that many children diagnosed with pervasive developmental disorders or autism have severe processing difficulties, which can impair both the child's comprehension (input) and the ability to respond to what has been taken in through the senses through expression or action (output). The term Multisystem Developmental Disorder (MSDD) reflects the multiple sensory and sensory-motor interactive processing systems that are involved.

Even at this time, more than a half-century after infantile autism was first described, the etiology of pervasive developmental, sensory, and motor processing disorders is hardly understood. Initially, the prevailing theory concerning etiology implicated the mother's behavior (the "refrigerator" mother) as the cause of autism. Later, both theory and research shifted to supporting a biological or neurological basis for these disorders. Currently, researchers are investigating a number of theories designed to explain the etiology of serious disorders of relating and communicating. The following discussion does not address etiology but focuses instead on the assessment of the specific functional abilities of very young children with severe difficulties in relating and communicating and the treatment required to help children overcome specific patterns of difficulties.

The diagnostic process and MSDD: Special considerations

Observation and clinical assessment are essential for the diagnosis of MSDD. The very nature of the disorder usually precludes the use of standardized or even criterion-referenced assessments. For example, a child having difficulty processing and comprehending what he/she hears, will, by definition, have difficulty following an examiner's verbal directions during an assessment. If motor planning difficulties prevent a child from imitating an examiner's actions because the child has difficulty planning what to do first and what to do next in a sequence of actions, he may even fail on nonverbal items in an assessment protocol. Nor is it likely that a child will be able to complete an unfamiliar interactive test who cannot readily form a cooperative alliance with an examiner in a new situation. Thus formal testing of children with presenting problems in relating and communicating may reveal something about the children's test-taking ability but little about their attachments and ways in which they relate to their parents, their skills and adaptations in daily functioning, their ability to initiate and sustain purposeful communication and play, or their potential for growth. Instead, a continuous diagnostic process is necessary, in which the clinician can: a) observe the child and family interacting several times; b) suggest ways in which the parents can facilitate the interaction with the child in order to see how the child does with support; and c) also interact with the child to further explore his capacities (Greenspan, 1992; Greenspan & Wieder, in press).

The diagnosis of a relationship or communication disorder must utilize observation of infant-parent interaction in order to see the relationship "in action," where emotional cues and gestures and communication can emerge. What will emerge is an understanding of both the child's attempts and the parents' attempts to cope with sensory processing difficulties and the barriers they present to successful relating and communicating.

Clinicians must be wary of using traditional criteria in judging the relationships or attachments of children who may have sensory processing difficulties. For example, a child who averts his gaze or moves away from his mother's shrill voice or his father's long, rapidly uttered sentences may be avoiding auditory input that is aversive or that he is unable to comprehend. The child's action may reveal nothing about his awareness of or attachment to either parent, which he will initiate and express quite clearly under other conditions. Furthermore, since no single sensory system operates independently, a child's apparently avoidant behavior to certain stimuli or situations may represent an in-the-moment attempt to cope with the situation or reflect a pattern based on the child's previous experiences. Multiple observations, preferably in several settings (home, child care, preschool), and parent reports are therefore critical for understanding the impact of the sensory processing difficulties.

Whenever a developmental disorder is being considered, the parents' fears and concerns are often overwhelming. As with all children, the diagnostic process not only needs to be sensitive and responsive, but focused on the child's and family's adaptation. The clinician should allow the parents to first tell their story and share their concerns. Observations of interactions will usually follow, but may precede, this presentation and will be repeated as the clinician continues interviews until information is gathered in all the areas noted below.

1. Engagement and communication: The following basic questions need to be asked concerning each stage of development, starting with the first few months of infancy, and every few months thereafter as the infant develops new capacities to communicate, gesture, vocalize, and so forth, which allows her/him to relate and communicate in more active and intentional ways. The clinician should ask parents: Describe how your baby related to you. Was your baby affectionate? Did your baby look at you, follow you with his eyes, turn to your voice, and so forth? When did you feel close to your baby? What did you enjoy most, least? How did you play with your baby? How did you know what your baby wanted? When did your baby point to something she wanted? When did your baby point to show you something out there? Did your baby wave "Hi" or "'Bye"? Did your baby want to play or do some things over and over again? Did your child stop doing something he had been doing up to that point?

2. The course of the child's health and development from conception, including birth, and subsequent milestones, growth, allergies, illnesses, medical interventions and nutrition.

3. Individual differences in sensory and sensory motor processes, including history of the child's regulatory capacities, including sleeping, feeding, attention and self-regulation.

4. The child's attempts to adapt and cope with the demands and sensory impact of the environment as well as internal needs, and how well these attempts worked.

5. Caregiving approaches and solutions that have been used to keep the child calm, engaged, and responsive.

6. Parents' personal, history of similar difficulties in the family, and the way their child's difficulties have affected them; parents' relationship with each other; and the availability of extended family to support them.

When the child can respond to more structured assessments, speech and language, occupational and physical therapy, educational, cognitive, and neuropsychological assessments should be used selectively to answer specific questions about the child's functioning and current abilities that were raised in the course of the observations and interviews. Sensory-motor processing and adaptive function checklists may help identify difficulties. Developmental pediatricians, child psychologists and psychiatrists, and neurologists who diagnose this disorder will specify or rule out various contributing factors as they consider the various assessments and evaluations in a team or through reports and other forms of collaboration.

DC: 0-3 lists the following defining characteristics of MSDD:

• Significant impairment in, but not complete lack of, the ability to engage in an emotional and social relationship with a primary caregiver;

• Significant impairment in forming, maintaining, and/or developing communication;

• Significant dysfunction in auditory processing; and

• Significant dysfunction in the processing of other sensations and motor planning.

Three different patterns are suggested for the MSDD diagnosis. Although these frequently observed patterns are not yet intended to suggest specific subtypes, they reflect the wide variations in processing seen in children with this disorder, as well as the different effects on relating, communicating, and learning. The three case studies presented below will represent children with these different patterns and the implications of the diagnosis for intervention, using integrated approaches that consider the multiple aspects of MSDD. In each case, the evaluation consisted of a series of observations and interviews, as well as additional assessments geared to identifying the treatment approaches to be used.

JODY, AGE 2

Reason for referral

Jody's nursery school teacher was concerned about this two-year-old boy's behavior after the second day of school. Jody had not seemed aware of anything going on in the classroom and had not even responded to his name. He ran around excitedly all morning singing the alphabet song, but ran away when approached. The teacher suggested a developmental evaluation to Jody's parents, who quickly consulted their pediatrician. He had noticed that language was slow in coming but had not yet become concerned, since Jody had only turned two. Jody otherwise enjoyed good health, was a robust toddler growing well, and was always described as a happy and quite adaptive little boy. Jody had one sister, three years older, who appeared to be developing well. There was no family history of developmental or learning difficulties. Jody's parents were professionals; his mother had only recently gone back to work part-time. Jody also enjoyed a young live-in nanny, who had helped care for him since infancy. The extended family lived nearby, and the families were close.

Jody was referred to a neurologist, who suggested he might have autism, performed a neurological evaluation, and ordered a series of laboratory tests. The findings were nonspecific. Jody was also given the Bayley Scales by a developmental psychologist, and obtained a Mental Developmental Index of 54, in the retarded range, although the validity of this assessment was questioned in the report, since Jody could hardly take the test. He was diagnosed as having pervasive developmental disorder. Still disbelieving, Jody's parents sought a third opinion from a child psychiatrist, this time also looking for someone who could help them organize an intervention program.

Assessment process

Jody's evaluation included observations and interviews by a multidisciplinary team of clinicians in private practice. The child psychiatrist initially seen by Jody's parents continued to provide consultation and leadership. A clinical psychologist used observation and guided interaction to both assess Jody and start the intervention. Additional evaluations with a speech/language pathologist and an occupational therapist who could continue working with Jody were arranged. They, too, combined evaluation and intervention, finding the ways Jody would respond and learn, and explaining to his parents the meaning of what they were looking for. Both the speech/language pathologist and occupational therapist were highly trained in evaluating and treating sensory processing difficulties. They brought this perspective to evaluating communication and auditory processing, as well as the various sensory, sensory-motor, muscle tone and motor planning functions. Following one month of evaluation-intervention efforts, the parents and team met to discuss the diagnosis and define the intervention program.

Assessment findings

Observations

Jody ran into the playroom in the office of the clinical psychologist without looking back to see if his parents were following. Nor did he look forwards to see if anyone was in the room. As if by telepathy, without even looking around the room full of toys, he saw an ABC board on the couch, ran over, and began to sing the alphabet in a loud and excited voice, waving his arms up and down to his sing-song rhythm. As soon as he finished "XYZ," he began again, each letter as clear as a bell, his voice intense and hurried, as if he were rushing to start again. Each time he completed the alphabet, his parents clapped and cheered, "Yay, Jody!" Jody, however, did not turn around, pause, or even appear to hear them, but continued singing the alphabet four or five times, with increased vigor, before he turned around and started to run across the room. Even his parents' outstretched arms did not deter him as he ran back and forth. Finally, his mother swept him up and started to sing "Baa, baa, black sheep," holding on tightly to his squirming body. As she danced and sang this familiar song, Jody relaxed a bit in her arms, but when she leaned over to give him a kiss, he lurched backwards without notice, almost causing her to drop him. As soon as she put him down, he started to run away, jabbering to himself. The garbled vocalizations almost sounded like, "I gotta go, I gotta go!" But, of course, there was no way to get Jody to repeat or clarify what he had just muttered.

As if to stop his own frenetic movement, Jody squeezed between a chair and the filing cabinet. He looked up at a picture of a woman with long dark hair just like his mother's, seeming to say, "Mommy," but she did not hear it. When Jody's father approached with an Ernie puppet, Jody banged it on the nose five or six times, squirmed out from behind the chair, and ran off. Jody would stop himself momentarily to look at something that appeared interesting—especially anything decorated with numbers or letters—but he did not even pause when called or approached by his parents. Only by sweeping him up in their arms and playing baby games, such as tickling or swinging up and down, could they evoke some pleasure, which Jody expressed through laughter. His parents could not elicit eye contact from Jody.

This two-year, three-month-old little boy was adorable, with long curly hair, sparkling eyes, and an effervescence that elicited admiration but also a "watch-but-don't-touch" message. His parents described him as a bubbly and happy toddler, running around, seeking familiar letters and numbers, and always eager to sing and dance. They had been shocked by the nursery school teacher's call.

On a subsequent visit, Jody found a Main Street toy. This toy street had seven stores with "letters," each decorated with a different number, which could be delivered by the mail carrier. Jody instantly dropped to the floor and started to line up the letters in order. His mother quickly joined him and tried to deliver the letters to the stores, urging him to look at the mail truck and the stores. This was to no avail, as Jody simply undid what she had done, took his letters, and resumed lining them up. He never looked at her, let alone acknowledged what she had said. Somehow, he managed to get all the letters in a row. When his mother was encouraged to help him do what he wanted to do and join his intentions, she handed Jody the letters he wanted one at a time.

After a few moments, Jody became less defensive and appeared to have recognized the change in his mother's approach. He began to take the letters from her, even waiting until she found the next letter to give him. Jody still did not look at her but saw her hand reaching out to him. Jody's mother was then encouraged to put down a letter exactly where he would have placed it. Jody reacted violently, messing up the whole row and protesting vocally for just a moment before resuming his task. When she tried again, this time he roared! When she backed off, while reassuring him that she was only trying to help, he continued his task, and she again began handing him the letters. A minute later she put down a letter, explaining in a soothing voice that she wanted a turn. This time Jody left the letter in place, as his mother quickly gave him a letter, too. At no point did they exchange looks. In fact, Jody had his back to his mother through the entire sequence. But they were interacting, with Jody opening the circle of communication as well as closing it when he responded to what his mother did.

Although Jody did not look at his mother directly, call her name, respond to his name, or do anything she asked, he seemed to be aware of where she was, depending on his peripheral vision to track her. During the next observation, while his father was attempting to engage him with a puppet, his mother left the room to go to the bathroom. Within a split second, Jody burst into tears and started to cry passionately, running to the closed door and attempting to turn the knob. Though shocked by the intensity of his reaction, Jody's father quickly tried to reassure him, but to no avail. When Jody's mother returned a few moments later, Jody simply walked off, as if to search for a toy, but did allow his mother to pursue him and accepted her hugs and kisses briefly before squirming out of her arms. He quickly found the numbers on a toy cash register and started to count from one to ten repeatedly. Both parents reported they had never seen him react quite like this and asked if this meant he was in fact attached to them.

Each subsequent observation involved more and more guided interaction in order to assess how Jody would respond to various techniques of attempting to interact with him. By observing what he initiated, when he was avoidant, what he responded to, what he found pleasurable, what he found frustrating, and how he conveyed all this and communicated what he wanted, the team could formulate a clinical diagnosis and treatment plan. During this process, Jody's parents developed a better understanding of their son's adaptations and difficulties. They realized it would be possible to challenge these in order to move his development forward, and that they could integrate the multiple efforts and intensive interactions needed to get their child's development back on track. Each aspect of his treatment now had meaning and relevance to their day-to-day lives together.

Diagnosis

Although Jody met the criteria for the diagnosis of autism under other classification systems, this diagnosis was rejected at this time because the team's observations and assessments indicated that: a) he had treatable processing difficulties which were contributing to his difficulties; b) he had formed attachments to his parents; c) he could be responsive to interaction when encouraged in certain ways; and d) that he responded quickly to intervention that took his processing difficulties into account and addressed his underlying needs.

A discussion of Jody's diagnosis along the five *DC: 0-3* axes follows, with specific reference to the diagnostic criteria for MSDD (*DC: 0-3*, pp. 43–45).

Axis I: Primary Diagnosis

The defining characteristics of Multisystem Developmental Disorder follow with a side-by-side description of Jody.

1. *DC: 0-3:* Significant impairment in, but not complete lack of, the ability to form and maintain (and occasionally form) an emotional and social relationship with a primary caregiver, i.e., the capacity for emotionally connecting, evidencing pleasure and warmth with another person, and/or exchanging social gestures, is significantly delayed or impaired.

Jody: Although Jody was so avoidant and had developed peripheral ways of relating, he was very much aware of his parents (he needed to be in order to avoid them so effectively). His attachment was seen in his distressed reaction when his mother left the room, as well as in joyful giggles when he and his mother played baby games using movement, songs, and tickles. He enjoyed their emotional connection on his terms, when he could take in and understand his parents' intention by looking, feeling their tickles and movement, or recognizing the nursery rhyme they were singing. When he stood behind a boundary (between the couch and the wall), he also appeared to feel safe from unpredictable actions or words he could not comprehend and could interact face-to-face more joyfully. Even his brief expressions of joy, protest, and distress in reaction to his parents suggested an emotional range. While his pleasure in singing the ABC, a song he could count on wherever he went, appeared totally self-absorbed, it suggested satisfaction in what he chose to do. Nevertheless, Jody could not engage in social interactions or even use gestures to communicate. This constituted significant delay in a child his age.

2. *DC: 0-3:* Significant impairment informing, maintaining, and/or developing communication. This includes preverbal gestural communication, as well as verbal and non-verbal (e.g., figurative) symbolic communication.

Jody: Jody's best gestural communication was avoidance and flight, but he was on a one-way street. He did not even wave "Hi" or "Bye" or point. He fussed but could not signal why he was distressed. Nor did he use toys with any symbolic intent. Though he was quick to line up letters or numbers, it made no difference whether anyone was looking or applauding his efforts. His impairment was highly significant.

3. *DC: 0-3:* Significant dysfunction in auditory processing (i.e., perception, comprehension, and articulation).

Jody: Jody's ability to sing the alphabet and numbers and recognize nursery rhymes indicated he was perceiving some auditory input when predictable words were accompanied by melodies. He could also retrieve the words and melodies when prompted by some visual signal—i.e., when he saw letters and numbers—and these of course appear everywhere. It was also important to note that Jody could articulate the letters and numbers quite clearly, a positive sign for later speech. Furthermore, some evidence of processing language was suggested by his frequent jabbering. Jody was "talking" all the time, and sometimes his jabber approximated words even though they had no communicative intent. Although he did not "fill in the blank" when he heard nursery rhymes, he recognized the gestures or movements which his parents used when reciting them and tolerated the contact, although he squirmed away instantly afterwards. He did not present as hypersensitive to sounds and in fact had a very high threshold for registering spoken language, not even responding to his name or saying "Mommy" or "Daddy." Although he had made numerous consonant sounds as an infant, his parents did not report Jody's having "lost" real words. Just several weeks into the intervention, it was promising to see that Jody could stop and listen to someone else continue singing the next letters in the ABC song he had started when they could intercept him on a pause between sets of letters, going on to the next phrase without just repeating what the other person sung. This was his first verbal interaction.

4. *DC: 0-3:* Significant dysfunction in the processing of other sensations, including hyper and hyporeactivity (e.g., to visual-spatial, tactile, proprioceptive, and vestibular input), and motor planning (e.g., sequencing movements).

Jody: Jody demonstrated significant difficulties in all these areas, being both over-and under-reactive to sensations. He was very sensitive to touch, squirming away as quickly as he could, unless held very tightly. Jody liked to squeeze into tight spaces, as observed when he was behind the couch, giving himself pressure which helped him locate his body in space. He was frequently in motion, darting back and forth (as if to keep himself revved up), and craved swinging and jumping. Jody also waved his hands up and down when singing the ABC, not able to contain his own excitement. He was unable to modulate his energy or organize his movements. His need for excessive input could be seen in his continuous motion and cravings for sensation. Low muscle tone may also have contributed to this. He could, however, briefly regulate some of this craving for input when he was intentional, as with singing the alphabet, eating, or watching a video. It is also important to note what Jody did **not** do in the playroom. He hardly noticed any of the toys, did not explore objects visually or through touch, did not appear interested in puzzles or building, and had to be wooed into pushing down a lid on a pop-up toy by putting a hand over his hand. In fact, his only use of objects initially was lining up the letters or numbers or dumping the toys out of a basket. Later, he mouthed pretend food with great voracity, craving the oral input. The absence of purposeful use of objects suggested severe difficulties with motor planning, i.e., the ability to sequence actions to execute an idea or use of an object. The absence of any imitation of gestures to accompany songs or even waving and the inability to point to objects he desired also indicated motor-planning difficulties.

Multiple observations of Jody suggested that he met the general criteria for MSDD. Interviews with his parents further clarified how his difficulties were expressed in day-to-day functioning and regulation. The last step in making the Axis I diagnosis of MSDD involved determining whether Jody fit any of the three proposed MSDD patterns in *DC: 0-3*. He came closest to Pattern B.

702. Pattern B

These children are intermittently related and capable some of the time of simple intentional gestures. In this group the affect appears accessible, but fleeting, with small islands of shallow satisfaction or pleasure, but no consistent interpersonal joy or warmth. These children tend to enjoy repetitive or perseverative activity with objects (rather than only self-stimulation) but are very rigid and react intensely to any changes in their lives. Children who fit this pattern show mixed patterns of sensory reactivity and reduced muscle tone, and are much more organized than children with pattern A in the way they seek sensation or avoid sensation. Most of the time they try to express their intentionality in patterns of perseveration. They often do this to control the amount of sensory and affective input they can take in.

Jody was referred to speech and occupational therapists for evaluation and help in the development of a comprehensive treatment program. Prior laboratory tests and a neurological evaluation had ruled out specific metabolic or neurological findings.

Axis II: Relationship Disorder Classification

When a diagnosis of MSDD is being considered, Axis II requires special consideration because of the severe nature of the disorder and its impact on the parents and family. There was no question that by the time Jody's parents saw the child psychiatrist and clinical psychologist they were extremely anxious and tense, overwhelmed by fears for their child. They could not believe what they understood as the implications of the initial diagnoses of autism or pervasive developmental disorder—that their child could not relate to them or that he would grow up without being able to marry and have a family. They could not believe he might be mentally retarded. When Jody's parents were seen alone, their anxiety was coupled with despair as they expressed their fears for the future.

When the child psychiatrist and clinical psychologist met them, Jody's parents were clearly reeling from the shock of the referral and diagnostic process they had experienced. In their eyes, Jody had been a responsive, cute baby, and quite easy to care for, especially compared to their first child, who was much more "wired" and demanding. Even as a toddler, Jody always appeared so happy—they had hardly noticed that he was spending more and more time absorbed in his own little games. He seemed so independent and so smart, already singing his letters and numbers. Mostly, he seemed happy and bubbly, running here and there. He didn't talk, but they had just assumed he would be a late speaker, and their doctor was not concerned either.

Because of Jody's difficulties, their interaction with him was stilted, fragmented, and almost desperate as the parents chased, swung, blocked, and tried to give things to Jody. Somehow, he always got away. The best they could do was hold him tight and dance to a few nursery songs they had sung since he was a baby. He did enjoy those. They worked exceedingly hard to pursue their child in attempts to interact and relate to him. Asked to reflect on their interaction with Jody, the parents said that most of the time they felt intrusive, confused, and helpless. They felt out of tune and even rejected by their son, who avoided and fled their overtures continuously. Interestingly, the parents said that these feelings had developed only after they received the initial diagnosis of autism and were prompted by their image of the disorder; before the diagnosis, they had felt connected to Jody.

Clearly Jody did have a relationship with his parents, one which seemed currently impaired by Jody's multiple difficulties. But even the team's multiple observations of Jody and his parents could not reveal what their relationship had been like earlier in Jody's life, or how the parents would relate to a typically developing child. The parents remembered, for example, that in Jody's first year he had been a lovely baby who would look at them and enjoyed tickling and dancing. When he began to walk, he even took their hands when he wanted something and pulled them over to what he wanted. They never understood, however, why he would use *their* hands instead of his own to reach something. They had continued to enjoy Jody; he came to all the extended family's functions. He loved to eat, and even in restaurants he sat quite patiently in his high chair, waiting for his food. Perhaps recently, they thought, he had stayed more with the nanny when they went shopping at the mall, but he loved to swing at the park. He did not play with other children or pay much attention to his sister.

It was an observation of Jody's parents playing and talking with his sister that gave the best impression of how they would relate to a child under normal circumstances. This observation helped tease out the possible contribution of a relationship disorder to Jody's diagnosis. Both parents appeared to enjoy a very good relationship with their daughter, the mother tending to be more tentative and the father somewhat more controlling. They could step away from their anxiety about Jody to enjoy her. This five-year-old was a very "take charge" child, insisting that her parents "play some more."

While their current stress was certainly affecting their relationship with each other when the team met them, Jody's parents appeared to be totally focused on what to do for Jody and united in the goal of assisting him.

Although many of the interactions between Jody and his parents at the time of the team's evaluation could be described as anxious and tense, a relationship diagnosis as defined in *DC: 0-3* is not applicable in this case.

Axis III: Medical and Developmental Disorders and Conditions

Jody's difficulties included sensory and motor processing disorder, receptive and expressive language delay, dyspraxia, and reduced muscle tone.

Axis IV: Psychosocial Stressors

It is difficult to ascertain how much stress Jody was experiencing at the time of the assessment. His parents thought he might have become more intense and active during the weeks he started and stopped school and underwent numerous evaluations in many different settings with many different people, suggesting at least moderate effects. The parents' own stress made it difficult for them to step back and judge the impact on Jody, but they did feel they perceived and interacted with him differently now that they were aware of his developmental challenges, and he was now unpredictable to them. They worried that their concerns and anxiety would make him worse. Their distress was extremely high because the course and outcome for Jody was unknown and would be for some time. Although Jody's strengths and indicators for a good prognosis were discussed, it would only be his real improvement that would be encouraging. Also, the nature of the disorder and its treatment put enormous stress on the parents every day since they had to learn to interact with their child continuously as well as implement the specific recommendations of the therapists. Marital stress was to be anticipated since the parents already appeared so depleted and might have few resources left for themselves. Fortunately, Jody's family could call on the extended family for some support and were relatively stable financially. It was not clear how Jody's mother would respond to the change in her work and social expectations, since she had quickly set aside her goals to help Jody. Overall, the family would be very vulnerable for several years to come.

Axis V: Functional Emotional Developmental Level

This axis is used to describe the developmental level at which the infant organizes affective, interactive, communicative, cognitive, motor and sensory experience. The concept of Functional Emotional Developmental Level captures how well the child is actually able to function, given his or her constitutional make-up—i.e., how well the child takes in and integrates information, how effectively the child can take action, and how well the child self-regulates, as well as the child's level of cognitive and emotional processing. These interrelated processes emerge developmentally following each other, but each of them continues to develop and become more complex as the child grows older. This axis also takes into account how well caregivers and the larger environment support these processes. (See pp. 26-28 for descriptions of each level.)

The assessment of Jody's Functional Emotional Developmental Level was based on observations, described above, of Jody interacting with each of his parents. Ratings are also included for his interactions with one of the evaluators.

As described in *DC: 0-3*, the following ratings are used to assess a developmental level:

1. Has not reached this level.

2. Barely evidences this capacity even with support.

3. Needs some structure or sensorimotor support to evidence capacity; otherwise manifests capacity intermittently/inconsistently.

4. Has the capacity but not in keeping with age-expected forms of the capacity; e.g., relates but immature.

5. Age-appropriate level but vulnerable to stress, with constricted range of affects.

6. Age-appropriate level under all conditions and with range of affect states.

	Mother	Father	Other	Evaluator

Mutual attention: *Ability of dyad to attend to one another (all ages).*
At best, mutual attention with Jody was very brief and only possible with sensory motor support—while dancing, for example. Eye contact was only observed briefly—for example, when Jody was wedged behind the couch and could safely peek at his mother. Although his father held a puppet in front of him and Jody tapped for its sensory feel, the attention was not mutual. The evaluator could not elicit mutual attention at all.

Mother 3 Father 2 Evaluator 1

Mutual engagement: *Ability for joint emotional involvement, seen in looks, gestures, etc. (over 3 months).*
Jody was given the benefit of a higher rating with his mother because his best responses were the fleeting pleasure he showed when they danced to "Baa, Baa, Black Sheep" and his distress when she left the room.

Mother 3 Father 2 Evaluator 1

Interactive intentionality and reciprocity: *Ability for cause-and-effect interaction, where infant signals and responds purposefully to another person's signals; involves sensorimotor patterns and a range of emotional inclinations (over 6 months).*
Jody was purposeful, in that he could pull his parents over to get something or undo (dump or throw) something they did, but the interaction would stop there, with his usually taking flight and avoiding them further. He could open and close one or two circles of communication when he really wanted something—and in his attempts to avoid his parents when they pursued him—but direct interaction did not develop further.

Mother 3 Father 1 Evaluator 1

Representational/affective communication: *Capacity to use mental representations, as evidenced in language and play to communicate emotional themes (over 18 months).*
There was no evidence of this capacity during the evaluation. Jody did not reach this or any further levels (i.e., **Representational elaboration** or either level of **Representational differentiation**). It should be noted that these levels should have been emerging, since Jody was 27 months old at the time of the evaluation.

Mother 1 Father 1 Evaluator 1

Diagnostic summary

Axis I: **Primary Diagnosis**
Multisystem Developmental Disorder, Pattern B.

Axis II: **Relationship Disorder Classification**
No diagnosis.

Axis III: **Medical and Developmental Disorders and Conditions**
Sensory and motor processing disorder, receptive and expressive language delay, dyspraxia, reduced muscle tone.

Axis IV: **Psychosocial Stressors**
Moderate effects.

Axis V: **Functional Emotional Developmental Level**
Has not reached expected level of representational/affective communication; barely evidences capacity for mutual attention, mutual engagement, and interactive intentionality and reciprocity, even with support

Discussion with caregivers and treatment planning

The parents and team discussed the meaning of Jody's diagnosis and the implications for intervention. Family patterns were explored to determine the flexibility and resources needed to implement an intervention program. The clinical psychologist, an interactive developmental therapist, who had assessed Jody was enlisted to work intensively with him and his parents, as well as to coordinate team meetings to discuss treatment plans and monitor progress.

Jody was a very appealing toddler. Even when one was not interacting with him, he exuded a joyfulness and energy that pulled one in and made one smile. He had a glimmer in his eye which seemed to say, "Get me if you can!" as he would run away. It was also impressive to see him stop and regulate himself when he found his goal! For example, he would stop running to happily sing the alphabet or get on the floor to line up his numbers, focusing intently at the task at hand. He also seemed to quickly grasp the change when his mother shifted to helping him do what he wanted to do rather than pursue her own agenda. Although Jody's cognitive potential could not be ascertained, there was something "sharp" about this little boy and his speedy perceptions of the world about him. Another strength was that he had spontaneous jabber, which was beginning to sound like word approximations. This behavior suggested strongly that Jody would be able to speak. While his auditory processing difficulties were certainly severe, music and language were getting through and could be retrieved with certain prompts. As noted above, he certainly seemed attached to his parents, although very limited in the ways he could express this. Jody's parents were very determined to help him and had the resources to do so.

On the other hand, it was also evident that this very excitable little boy had significant difficulties with regulation and had to work very hard to compensate for his under-and over-reactivity to various sensory stimuli. His significant difficulties with motor planning impeded spontaneous imitation of gestures and his ability to carry out complex actions. Thus, he was confined to lining up objects or simple one-step actions. It appeared that Jody would have difficulty with eye/hand coordination and visual/spatial learning. These difficulties were identified and could be effectively treated over time.

The most important recommendation was for the parents to learn how to interact with Jody every waking hour. It was recommended that Jody and his parents see a psychologist three times a week to learn how to interact more effectively in order to achieve the functional levels described above. The parents and team agreed that Jody was not to spend time alone during the day. In addition to routine caregiving, his mother, father, and nanny would schedule "floor time" sessions in which each caregiver would play as interactively as possible with Jody, following his lead. Jody was to participate in the family's daily life and be taken everywhere they would ordinarily go as a family; he would also have excursions to the park, playgrounds, and other family and community activities.

Some time during the sessions with the interactive developmental therapist would be used to address the parents' feelings and concerns. The parents and Jody would also be seen for monthly consultation with the child psychiatrist. It was further recommended that Jody begin speech and occupational therapy twice a week with therapists who had a sensory-processing focus and that programs be developed to carry out at home in order to strengthen Jody's capacities.

The team suggested that Jody not attend his current nursery school for the remainder of the school year. Following several months of the intensive intervention and an assessment of Jody's rate of progress, an appropriate school program would be identified. The strengths outlined above left open the possibility of having him attend a regular preschool, where he would be immersed in an interactive and communicative environment. Finally, the parents and the therapeutic team (then consisting of a clinical psychologist, a child psychiatrist, a speech/language pathologist, and an occupational therapist) would meet once a month to monitor Jody's progress, address concerns, and plan further intervention.

Intervention

Jody participated in intensive intervention for the next four years. This consisted of interactive therapy with his parents, play therapy with one or two other children in small group sessions, speech and occupational therapies, and monthly psychiatric consultations. He was enrolled in a regular preschool, with an aide, during the first two years of intervention. For the next two years he received weekly cognitive/educational tutoring. He also underwent auditory training (Tomatis method) during the fourth year of intervention, when it became available. Jody's parents were discouraged from giving him refined sugar, chemicals, and salicylates. To facilitate social inter-action Jody also participated in creative drama classes and sports programs in his neighborhood. His parents also arranged play dates with other children several times a week throughout the intervention period. Team meetings were first held monthly and then every two to three months . These were especially important to support the family's remarkable efforts through "thick and thin" and keep them on the forefront of the intervention.

Jody progressed rapidly throughout this course of intensive intervention, with each day spent interacting with parents, children, teachers, and family members, as well as therapists. He became an exceptionally well-related, very bright, and creative child. Jody is now a very happy child, can put himself in someone else's shoes, and expresses warmth and empathy. He is aware of his tendency to get excited and insistent, but is able to reflect, anticipate his reactions and modify them, and monitor himself. He has complex opinions about everything and uses symbolic play to work through and understand emerging feelings and impulses. He entered first grade in a highly competitive school and is doing extremely well.

Prognosis

Were he to be assessed today, Jody would not receive any diagnosis of mental health or developmental disorder. He has attained all functional developmental levels.

MARY, Age 28 Months

Reason for referral

When Mary turned 28 months old, her parents became concerned because she was not yet speaking to them, although she knew the words to many songs and was interested in watching videos. Mary would occasionally ask for something she wanted, using single words, but she did not answer any questions or even respond to her name consistently.

When her parents became concerned about her delayed language, they had Mary evaluated through Child Find (a component of infant/toddler services available under the Individuals with Disabilities Education Act). She was placed in a special education toddler speech and language program three mornings a week. Her teachers, however, noticed Mary's self-absorption and found it difficult to engage her in the group. They referred her for further evaluation. Although her parents agreed to follow through with Child Find's recommendations, they found it hard to grasp that anything could be seriously wrong with their pretty little girl. She had always enjoyed being affectionate and, though undemanding, was responsive to their dances and tickle games. Their nanny never reported any difficulties, and Mary certainly seemed pleased to see them at night when they returned from work and put her to bed. Until now, their biggest concern had been her numerous ear infections, but recent hearing tests had indicated no problems. Mary's parents now started to make inquiries regarding further evaluation and consulted a clinical psychologist, who brought in an occupational therapist and speech/language pathologist for further evaluation.

Assessment process

The assessment process was similar to that used in the assessment of Jody, described above.

Assessment findings

Observations

At 28 months, Mary sat on the floor of the clinical psychologist's office, arranging a row of Sesame Street figures, placing the figures in a line but continuously changing their positions. She seemed to stop, look, and consider where to put them but never looked up as her mother gently asked her questions about what the figures were doing. When her mother tried to use one of them to jump into a nearby, small pretend swimming pool, Mary simply retrieved the figure after her mother put it down and put it back in her line. When her mother gently commented, "Oh, you don't want them to go swimming!," Mary gave no indication that she heard her and just continued her own scrutiny of the figures, turning sideways. Although her mother persisted in trying to join her, Mary did not respond. Finally she gathered as many figures as she could hold and took them over to a table facing the wall. This time her mother was not be able to get in front of her. She again started to line the figures up and rearrange them. Suddenly, a screechy high-pitched voice could be heard attempting to sing, "Happy birthday to you!" The melody was distorted and the words distended, but still recognizable. The therapist quickly gave Mary's mother a Cookie Monster figure holding a birthday cake and urged her to go over to join Mary. She was told not to give the figure to Mary, but to hold it in front of her near her line and move it up and down as if dancing to Mary's song, while she urged Mary to look at Cookie. Mary did in fact see Cookie very quickly but since he was "dancing" did not grab it; instead, she brought over the Big Bird figure she was holding and started to imitate the dancing action with this figure. She could not sing at the same time, but Mary's mother sang for them all. As soon as she stopped, Mary took the Cookie Monster figure and turned back to her line.

At the next observation, Mary gathered a bunch of jungle animals and placed them in a line on the couch, her back to her parents. This time her mother was encouraged to offer her more animals for her line. When she came to the gorilla, she placed him on the tiger as if to ride. Mary quickly noticed this and took the gorilla off the tiger but a moment later put him on her lion and started to move it across the couch. She gave no indication that she appreciated her mother's praise, as she followed Mary again. A little while later, Mary took her cache of animals, lined them up in front of the door, and lay down facing away from everyone. The therapist placed a large plastic mirror against the door so that when Mary's father joined her, both their images were reflected in the mirror. Mary was a bit surprised by the mirror image, but also curious; she did not move away. She let her father add and move some of the animals and again imitated riding on the tiger. Her glances were very brief at first, but she then started to look into the mirror and at her father when she moved the animals. She gave no indication she heard anything he said, until he started to sing "Eentsy Weentsy Spider" when handing a gigantic spider to her to add to the line. Then she looked up for a moment.

Although Mary appeared curious and alert in a subdued way, she never smiled or showed any pleasure in what she was doing. When the therapist asked her father to show her what Mary liked or enjoyed doing with him, he started a tickle game. Mary rolled onto her back as her father excitedly called her name and said he was going to "get her belly button." Suddenly Mary's eyes widened, she smiled and said, "Pilllll-ooohh," as her father put his head on her tummy and protested, "No, no, no . . . pillow!" They repeated this again and again with great delight and finally some giggles.

Parents' observations

Both parents reported that Mary was a very content 28-month-old who enjoyed watching videos, loved music, and could sing quite a few songs. She enjoyed lining things up and always appeared busy with her little toys. Mary was also quite cooperative and did not mind going on outings with her parents. She was always quiet and well-behaved, and very undemanding. She kept herself busy and often went to her room, where she would lie down and suck her pacifier for long periods. Mary did not pay any attention to her five-year-old sister, but the parents felt she was aware of her family and pleased when her grandparents visited. Mary also had a very loving nanny, who had been with her since birth. Both parents worked full time but were sure to spend time with the children before bedtime on weekdays. Her parents had noticed that Mary did not run around as much as other children in the playground, although she liked to swing.

Developmental and family history

Mary had been an easy, low-keyed baby who almost never cried, slept well, and patiently waited to be cared for. Pregnancy and delivery had been normal. She had been bottle-fed since her mother returned to work two months after her birth. Motor milestones were a few months delayed, but this did not worry her parents or the pediatrician, since her older sister's developmental course had been similar. Mary had enjoyed good health except for repeated ear infections and occasional strep throats, which started at eight months; these were cleared up each time with antibiotics. She was a fair eater and craved juices and her pacifier. She did not attend to other children but loved to roughhouse with her sister and father.

Diagnosis

On the basis of their observations, the clinical psychologist, occupational therapist, and speech/language pathologist agreed that Mary had difficulties in several areas, going beyond delayed speech, and met the criteria for Multisystem Developmental Disorder. A discussion of Mary's diagnosis along the five *DC: 0-3* axes follows, with specific reference to the diagnostic criteria for MSDD.

Axis I: Primary Diagnosis

1. *DC: 0-3:* Significant impairment in, but not complete lack of, the ability to form and maintain (and occasionally form) an emotional and social relationship with a primary caregiver, i.e., capacity for emotionally connecting, evidencing pleasure and warmth with another person, and/or exchanging social gestures is significantly delayed or impaired.

Mary: Mary had moments of intense engagement and pleasure relating to her father, when she could lay on her back (and feel supported) and be tickled intensely (she was very underreactive and needed intense input to register the experience). At such times she could look at her father and hear his high-pitched voice saying "tummy" or "pacifier" and responded with her own high pitched "tummy." Mary came to life when provided with the appropriate supports to take in the relationship her father offered, including intense affect, single words expressed in a high-pitched voice, positioning which compensated for her low motor tone, compression which supported her body awareness, and a familiar repertoire. She not only expressed joy and delight with her playful father, but also used words to request that he go on. Pursuing Mary in such a way only occurred from time to time, usually at bedtime, since the parents thought she might be too old for such baby games. But, in fact, they realized that these were their best moments with Mary and were encouraged to play with her this way much more often.

This account underscores the importance of multiple observations and close attention to the reports of parents and other caregivers, since Mary could appear very distant, remote and unresponsive to relationships if observed under one set of conditions and quite different under other conditions.

2. *DC: 0-3:* Significant impairment in forming, maintaining, and/or developing communication. This includes preverbal gestural communication, as well as verbal and nonverbal (e.g., figurative) symbolic communication.

Mary: Mary could certainly let others know what she did not like by undoing what they had done or by moving away. She would respond "More" to tickles or a question about whether she wanted more juice. But most of the language she had learned consisted of memorized fragments from video scripts. These fragments of scripts were not used with any communicative intent, and she did not seek an audience for her "performances." Instead, she appeared to repeat songs or fragments of stories she had seen to herself while playing with figures related to her words. Perhaps she "knew" or at least recognized what the words meant. However, with the exception of very familiar phrases related to her daily life, she did not appear to comprehend what other people said to her. There was the suggestion that she was beginning to use fragments of script to connect to others, since they might recognize what she said and meant at the moment. For example, when Mary no longer wanted something, she had used the word, "Bye-bye," to tell her mother to take it away.

3. *DC: 0-3:* Significant dysfunction in auditory processing (i.e., perception, comprehension, and articulation).

Mary: Mary was able to sing songs and repeat fragments of scripts from videos she had heard many times. She also responded to words repeated in her daily life that were related to high-affect desires and pleasurable experiences, as well as to the names of the family members. These words often had to be repeated, exaggerated or sung to get through to Mary because she was so under-reactive to sounds. Her articulation was not always clear, and when she said anything it was always in a high-pitched voice. The extent of her comprehension of videos or songs was not clear, since she was not able to communicate her understanding. She would sometimes repeat a single word attached to an action she was doing, just as she echoed "jumping" in the observation above. While her auditory processing difficulties were quite significant, the auditory channel was open, and it certainly appeared that she would be able to learn to speak and communicate.

4. *DC: 0-3:* Significant dysfunction in the processing of other sensations including hyper-and hyporeactivity (e.g., to visual/spatial, tactile, proprioceptive, and vestibular input), and motor planning (e.g., sequencing movements).

Mary: Mary was a very underreactive child in most areas. She had low muscle tone and low energy, tending to find places where she could lie down and become absorbed with a few toys or watch her videos. She was underreactive to movement and craved swinging, but did not like to run, climb, or jump, and had to be urged out to the playground. It was here that her motor planning difficulties were most evident. She was poorly coordinated and had difficulty climbing on the equipment. She also did not like to do puzzles or build, preferring to line up her figures or animals and move them about. She did however wave good-bye and imitate simple gestures such as clapping or peek-a-boo, although others were more difficult and required lots more hand-over-hand facilitation. Mary also showed tactile defensiveness. She hated to have her hair brushed, hated shampoos, got alarmed at an unexpected touch, and only ate soft foods.

If it were not for the delay in Mary's language development, she might have passed for a very shy or quiet little girl who liked to play by herself and was just going to be a late talker. In fact, it was finally the language delay which prompted her parents to get help. Otherwise, she appeared to them to be quite comfortable at home, would relate to tickles and giggles, seemed to enjoy tapes and videos like other children do, and was easy and undemanding. The fact that she was so different from her older sister was attributed to the older child's being more like the father and Mary more like her mother, who was also a quiet, low-keyed person.

What her parents had overlooked was not her quiet, self-absorbed manner, but her difficulties relating to them and the high degree of accommodation they made to her, guessing her needs and providing a stable, predictable, very organized environment. This environment kept Mary's anxiety at a minimum, because she had a secure sense of her routines, was allowed to watch videos and do what she chose most of the time, and was able to avoid challenging environments, such as the playground or preschool, where other children and far greater stimulation might have impinged on her. The absence of other symptoms made it easier to "wait" for her language to catch up.

The next step is to consider whether Mary fit into one of the proposed patterns for MSDD. Mary's disorder is most nearly characterized by Pattern C.

703. Pattern C

These children evidence a more consistent sense of relatedness, even when they are avoidant or rigid. They also still tend to pull away but have islands of warm, pleasurable affect and are more consistently able to use simple social gestures (e.g., reaching, looking, vocalizing, exchanging objects), and intermittently capable of complex interactive behavior and gestures (e.g., taking a parent to the door to leave). These children also resist change, tend to be very perseverative and be preoccupied with certain objects, but will allow another individual to join them in their perseverative behavior and make it interactive (e.g., they will somewhat playfully try to remove a person's hand from the door, as they keep trying to open and close it repeatedly.) They evidence a mixed pattern of sensory reactivity and motor planning difficulties, with a tendency towards overreactivity to sensation. They may use some words or phrases in scripted or rote form, i.e., repeating words from a video or song.

Mary fit much of this profile, although she was more underreactive to sensation, had reduced muscle tone, and was just beginning to show some symbolic and communicative intent.

Axis II: Relationship Disorder Classification

Mary's father was an optimistic, energetic, and outgoing person who could engage his daughter in more affective and pleasurable ways. A busy professional who worked very long hours, he usually did not see Mary until bedtime, when he would enjoy putting her to bed. He had not noticed that it was he who had to initiate their interactions all the time, since this was his inclination anyway. He enjoyed Mary's beauty and found her undemanding nature a relief after their first daughter. Although very concerned at the time of the evaluation, he had not been particularly anxious about her development and related to Mary in a positive and sensitive way, deliberately enticing her with objects or ideas he thought she liked, as well as roughhousing and tickling, to which she always responded.

Mary's mother was a successful professional woman who worked very hard at everything she did. She was the first in her family to "make it" by sheer determination and will power. She was very organized and precise in all she did and approached everything with a list of specific goals to be accomplished. Her work, her parenting, and her relationships were all approached the same way. It was clear that she took her responsibilities very seriously and that she would probably work harder to overcome obstacles before she would confront or ask assistance of others. Although she appeared subdued and spoke softly, anxiety appeared to underlie her gentle composure. She responded openly to questions about her daughter but was much more reluctant to talk about her own feelings and what it was like to find out that her daughter was having difficulties.

Mary's mother could acknowledge that she often felt rejected or inadequate trying to engage Mary, but she also identified with her shyness and self-absorbed nature. She had not been concerned about her language delay because she could think of no reason Mary would not eventually speak. She also felt very confident in their nanny, who was highly educated and an experienced mother herself. Because Mary's mother had had the children in her late thirties and was very established in her career, she had never considered not working full time. However, she always had the flexibility to keep appointments when needed.

It was hard for Mary's mother to identify times when she really enjoyed Mary. She wondered now if this was because Mary was in fact so hard to engage. She would sometimes just want to go shopping to find Mary pretty things to wear in order to feel good about her. It was very hard to "push through" to Mary. She depended on their caregiving routines as occasions to be with her. Mary's mother seemed sad as she spoke, but downplayed her feelings, saying she just felt worried and hoped Mary could be helped. This anxious concern was expressed in a bland way, her calm face almost impassive. Her interactions with Mary were hesitant and reticent, as if she had to respect Mary's lack of responsiveness and not intrude upon her. When this mother was observed with her older daughter, her reserve was less evident. In fact, she became more lively and energetic as her older daughter made her laugh or engaged her in interesting questions they could explore together.

The use of the Relationship Disorder Classification axis in this case requires consideration of the child's effect on the parent, reflected here by the anxiety, inhibition, tension, and stress related to engaging this child. The periods of engagement were very short and intense, but the overall quality of care was extremely loving and supportive. Although Mary did not initiate interactions often, she was certainly aware of and even kept track of the important relationships in her life.

Axis III: Medical and Developmental Disorders and Conditions

Mary experienced recurrent ear infections and had sensory processing disorder, receptive and expressive language delay, low muscle tone, and dyspraxia.

Axis IV: Psychosocial Stressors

Mary appeared to increase her avoidance when pursued by others, although she did not appear terribly distressed. Nevertheless, given her underreactive nature, it would take very intense input before she was likely to show a response. The effect of Mary's disorder on the family at the time of the assessment was moderate, although it did occasionally become severe, depending on how responsive she was at any given period. The family enjoyed considerable stability and was not dealing with other stressors at the time.

Axis V: Functional Emotional Developmental Level

The assessment of this axis is based on observations of Mary interacting with each of her parents as was described above. Ratings are also included for one of the evaluators.

The following ratings will be used to assess developmental level:

1. Has not reached this level.

2. Barely evidences this capacity even with support.

3. Needs some structure or sensorimotor support to evidence capacity; otherwise manifests capacity intermittently/inconsistently.

4. Has the capacity but not in keeping with age expected forms of the capacity, e.g., relates but immature.

5. Age-appropriate level but vulnerable to stress, with constricted range of affects.

6. Age-appropriate level under all conditions and with range of affect states.

	Mother	Father	Other	Evaluator

Mutual attention: *Ability of dyad to attend to one another (all ages).*   2   3   1
Mutual attention was best with Mary's father, who would rough-house and tickle and seduce Mary by his own energy and affect. Mary's capacity was less apparent with her mother, who relied on more ritualized songs and postures to capture her attention. Mary's quick response to undoing what her mother or others did suggested that she was attentive to keeping the world the way she set it up or was familiar with, but this did not have a mutual quality.

Mutual engagement: *Ability for joint emotional involvement, seen in looks, gestures, etc. (over 3 months).*   2   3   1
As described above, Mary was at her best with her father, who appeared to lend her his spontaneity and pleasure. Mary could best join him when she had the sensory-motor support to compensate for her low muscle tone and underreactivity. Her engagement with her mother was weaker and more intermittent, as noted above. She was not responsive to new people, whom she appeared to watch out of the corner of her eye. However, it was possible to develop mutual engagement by gently obstructing and then helping Mary do what she wanted; she would quickly begin to anticipate the therapist's actions and responses. It was important to remember that Mary's expression of affects was very subdued and low-keyed, due, in part, to her low muscle tone and underreactivity. Even when she felt strongly about something, her expression appeared mild. She was not a child who would tantrum to express opposition, but rather became more avoidant.

Interactive intentionality and reciprocity: *Ability for cause-and-effect interaction where infant signals and responds purposefully to another person's signals; involves sensorimotor patterns and a range of emotional inclinations (over 6 months).*   3   3   2
Although intermittent and inconsistent when not supported intensely by others, Mary was capable of reciprocal interaction. Her actions, however, were fairly simple. She could repeat or undo what others did, and she could do simple imitation.

Representational/affective communication: *Capacity to use mental representations, as evidenced in language and play to communicate emotional themes (over 18 months).*   2+   2+   2
Mary's ability to re-enact fragments of songs and actions from videos suggested these were meaningful to her. She also allowed others to join her when they recognized what had "popped" into her head. However, while she did not appear to do any of this with communicative intent, it did suggest she had very good symbolic potential and that this capacity would develop relatively quickly once mutual attention and engagement improved. She did not demonstrate any higher abilities at this time.

Functional Emotional Developmental Level Summary—Mary has not reached age-expected levels and demonstrates only intermittent capacities at lower levels. However, with various kinds of support, she already shows the potential to respond at higher levels, with the door open to communicative language and symbolic play.

Diagnostic summary

Axis I: **Primary Diagnosis**
Multisystem Developmental Disorder, Pattern C.

Axis II: **Relationship Disorder Classification**
No diagnosis. Anxious/tense tendencies.

Axis III: **Medical and Developmental Disorders and Conditions**
Recurrent ear infections, sensory processing disorder, receptive and expressive language delays, low muscle tone, and dyspraxia.

Axis IV: **Psychosocial Stressors**
Mild effects.

Axis V: **Functional Emotional Developmental Level**
Has not reached age-expected level of representational/affective communication. With various kinds of support, shows capacity for mutual attention, mutual engagement, interactive intentionality and reciprocity, and representational/affective communication.

Discussion with caregivers and treatment planning

It is interesting to note that because Mary's difficulties were not disruptive to the family's functioning, her difficulties were identified at a later age than those of many children with MSDD, and then seen primarily in terms of language delays. Her self-absorbed and compliant nature masked the multiple processing difficulties she was having.

A critical feature of the MSDD diagnosis is that it requires identifying the various processing areas that may be undermining relating and communicating, and treating these. The first question is: Which intervention modalities are needed? The next challenge is to integrate the various interventions and maintain communication between the family and various intervenors on an ongoing basis. This can be done with periodic meetings, phone calls, communication notebooks, and, most importantly, discussion with the parents, who are participating in all aspects of the program and implementing the interventions in an ongoing way. A second question that arises concerns how much hands-on intervention by therapists is needed, and how much can be supported through school and home programming. The answer depends on several factors, including the resources available and the family's ability to follow through, which depends in turn on their talents, time, and personal resources. Even when an appropriate school program can be found, as was the case with Mary, the severity of this disorder often requires additional interventions after school hours and throughout the day to assure that the child will progress at an appropriate rate. Although some express concern regarding the number of therapists, it is important to remember that each offers a relationship to the child and it is with relationships the child needs most practice. All these relationships strive towards an overall goal.

It is the **rate** of progress once intensive intervention has started that is usually most indicative of outcome. The assessors and Mary's parents agreed that Mary would need speech and language therapy twice a week with a therapist experienced in interactive approaches, as well as sensory integration approaches to address her low muscle tone, oral-motor, and motor planning difficulties. Similarly, the occupational therapist would use interactive relationship approaches while treating the above concerns at least twice a week. Mary was also enrolled in an inclusion preschool with teachers who first developed their relationships with her in one-to-one interaction, prepared her for group activities by practicing songs and gestures, provided visual props during circle or story time, and facilitated interaction with other children. A nutritional assessment was also suggested, since Mary craved certain foods and might also benefit from certain supplements.

Most important, interactive developmental therapy (twice a week) with Mary, her parents, and her nanny would support the integration of her abilities through relationship-based interactions. A home program would be developed which would insure that Mary was engaged throughout the day with frequent floor-time play sessions; continuous interactions around daily needs, such as requests for food, diaper changes, and baths; and occupational therapy activities to organize her body, movements, and energy to enable her to participate more actively in all she did.

Intervention

Mary made consistent progress during the course of the intervention. Since she was already enrolled in a speech and language special education program, she continued to attend for the rest of the year and then transferred to a full-inclusion nursery school program. She also received interactive developmental therapy, speech and occupational therapies, Tomatis auditory training, and psychiatric consultation. Frequent play dates were provided. After she entered kindergarten, Mary was also enrolled in a soccer class and later Tai Kwon Do. Mary made consistent progress throughout the next four years, becoming a friendly, warm, related, and bright child. She was admitted into one of the Kindergarten-3rd grade schools, where she is doing very well academically, somewhat stronger in math than in reading and comprehension. She enjoys drama and loves to perform, creating her own scripts and directing productions. She tends to be somewhat reticent in new situations but adapts quickly and enjoys communicating with adults, curious about everything and always asking questions. She prefers playing with a few close friends rather than in large groups. Mary is very involved in her family life and greatly enjoys her relationships.

Prognosis

Mary no longer meets the criteria for a mental health diagnosis. She has attained all functional developmental levels. It is expected Mary will continue to do well.

TIM, Age 25 months

Reason for referral

From the time he was about 19 months old, Tim's parents noticed that he was changing a great deal. They worried especially about his passivity and lack of initiative. The parents had been afraid to express their concerns to each other, but when they visited the pediatrician for Tim's 24-month checkup, the pediatrician also expressed concerns about Tim's development, especially when he noticed him lying on the floor, biting his arm repeatedly. Now "the red flags were up," and Tim was sent to a neurologist for further assessment. All the metabolic and neurological tests were negative, but the doctor said he thought Tim might be autistic and referred him to an early intervention program. The parents immediately sought additional opinions.

Assessment process

The process used to assess Tim's development was similar to that used with Jody and Mary.

Assessment findings

Observations

Tim, an adorable, dark-haired 25-month-old, followed his parents into the room slowly and immediately went over to the couch and plopped down. While his parents were talking, he crawled under the pillows and lay passively, occasionally twisting his hands together and staring at the light. When his father went over to play with him, Tim showed a weak smile and started to move about, but did not quite signal that he wanted something. When his father called Tim's name and asked him to play, he did not appear to hear. He became more restless and started to bite his arm. When the therapist asked his father what Tim might want, Tim's father appeared embarrassed and finally said, "To sit on him!" He proceeded to press down on Tim with his upper body, and Tim smiled. When his father stopped, Tim again started to bite his arm, this time making a few sounds, until his father squashed him again. Then the father asked if he wanted more, and Tim looked directly at him with an expectant look. They continued this interaction for three or four minutes until his father said it could go on for hours. The most pleasure he ever saw in his son was when he was being pressed down, squeezed into, or pushed against something or someone.

Encouraged to play, Tim's father noticed a Slinky and handed one end to Tim, urging him to get up while he began to swing the toy up and down. Tim sat up and moved his arm up and down a few times, following the motion his father had started. Then he dropped the Slinky. He noticed two small plastic boxes on a shelf, dumped the toys inside them on the floor and started to bang the boxes together. Seated across the room, his mother groaned.

When asked what Tim enjoyed playing with her, his mother responded, "Tickle games!" Before she could begin explaining, Tim had dumped the contents of two more baskets on the floor and was stepping on the Sesame Street figures they had contained. He did not appear to notice them underfoot. His mother called Tim, saying, "I'm gonna get you!" He did not seem to hear her until she was right in his face, wiggling her fingers. He smiled and lay down on the floor while she hovered above his head, building anticipation with her voice and motions. He looked at her eagerly and actually laughed when she tickled him. She then picked up a puppet; he extended his arm so that the puppet could "bite" him. When the therapist suggested she expand her engaging tactile play that Tim appeared to like so much, she planted Koosh balls in Tim's socks, under his sleeves, behind his neck, in his pocket, and any other place she could get into in a rapid, excited game. Tim also became excited, picking up on her affect cues, and sat up and started to actively search for the Koosh balls, purposefully removing them one by one, even eager to do the next task. When he had found them all, he sat passively again.

Tim was offered a box of Disney movie figures and brightened. He picked up a few, looked at them, and dropped them on the floor. He then noticed a Disney book and opened it eagerly, turning the pages slowly. Tim's mother tried to point to figures and described the pictures, but Tim did not respond, although he kept turning the pages.

Developmental history

His parents reported that Tim had changed a great deal in the last six months, "as if once he had learned to walk he did not have to do anything else." They said that he had once been able to use a few words, had responded to his name, and had loved to listen to music, but not in recent months. It was not his lack of language that concerned them (although they worried about a year-long series of ear infections), but rather his passivity and lack of initiative. They wondered why he liked being squashed, why he was always lying down, and why he would rather watch videos than go outside and run around. Tim's five-year-old brother used to play with him but had pretty much given up, although he would sometimes join a tickle game. Mostly, the brothers watched videos together.

Reviewing his developmental history, Tim's parents said that he had been born by cesarean section because the umbilical cord had been wrapped around his neck. He was full term and weighed over ten pounds at birth. His mother had to stop nursing him within a month because he had difficulty latching on and sucked weakly. He required predigested formula and was often irritable and fussy. He did respond well to being swaddled tightly and rocked gently, but more often than not Tim's parents had to drive around the neighborhood in the car to help him fall asleep. Tim achieved motor milestones somewhat slowly, but he did sit, stand, and walk within the expected age range. However, he did not crawl and did not like being put down on the carpet at home. His parents thought they remembered him smiling, following them with his eyes, and even turning when called. He liked looking at mobiles but did not seek out toys, although he would push a knob on a toy if someone handed it to him. Although he had difficulty falling asleep and tended to become overtired, Tim was not a demanding baby. Except for frequent ear infections, for which he was treated with broad-spectrum antibiotics, he was healthy. There was some family history of delayed speech and learning disabilities on the father's side, but his parents had not thought that this history would necessarily be relevant to Tim.

Interaction with parents

Both mother and father appeared anxious and subdued as they talked with the therapist. They had been afraid to express their concerns to each other for some time now. Tim's father was coming home late from work; he admitted that he was avoiding Tim. His mother had returned to work full time when Tim was a year old. She now felt very guilty that she enjoyed being at work much more than being with Tim, but she came home on time so that her older son would not suffer. The parents were aware that they were arguing with each other more than usual, ostensibly about the wing they were planning to add to their house.

Before the 24-month check-up that had resulted in the referral to the neurologist, the family's pediatrician had checked Tim's hearing several times and thought they could wait before seeking further evaluation.

Tim's parents asked if they could raise some questions that they had been afraid to pose to other examiners, fearing that they would reveal indications which would suggest that Tim was even worse than he appeared. Why did he lie on the floor or couch so much? Why did he bite his arm? If he could hear, why didn't he respond to his name? Why was he more hyperactive when on antibiotics? (He didn't mind taking the pink sweet medicine!) Why didn't he play with toys? How could he be considered autistic when he was so affectionate with them? What had they done wrong?

Tim's parents struggled against tears and asked if he could get better. No one had given them much hope. Tim, meanwhile, had picked up a Koosh ball and come over to his father, pushing against his leg. When his father pushed back, a small smile appeared on Tim's face, and he pushed again. His parents looked up and smiled.

Diagnosis

Axis I: Primary Diagnosis

DC: 0-3 criteria for MSDD are presented, followed by observations of Tim.

1. *DC: 0-3:* Significant impairment in, but not complete lack of, the ability to form and maintain (and occasionally form) an emotional and social relationship with a primary caregiver, i.e., the capacity for emotionally connecting, evidencing

Tim: Tim had significant difficulties expressing social relatedness. He was so passive, had such difficulty even holding his body erect, and made such weak gestures. Even his smiles were fleeting. His reaching out was so brief, and his desires were so nearly imperceptible that only very close observation could detect his efforts

pleasure and warmth with another person, exchanging social gestures is significantly delayed or impaired.

to connect to his parents. Yet connected he was, allowing them to get close, depending on their pressing and squashing to find himself, and coming over at times with an offer to engage. Tim could relate in very few ways; yet he conveyed recognition and appreciation of his parents. Without their support, organizing and "revving up" his responsiveness, he was often helpless and immobilized. Tim's parents had discovered ways to elicit his smiles and could comfort him when distressed. But his subtle form of relating was not so evident to others in medical offices, where he had been tested and sedated for brain scans. In these assessments, Tim's parents had been asked many questions but had never been asked to play with him. Few evaluators had persisted in trying to engage Tim for more than a minute. Tim's parents indicated that he had been at his best during this assessment in an office with toys everywhere and a big, soft couch to lie on. It was almost like home.

2. *DC: 0-3:* Significant impairment in maintaining, and/or developing communication. This includes preverbal gestural communication, as well as verbal and nonverbal (e.g., figurative) symbolic communication.

Tim: Tim could express pleasure and distress through weak smiles and fussing, but he was so underreactive that it was easy to miss his cues. He did not compensate well for low muscle tone and poor sensory registration, depending on others to figure out what he needed. Once someone "got him going," he could gesture for more interaction, using smiles, looks, reaching his arm out, and responding to what someone had done. He even could initiate interactions occasionally, as when he came over to his father and pushed against his leg.

3. *DC: 0-3:* Significant dysfunction in auditory processing (i.e., perception, comprehension, and articulation).

Tim: There was little indication that Tim was processing very much auditory input, although he had been doing so prior to his series of ear infections. Even music was no longer engaging him. He barely noticed the sirens of fire engines or ambulances. He did, however, enjoy watching musical videos and noticed babies who cried intensely. Of all Tim's processing systems, the auditory was most shut down.

4. *DC: 0-3:* Significant dysfunction in the processing of other sensations, including hyper- and hypo-reactivity (e.g., to visual/spatial, tactile, proprioceptive, and vestibular input) and motor planning (e.g., sequencing movements).

Tim: Tim relied on his vision to survive, but did not appear to use his eyes well together (binocular) often tilting his head to one side to look. His "body senses" (tactile, vestibular, and proprioceptive) were not reliable since he was so underreactive and did not compensate on his own by seeking sensation more actively. As a result, he had become very passive and almost helpless, spending long periods lying down and, at best, finding things to bang. Even his efforts to bite himself were not intended to be self-injurious, but rather stimulated his tactile system so that he could feel and respond. Low muscle tone made it difficult for him to deal with antigravity responses like standing up, running and jumping to "rev himself up." Instead he sought compression and "squashing" to find himself in space. Then he could respond more to others. Although he did not wander very much, he was not very purposeful with toys, resorting to picking up and dropping things and simple, single actions. Motor planning was very poor. He could not point or wave.

The profile of pattern A described under MSDD best describes Tim.

701. Pattern A

These children are aimless and unrelated most of the time, with severe difficulty in motor planning, so that even simple intentional gestures are difficult. They usually show flat or inappropriate or unmodulated affect but at times, with direct sensory play, can evidence moments of pleasure or, if over-stimulated, a tantrum. These children show a great deal of self-stimulating, rhythmic behaviors rather than more organized, perseverative behavior with objects. Many also have poor muscle tone and tend to be underreactive to sensation, requiring more and more intense input to respond. These children may also have selective patterns of overreactivity to sensation, such as touch or certain types of sound. Some children who evidence this pattern of aimless behavior do not have low motor tone but are overly active and extremely distractible.

With interventions that provide the necessary levels of sensory and affective involvement and deal with the underreactivity and motor planning difficulties, these children may evidence gradually increasing relatedness and purposefulness.

AXIS II: Relationship Disorder Classification

Tim enjoyed being affectionate with his parents and had ways of indicating that he wanted them. He felt secure with them and kept track of where they were, ready to follow if necessary. He could use very simple gestures to pull them over to what he wanted and smiled when they understood his needs, especially sensory-motor ones. At first, he did not readily relate to the evaluator unless she employed one of the strategies the parents used to engage him. Over the course of the evaluation, Tim did convey familiarity with the new setting he was in, would run into the playroom and seek something he had used previously, would glance briefly at the evaluator every so often, and welcomed contact through sensory motor play and just being "in his face" where affect cues could be exchanged. His tolerance for frustration increased as the problems he confronted (including those created intentionally by his parents or the evaluators) yielded to solutions. In the course of interacting to solve problems, Tim began to relate more warmly. Although he could not initiate many interactions, he was not particularly avoidant, but tended, rather, simply to collapse wherever he was.

Once again, the nature of Tim's disorder makes it important to observe interactions carefully and interpret them with caution. Thus Tim's mother could be seen as over-involved, since she was always trying to engage and get him to respond more purposefully. However, this was her way of spontaneously helping Tim compensate for some of his own difficulties. Tim's father appeared more generally anxious and tense, finding Tim's behavior more bewildering, feeling more helpless, and resorting again and again to the same few sensory motor interactions to connect to his son.

Axis III: Medical and Developmental Disorders and Conditions

Tim had sensory-motor processing disorder, developmental language delay, hypotonia, and dyspraxia.

Axis IV: Psychosocial Stressors

As with the children described above, it is difficult to ascertain the stress Tim may have experienced as his parents became more distressed realizing the significant difficulties their son was having. There were few, if any, apparent changes in his behavior.

Axis V: Functional Developmental Level

The assessment of this axis is based on observations of Tim interacting with each of his parents, as described above. Ratings are also included for one of the evaluators.

The following ratings will be used to assess developmental level.

1. Has not reached this level.

2. Barely evidences this capacity even with support.

3. Needs some structure or sensorimotor support to evidence capacity; otherwise manifests capacity intermittently/inconsistently.

4. Has the capacity but not in keeping with age expected forms of the capacity, e.g., relates but immature.

5. Age appropriate level but vulnerable to stress with constricted range of affects.

6. Age appropriate level under all conditions and with range of affect states.

	Mother	Father	Other	Evaluator
Mutual attention: *Ability of dyad to attend to one another (all ages).*	2+	2		2

Mutual attention was best with Tim's mother, who used a greater variety of ways to get Tim to attend, including sensory-motor infant games and songs. His father could get him to attend through more "heavy duty" proprioceptive input.

	Mother	Father	Other	Evaluator
Mutual engagement: *Ability for joint emotional involvement, seen in looks, gestures, etc. (over 3 months).*	2	2		1

As described above, his parents could engage Tim through infantile games and tactile/proprioceptive pressure as well as by meeting his direct needs when he wanted something. At best, this involvement was inconsistent and required guesswork.

	Mother	Father	Other	Evaluator
Interactive intentionality and reciprocity: *Ability for cause-and-effect interaction where infant signals and responds purposefully to another person's signals; involves sensorimotor patterns and a range of emotional inclinations (over 6 months).*	2-	1		1

Intermittent and inconsistent when not supported intensely by others, this capacity was very limited.

	Mother	Father	Other	Evaluator
Representational/affective communication: *Capacity to use mental representations, as evidenced in language and play to communicate emotional themes (over 18 months).* Tim did not evidence any capacities at this level.	1	1		1

Functional Emotional Developmental Level Summary

Tim has not reached age-expected levels and demonstrates only intermittent capacities at lower levels. While he is sometimes capable of mutual attention and engagement, there is very little interactive reciprocity and no representational communication in evidence yet.

Diagnostic summary

Axis I: Primary Diagnosis
Multisystem Developmental Disorder, Pattern A.

Axis II: Relationship Disorder Classification.
No diagnosis.

Axis III: Medical and Developmental Disorders and Conditions
Sensory Processing Disorder, hypotonia, static encephalopathy.

Axis IV: Psychosocial Stressors
Mild effects.

Axis V: Functional Emotional Developmental Level
Has not mastered any of the Functional Emotional Developmental Levels expected for his age. With considerable support, shows some capacity for mutual attention and mutual engagement. With intense support, shows very limited capacity for interactive intentionality and reciprocity.

Discussion with caregivers and treatment planning

Developing an appropriate program for Tim required consideration of each of his difficulties as well as how to integrate the multiple efforts which would be needed. Guided by the Functional Developmental Levels, Tim's parents, other caregivers, and therapists needed first to strengthen Tim's capacities to engage and attend to others. To start with, floor time was recommended for eight 30-minute sessions each day. In this approach, Tim's caregivers would follow his lead and woo him into rapid affect cueing, through which he would become consistently engaged for longer periods. This would provide the foundation for his taking action on his own, developing his initiative and ability to be purposeful. Tim's parents and caregivers were encouraged to build on the sensory-motor and pleasurable games they already used but to challenge Tim to communicate his desire for more; to create problems for him to solve in order to get what he wanted (for example, to keep his marbles in a closed container rather than in a basket, so that he would need help opening it); to use augmentative communication (basic sign language, photographs, and communication boards) to help him understand and respond with simple symbols; and to use more singing and ritualized language (e.g., "Ready, set, go!") to communicate with him. These floor time sessions would be interspersed throughout the day.

Because of the severity of Tim's auditory processing and motor planning difficulties, the team recommended that he receive 30 or more hours of one-to-one interaction using a combination of behavioral intervention weekly and floor time. The structure of the behavioral approach would help Tim get started on learning through discrete trials. The floor time interactions would continue to support his initiative, spontaneity, and generalization. His parents would explore whether this program could be provided through their school special education programs or in a home program, or both. Tim's parents would undertake scheduling and integrating these efforts and conducting frequent meetings with all the intervenors. Such an intensive program would have Tim interacting with others continuously throughout the day, learning through various modalities. Given the severity of his difficulties, it was essential to implement an integrated intensive program as soon as possible.

The team also recommended that once Tim was more fully engaged, he receive occupational and speech therapy a minimum of three hours a week, with home programs to be implemented daily, in addition to floor time sessions. This intensive approach was essential to deal with Tim's hypotonia, and oral-motor, tactile, visual, proprioceptive, and vestibular needs. Tim would be evaluated for nutritional intervention, supplements and auditory training.

Intervention

Tim moved slowly but made steady progress over the next few years. His engagement, relatedness, and affects expanded readily with the intensive interactions offered him day in and day out. As his body became more able to support his efforts and motor planning improved, his initiative expanded, and he became eager to interact and play with others. Tim also responded well to the behavioral work. He was soon imitating gestures and able to follow various verbal commands; he could also imitate block designs and learned to use picture symbols to communicate what he wanted or where he wanted to go. Within a year he was beginning to imitate sounds, and soon words. The behavioral work focused on actions and language that was meaningful to him and helped him express what he wanted. Executing a series or sequence of actions to express a symbolic pretend idea remained very difficult for him, but he learned to read, which improved receptive and expressive abilities. Floor time and behavioral work were complementary, with floor time promoting more spontaneity and generalization. Tim was also put on nutritional supplements and treated for significant allergies.

Three years after starting the intensive intervention program, Tim entered an inclusion kindergarten program at his local school. He was an appealing little boy, and children reached out to him readily. He could express his wishes spontaneously and enjoyed playing games and semi-structured activities with other children. He was attentive in class and developed strategies for watching and imitating the other children. When prepared ahead of time for more complex class verbal content, he could participate actively. He works on language and math with his inclusion teacher in a small group part of the time. Handwriting is quite hard for him, but, not surprisingly, he has become a whiz on the computer.

Tim continues with floor time, speech therapy (individual and pragmatic group therapy) and occupational therapy, as well as cognitive tutoring to develop his thinking and comprehension skills. After school, he plays with friends and practices riding his bike; he has just joined the T-Ball team in his neighborhood. He is always ready to join friends and family on new adventures. He also loves to read and be read to, beginning to understand the more abstract meanings of old fairy tales he heard so many times. His pretend play now includes the "good guys and bad guys" as he figures out how to use their powers and elaborates on his fantasies. Tim's parents continue to work with the evaluator, who became the consultant who guided the intervention program and provided support to Tim's parents through the years as they dealt with the extraordinary challenge their little boy presented.

Prognosis

Tim relates warmly to those he knows and is always eager to interact and play. Tim is progressing at a slower rate academically but is moving on all fronts. He works hard at school and in his therapies but also readily expresses his negative feelings when frustrated or angry. There is always a glimmer in his eye, which endears him to everyone. Tim should be able to keep climbing the developmental ladder to more differentiated and elaborate representational stages. With relationships and communication well established, and with continued intervention Tim should be able to reach these higher levels with time.

Discussion

The cases of Jody, Mary, and Tim illustrate the use of new diagnostic conceptualizations to guide the assessment and treatment of young children with severe disorders of relating and communicating. Consideration of the issues raised by each of the five axes of DC: 0-3 prompts the clinician to develop a complete profile of the child and caregiving environment. This profile then becomes an invaluable foundation for the creation of an individualized, well-conceptualized, and integrated intervention plan.

Axis I: The Axis I criteria for the primary diagnosis of Multisystem Developmental Disorder provide a framework for the clinician's assessment of children's behavioral patterns and of the ways in which specific impairments may affect relatedness and communication. When children are observed carefully, over time and in interaction with familiar caregivers, it is possible to see how they attempt to adapt to their difficulties and how they learn. How parents try to cope and compensate for their children's difficulties also becomes evident.

Axis II: Axis II, Relationship Disorder Classification, requires special attention when a child has MSDD. Although this axis is designed to help the clinician characterize a specific relationship—that of the child being assessed with a parent or other primary caregiver—to gain perspective, it is helpful to observe the parents of a child with severe difficulties in relating and communicating with their other children, if there are any. It is also helpful to talk with parents about their feelings regarding their relationships with all their children, to better understand the effect of the target child's disorder on them and their responses to this child. In the cases described above, it was evident that the parents had been making heroic efforts to help their children. Their anxiety, tension, and "overinvolvement" were appropriate to the circumstances rather than evidence of a disorder. Of course, it may also be the case that parents of children with severe disorders of relating and communicating may, either temporarily or consistently, withdraw from or avoid their children, or become too angry or depressed to be consistently available to their children. In these circumstances, an Axis II diagnosis may be warranted, and intervention planning should address relationship issues. Whenever a child has severe difficulties in relating and communicating, a therapeutic alliance and supportive relationship are crucial for the family facing such challenges.

Axis III: Identifying the specific processing difficulties and other medical conditions of children with severe problems in relating and communicating is critical in order to understand the child's situation fully and to develop a comprehensive treatment plan. Ear infections, allergies, and regulatory difficulties are the most common conditions found in young children with MSDD. These are important to note and may require additional interventions or medications.

Axis IV: It may be difficult to assess the impact of psychosocial stressors on a child with MSDD because of the nature of the under-and overreactivity. Their family environments may become much more highly charged or subdued, depending on how the family copes with their concerns about their child's atypical development. However, there is no doubt that each of the families described above experienced severe stress as a result of their child's disorder.. While the impact of stress on the child may not be obvious in the usual sense, the stress should be noted in Axis IV. Its presence indicates that the family will need considerable social support and therapeutic relationships in order to understand and cope with their feelings as well as to endure the long and uncertain duration of the child's recovery period.

Axis V: Careful assessment of the child's Functional Emotional Developmental Level provides a solid basis for treatment planning and for evaluating the effectiveness of intervention. Since there are many current approaches to treating children with severe disorders of relating and communicating, improvement in a child's functional developmental capacities can serve as both the long-term goal of treatment and the criterion against which all interventions can be measured.

An integrated approach to the treatment of MSDD requires both intensity and long-term efforts to achieve positive results. The *DC: 0-3* diagnostic conceptualization provides clinicians with a framework for identifying a child's capacities and difficulties, and also offers guidance in planning an intervention approach that will promote recovery and get development back on track.

References

Greenspan, S.I. (1992). *Infancy and early childhood: The practice of clinical assessment and intervention with emotional and developmental challenges.* Madison, CT: International Universities Press.

Greenspan, S.I. and Wieder, S.(in press). *The child with special needs: Emotional and intellectual growth.* Reading, MA: Addison-Wesley.

Kanner, L. (1943). Autistic disturbances of affective contact. *Nervous Child 2,* 17-150.

ZERO TO THREE. (1994). *Diagnostic claasification of mental health and developmental disorders of infancy and early childhood.* Arlington, VA: ZERO TO THREE: National Center for Clinical Infant Programs.

702. Multisystem Developmental Disorder (MSDD) Pattern B

702. Pattern B

Rebecca Shahmoon-Shanok, M.S.W., Ph.D.*

Multisystem Developmental Disorder (MSDD) is characterized by significant impairment in, but not lack of, the ability to form and maintain emotional and social relationships with the primary caregiver; significant impairment in forming, maintaining and/or developing communication; and significant dysfunction in auditory processing, the processing of other sensations, and motor planning. Children who fit the "B" pattern of MSDD tend to seek repetitive or perseverative activity with objects (in contrast with children who repeat self-stimulating behaviors), but are very inflexible and react intensely to any changes in their daily habits. Children who fit this description evidence mixed pictures of sensory reactivity and muscle tone, and are more organized than children with Pattern A in the way they seek or avoid sensation. Most of the time they express their intentionality with purposeful avoidance or negativism. They often do this to reduce or avoid sensory and affective input. Yet, as may be seen through the evolution of this case, with the help of interventions which extend interactive sequences, these children often begin to evidence increasingly complex behavioral and affective interactions rather quickly.

This report covers six years of work with Simon and his family, begin-

* Author's note: Assessment and intervention with Simon began several years before the publication of *DC: 0-3* in 1994. Thus, the writing of this chapter from the diagnostic perspective of *DC: 0-3* has involved a bit of creative historical revisionism. It is the author's hope that this contribution to the casebook will be useful, nevertheless, since the principles that govern the MSDD classification are those that guided the work with Simon and his family. Readers should be aware that Simon's intensive treatment was costly, and required enormous effort by his family to coordinate. The approaches described here could be implemented in an integrated manner more easily, and at less financial and energy cost to families and the community, in community-based early intervention and family support settings.

It is with enthusiastic gratitude that the author acknowledges all she learned from the collaboration with each family and team member and with consultant, Stanley Greenspan, M.D.

ning when Simon was 39 months old. It focuses primarily on diagnostic issues as they shaped treatment initially, as they emerged during the accelerated developmental process, and as they influenced treatment decisions (See Shanok, [1992] for more extensive description and discussion of the first third of the intervention process.) Descriptions of Simon at successive stages of his progression may help readers to recognize children with challenges similar to Simon's who come to professional attention at different points in their developmental trajectory.

Reason for referral

When the therapist first met Simon, he was an adorable, slender, white-blond child, 3 years, 3 months old. His parents felt that his developmental progress had virtually halted well over a year before. Simon had almost no language and was obsessed with hinges and the movement of doors. When not studying the moving parts of doors, Simon himself was on the move, going from, looking at, or briefly handling one object or another, in frequent, driven succession. Most language appeared to wash right past him. He said few words, but would fill in an approximation of the sound of syllables to some songs when a familiar person, like his mother, sang the song and paused expectantly at key intervals. Simon did not respond to his name or to any other words or sounds, except to select from among a few familiar foods. Simon rarely interacted with his older brother; while he made almost no eye contact with his parents, grandparents, or au pair, he seemed to know these key caregivers and want them nearby. Although he had seemed to be developing typically earlier in his life, now his parents were increasingly unable to go places with him, since he would investigate every door he encountered for 15 minutes to half an hour. They felt it was not possible to begin toilet training.

Just prior to his third birthday, Simon's parents, Amanda and John Taylor, requested an interdisciplinary assessment at a well-known hospital early evaluation unit. The psychological report described Simon as an:

active boy who is functioning in the 24-29-month (mental) age range . . . his strengths were in his ability to accurately solve puzzle type tasks . . . and in his gross motor skills. His weaknesses were his inability to process information due to the severe delay in both his expressive and receptive language and in his inability to engage in meaningful problem-solving tasks which required following simple commands. . . . His attention span is short . . . he had a noticeable lack of interaction with anyone (besides family).

The psychiatrist there diagnosed Simon as having "expressive and receptive language delay; rule out pervasive developmental disorder." Consultation at another major hospital early assessment unit just following the first yielded several separate reports by members of the interdisciplinary team which were fairly consistent with the initial psychiatric diagnosis, but staff at that center did not make an overall integrated diagnosis.

Simon's parents believed that the professionals who had, as strangers, assessed their child in unfamiliar settings did not see him at his best. Thus, they questioned the basis for the recommendations made—each center suggested placing Simon in its own therapeutic nursery school, with adjunctive language therapy—and they doubted the sufficiency of the prescription, as well. So, when a park-bench acquaintance in the early intervention field told Simon's mother, Amanda, about promising intensive, multifaceted treatment approaches for children with difficulties similar to Simon's, Amanda arranged for an appointment with the therapist, a clinician in private practice.

Assessment process

Given a commitment to beginning intervention as early as possible, the assessment phase was kept brief. In fact, since the symptomatology is quite obvious, diagnosing children with severe developmental disorders is not difficult; it was, thus, not seen as necessary to have every discipline's evaluation finished, or even begun, before some components that would clearly need to be part of any treatment plan got started.

Believing that the promotion of mutual trust between parents and therapist during the assessment process must be accorded as high a priority as diagnosis itself, the assessor-therapist presented these early sessions to the parents as opportunities to observe and think together, to gather and exchange information, and to spend enough time with each other to decide if all felt they could work together productively on Simon's behalf.

The initial assessment process involved two 75-minute sessions with Simon's parents, an observational home visit of almost two hours, and a follow-up 75-minute office visit with the parents to discuss the visit and recommendations.

Assessment findings

Office interviews with Simon's parents

The Taylors were pleasant, devoted parents who had tried everything they could think of to help their young son. They seemed frustrated, deeply worried, and very sad, but not yet clinically depressed. Both of them had grown up in sprawling, upper-middle-class suburbs adjacent to different large cities in the eastern United States. Amanda, like her mother and mother-in-law, was energetic, garrulous, and high-spirited. In contrast, the men on both sides of the family, and particularly Simon's father, seemed quieter, more placid, somewhat careful or compulsive, and, in the case of John, somewhat muted emotionally. Amanda and John described their initial attraction as "love at first sight." Once they met, the courtship progressed quickly, and they were married with the blessings of both families within a year and a half. Amanda continued working in the marketing division of a large discount drugstore chain, and John pursued his legal career. They saw friends and extended family often, with interests centering on sports and movies.

Amanda and John described their first child, Ben, as "robust" and ""easygoing." All Ben's developmental milestones were within typical limits. As a nine-year-old, he excelled in sports, especially soccer and basketball, his father's games. Life for Amanda and John Taylor was abundant, busy, and fun, with close ties to both families of origin. But it was increasingly darkened by the shadow of four miscarriages, beginning 19 months after Ben's birth. In the process of attending to her reproductive health concerns, Amanda gradually reduced her hectic work schedule. By the time she became pregnant with Simon, Amanda had a somewhat less demanding routine, and she ate and exercised carefully.

Amanda and John reported that Simon had been a joyfully welcomed infant. He was born full-term, weighing just over 7 and $1/2$ pounds, after a closely watched pregnancy. Simon had been a vigorous, though sometimes cranky baby, doted on by his parents and their large network of extended family members. His achievement of social and motor milestones in the first 18 months had all seemed to be appropriate. Indeed, Simon had reached landmarks of gross motor development rather early. Yet, looking at family videotape of Simon's early months, Simon's parents, together with the therapist could recognize that as a one-year-old, Simon had been somewhat irritable and fussy, tending to entertain himself on the periphery of the frequent, large social gatherings held by family and friends. A parent or key caregiver would always linger nearby, shadowing him, in order to insure his safety as he absorbed himself with one physical detail or another of the room or hallway; elevator buttons became a long-term favorite.

Given Simon's almost precocious motor unfolding, along with their hearty, energetic, outward-looking style, his parents began to notice that his development was "off" only after the middle of his second year of life. From that point forward, in their retrospective accounts, his parents observed that Simon's social interaction, gestural communication, and general progress began to slacken. Again, the view of his vulnerability was obscured initially by Simon's excellent large-muscle coordination. By the time the therapist met him, at age 3 years 3 months, Simon could manipulate a small top; climb and descend steep stairs, alternating feet and without holding the banister; throw and catch a small rubber ball; and hit a tennis ball with a racket (!).

Gradually, it dawned on Amanda, and then John, that Simon was not learning new words. When some of the few words Simon had learned seemed to disappear at about 26 months, they grew increasingly concerned. At this time, also, Simon's interests became more circumscribed, and his parents began to feel a strange sense that he was eluding their attempts at playful contact. When Simon was 31 months old, his pediatrician, who a few months earlier had advised a wait-and-see strategy, recommended a language assessment. Having made some inquiries themselves, Simon's parents opted instead for a multidisciplinary developmental assessment at a large hospital center. Unsatisfied with that first evaluation, they sought a second at another hospital and then came to the therapist.

The observational home visit and follow-up

Toward the end of the second information-gathering session with Simon's parents, the therapist asked to make an observational home visit. Although the Taylors acknowledged some discomfort about having the therapist "watch" them at home, they expressed relief that a professional actually wanted to see Simon where he was most relaxed and at his most resourceful. In preparation, the therapist said she would be in their home mostly to learn and would probably interact very little, but to minimize their discomfort, she scheduled an office session for them soon after the home visit with the expressed purpose of discussing what each had perceived. The visit was planned for a time when both parents, Simon, and Ben would all be home.

The therapist entered the Taylors' family room quietly and sat to one side; Simon glanced toward her fleetingly but otherwise seemed not to notice her presence. He and his parents were taking turns spinning a small top inside a large, flat box-top. Amanda and John managed to keep Simon's attention on the spinning top for five or six minutes. Simon seemed pleased when his parents made the top spin, and he watched intently. Occasionally, he was able to make the small top spin himself. He made no eye or vocal contact with his parents, but he did brighten or smile, especially when he succeeded in spinning the top himself.

During the greatest portion of the hour and 50-minute visit, Simon inspected the unusual latch to a nearby cabinet and swung the door back and forth. He seemed oblivious to his parents' or brother's attempts to get his attention, let alone involve him in something. He did not respond to his name. Over the course of the visit, however, each parent was able to draw Simon into a game of fill-in-the-missing-sounds, using familiar songs. Once he had started the game, however, John, himself, seemed stuck, going over the same song phrase a dozen or more times. Ben, Simon's older brother, was curious about the therapist and stayed around for almost half an hour before retreating to his room; this animated and well-developed youngster was not able to hold his little brother's attention for long.

As Amanda sat cross-legged on the floor, Simon climbed on her back and, as she leaned over, scrambled to sit on her neck. He seemed oblivious to the effect of his movements on his mother. Similarly, several times Amanda swooped down on Simon with whoops, kisses, and tickles, which he *appeared* to tolerate, yet the therapist thought she had glimpsed a fleeting grimace on his face on one of these occasions. Frequently active, Simon could manipulate the buttons on his tape recorder and seemed pleased at hearing familiar songs before moving on to another repetitive activity. His face almost always registered a pleasant-neutral expression, occasionally showing pleasure. In running across the room, Simon tripped and scraped his calf hard enough that tears would be expected, but he just got up and kept going. His parents expressed pride in this evidence of what they saw as "big-boyishness." Toward the end of the visit, Simon accepted hands and circled in ring-around-the-rosy; he tolerated the therapist's joining the family circle.

A few days after the home visit, Amanda and John met in the therapist's office, where they all exchanged impressions. They compared what the therapist thought she had seen with the parents' knowledge of Simon's day-to-day behavior. From this, the therapist learned more about how they understood the range of his behaviors, about details of their typical days together, and about his and their histories.

Diagnosis

The *DC: 0–3* classification system emphasizes constitutional, developmental, social, and emotional factors in the child (especially Axis I, Axis II, and Axis V); the relational factors that are so key to development in the earliest years of life (especially Axis II, Axis V, and the Parent-Infant Relationship Global Assessment Scale [PIR-GAS]); and the impact of direct and indirect psychosocial stress on the child (Axis IV). The impact of the child upon his parents is critical to their moment-to-moment, day-to-day interaction with him which, in turn, is pivotal to discovering the nuances of their interventive resourcefulness; this is implicit in Axis II. When a clinician integrates information from all the axes into a diagnostic profile of an infant or young child, the intervention approach implicit in it holds explanatory value, direction, and some hope for the family.

The limitations of the evaluation reports given to Simon's family by two leading assessment centers in a major metropolis suggest the challenges before our field as we move to better understand and treat young children with severe disorders of relating and communicating. Using an obvious choice, one hospital-based team assessed Simon's difficulties as "Expressive and Receptive Language Delay: rule out Pervasive Developmental Disorder" (PDD, a DSM-IV category). Simon's impaired language processing and expression were certainly important components of the diagnostic picture, but this diagnosis failed to reflect or suggest the need for further evaluation of his complex sensory processing/integration difficulties. Given that Simon's gross motor and motor planning skills were excellent and that his fine motor capacity seemed relatively adequate, his sensory integration deficits were apparently not suspected.

A diagnosis of Pervasive Developmental Disorder, were it to be applied to Simon, would offer little more than a label for what was obvious to his family and others: that Simon was seriously "disordered" or "delayed" in the development of several key functions. In neither evaluation of Simon were the findings of the various professionals who saw him integrated into a comprehensive developmental profile (which would have included an evaluation of his sensory systems), nor was a rationale offered for the interventions proposed, that is, placement in a therapeutic nursery school with supplementary language therapy. In contrast, the *DC: 0-3* diagnostic profile, completed after three interviews with Simon's parents and an extended home visit, allowed the therapist and the Taylors to set initial treatment goals and formulate an intervention plan, parts of which could begin immediately. The profile also pointed out areas (sensory processing and language) where further evaluation was needed; as the informative details from these findings became available, the diagnostic profile was elaborated and intervention planning could be refined.

Axis I: *Primary Diagnosis:* Criteria for MSDD include "Significant impairment in, but not complete lack of, the ability to form and maintain emotional and social relationships with the primary caregiver" and "significant impairment in forming, maintaining, and/or in developing communications."

Simon almost never made eye contact with a parent and spent much of his time eluding contact with them. His affective range was extremely limited: mostly his face registered pleasant-neutral or, his parents told the therapist, he would quickly escalate to a tantrum when opposed. Still, there were some circumscribed islands of pleasure with one or the other; for example, his smiles when he and his parents took turns spinning the top and when they paused in their rendition of a familiar children's song, and he would brighten as he filled in by approximating the missing words. Furthermore, he had a significantly greater repertoire of interactiveness with his parents than with people unknown to him. In observing his interaction with his mother, the therapist thought she had glimpsed a fleeting grimace when she (over)stimulated him; he did appear to want to climb on her back, oblivious though he was to the effect of his movement upon her.

Simon lost ground in his development of language somewhere in the second year of life. Similarly, gestural communication and the turn-taking of interactive play that began to be evident in the first year slackened and finally came to a halt, becoming circumscribed to a few known and repeated sequences, with familiar children's songs, for example. Occasionally, new, but still circumscribed, chances for turn-taking could develop, such as in the back and forth play with the small top.

There was severe paucity of eye contact, few words, and Simon's repertoire of gestural communication was very limited; he tended to rely on grasping the caregiver's hand and moving it towards whatever it was he wanted.

Language therapy began about six weeks after the therapist's first contacts with Simon. The language therapist noted that:

Simon evidenced a severe language processing difficulty, as well as difficulties in relating with fleeting eye contact and a limited range of affect. His self-generated language was limited to single word utterances and a few two-word combinations. His expressive vocabulary consisted of approximately 100 single words. The rest of his language consisted of echolalia or delayed echolalia (rotely learned phrases or recitation of memorized portions of videotapes which he repeated without comprehension). Comprehension of language spoken to him was minimal. His primary use of language was to request objects and protest, and to comment on or call attention to his own actions or something in the environment, which are more social aspects of language use. When he did comment or call attention, it had the quality of a repetitive language routine. The frequency of his language production was low. Simon's attention was very poor. He often did not turn to his name. He flitted from one thing to another or got "stuck" on one activity or routine and could not extricate himself from it. It was very difficult to establish shared attention and shared activity. Other than repetitively rolling a car back and forth and saying, in a chant, "Here we go," Simon did not know how to play. He had no understanding of a "pretend concept." He was often preoccupied with opening and closing doors.

Significant dysfunction in auditory processing and in the processing of other sensation and motor planning is also characteristic of MSDD. Unlike many children in this diagnostic category, Simon's motor planning in large muscle activities was excellent, even precocious: he could throw and catch a small ball; could alternate his feet going up and down steep stairs without holding on; and could return a tennis ball with a racket. Because he avoided holding a pencil or marker, scissors, or the like, it was difficult to judge his motor planning in small muscle activities. Although he learned to manipulate latches on doors, he could not sequence actions in symbolic play, resorting to the repetition of simple or practiced actions.

Simon appeared unable to grasp even very simplified language. Moreover, his avoidance of eye contact and his lack of overt reaction to a fall and scrape suggested significant dysfunction in both visual and tactile processing areas, and possible involvement of other perceptual systems. These impressions were confirmed a few months later in two separate occupational therapy/sensory evaluations, which found him to be hyperreactive to tactile, auditory, and visual stimuli, recoiling, for example, from the volume and intonation of speech or the touch of soft substances, such as playdough or squishy balls. Compounding these profound challenges, Simon suffered from encumbered abilities to process and sequence auditory input and from difficulties in sequencing, word-finding, and producing language.

Axis II: *Relationship Disorder Classification:*There was little to suggest that relational factors were the cause of Simon's difficulties. Ben was doing well. Overintensity and volubility did characterize some of his mother's interactions with Simon; his father would sometimes get stuck in Simon's perseverations, repeating sequences and songs well past most people's tolerance; both parents sometimes seemed a bit automatic, tense and either super-pleasant or almost abrasively upbeat with Simon. However, these reactions seemed natural for committed parents, so worried about their child's predicament, yet trying to keep their courage up. It appeared likely that the parents' automatic hollowness covered over deep sadness and fear for Simon's future, and it probably also was a manifestation of the feelings of boredom and of being trapped, which not infrequently accompany giving care to a child with delays, especially when one doesn't know how, or even if it is appropriate, to try to move a child past perseveration.

These initial clinical impressions were confirmed as Amanda and John quickly began to utilize the therapist's perspective and suggestions; even during the brief evaluation period itself, some such responsiveness was evident.

Axis III: *Medical and Developmental Disorders and Conditions:* The initial diagnostic impression of Simon, as outlined above, included recognition of his profound language disorder and his sensory motor integration disorder. For a clinician experienced with this range of disorders, the symptoms are dramatic enough that an accurate diagnosis, based on observation in natural settings and discussion with parents alone, can be made by a lead assessor without having to wait. The evaluations of specialists could follow, as noted above, and provided both verification and the detail essential to a good, integrated, and wide-ranging intervention program.

While there has been controversy about the linkage of particular foods with certain syndromes or behaviors, the research is not conclusive. Following Greenspan's suggestion to take an "open conservative position by checking out each patient" (1992, p. 377), it appeared worthwhile to investigate whether or not Simon's sensitivities and the driven quality to his behavior could be modified by dietary restrictions.

Axis IV: *Psychosocial Stressors:* There were no particular stressors on either the family or Simon since his birth just over three years earlier.

Axis V: *Functional Emotional Developmental Level:* Given that this category "is based on the child's most optimal functioning even if this level is not consistent with all caregivers" (*DC: 0-3,* p. 66), it was important to see that while Simon had significant challenges and had not mastered even the first level, mutual attention, in observing him at home with his parents, one could fleetingly glimpse fragments of greater capacities which denoted the next two levels, mutual engagement and interactive intentionality and reciprocity. Notable, for example, was the mutual enjoyment and shared attention seen when Simon and his parent took turns spinning the top (which provided sensory support) and "singing" the familiar songs (which provided structure).

The functional emotional developmental stages of this axis made it crystal clear where the work with Simon needed to be focused at the outset of treatment; his capacity for mutual attention needed to be strengthened and expanded in order to provide the base so crucial to the achievement of further solid interpersonal, intrapsychic, and ego capacities.

Diagnostic summary

Axis I: **Primary Diagnosis**
Multisystem Developmental Disorder (MSDD)—Pattern B.

Axis II: **Relationship Disorder Classification**
No diagnosis.

Axis III: **Medical and Developmental Disorders and Conditions**
Receptive and Expressive Language Disorder; rule out Sensory Motor Integration Disorder; rule out food sensitivities.

Axis IV: **Psychosocial Stressors**
No obvious effects.

Axis V: **Functional Emotional Developmental Level**
Had not reached age-expected capacities but did show some capacities for mutual attention, mutual engagement, and interactive intentionality and reciprocity when provided with structure and sensory-motor support.

Discussion of diagnosis and implications for treatment

Simon was not only overly responsive to environmental stimuli but also lacked the effective processing and integration capacities that help a child make sense of and respond to the varieties of perceptual information coming from contact with his environment.

In his world, signals, sounds, and touch were experienced as abrasive; most often, he could not organize responses. He could not have coped with even the most sedate family, but his own environment, which included his family's enthusiastic energy, volubility, and bustling social schedule in an intense urban context, was perhaps particularly overwhelming. In a youngster whose eyes, ears, touch, vestibular, proprioceptive, and processing systems bombard, whisper, and confuse, behavioral organization and regulation tend to become stereotyped or driven, or both, while attention and engagement are compromised. So, when not zooming from one thing to another, Simon retreated to his island of predictability and calm: absorption with doors, hinges, latches, and buttons on mechanical objects.

While he was basically engaged with his family, Simon warded off visual exchange and cueing, even from them, through his driven and often aimless, often repetitive behavior. In terms of the continuum of multisystem developmental delays, represented in *DC: 0-3* by Patterns A, B, and C, it was encouraging to note that Simon appeared to have positive expectations of the people he knew. He could share eye contact, however, briefly and unreliably, more readily with his family than with strangers. He often seemed to want them nearby. Reciprocal games, such as turn-taking songs, also brought pleasure, contact, and some limited, routinized two-way communication with family members. This put him in Pattern B.

Not surprisingly given the abrasive effect of stimulation on his senses, coupled with his inadequate, encumbered processing abilities, Simon was extremely stressed by novelty. So, as will be seen by comparing his behaviors in the home visit to that of his first office visit, his behavioral range was more shallow, repetitive, and driven outside of very familiar surroundings. He also was unable to generalize his fragile and fragmentary capacities for mutual attention and mutual engagement with anyone who was not very familiar. This last point seemed to be one appropriately pitched place to begin intervention proper; that is, for the therapist to work towards becoming part of his inner circle, helping Simon to shore up his fledgling capacity to share attention and engagement and to exercise it with a new person. At the same time, his parents needed help to discover how to be with him so that he— not they— could incrementally maximize his abilities to *be* and to *communicate* with them.

Discussion with caregivers and treatment planning

Within the first two 75-minute interviews with Simon's parents and one home visit, it became clear that an intensive treatment plan could be helpful to both Simon and his parents. The various specialists' evaluations, which had been written only a few months earlier at the hospital centers, offered certain details, especially the levels at which Simon could or could not achieve when under some stress. But even without that data in hand, meaningful intervention with Simon and his parents could begin once the family and the therapist had all achieved the sense that they could collaborate openly and energetically on Simon's behalf. So, in the third interview, ten days after the first, the therapist was straightforward in outlining what she thought the next steps should be, what the components of Simon's extensive treatment would likely become, and what her role would be within it.

Acknowledging the range of Simon's challenges, the assessor-therapist nevertheless focused on his strengths, given her conviction that how parents come to define what is hindering the appropriate unfolding of their child's unfolding affects how they handle him and how they feel when they interact with him. In turn, parents' perceptions and feelings, shifted as a result of an assessor's feedback, counsel, and tone, influence how their child responds to them, even when a youngster is as difficult to engage as Simon was at that time (cf. Shahmoon-Shanok, 1997). Simon's parents engaged easily within this context and were eager to begin.

From the outset, Simon's treatment was intense: it consisted of four times weekly treatment with the therapist, usually with the participation of one of his key caregivers, that is, his parents, his au pair, or grandparent. Occasionally, his older brother attended a session along with one of his parents. In addition, his parents were each seen weekly on their own. At the outset, the goals of his psychotherapy were to:

1. Help Simon expand and solidify the range of his capacities for mutual atten-

tion, engagement and intentionality with the people in his daily world.

2.   Help Amanda, John, and the others in Simon's life learn how to understand his challenges and, even more crucial, how to more successfully and frequently elicit his fragile attentional and relational capacities. A fundamental goal of the treatment was to get and keep their relationships with him contingent and working as the force to pull development along, just like what happens relationally for typically developing children. Because a young child's family will always be a more central referent than any professional member of the team could ever become, this is a crucial, paradigmatic shift in professional focus, for it is not only the child who needs "fixing," and not only the therapist who can "fix."

3.   Help Simon allow an adult outside of his familiar family circle into his sphere of tolerance.

   Within about six weeks after psychotherapy with Simon and his parents began, relationally based language therapy began twice a week. Later, occupational therapy, with an emphasis on sensory processing and sensory integration, began to occur twice weekly. After several months, Simon was placed in a small preschool with typically developing youngsters six months to one year younger than he, for three hours a day, five days a week, with a designated assistant teacher (sometimes called a shadow). Again, in all of these plans for specialized support, a fundamental element of the work was to weave in the basic relational elements of mutual attention, engagement, and interactive intentionality.

   Another component of his treatment plan became an increasingly significant element which we all watched carefully: several months after treatment began, Simon's mother became ready to implement an elimination diet with Simon. Dietary restrictions yielded impressive modification of the driven quality to Simon's behavior. The result was a dramatic reduction in his moves from one thing to another and a consequent greater ability for him to concentrate on things other than doors. While Amanda had initially balked, crying at having to deny her son "who already has had so much denied him" a variety of foods, she came to agree that it had been worth carefully observing the effect of foods on Simon's behavior through the elimination diet (Greenspan, 1992, chapter 8). Indeed, his parents much preferred this approach to the possible alternative of medication; medication was never utilized with Simon. Finally, part of the initial prescription for Simon also included frequent play dates with typically developing children.

   What tied all of these components together and was crucial to the enormous, integrated progress which Simon has made, were regular, frequent, and concentrated team meetings. These took place every six to eight weeks over the first four years of treatment, and every three and then every four months or so thereafter. As case manager, the therapist chaired the meetings, inviting all team members to describe details and nuances. The environment was one of mutual sharing, with each member teaching the others which of the subtle successes with Simon could be generalized into the others' settings. Especially with a child like Simon, who requires evaluation and intervention from the perspectives of multiple disciplines, lively meetings of team members and the family are essential, to exchange observations of intervention techniques that are proving to be effective with this particular child and, later, to exchange observations that lead to modifications of the initial diagnosis. Recalling that no stage can be skipped, the team used the functional emotional developmental levels as an overall guide to goal-setting. All members of the team, including Simon's regular teachers and his special teacher, were active contributors. Subunits of the team also had informal and frequent conferences, as needed.

Intervention

In order for the reader both to contrast Simon's behavior at home and in the therapist's office, and to capture the course of his progress, notes of his first office visit are included here. This visit took place after the decision to treat him intensively had been agreed upon by parents and therapist. In terms of assessment methods, when the reader compares how much better Simon could function in his home than he did with a stranger in a new setting even with his mother's presence, and recalls how essential it is to search for best, even if only fleetingly glimpsed, developmental levels, the significance of observing in settings most familiar to the child (and his caregivers) becomes obvious.

Following the description of the office visit is a summary of Simon's unfolding development, with occasional brief session vignettes so the reader can "observe" and feel how his progress advanced.

Notes from Simon's first office visit—age 3 years, 3¹/₂ months

Simon and his mother almost burst into the office. He immediately went to the toy telephone, picked it up for a moment and dialed, dropped it, and moved to the rocking chair which he pushed for a few seconds. By this time, the therapist talked about taking his heavy jacket off, which he permitted his mother to do. Simon seemed to have no appreciation for the limits of the office; he was fascinated with the mirrored French doors and kept returning to them, opening and closing them, during the entire session.

He also opened and closed the inner front entrance door to the waiting area several times and tried the locks on the outer door. Perhaps most striking was a driven but somehow aimless quality which sent Simon first to one thing, then to another, moving from space to space. The only thing that he lingered at and repeated was door "play." About halfway through the session, he noticed the steep staircase just outside the office door, walked jauntily (alternating his feet) to the top, looked in the bathroom, opened and closed its door, opened a closet door slightly, seemed disinterested in the contents, and evaded the therapist's efforts to let him know that the closet was off-limits. He was clearly more drawn to the doors and the stairs than to anything else, including toys and the therapist. Simon's emotional displays stayed mostly the same, pleasant-neutral, and he made virtually no eye contact with the therapist and very rarely and fleetingly with his mother. His mother was unable to engage him in any back and forth play. Simon's behavior was much more driven in the new setting than at home; in fact, it was not possible to glimpse his best functional emotional developmental levels in the office until it became quite familiar to him over the next several appointments.

Abbreviated treatment summary

Simon was seen in psychotherapeutic play therapy for close to 6½ years; of course, the other components of his treatment plan changed a lot given his rapidly improving diagnostic picture, especially over the first 3 or 4 years. For example, in order to help him generalize language and social gains made with adults to peer interaction when he was 4½ years, Simon's language therapist began to work with him and another child at school, and did so weekly for a year and a half. Changes in the plan were made over time and very carefully in response to Simon's growth and shifting needs.

Simon's psychotherapy can be loosely organized into stages. The first ones had relational engagement as a key goal, since human relationships are the central organizing feature which move children into reciprocal interchange and learning from the immediate environment. Thus, the first task was to help Simon discover this lifeline—ways of making greater contact with his key caregivers—by helping *them* find ways to make greater contact with him for more and longer periods during most of his waking hours.

All of the interveners, which included his parents and baby-sitter, took on this goal and shared the nuances: what would be effective with one of us in one situation, the rest of us would endeavor to utilize with Simon in the next. When motivating Simon to touch uncooked rice, for example, an experience Simon initially avoided, his occupational therapist would bury something he wanted in it, and also try to extend this experience by discovering the "right" distance from which to make eye contact or a verbal comment. That is, she would endeavor to include herself in his experience to the degree he could bear. Similarly, the therapist found that if she included a joint compression game, like jumping down her staircase, she could more readily find Simon's gaze and work to extend it for first one second and then two. Thus, this period was characterized by attempts and then successes at making contact with Simon, bringing the team into his sphere of toleration by trying to make eye contact, imitation, following him, joining his activities and, occasionally, by getting in his way. In these ways, all the therapists gradually came to join his inner circle as key caregiving influences.

Once he was relatively comfortable with the team and began making contact more reliably for a couple of seconds at a time, it was time to "up the ante" in terms of communication. Because communication processing and production were so hard for him, Simon had to be quite motivated in order to produce a spontaneous behavior or sound that had communicative intent or potential. Yet it was precisely this facility which the team was working to promote, always searching for ways which followed from his own initiative and motivation. Thus, if he wanted his psychotherapist to open a window (a variation on the theme of doors, and something he very much wanted to master), he would take hold of her arm as though it were wood, pulling it in the direction of the window without making a sound or glancing at her eyes. As this was no longer sufficient to garner the therapist's immediate cooperation, she might extend the interaction by using her hand first to scratch her nose, a gesture which could bring his eyes to her face. By taking enough time in that delay, he would look at her and emit a sound, to which she would then smile slightly and murmur reassuringly, "Yes, open window. " How careful the team had to be with those smiles and words, not to overwhelm his fragile and hard-won, increasing toleration of human contact! The team had its own door to open, and that had to be done bit by bit by bit, over time.

During this period, the team worked actively to help Simon increase his ability to reciprocate in gestural and sound communication, not necessarily with words, trying to help him get accustomed to the back and forth pattern that undergirds all spontaneous interchange. We helped him move from one to four communication circles in a row to five, six, seven and then more circles of communication (Greenspan, 1989, Chapter 3); first, Simon was the initiator, but soon one of us would take the lead about something we knew he would want. By this time, Simon was moving up the functional emotional developmental ladder; he was solidly into the third level, interactive intentionality and reciprocity (*DC: 0-3*, p. 65).

When Simon was about four, he began to evidence a remarkable capacity to remember certain things. The therapist first noticed this when they were together at the top of a staircase of a neighboring building looking out on the street from inside the glass-paned front doors. A truck sped by, which the therapist hardly noticed, except that Simon "read off" all the letters, perhaps a dozen or more, on its long sign *after* it had moved to the end of the block. The therapist had to stick her head out the door to catch sight of the truck's sign again to realize that he had actually done what he did. Similarly, he began to memorize—it seemed as though he automatically knew——a wide variety of bus and subway routes during this period.

His family naturally responded with enormous enthusiasm to these displays of what they saw as remarkable intelligence. It soon became clear, though, that bolstering these feats, which were so easy for Simon, would support the growth of fantastic skills split off and leaping way ahead of any real meaning in or association with the larger world. Rather, what Simon needed was support to do what was hard for him: communications created within the spontaneity of regular, everyday interaction and, what is hardest still for children with processing challenges, beginning representational abilities in the social-emotional-communicative spheres. With the first three levels on increasingly solid foundation, the team aimed to exercise and strengthen Simon's capacities to use mental representations to communicate emotionally endowed themes through play and language.

With tactful, supportive but also authoritative direction from the therapist *not* to encourage what too easily could have become typical of an idiot-savant—prodigious, but decontextualized and, therefore, totally useless knowledge—Simon's parents did manage restraint. Hard as it was for them at first, they accepted Simon's feats with moderate interest but then tilted their attention to something contingent to what Simon was attending to, something that would demand improvisational interchange. Increasingly, Simon could be counted upon to follow the attentional lead of another, if he or she managed to stay close to his original interest. So, the team began to work actively at representational capacities in language and pretend play as he became ready, following his lead, with very familiar sequences at the outset, such as, for him, pressing the buttons of an imaginary ATM machine or walking up the stairs of a pretend bus, putting in the change and sitting down on the seat.

As the team came to understand more about Simon's bodily sensitivities, and as it discovered ways to help these come under his control and maturation through the sensory approaches and the elimination diet, Simon's progress burgeoned. Gradually, and with considerable effort to help him pay attention to his own tactile and internal organ feedback (which tend, paradoxically, to be overtly ignored by children with MSDD), Simon began to register and react to pain and other sensations more typically. After $2^1/2$ years Simon no longer required occupational therapeutic intervention, although, for about a year afterwards, his occupational therapist remained a member of team meetings to offer occasional ideas to the rest of us. (For a more detailed description of interventions through the first 26 months of treatment, see Shanok, 1992.)

The work outdoors, begun to follow his desire to be outside in the spring and to evade what the therapist sensed was a powerful oppositional potential, moved from elaborations of the stair play begun indoors to turn-taking imitation games through the glass panel doors of the brownstone houses on the therapist's street. Then Simon became interested in the routines and paraphernalia of her neighborhood mail delivery person who, after all, worked purposefully and reliably, almost ritualistically, opening and closing regular front doors, as well as a whole new category of doors, namely apartment mailbox doors, which had keys galore. Therapist and child followed this tolerant gentleman of few words on his rounds for several months, coming to know every detail of his daily business, and after a while taking the turns he offered to put mail in some of the slots.

Then one day, their kindly friend did not appear. Fully knowing that it was a stretch for Simon, the therapist nevertheless felt it natural to suggest/demonstrate that they could *pretend* the routines they knew so well. He caught on! Over the next many weeks, he became increasingly fascinated by the imaginary mail delivery play as his interest in the actual delivery person and his activities waned.

By 2 years and 2 months into treatment, when Simon was almost 5¹/₂ years old, the therapist noted, "Simon is a warm, animated and eager youngster who speaks in full sentences. His language and cognitive strides, his affective vivacity, his widening interests, his relatedness to important people in his life, and his increasing social skills are heartening" (Shanok, 1992, p. 35). Often loving and joyful, he can be mildly provocative and come up with some ideas. He can make jokes and utilize play, "but he continues to be somewhat self-centered and unimaginative, focusing on the familiar. Perhaps partly in response to his parents' pleasant, friendly style, and the muted quality of any sad and anxious affects by family members, Simon is disinclined to express negative emotions—except when they overwhelm him. He resists integrating affect into play" (Shanok, 1992, p. 18).

The team worked together to help Simon get his tendency to too much energy—which, for example, might promote his being heavy-handed and demanding, or his tendency to race through school-work—under his own restraint. Although he resented the need for restrictions, he usually cooperated with dietary restrictions because he knew he felt better being "more in control." Similarly, his vigorous extracurricular athletics were selected thoughtfully. When Simon was almost seven, he also had auditory-integration training, which appeared to have a salutary effect on his ability to focus.

The next stages of Simon's treatment more closely resembled play therapy with a typically developing but immature and egocentric youngster, a boy evidencing uneven cognitive functioning with delineated strengths, weaknesses, and social challenges. Progress became far less dramatic; it slowed and plateaued for a time here and there as Simon increasingly caught up with his age-mates along the various domains of development.

An example of work at this stage is drawn from the therapist's notes of Simon's preoccupations, 3 years and 4 months into treatment, when he was coming to the end of his kindergarten year in a private, progressive elementary school for typically developing children, his first school year without a special teacher:

Simon has complained consistently in the past few months about two boys in class named Michael and Billy. He says that they don't follow the rules, are wild, chase other children, say bad words; and "take three turns when they're only supposed to have two." I have felt that Simon is troubled by these boys because they get away with exactly what he would like to be able to get away with, that is, they're immature and self-centered, sometimes impulsive, and he's only one small step away from those kinds of behaviors, but is too dependent and concerned about an adult's admonitions to be free enough to try those things anymore. He remembers too well the beginning of the school year, which was largely characterized by his grabbing from other children and running to the front of the line; those impulsive, greedy behaviors have subsided through the consistent limit-setting of his teacher, his growing attachment to her and, related to this, his dependence on female adults in general.

Noted from a psychoanalytic perspective, Simon evidenced enduring Oedipal interests for several months, on the late side of normal limits. He could be quite creative as he schemed to put his father aside. When his grandfather had to stay off his feet following knee surgery, for instance, Simon announced to the family that at the upcoming large family wedding they would all be attending, his father would simply have to dance all night with his grandmother since grandpa couldn't. "And then," he added with a great flourish and jaunty satisfaction, "*I* will dance with Mommy *all* night!"

John and Amanda had difficulty setting limits for Simon at this time; separations at night were particularly troublesome. They were unable to find a way for him to fall asleep by himself: John would lie on the floor by Simon's bed as Simon fell asleep, frequently falling asleep himself; later, when Simon would wake up in the night, he would frequently wander into his parents' room and climb into their bed, usually between them. Many months of encouragement, based on the idea that Simon was now securely related enough so that his capacities for symbolism would benefit from a push to more autonomous functioning, finally allowed John to insist that Simon could manage to fall asleep on his own. Soon, Simon was not only falling asleep alone in his room but, within two months, he was rarely coming into his parent's room in the middle of the night any longer.

A few months later, when Simon was 6¹/₂, he and the therapist struggled to get some greater expression of symbolized aggression available. He was angry at Kenny, the resource room teacher, who he felt was making him practice the difficult "th" sound too much. In his psychotherapy, he wanted to play yet another version of the rolling a ball back-and-forth game, which we called "Good-bye, eight cents!" He began chanting things in his turns like, "Good-bye, Kenny!" or "Good-bye, 'th'!" The therapist and Simon began thrusting the ball across the floor harder and harder. Careful to follow his lead, the therapist joined his high-spirited gusto, but once added, "Good-bye, Kenneth!" Simon began to gleefully call out things in his turns like, "Good-bye, doody-Kenny!" At some point, he escalated to, "You fall out the window and crack your head and the blood comes out your head," and laughed heartily.

Amanda, who had been watching quietly, admonished, "That's not nice." The therapist had never directly contradicted her before, and certainly never in front of Simon, but this seemed too important. The therapist interrupted and asked, "Don't you think it's okay to think it and say it, especially in privacy, just not okay to **do** it?" Because she and the therapist had been talking about these issues, Amanda trusted her shift and caught on right away. She agreed, "Yes, I see what you mean," and smiled at Simon. He recognized that the therapist had sided with his dawning ability to enjoy a wider emotional range and to fantasize. He seemed very relieved, and continued to send "Kenny" crashing out the window, smashing him on the imaginary sidewalk far below.

At the end of the session, the therapist was careful about not only "putting away the toys," but also "putting away our teases" as a way of helping Simon feel some sense of control over his aggressive wishes. He quickly asked, "Why are we doing this? Because Kenny would get upset?" In this question, we can discern Simon's struggle to ascertain the degree to which his thoughts and impulses might actually wound.

By this point, Simon's pretend play and symbolic communication went beyond basic needs and dealt with more complex feelings and wishes. His ideas were logically related, but the difference between real and pretend was still fragile. Thus Simon's functional emotional developmental level was then best described as representational differentiation.

Independent psychological evaluations when Simon was 5 years old and later at 7 years 4 months

As the team engaged in school planning, it engaged an examiner previously unknown to Simon do a psychological evaluation of him. The report documents Simon's growth by age 5:

This attractive, charming lad currently demonstrates a solidly average level of intellectual, cognitive achievement . . . his ultimate potential is (probably) somewhat greater. . . . In spite of his articulation problem, Simon makes himself easily understood through syntactically accurate and coherent conversation. He had (1) word knowledge, (2) expressive abilities, (3) visual-analytic and organizational ability, (4) mathematical and reading readiness, (5) capacity for abstract thinking and (6) fund of general knowledge. His cognitive skills, his readiness and eagerness to absorb information like a sponge, and to participate with others have been marching out ahead of the maturation of his internal representations of feelings and relationships between himself and his world.

At age 7 years and 4 months, Simon had a complete neuropsychological workup by another evaluator to identify and delineate his cognitive strengths and weaknesses since it had become clear that, as the team expected, his learning competencies were unusually variable. The report stated:

(Simon). . . demonstrated many strengths. Measures of academic skills indicated that he has powerful ability to decode and produce language through phonology, and that he has acquired mathematics concepts. . . . Simon has made remarkable gains since his last assessment. Presently, all tests of language functioning were at the low end of the normal range, his memory for information presented visually and verbally was above average when repeated presentations were provided, letter and number reversals were not evident, and visual motor integration was above average. Difficulties were evident on tasks which required an integration of abilities or the capacity to organize information. Simon was unable to comprehend passages which he could decode with great accuracy . . . he tended to be distractible. . . . Brief projective assessment indicated that Simon is becoming aware of his difficulties. It appears that he has developed the language which will permit him to begin understanding his experience. One result of this developing awareness is that he feels he is being observed. In addition, Simon models his behavior on that of his peers and is particularly focused on a child who is experiencing problems in this domain. . . . He is acquiring language which will enable him to develop an understanding of his unique experience and learning style. . . . Simon has had problems with the integration of information. He will require assistance processing the information which comes from his academic, social and emotional worlds. [Continued] treatment should help Simon to increase his capacity for sustained attention and reduce his distractibility, while learning to not become enmeshed in detail. . . . The greatest challenges facing Simon will be to improve his reading comprehension. . . . Simon needs to develop an awareness of the main themes that connect information. . . .

Abbreviated treatment summary, continued

In the fifth year of treatment, the weekly play therapy sessions dropped from four to three times a week, once for a session and a quarter, at his request. For about eight months, Simon also had a joint (overlapping) session for 15 to 20 minutes once weekly with another child whom the therapist also saw in intensive treatment. One time a week he was often with his father, one time a week he was usually with his mother. The au pair brought him to other sessions. When his parents brought him they would be in the sessions, but this involvement had tapered off gradually. In addition, the therapist saw each parent every other week; this was the first period during which Amanda was not seen weekly. Simon remained on a strict diet; his mother supported his diet by being imaginative and resourceful. For instance, she supplied alternative but similar snacks to those being offered at birthday parties. She even supplied alternative treats for neighbors to give to Simon on Halloween. His mother had also been careful to promote the recommended frequent play dates with typically developing children.

If any affect was circumscribed in Simon's representational world, it was fear. Simon had consistently avoided frightening material, and only at age 8 $^1/_2$ did he begin to enjoy Halloween and the range of children's video tapes and movies. His tolerance for those things grew impressively, however, between the ages of 8$^1/_2$ and 9. Further, while he still preferred to keep things pleasant and playful, he became somewhat more exploratory with playthings. For example, in setting up the playhouse, the mother and father often were basically kind to the children, but sometimes they left them alone, rejectingly.

In his sixth and final year of treatment, Simon attended psychotherapy sessions without an adult joining in, twice a week, and his parents saw the therapist jointly, without Simon, every other week. Work with the language therapist had ended when he was 7 $^1/_2$, at about the time that Simon began to work with a neuropsychologist/tutor for his learning challenges twice a week. There, he worked on strategies to deal with the areas most difficult for him: reading for comprehension, richness of understanding, nuance and theme, and slowing down to take sufficient time and care to attend to all aspects of the assignment before him. The neuropsychologist often worked with him at school. About that she said:

> At school, he is increasingly aware of what is going on socially and in general seems to be more aware. In (terms of) inferencing skills, he is coming along in understanding emotions and motives of characters and the practical relationships between people. Of course, it is still harder for him to understand the more abstract concepts but, in general, his thinking is less concrete and tangential.

Simon continued to be on a restricted diet, which helped him with his tendency to attentional variability and impulsiveness. Understandably he had mixed feelings about this, given that he rightly saw himself as competent and strong across a variety of age-appropriate age expectations. For instance, he said of his psychotherapy, "This sucks. I could be at home watching TV or having a play date instead." Yet, in the same session, Simon provided evidence of his contradictory feelings when reminiscing about fun in sessions past and in spontaneously cozying up when he and the therapist sat side-by-side on the sofa to look at something together. In the next session, when he and the therapist used a tape recorder for the first time to devise a radio program, Simon laughed and laughed over the expletives he managed to fit into the "show," words he would not be allowed to say at home or school. He seemed to catch on that one goal of the work in the last period of psychotherapy was to boost his still fragile expansiveness and abilities for imaginary gratification while, at the same time, the therapist worked with him to modify his narcissism and to delimit his driving competitiveness to situations in which it is appropriate, such as athletics.

On a trip to a large theme park hotel, which Simon and his parents took while Ben was away on a class trip, all three evidenced new-found competence in terms of separation. John and Amanda were able to leave him with a hotel sitter, and when that sitter was not able to come on their second evening out he stayed with another stranger, a second new sitter, and managed to have a good time.

While he tended to continue avoiding affects which might disturb him, particularly fear, Simon began to show evidence of greater ability to engage with potentially stressful information and circumstances. For example, when his grandfather inadvertently mentioned an anticipated hospitalization of Simon's father, Simon acknowledged that he didn't know about it. Later, when with his father in relaxed circumstances, he asked, "Grandpa told me that you had something that you were worried about," offering his father the opening he needed to explain.

In some situations, Simon still seemed egocentric and competitive; this could occasionally be compounded by a sense of entitlement. However, he was quite responsive to criticism, and even when angry or being criticized, he usually could listen to another's viewpoint and either work out a conflict or be responsive to compromise. He had a gusto for life, labored hard at schoolwork, and had a great sense of humor and of fun.

At age nine, Simon was enjoying his good, progressive, private school, where he continued to get good report cards. He was doing well enough at school that no meetings with his new teachers were sought by either the therapist or them that year. He was liked by a range of peers and, not infrequently, was a sought-out play partner at school, in family-oriented play settings, and at day-camp. A handsome and very appealing youngster, he was an excellent athlete and was very good at tasks which require memory and skill, such as board games and computer games. Simon's articulation problems faded to the point where they were no longer apparent. He was ambitious and exceptionally well-organized and oriented in time and space, knowing, for example, a lot of detail about public transportation. He preferred play in which the rules are evident, and, at that point, had less tolerance for fantasy play, although he liked to read imaginative stories or watch them on TV or at the movies, as long as they were not too frightening. Simon had completed psychotherapy and saw his neuropsychologist/tutor once a week.

Diagnostic summary, updated

Axis I: Primary Diagnosis
No longer applicable.

Axis II: Relationship Disorder Classification
No longer applicable.

Axis III: Medical and Developmental Disorders and Conditions
Relatively mild and circumscribed learning challenges in language comprehension and symbolic thinking which are responsive to strategies learned in one-to-one tutoring; tends towards concrete memorization of facts as distinct from recognition of integrated and nuanced themes; dietary restrictions promote sustained attention.

Axis IV: Psychosocial Stressors
Family and child have handled a variety of recent stressors without compromised function.

Axis V: Functional Emotional Developmental Level
At expected representational level with some egocentrism and some constriction of affect and theme.

PIR-GAS: 80 (Adapted)

Using DSM-IV nomenclature, Simon also would no longer receive a diagnosis. In professional parlance, he would be described as having some narcissistic features to his personality, but not nearly to the extent that he would be seen as moving in the direction of a narcissistic character disorder. Likewise, Simon obviously no longer met criteria for Mixed Receptive-Expressive Language Disorder, nor did he meet criteria for the learning disorders.

While somewhat distractible at times, Simon was usually capable of sustained attention to a wide variety of materials and activities, including demanding school-work. When his diet was maintained, the only visible residue of his former drivenness and hyperactivity was that he tended to hurry through his school-work. At the same time, the energy, drive, and gusto which characterized his personality seemed to be a testament to the idea that what had been a serious problem became transformed into strength.

Prognosis and discussion

At age 3 years, 3 months, Simon suffered from a primary communication processing disorder with several processing and integration challenges that resulted in a downward spiral of the human interconnectedness that civilizes and infuses life with meaning. His diagnosis was Multisystem Developmental Disorder (MSDD), Pattern B.

Six years later, Simon's prognosis was excellent. Because of earlier school placement decisions, Simon was a year older than most of his classmates. Compared with them and functioning in a supportive but demanding private school setting, Simon was achieving beyond grade level in many areas, was at grade level in literal reading comprehension, and was approaching grade level in inferential thinking. His study and organizational skills were excellent, and he was less apt to race through his work. He had increasing awareness of his effect on others and of their emotional motivations. Simon also enjoyed a wide range of competencies, including computer skills, many types of athletics, and board games. He loved singing, woodworking, day camp, and family trips. He was increasingly able to function and amuse himself independently, although his parents needed continued bolstering to promote his optimal independence.

It seems likely that Simon will move into pre-adolescence as a popular, energetic, ambitious, and attractive, if somewhat self-centered, boy who continues to achieve in school, and to enjoy a wide range of interests. If love and work are the sine qua non of a full adulthood there are, at this point, many reasons to hope that Simon's development will continue to unfold in ways that will enable him to thrive and his family to take deep and enduring pride, not only in him, but in their roles as the central organizers in his life.

References

Greenspan, S. I. (1992). *Infancy and early childhood*. Madison, CT: International Universities Press.

Greenspan, S. I. & Greenspan, N. T. (1989). *The essential partnership*. New York: Viking Press.

Shahmoon-Shanok, R. (1997). Giving back future's promise: Working resourcefully with parents of children who have severe disorders of relating and communicating. In S.I. Greenspan, B. Kalmanson, R. Shahmoon-Shanok, S. Wieder, G.G. Williamson, & M. Anzalone, *Assessing and treating infants and young children with severe difficulties in relating and communicating*. Washington, DC: ZERO TO THREE: National Center for Infants, Toddlers and Families.

Shanok, R S. (1992). Simon: intensive, multifaceted treatment with a developmentally delayed little boy. *Zero to Three*, 13, (2), 16-20, 31-36.

ZERO TO THREE (1994). *Diagnostic classification of mental health and developmental disorders of infancy and early childhood*. Arlington, VA: ZERO TO THREE/National Center for Clinical Infant Programs.

Axis II. Relationship Disorders

905. Mixed and 902. Underinvolved

Roseanne Clark, Ph.D.
Mary Seidl, M.S.
Andrew Paulson, Ph.D.

Infants and young children's sense of themselves and of themselves in relation to others develops within the social-emotional matrix of the parent-child relationship (Winnicott, 1965; Stern, 1985). The primary relationships of infants and young children contribute not only to the development of children's personality and structure of psychological defenses but also to young children's beliefs about what is possible to expect in relationships with others (Bowlby, 1982; Bretherton, 1987; Main, Kaplan & Cassidy, 1985). Sameroff and Emde (1989) have underscored the strength and importance of relationships in the life of a young child, stating that the "relationship frames all individual experience" (1989, p. 34), and Lieberman and Zeanah emphasize the importance of the primary attachment relationship in suggesting that "the infant-mother relationship has the power to promote mental health or serve as the genesis of psychopathology in the young child" (1995, p. 571).

Understanding the quality of the parent-infant relationship within which the infant or young child is developing plays an important role in formulating a diagnostic profile for infants and young children. In recognition of this, Cicchetti (1987) asserted that, "disorders in infancy are best conceptualized as relational psychopathologies, that is, as consequences of dysfunction in the parent-child environment system" (1987, p. 837). Further, the Committee on the Family of the Group for Advancement of Psychiatry has argued that in general, important and common relationship conditions can exist independent of severe individual psychopathology and that these conditions should be described in relational terms, with specific diagnostic criteria (The Committee on the Family, Group for the Advancement of Psychiatry, 1995).

Including relational diagnoses as part of a diagnostic classification system serves to inform and help focus intervention approaches (Sameroff & Emde, 1989). In the field of infant mental health, the parent-infant relationship is often the focus of therapeutic work (Fraiberg, Adelson & Shapiro, 1980; Lieberman, 1985; Clark, Paulson & Conlin, 1993). Thus it is important to think about and conceptualize primary relationships as entities to be assessed, and, when indicated, diagnosed and treated.

Parent-child relationship disorders are characterized by perceptions, attitudes, behaviors, and affects of either the parent, the child or both, that result in disturbed parent-child interactions. When a disorder exists, it is specific to a relationship. A diagnosis of relationship disorder is warranted when significant relationship difficulties of long duration and/or intensity are identified, through assessment of the behavioral quality of the parent-child interaction, the affective tone of the dyad, and the nature of the psychological perception of, or involvement of the parent(s) with, the child—that is, the meaning of the child or child's behavior to the parent.

The categories of relationship disorders described in Axis II of *DC: 0-3* should be used only to diagnose significant relationship difficulties. The relationship axis does not address the full range of relationship quality, from well-adapted to disordered. In other words, readers should be aware that an Axis II diagnostic classification is appropriate only when a clinician would rate the relationship being assessed as below 40 on the Parent Infant Relationship Global Assessment Scale (PIR-GAS) (see p. 28-30). An infant with a primary (Axis I) diagnosis need not have a relationship (Axis II) diagnosis, nor does an Axis II relationship diagnosis for an infant-parent dyad suggest that an Axis I disorder must present in the infant. The case reports below illustrate these variations.

Some parents may have tendencies toward relationship difficulties described in Axis II—toward, for example, over involvement or hostility. Milder forms of relationship disorders may be triggered by the child's disorder (see Wieder, this volume), family dynamics, or other stresses that challenge parents' usual balance between nurturance and more problematic parental functioning. Clinicians should be careful not to overdiagnose a relationship disorder when such milder and transient forms related to stress are observed. However, the diagnostician will want to keep the relationship diagnostic categories in mind even when they appear in milder or transient forms, in order to understand the dynamics of the family, monitor relational problems over time, rule out a relationship disorder, avoid underdiagnosing, and guide relationship-focused interventions.

The two case reports below provide examples of differences in parent-child relationship histories, in parents' expectations for their relationship with their child based on their past experiences of being parented, in temperament/personality dynamics, and in behavior that both infants and parents brought to the relationship. In both cases these factors interacted to create difficulties that are serious, intense, and sufficiently long-standing to warrant a Relationship Disorder diagnosis. In addition, in the first case, the child's functioning also warranted an Axis I diagnosis.

CODY, Age 25 Months

Reason for referral

Cody and Marcia were referred for a mental health evaluation by Cody's pediatrician when Cody was 25 months old. Marcia had asked for more support with parenting. The pediatrician was very concerned about Cody's lack of expressive language and Marcia's lack of parenting skills, observed when she was unable to set limits and respond to Cody's needs (manage Cody's behavior) during office visits. Describing Marcia in his call to the Parent-Infant Clinic, the pediatrician noted, "She appears overstressed, inconsistent, at times inappropriate—I just have concerns about this family."

During the initial discussion with the pediatrician, a Parent-Infant Clinic clinician encouraged a simultaneous referral to the local birth-to-three early intervention program for a developmental evaluation to see if Cody was eligible for publicly funded early intervention services.

Assessment process

In the Parent-Infant Clinic, a therapeutic evaluation typically involves four to six sessions. The process begins with a $2^1/_2$ hour clinic intake session, which includes a family interview and videotaping of parent-child interactions during feeding, structured-task, and free play situations, as well as a brief separation/reunion episode (Clark, Paulson, & Conlin, 1993). During a second session, the clinician and the parent(s) watch the videotapes from the first session together. This process has proven to be helpful in engaging parents in looking, with the clinician, at the meaning of the child and his or her behavior to the parents, and in thinking through possible approaches to elicit more functional behavior and to enhance the quality of the parent-child relationship. Parents are encouraged to reflect on their parenting, their experience of their child, and their interactions and relationship.

The evaluation process also includes the following:

1. The Parent-Child Early Relational Assessment (PCERA) (Clark, 1985)—an assessment instrument which includes both objective and subjective components. The objective rating scales are used to assess the affective and behavioral quality of the parent-child interactions from videotapes, while the subjective aspect of the assessment involves the parent in reviewing the videotaped situations with the diagnostician/therapist (as described above). Parents are videotaped at the intake session. The diagnostician/therapist uses the ERA to guide his or her observations and in providing information to the parents as part of the assessment process.

2. Self-report instruments completed by the parents, including:
   a. Symptom C.Checklist-90 Revised (SCL-90 R) (Derogatis, Lipman, & Covi, 1973)—a checklist measuring the frequency and severity of a variety of psychiatric symptoms;
   b. *Achenbach Child Behavior Checklist* (Achenbach and Edelbrock, 1983)— a measure of parents' perceptions of their child's behavior problems;

c. *Beck Depression Inventory* (Beck, Ward, Mendelson, Mock, & Erbaugh, 1961)—an instrument that measures the amount and severity of depressive symptoms;

d. *Parenting Stress Index* (Abidin, 1986,1990)—an instrument assessing parental stress associated with characteristics of their child (e.g., demanding, adaptable), characteristics of the parent (e.g., depression, competence in the parenting role), and various life events; and

e. *Developmental Questionnaire*—a questionnaire asking parents to record aspects of temperament, developmental milestones, and significant events in their child's early development, such as illness and separations.

3. A developmental/psychological assessment of the child, consisting of:

a. *The Bayley Scales of Infant Development* (Bayley, 1993) or *The Stanford-Binet Intelligence Scale* (Thorndike, Hagen, & Sattler, l986);

b. *The Developmental and Psychosocial Screener* (Clark, l986)—a rating instrument measuring social-emotional aspects of the child's functioning during the developmental testing, including the child's manner of relating to the assessor (e.g., the amount of eye contact, social initiative and responsiveness), ability to focus and attend to the testing, frustration tolerance, and maintenance of an appropriate energy level and organization.

c. *Diagnostic Classification of Mental Health and Developmental Disorders of Infancy and Early Childhood* (ZERO TO THREE, 1994)

4. A diagnostic play session with the child in which themes, level, and quality of play are assessed as well as ways in which the child relates to the diagnostician;

5. Assessment of the parents' current psychosocial functioning, developmental, and relationship history; and

6. A home visit to assess the provision of developmentally appropriate play materials, interactions and safety. During the home visit, the Caldwell *HOME Inventory* (Caldwell & Bradley, l978) and *Safe Home Checklist* (Massachusetts Department of Public Health, 1986) are completed.

Assessment findings

Developmental history

Cody entered the clinic family interview room wild-eyed, darting from toy to toy and exploring every corner before acknowledging the clinician's greeting with a fleeting glance. Marcia, a 26- year-old single parent, with a depleted look that seemed to signal, "See what I have to deal with?", attempted to settle Cody, but to no avail. Eventually, Cody became occupied with some building blocks, and Marcia began to share her parenting story.

She described an infant whose early development had been unremarkable. Cody was born at term, an alert and engaging baby. He had been easy to care for and to soothe. However, as a toddler he became increasingly more difficult to manage; this problem was exacerbated by his delays in language development. Describing his current behavior, Marcia lamented, "He whines and points, he won't nap, won't listen, darts into the street, breaks all his toys, I can't take him anywhere." When asked to describe Cody's strengths, Marcia replied, "He can be loving, he is curious, and he is cute."

Marcia did not specifically recall when Cody's difficulties began but loosely associated them with Cody's early walking (reported at 10 months) and the significant conflict between Marcia and Cody's father, Mike, at about the same time, and this conflict resulted in Mike's leaving Marcia and Cody. The couple were not married.

The local Birth-to-Three Early Intervention Program had conducted a preschool language assessment, which revealed that Cody had significant expressive language delays. Although his cognitive skills were age-appropriate, his disruptive, impulsive behavior was described as interfering significantly with his capacity to learn new material.

Parents' history and family functioning

During the initial family interview and follow-up sessions, Marcia spent a great deal of time discussing her own psychological story, but had difficulty joining with the clinician in exploring her experience in the parenting role and her relationship with Cody. When asked about her initial feelings about Cody at his birth, for example, Marcia remembered being flooded by her own memories of being abused. Marcia remembered feeling intense concern that she would be unable to interact with her infant son, Cody, fearing that she would repeat the abuse that she had experienced. She also said that she had general concerns about her ability to be a good parent and that she feared that as Cody grew and developed he would reject or hurt her in some way.

Marcia had participated in therapy for depression and other problems on two previous occasions. While she was a college student, she had become depressed, was unable to perform most of her routine activities and obligations, and considered suicide. She entered treatment, which she found helpful. Several years later, after a move, Marcia again sought treatment for depression for approximately one year. She said that she had never been able to resolve some issues with her therapist and had terminated treatment, feeling dissatisfied.

Marcia is an only child who had lived with her parents in a small Polish-American, Catholic, working-class community. She described her parents' 30-year marriage as "completely dysfunctional." Marcia described her mother as having chronic and severe mental illness, characterized by obsessions with dirt and the sexual promiscuity of others. Marcia's descriptions of her mother suggested a high level of paranoia and tangential thinking, occurring in conjunction with frequent episodes of rage and verbal and physical abuse. Marcia said that her mother had never received any psychiatric assessment or treatment.

Marcia noted striking inconsistencies in her perception of her mother's care. She remembers that her mother adored her when she was a little girl and vividly recalled being given a beautiful Easter dress and having her hair carefully brushed by her mother. She also recalls her mother wanting her close, sleeping with her, encouraging Marcia to touch her in sexualized ways. She also reports stinging statements made by her mother regarding her physical development at puberty, and being called a "slut" when she dressed up as a young adolescent. Throughout Marcia's childhood she was physically and mentally abused. Marcia remembered her mother holding her head under water during bathing, as well as slapping, beating, and verbally abusing her. Marcia said that in contrast to the intense closeness and abuse she experienced with her mother, her relationship with her father was characterized largely by distance. She said that her father was also critical and unsupportive, but was less hurtful in his interactions with her.

Marcia said that she had been greatly affected by her parents' dysfunctional marriage. She witnessed regular, intense conflict, including some physical abuse, between her parents. When her mother turned to Marcia for intimacy and support, Marcia became the enmeshed partner and caregiver for her mother, while being required to sacrifice attention to her own needs. Marcia expressed extreme ambivalence about caring for her mother. She felt needed and enjoyed her special confidante status with her mother, yet could never be fully secure about her relationship. She was often overwhelmed by the intensity of both her love and her anger for her mother. Marcia has, by psychiatric report, a history of recurrent major depressive episodes with ongoing dysthymia between episodes. She also exhibits traits associated with avoidant, sociopathic, and borderline personality disorder and has intense, at times paranoid, anxiety. She has no history of alcohol or other drug abuse nor do either of her parents.

Marcia's mental health status made it difficult for her to maintain ongoing employment. At the time of the evaluation she was receiving AFDC and limited, irregular financial support from Cody's father. Marcia said that she seeks financial help from her parents as well; but that their gifts are often contingent upon frequent visits, which, according to Marcia, serve to maintain negative and destructive patterns of interaction between herself and her parents. Marcia suggested that her attempts to define herself as a parent were stressful, as the specter of her own relationships with her parents comes to the fore. She said that her relationship with Mike, Cody's father was highly conflictive. They had lived together briefly, separating when Cody was approximately 10 months old. At the time of the assessment, Cody was having infrequent, unplanned visits with his father, generally to provide respite for Marcia. Marcia resented Mike's failure to provide adequate, regular financial support. Marcia said that she had few friends. Given her descriptions of her primary relationships, she had few, if any, unambivalently experienced supports of any kind.

On the various self-report instruments, Marcia indicated significant feelings of depression, particularly loneliness and isolation. She reported feeling easily annoyed and irritated, never feeling close to another person, extreme guilt, and significant nervousness, tension, and shakiness. She reported finding little pleasure in her role as a parent, questioned her competence, and described Cody as extremely challenging, impulsive, aggressive, and distractible.

Parent-infant interaction

Results from the Parent-Child Early Relational Assessment indicated that there were several strengths in the interaction between Marcia and Cody. Marcia used a warm tone of voice and smiled frequently. She made eye contact at times and initiated a number of interactions. However, her overall resourcefulness and creativity were limited, and she quickly became frustrated with Cody's lack of attentiveness. This was particularly the case during more structured aspects of the videotaped interaction. Marcia appeared to resent the evaluator's telling her what to do with Cody, and when Cody failed to comply with her requests, she dismissed him with a rather hostile tone. It is possible that Marcia's apparent resistance and anger towards the evaluator's request reflected her own past experience with her mother's intense demands.

It was during the free play segment of the videotaped interaction that Marcia appeared warmer and at ease. For example, Cody brought her a book and she read to him in an animated fashion, showing the capacity to keep him engaged and interested, not only in the book but in herself. During the same free play section, the positive interaction moved into tickling and an intense closeness that quickly over-stimulated Cody. He became more agitated and disorganized, pushing his mother away and running around the room. This resulted in Marcia again dismissing Cody in a rejecting tone. Overall, Marcia was inconsistent in her interactions, seeming to prefer observing Cody (in an apathetic, somewhat hostile fashion) to interacting with him. Marcia's self-absorption, which interfered, at times, with her ability to interact with Cody or to perceive and respond to his cues and needs, was worrisome.

Cody, for his part, was extremely noncompliant and anxious. He often resisted his mothers' attempts to interact. Although he did engage in a brief positive interaction during the free play time, more characteristically he appeared to want to play by himself in a rather rigid, repetitive fashion. He communicated by whining and pointing, and made no other verbalizations.

The interactions between Marcia and Cody were usually tense. Although there were brief periods of enjoyment and fleeting moments of reciprocity in their interactions, mother and son appeared unable to maintain a regulated, contained, safe interaction. Cody's response to the separation and reunion reflected ambivalence. At the time of reunion, he initially attempted to engage his mother in his play and then threw a toy car at her when she did not respond.

The video-replay interview indicated that Cody represented both hope and fearsome challenges to Marcia. She saw in him the opportunity to parent in a more nurturing way than she had experienced. At the same time, she feared the power he would have to reject her as he became more and more independent. Of interest was Marcia's particular fear of Cody's becoming verbal, a fear likely to be connected to the intense and ongoing verbal abuse she had experienced and was still experiencing with her mother. Cody's significance to Marcia as a vehicle for her own recovery was tremendous. Howover, Cody could be cast in the role of either a savior or destroyer for Marcia. In either case, Cody's identity as a separate person was at risk.

The home visit

The home visit revealed a generally appropriate, safe environment for a toddler. Cody and Marcia share a bedroom; Cody still slept in a crib. Although there were many age-appropriate toys and books, all of Cody's infant clothes, toys and other items were in piles throughout the apartment. When the evaluator commented on this, Marcia responded, "I can't think of him growing up; he's still my baby." This sentiment was in striking contrast to her anger (at times, even rage), as she described during the same visit how Cody limited her freedom to pursue dating relationships. Pointing out the window, Marcia went on to describe how she allows Cody to cross a busy, dangerous parking lot to get to the playground by himself. Though it was clear that she was aware of the danger, she seemed confused by her conflicting desires, which included both a need to protect herself from her own destructive feelings toward Cody and a wish to provide him with a safe place to experience his emerging autonomy.

Diagnosis

At 25 months, Cody displayed pervasive, consistent, cross-situational (at home, in child care, during a clinic assessment, and in other public places) difficulty with impulsiveness, aggressiveness, and overactivity. His behavior had a driven quality, and his capacity for social relatedness was delayed. He appeared to crave stimulation, but his low threshold for intense stimuli often led to his becoming overwhelmed and disregulated. At such times, he was unable to focus and quickly became frustrated by relatively benign inputs from the environment. Cody was an extreme risk-taker and was underreactive to pain and touch. For example, he did not cry or express distress upon running into a table and bumping his head. He had significant expressive language delays, which included deficits in his articulation capacity. Cody's basic sensory difficulties, including stimulation-seeking behavior, underreactivity to pain and touch, poor motor planning and judgment, and limited attentional focus made Regulatory Disorder–Type III: Motorically Disorganized, Impulsive the most appropriate Axis I diagnosis at this time.

Cody appeared anxious at times, particularly with his mother. His disregulated behavior could be seen in part as a product of their disordered relationship. Marcia's ambivalent feelings of wanting Cody to remain a cuddly, responsive infant and rejecting any attempts he made towards autonomy may have contributed to his language delay

Marcia suffered from intense anxiety, reflecting a poorly organized sense of self, and had difficulty maintaining close relationships. Problems with dependency, empathy, and self-esteem were among her difficulties. Marcia had significant periods of depression during her life and had thought of suicide at times. Her overall internal instability had contributed significantly to a relationship with her son Cody that could be characterized behaviorally as unstable, unpredictable, and poorly regulated.

The behavioral quality of Marcia and Cody's relationship fluctuated between periods of intense overinvolvement, overcontrol, and inappropriate demands and periods of withdrawal, lack of limits and assurance of safety, and overall emotional neglect. Lack of predictability also characterized the affective tone of Marcia and Cody's relationship. Interactions ranged from expressions of anger to poorly modulated and inappropriate hugging and kissing to periods of lifelessness and absence of pleasure. Psychologically, Marcia seemed to alternate between experiencing Cody as abusive and viewing him as a potential savior who could make her psychologically whole. She frequently commented on her need to see Cody as an infant, a need attested to by her inability to remove any infant items from Cody's room and her frequent infantile interactions with him, which were often intrusive and developmentally inappropriate. Both representations of Cody restricted Marcia's ability to respond to him as a separate individual. His emerging autonomy was experienced by her as potential abandonment, while his neediness and dependence evoked resentment ("Why should he get things that I never had?"). Because the significant variation in behavioral quality, affective tone, and psychological involvement are representative of several relationship classifications, the Mixed Relationship Disorder would be the appropriate Axis II diagnosis.

Diagnostic summary

Axis I: **Primary Diagnosis**
Regulatory Disorder—Type III.

Axis II: **Relationship Disorder Classification**
Relationship Disorder - Mixed (Angry/hostile and Overinvolved).

Axis III: **Medical and Developmental Disorders and Conditions**
Expressive Language Disorder-315.31 R/O Attention
Deficit Hyperactive Disorder-314.01.

Axis IV: **Psychosocial Stressors**
Moderate effects (parental conflict, maternal psychiatric disorder, multiple moves, financial stressors).

Axis V: **Functional Emotional Developmental Level**
Has achieved age-appropriate levels of mutual attention, mutual engagement, and interactive intentionality and reciprocity, but vulnerable to stress. Needs structure and sensorimotor support to achieve representational/ affective communication.

PIR-GAS:30 (Disordered)

Discussion with caregivers and treatment planning

Marcia gave the impression that she was eager to begin treatment. The treatment approach utilized was both multisystemic and multimodal. The treatment team included therapists from the Parent-Infant Clinic, a speech and language therapist from the birth-to-three program, and parent support from a local prevention agency. It was felt that Marcia's individual needs were significant enough to warrant an individual therapist separate from the therapist conducting parent-toddler dyadic therapy. Individual treatment focused first on developing a trusting and open relationship with the therapist, as a prelude to connecting interpersonally with others. The therapeutic relationship was used as a context for understanding and interpreting the significance of feelings engendered in past relationships, particularly with her parents. This focus attempted to help Marcia become more consistent and predictable in her expression of feelings and more able to take a child centered focus in the parent-child dyadic therapy.

Dyadic therapy focused on helping Marcia to develop an understanding of Cody's needs and predictable developmental course, so that developmental issues did not become conflictual. Therapy was also designed to promote more mutually satisfying interactions, specifically interactions that would support Cody's emerging competencies. The primary mechanism for attempting to reach these goals was focused, child-centered play. This approach involved Marcia joining Cody on the floor, reflecting on his play activities, attempting to build and facilitate his play, and attempting to avoid directives or punitive statements.

Communication among Marcia, her individual therapist, and the dyadic therapist was necessarily frequent in order to keep treatment goals focused and consistent. These treatment review meetings also functioned to prevent Marcia's tendency to play one therapist against another, in a repetition of her interaction with her parents. For example she would frequently attempt to discuss the "mistakes" of her individual therapist during dyadic sessions and ask each therapist their opinion of the other. This parental triangle became an important therapeutic focus during joint meetings, which served to provide Marcia with a consistent, responsive holding environment.

At the same time, Cody was referred and accepted into a specialized educational program four mornings per week. Here he received both group and individual speech and language therapy as well as an educational program to help him develop social and school-readiness skills.

Cody and Marcia also participated in an in-home parent support program which matched Marcia with a parent from the community who could offer Marcia general assistance in her parenting role. This included evenings out with Marcia, providing respite care for Cody, help with educational pursuits and job finding, and being available by phone for support and crisis intervention.

Intervention

Treatment to date is best described as a ride on a roller coaster. Marcia's strength has been her capacity to maintain consistency in Cody's treatment. She has gotten him to high-quality child care settings, speech and language appointments, and, beginning at age 3, to early childhood special education. She has regularly attended multidisciplinary staffings, where she advocates appropriately for her son. This consistency and involvement have resulted in significant improvement in Cody's overall developmental functioning, specifically in the area of expressive language. Cody's behavior is still problematic, however, particularly in relation to Marcia. At school, he is relatively able to tolerate frustration and remain appropriately task-focused. However, with his mother, Cody appears more impulse-driven and chaotic.

Marcia's own treatment and the dyadic sessions illustrate how powerful past representations of relationships can be. Most challenging therapeutically has been the previously discussed "splitting" between individual and dyadic therapists. This splitting has necessitated frequent therapeutic team meetings, which include Marcia, to help clarify roles, provide a more unified perception of her therapeutic "parents," and develop and modify therapy goals. In the dyadic treatment, Marcia has strongly resisted the child-centered play, often bringing in magazines to read and shutting out the attempts to have her interact with her son. She has said quite explicitly that Cody does not deserve the kind of attention she never received. Despite this resistance, Marcia keeps attending sessions and has recently become more involved since she began bringing toys for Cody from home in order to avoid having to use the "stupid" toys in the therapy office.

Rediagnosis

After 12 months of treatment, the diagnosis of Mixed Relationship Disorder remained appropriate. The "mixed" element of the diagnosis was particularly significant, supporting and confirming the features of Marcia's personality disorder. Marcia's overall internal instability continued to be manifest in her relationship with Cody, which, at some times, was characterized by over-involved intrusiveness, with an overall seductive tone; at other times, by rage and anger; and, at still other times, by a sense of neglect and resignation, and an overall lack of emotional attunement or sensitive caretaking.

Following treatment, Cody's diagnostic profile looked different than it did initially. The disregulatory aspects of his behavior now appeared more situationally relationship driven. Although he was still quite vulnerable across settings, given cues and ego support, such as that provided in his school setting, Cody demonstrated near age-appropriate expressive language, and the capacity to learn, to make friends, and to tolerate frustration (at age-expected levels). Was the Axis I diagnosis of Regulatory Disorder still appropriate? Our answer is, "Yes," but to a lesser degree, suggesting that a diagnostic classification by itself does not speak to a child's capacity for growth and change. Cody still had the underlying components of the disorder, but in "good enough" relationship environments he could successfully manage the demands made upon him.

Prognosis and discussion

The prognosis for Marcia and Cody is guarded. Cody has made solid developmental gains in his early childhood classroom. He has demonstrated the capacity to learn and establish appropriate relationships with peers and teachers. His communication skills are generally age-appropriate. However, his interactions with his mother continue to be conflictual and anxiety driven, as confirmed by the continuing concern of school professionals involved with the family. Marcia does have the capacity to acknowledge Cody's developmental gains but rigidly hangs on to her representation of Cody as abusive, resisting attempts by therapists to both indirectly and directly reframe and alter the quality of their interactions. Unfortunately, Cody's behavior in his mother's presence continues to reinforce her beliefs. Cause for therapeutic optimism lies in Marcia's capacity to allow Cody to grow, both in school settings and through the nurturing caregivers she provides for him in child care settings. Her ongoing commitment and struggle to continue her own therapeutic relationships also provide reason for hope. Perhaps being willing to receive consistent empathic therapeutic care will allow Marcia to understand the nature of her own early relationship conflicts, allowing for expanded perceptions of her son, Cody, and of herself in the parenting role. Reducing her ambivalent feelings could allow for a more modulated, positive affective tone and the kind of predictable care needed by a child with regulatory concerns.

SAMMY, Age 8 Months

Reason for referral

Jane, her fiance, Rob, and their eight-month-old son Sammy were referred by a pediatric social worker in Sammy's well baby clinic, to the Parent-Infant Clinic's mother-infant therapy group for mothers experiencing depression. She was worried about the quality of care Sammy was receiving from his mother, who had a history of depression and had seemed increasingly depressed after the birth of her son. During her first interview with the clinic therapist, Jane reported increased depressive symptoms, difficulty staying engaged with Sammy, and obsessive worrying about her son's well-being (e.g., "I worry he'll stop breathing"). She also expressed concerns that Rob might hurt Sammy, although she said that "he is good with the baby."

Assessment process

Group members typically participate in an intake process of two sessions, which include a clinical interview conducted with the mother, spouse/partner, and infant. The interview focuses on the mother's experiences of depression, family members' current functioning, current and past relationships, child's developmental history, the establishment of preliminary goals (individual, dyadic, and family), and completion of self report questionnaires, including psychological measures for the mothers to assist in recognizing their needs and those of their child. Measures are obtained both pre- and post-group, and include the following:

- *SCL-90* (Derogatis, Lipman, & Covi, 1973)
- *The Beck Depression Inventory* (Beck, Ward, Mendelson, Mock, & Erbaugh, 1961)
- *The Parenting Stress Index* (Abidin,1986,1990)
- *Infant Behavior Questionnaire* (Rothbart, 1986)—a measure of infant temperament
- *The Parent-Child Early Relational Assessment* (Clark, 1985)
- *The Bayley Scales of Infant Development* (Bayley, 1993)
- *The Developmental and Psychosocial Screener* (Clark, 1986)
- *The Structured Clinical Interview for DSM-SCID I & II* (Spitzer, Williams, Gibbon, & First, 1987)—Mothers complete this structured clinical interview prior to the group to assist in the diagnosis and in the development of a treatment plan for each family.

As part of the diagnostic process, Sammy was videotaped interacting with each of his parents in feeding and free play situations. These interactions were later assessed using the *Parent-Child Early Relational Assessment (PCERA)*; Clark, 1985). This instrument is used to assess the affective and behavioral characteristics of the parent, child and parent-child dyad. Group participants view this videotape with their therapist following two to three weeks after group begins. During this session, brief segments of the video-taped interactions are played back and viewed with the parent. A semi-structured interview is used with parents to gain a better understanding of their perceptions, attitudes, and goals during the interactions with their child. Interview questions focus on the meaning of the child and the child's behavior for the parent.

Assessment findings

Current family circumstances

At her initial interview, Jane presented as a slightly overweight Caucasian woman with flat affect who appeared older than her stated age of 20 years. She reported a long history of depression, beginning when she was an adolescent. Jane said that her most recent episode of depression had begun 16 months earlier, following the suicide of a close friend. She said that her depressive symptoms had worsened after Sammy was born. At the time of referral, she was seeing a social worker once a month for individual therapy, and she was taking anti-depressant medication prescribed by a psychiatrist.

Jane said that she had very little social support, commenting that, "No one really wants to hear about me." She said that she had been hospitalized for depression on three occasions over the past six years. Jane also reported having taken three different anti-depressant medications in the past; however, she felt that none were helpful in alleviating her symptoms. Jane's first hospitalization had occurred after the birth of Brittany, her first child. Her mother currently has custody of Brittany; Jane said that she felt as if her mother had "taken over" her own role as mother to her daughter. When asked why her mother retained custody of Brittany, Jane said that she had agreed to allow her mother to care for her daughter initially, while she lived with an aunt out-of-state so that she could finish high school. She tearfully recalled, "I was only 15, and I felt so embarrassed and ashamed that I couldn't stay in that small town . . . I just had to leave and try to get on with my life."

Jane said that, after graduating from high school, she had become involved with a man who followed The Grateful Dead and chose to tour with the band instead of returning to her mother's to reclaim her daughter. Jane said, "I realize now that I'm not taking responsibility for her."

Jane said that she and Sammy were living in a one-bedroom apartment with Rob, Sammy's father, a 24-year-old college student and resident manager of their apartment building. Jane said that she was unemployed and receiving public assistance, but that she wanted to open a jewelry business and was trying to accumulate enough capital to do so.

Child's developmental history

When asked about Sammy's conception, her pregnancy, and Sammy's birth, Jane said that Sammy was the result of an unplanned pregnancy following a year-long relationship with Rob. She said that she had met Rob at a Grateful Dead concert and moved in with him approximately one month later. According to Jane, when she informed Rob of her pregnancy he was surprised but "not completely disappointed." Jane said that although Rob had been supportive of the pregnancy, his family had not been and at one point had threatened to end their financial support of Rob. She said that she does not have contact with Rob's family, nor does she or her son receive financial assistance from them. Rob, however, continues to receive financial support from his parents and remains in monthly telephone contact with them.

Jane reported a difficult labor and delivery which lasted "30 hours." Sammy was born at 37 weeks; Jane reported no neonatal health problems. Since his birth, Sammy has had occasional ear infections. Jane said that Sammy had been a "fussy" baby who was colicky from 6 weeks to 3 months. She reported that during this time she had become frustrated and didn't know what to do to "get him to stop crying." She said that on one occasion she had shaken Sammy because "he would never stop crying." She reported feeling a great deal of guilt as a result of this incident. Jane said that she at times yells, "Shut-up—I can't take you anymore!" and subsequently feels guilty. She said, "He doesn't deserve a mother like me."

When asked who Sammy resembled, Jane replied that Sammy was a lot like his father. When asked how Sammy resembled Rob, Jane replied, "He looks like him, and he has his eyes and his temper. He knows how to push my buttons, just like his dad!"

At the time of the intake interview, Sammy appeared slightly smaller than his stated age of 8 months. He had long, uncombed hair and was dressed in a one-piece sleeper that appeared to be too small for him. His affect remained sober throughout the interview, and he evidenced poor fine motor control. When approached by the therapist, he was difficult to engage. He had notable lack of eye contact with his mother.

Mother's developmental and relationship history

During the first interview, Jane described an unhappy childhood in which she experienced verbal and physical abuse in her family of origin. She recalled vivid memories of her mother saying, "If I knew you were going to turn out this way I would have never had you!" She said that during her childhood her mother "beat her silly" approximately once a month, while her father hit her less often but with much more intensity, at times "knocking her to the ground." Jane said that her mother had been very controlling, telling her what she could wear, with whom she could develop friendships, and how she would spend her time. Jane reported that pattern had led to her being an "outcast" in school, with very few friends. Jane also said that her mother, whom she described as weighing 260 pounds, would often threaten to sit on Jane to punish her, and used medication to sedate her. Jane recalled witnessing her mother crushing a Valium into Jane's food when she was 12 years old.

Jane said that she considers herself to have been sexually abused by her father beginning at the age of 12 and lasting until the age of 15, when she became pregnant by a boyfriend. Her father would massage her breasts and rub himself against her. She said that he would try to fondle her "more than I would let him."

Jane's mother had forbidden her to date until she was 18; however, Jane's first pregnancy occurred when she was 15. Jane recalled her mother leaving her off at the doctor's office for an early prenatal visit, telling her not to come home. She also described her mother severely abused her during her first pregnancy, leaving bruises on her abdomen, back, and arms. Jane experienced a severe postpartum depression which required hospitalization following the birth of her daughter. After her discharge, when Brittany was three months old, Jane voluntarily gave custody of the baby to her mother.

Jane said that her daughter's father was in the military and had ended their relationship shortly after she delivered, leaving her with great feelings of loss and anger. Jane's feelings about Brittany remained ambivalent. She said, "I wish she lived with us, but she's better off with my mother. . . . Well, she is living with my mother . . . she may not be better off."

Parent-child interaction

Sammy was videotaped in interaction with his mother and with his father. In his interactions with Jane, Sammy appeared sober and serious. He did not initiate social interactions with his mother, nor did he respond to her initiations. Sammy's nonverbal communications were limited. During the 10 minutes of videotaped interaction, he glanced at his mother on only three occasions, and then only briefly. In contrast to his lack of interest in social contact with Jane, Sammy showed great interest in the toys available for free play. However, he demonstrated poor attentional abilities and only shallow explorations (i.e., he would pick toys up, turn around, and drop them, like a younger infant).

Of note in Jane and Sammy's ERA profile were Jane's depressed, apathetic mood and her lack of enthusiasm and animation when interacting with her son. Their interactions lacked enjoyment and pleasure; they seldom made eye contact. Jane was inconsistent when interacting with Sammy; she seemed unable to read his cues and respond sensitively. For example, during the feeding situation, Jane frequently removed Sammy's bottle from him to burp him, only to have him become upset and agitated. During play, she seemed unable to follow Sammy's lead and appeared to have her own agenda. Just as Sammy would become engaged with a toy, she would introduce a new one. For example, while Sammy was playing with a shape sorter she repeatedly tried to engage him in play using the baby doll and bottle, suggesting perhaps her difficulty with his competence and emerging autonomy and wishes for him to remain in a dependent role.

Jane also appeared to have difficulty recognizing and mirroring Sammy's internal feeling states, and in supporting his developmentally appropriate interests in play. For example, Sammy repeatedly attempted to place items in the shape sorter without success. When he did succeed in placing a block in the shape sorter correctly, his eyes widened, he looked up at his mother briefly, and he vocalized, "Ahh!" Jane, however, did not comment on his accomplishment or his pride in it, but again showed him the baby doll and bottle. Jane's depressed mood and inability to read and respond to her son's cues, combined with Sammy's lack of eye contact, paucity of communicative gestures, and sober mood, contributed to a constricted, flat quality in their interactions. Together, Jane and Sammy demonstrated a lack of mutual enjoyment in their interactions, with little reciprocity occurring between them.

As part of the *PCERA*, a brief separation/reunion was videotaped and observed by the therapist from behind a one-way mirror. Jane neither told Sammy that she would be leaving the room nor greeted him upon her return. During the separation episode, Sammy stopped his play, stared off into space, crawled to the door, and then returned to the toys before his mother returned. He did not appear overtly distressed by her leaving. When Jane returned Sammy did not acknowledge her arrival and remained near the toys with his back to his mother, suggesting an avoidant attachment pattern reflective of history of experiencing neglect.

In contrast to his interactions with his mother, Sammy's interactions with his father were more physical, reciprocal, and animated. Although he failed to initiate social interaction with Rob, he was more responsive to him. For example, Sammy looked at his father when he was held up in the air. Sammy also appeared less sober with his father, smiling briefly a few times and laughing when held up. However, Sammy could also be irritable with his father. For example, during the free play situation when Rob put Sammy down after holding him up in the air above his head, Sammy became quite upset, vocalizing fussily and crying.

At times Rob was both animated and positive in his interactions with his son. Of concern, were his cold tone of voice and, at times, awkward physical contact. Rob tended to interact with his eight-month-old son as if he were an adult. He never called Sammy by his name, always referring to him as "little man." In addition, when holding Sammy up in the air, Rob at times appeared unsteady. Sammy, however, responded to his father's unsteadiness with surprise and then laughter; he became irritable when his father discontinued this physical play. Although Rob could recognize the source of Sammy's irritability ("You liked going up in the air"), he failed to respond to it. Instead, Rob appeared to become frustrated by Sammy's inability to move onto a new activity. Eventually, Sammy's own frustration escalated into a cry, at which time Rob again began to play in a physically stimulating manner with his son. This resulted in curtailing Sammy's crying, however, he did not appear to experience pleasure. No smiling or relaxed body tone was observed.

Mother's psychological functioning and status

On measures obtained prior to group, Jane reported clinically significant levels of depression on the Beck Depression Inventory, SCL-90 and SCID I. Her self-reported depressive symptoms included feeling sad, discouraged about the future, and guilty most of the time as well as not enjoying things, crying often, feeling irritated, waking up several hours earlier than usual, and a poor appetite. Jane's responses to the SCL-90 also revealed a significant amount of hostility, including feeling easily annoyed or irritated and being prone to temper outbursts that she could not control. Jane also reported paranoid ideation on the SCL-90; she indicated that she felt most people could not be trusted and would take advantage of her if she let them. Not surprisingly, Jane's responses on the Parenting Stress Index revealed clinically significant levels of feelings of stress in several areas, including attachment with her son, lack of reinforcement value of her son, and competence in the parenting role.

A structured diagnostic interview (SCID I and II, Spitzer, Williams, Gibbon, & First, 1987) with Jane supported a diagnosis of major depression, with no indication of personality disorder.

Developmental status of the child

Sammy's developmental functioning was assessed using the Bayley Scales of Infant Development. Sammy was cooperative and interested in the test items, and capable of sustaining attention. However, consistent with his observed behavior with his parents, Sammy vocalized very little and did not initiate social interaction with the therapist. Sammy's performance on the mental scale was at his chronological age of 9 months with an MDI of 102, and a PDI of 96.

Sammy was interested in examining and manipulating test materials. His interest and curiosity may have been reflected in his passing items above age level, including fingering holes in a peg board (expected at 8.9 months), and searching for the contents of a box (expected at 9.5 months). Interestingly, Sammy had difficulty with tasks that required receptive and expressive communicative functioning, such as attending to scribbling and accompanying sounds "zip," "zap" by the examiner (5.8 months), vocalizing 4 syllables (7 months), listening selectively to familiar words (7.9 months), saying "da-da" (7.9 months), and not cooperating in games (7.6 months). Sammy's motor skills were relatively weak. Although he passed some items at and above his age level, such as partial finger prehension (7.4 months) and combining spoons (8.6 months), he failed much earlier items, such as sitting alone for 30 seconds or more (6.0 months), scooping a pellet (6.8 months), and sitting alone with good coordination (6.9 months). Sammy's inability to sit up without support suggested that he might not have been given the physical attention, structure, and support necessary to develop this ability; perhaps he was spending most of his time in a crib or playpen without the incentive to sit up on his own. These underdeveloped skills, along with his lack of social initiative, were of concern.

During an intake session, Jane was asked to identify goals for herself, her son, and her relationship with her son. She easily identified goals for herself: She said she would like to "feel less isolated and depressed" and "to learn how to not resent her son." She also was able to identify a goal for her relationship with Sammy as "to feel more close.'" However, Jane found it difficult to identify goals for Sammy, himself, stating "he's pretty good right now."

Videotape replay interview

During the third group session, Jane met with her therapist to review their videotaped interactions with Sammy. Before the tape was reviewed, Jane was asked how the interactions taped were alike or different from how things usually went. Jane replied that Sammy and she rarely found time to play together at home, but that when they did, their interaction was similar to how things went in the taping. When Jane was asked what part of the videotaping she had found most enjoyable, she responded, "Nothing, really," adding that she felt bad about her own appearance.

Throughout the video replay, Jane commented on her own appearance. When asked what had been the most difficult part of the videotaping session, Jane said, "Nothing in the taping—he was pretty good." When asked to elaborate, Jane responded, "Sammy can get really fussy and I just don't know what to do—it can be frustrating." One portion of the tape replayed for Jane included Sammy's attempts to place items in a shape sorter correctly. When Sammy correctly placed an item in the sorter, his eyes widened, and he vocalized, looked up at Jane, and smiled briefly. Jane did not respond to his attempts to engage her, but instead played with a baby doll. In reviewing this segment with Jane, she was asked how she had felt at the moment when Sammy looked up at her and smiled. She replied that she had never realized that Sammy was looking at her, stating "I guess I was too busy to notice." When Jane was asked how she felt now watching Sammy smile at her, she commented that she liked the fact that he smiled at her. When asked how she thought Sammy felt in that situation as he was smiling at her, she replied, "I bet it felt good to finally get that toy in the right spot." Her response suggests that Jane can accurately read her son's feeling states but has difficulty appreciating his need for her responsiveness.

As part of the replay interview, Jane was asked who Sammy was named for and who he reminds her of in appearance, temperament, and behavior. She said he was named after a musician hoping he would be creative. She continued, "He doesn't really look like anybody (note: the therapist thought he looked strikingly like Jane); he knows how to push my buttons just like his Dad does." When asked to describe herself as a parent, she commented, "I just don't feel like I'm doing a good job." When asked why she felt this way, she indicated that sometimes her depression and her own needs got in the way. She said that she felt guilty "for things that she hasn't done but that she thinks of doing."

At the end of this session, Jane was asked what she found most enjoyable about being Sammy's mother. She initially responded that she couldn't think of anything. Then she added, "I just want to enjoy being a family and wish that we could all get along."

Throughout the video replay interview, Jane seemed to need to avoid reflecting on what Sammy meant to her. This distance may have been a manifestation of her depressive symptoms including self-absorption, as well as serving a protective function for both herself and her child. It may have protected him from her frustration and ambivalence in relation to his autonomous and avoidant behavior. Not seeing herself in him or acknowledging meaning or intention to his behavior may have protected Jane from feelings of rejection and loss in relation to early experiences with her parents, which she had characterized as controlling and emotionally neglectful, as well as her loss of her infant daughter.

Diagnosis

Sammy was clearly an infant at psychological risk. However, at the time of this assessment he did not meet diagnostic criteria for an Axis I diagnosis. Sammy's reported developmental delays, his limited interest or ability to engage his mother, frequent irritability, and generally sober affect led the therapist to consider diagnoses of depression or reactive attachment deprivation/maltreatment disorder of infancy. However, since Sammy's developmental difficulties and worrisome behavioral patterns were most frequently manifested in his interactions with his mother, the team thought that a primary Axis II diagnosis would best capture Sammy's situation.

The team made the primary Axis II diagnosis of Underinvolved Relationship Disorder with a diagnosis of Mixed Relationship Disorder with underinvolved and angry/hostile tendencies to be ruled out. The underinvolved relationship diagnosis was warranted given the affective tone, behavioral qualities, and psychological involvement of Sammy and his mother. Observing the behavioral qualities of the interaction between Jane and Sammy, we had seen, on Jane's part, unresponsiveness to Sammy's cues, failure to mirror his behavior and internal feeling states, and an inability to protect her son (shaking him on one occasion). Looking at the dyad, we had observed underregulated interactions, with Sammy's cues often being missed or misinterpreted by Jane, and a lack of emotional connection between Jane and Sammy. Sammy's uncared-for appearance, avoidant tendencies, and delayed motor abilities also suggested an underinvolved relationship diagnosis. The affective tone of this mother-child dyad (i.e., constricted, withdrawn, and sober) provided further support for this diagnosis. The nature of Jane's psychological involvement with Sammy, including the intensity of her ambivalence toward Sammy and his emerging autonomy and perceived rejection of her support, warranted an underinvolved relationship disorder. In addition, the frequency of problematic interaction (observed, for example, in Sammy's lack of response to his mother's leaving and returning during the intake interview), and the duration of difficulties (illustrated by Jane's report that Sammy has been "trouble since birth") all pointed to this diagnosis.

The team considered three factors that suggested a diagnosis of Angry/Hostile Relationship Disorder might be warranted: (a) Jane's descriptions of the abuse she had experienced as a child and her current ambivalent relationship with her mother, characterized by unresolved anger; (b) Jane's projection of hostile intent onto Sammy's crying and his developmentally expectable exploratory behavior (e.g., pulling at her hair); and (c) Sammy's irritable behavior. More specifically, Jane's account of her frustrated shaking of Sammy and subsequent guilt fit an angry/hostile pattern, and the periods of frustration and tension observed occasionally in the interaction between Jane and Sammy reflected the affective tone seen in angry/hostile relationships. However, our observations during the initial evaluation did not yield enough evidence of intense, frequent, and enduring/anger hostility to support this diagnosis.

Diagnostic summary

Axis I: **Primary Diagnosis**
No diagnosis.

Axis II: **Relationship Disorder Classification**
Underinvolved Relationship Disorder.

Axis III: **Medical and Developmental Disorders and Conditions**
Speech, language, motor delays.

Axis IV: Psychosocial Stressors

Parental psychiatric illness, possible neglect (moderate).

Axis V: Functional Emotional Developmental Level

Demonstrates capacity for mutual attention but not for mutual engagement, or for interactive intentionality and reciprocity with his mother.

PIR-GAS: 30 (Disordered)

Discussion with caregivers and treatment planning

As noted above, Jane had been referred as a possible participant in the clinic's group therapy approach for depressed mothers focused on treating relational disturbances. This approach, in use at the clinic since 1988, has five overall goals: (a) to ameliorate depressive symptoms in the mother; (b) to address individual conflicts related to the mother's own experiences of being parented; (c) to reduce social isolation; (d) to provide an environment for the infant that is emotionally responsive and supportive of its development; (e) to facilitate positive mother-infant interactions; and (f) to support improved functioning within the family. The model involves 12 weekly group sessions that include separate simultaneous treatment groups for mothers and for their infants. Each session also includes a dyadic group time for mothers and infants together. Two of the 12 group sessions include spouses or partners as well. Sessions are structured in a two-part format. During the first $1^1/_2$ hours, mothers and infants meet in separate groups. Mothers meet with female and male cotherapists. In the infants' developmental therapy group, each infant is paired in an ongoing relationship with a therapist. In the last half hour of the session, mothers and infants reunite for dyadic group activities including interactive games and movement, baby massage, toys, and music. A group leader coordinates and conducts these sessions, in which each mother/infant dyad is joined and supported by a dyadic therapist. Fathers or significant partners are invited to two of the 12 group sessions. They meet together in a separate group and then join the mothers to discuss their mutual feelings, needs, and communication patterns. On these occasions, fathers also join mothers and infants in "triadic" activities.

The therapists believed that therapeutic involvement was warranted given Jane's depression, lack of emotional involvement and responsiveness with Sammy, and Sammy's sober affect, delayed development, and withdrawn behavior. They thought that the group therapy model would appropriately address this family's needs. Jane agreed to meet with one therapist from the Mothers' Therapy group, and one from the Infants' Developmental Therapy group to address issues in her relationship with Sammy and Sammy's needs. This process paralleled the therapeutic process that the team proposed to Jane and facilitated the development of a therapeutic alliance with her because it addressed her own issues first.

Jane agreed to participate in the group; however, she was initially opposed to Sammy's involvement, saying, "The problems I have are my own, and Sammy is doing just fine." However, the therapist from the Infants' Developmental Therapy group who conducted the developmental assessment with Sammy, provided concrete examples of Sammy's delayed motor functioning, lack of social gestures, few vocalizations, and sober affect. In addition, the mothers' group therapist, who had met with Jane to review her videotaped interactions with Sammy, reminded Jane of her comments regarding Sammy's desire to "distract" her and suggested that his irritability, and lack of attention and responsiveness to her could be addressed in the future therapeutic work. Jane was then able to identify some of her own concerns about Sammy, and agreed to try the infant group for two or three weeks.

The two therapists assured Jane that they would continue their involvement with her: one would be meeting with the group of mothers and the other would be working with Sammy in the group of children. Both of them would meet with Jane and Sammy together for dyadic therapy during the last half hour of each group session to support and facilitate more mutually enjoyable interactions.

Intervention

The mothers' group

Each of the mothers' group sessions is designed around a core theme, such as depression ambivalence, nurturance, communication, safety, self-esteem and competence, and independence/dependence. In the mothers' group, women are assisted in exploring themes and relationship issues in light of their own experiences of being parented. The mother's group offered Jane an opportunity to examine her relationship with her mother and the effects it might have had on her capacities to recognize and meet the unfolding needs of her son. In the group, Jane was able to focus on the details of her relationships with Sammy, her daughter, Rob, and her own parents. She spoke candidly of her mother's domineering influence on her life and her resulting anger and hostility. Jane described her relationship with her mother as "submissive, strained, beaten, hopeless, and awful." She said that her mother was very controlling and held unrealistic expectations for her; she was never satisfied with Jane. Jane spoke of ongoing conflict with her mother; she said she had never experienced a sense of her own self-identity. Although Jane reported being closer to her father, she said that she was closer to him because "he never really said anything . . . he left me alone." She said that she could count on the fingers of one hand the number of conversations she had ever had with him. Jane said that he was depressed, frequently sitting for hours watching television, clipping grocery coupons, and rarely speaking to anyone. Jane blamed her mother for her father's "introversion" because she was so controlling. She said that her father had often allowed her to spend time with friends ("He'd drop me off so he wouldn't have to spend time with me. I could do whatever I wanted because he didn't care as long as he was sitting in his chair."). Jane began to recognize how her anger toward her parents may have influenced her relationships with others, including her son and his father. In addition to exploring her relationship with her parents during the group, Jane also talked about her experience of Sammy's labor and delivery and the postpartum period, and reflected on the possible effects of her depressive symptoms on her view of herself and her relationships with Sammy and Rob.

The group experience helped Jane to gain insight and develop methods for reducing her symptoms and improving her relationships. Because the group process was designed to be therapeutic rather than educational, Jane was also provided with information on child development and parenting through printed handouts, including ideas for home activities.

Jane was able to make use of the therapist in the mothers' group. The therapist's role in the group is to be emotionally supportive, but also transferential—that is, mothers' interactions with their therapists allow them to begin to rework their own internal models of relationships. As Jane's needs for support, validation, and nurturance were addressed in the group sessions, she was better able to be supportive, validating, and nurturing in her relationships with Sammy and Rob. And as her insight into her relationship with her parents was enhanced, her ability to put "ghosts in the nursery" (Fraiberg, Adelson & Shapiro, 1980, p. 166) to rest was increased, thereby making her more emotionally available and responsive in interactions with her son.

The infants' developmental therapy group

While Jane participated in the mothers' group, Sammy was simultaneously involved in a developmental therapy group. These groups consists of five to seven infants, who may range in age from newborns to 2-year-olds. Each infant is involved in one-to-one consistent interactions with a therapist who provides affectively attuned, responsive caregiving, and developmental stimulation. Such interactions create a "holding environment" for the infant, making possible increased regulatory capacities, affective range, and social initiative/responsiveness. Because of their experience in group, infants are able to be more responsive and reinforcing with their mothers, making possible more reciprocal, mutually satisfying interactions.

During many of the group sessions, Sammy appeared sober and serious, as he had during the evaluation sessions. The first two times that Jane brought Sammy to group he was asleep, and she left him with his therapist while she attended the mothers' group. After Sammy had slept through much of the first two group sessions, the therapist talked with Jane, who agreed to have Sammy nap just before coming to group.

When Jane brought Sammy to the third group session, he was awake. She quickly left the room without saying good-bye. Sammy did not become upset at his mother's leaving but rather began playing with a rattle he found on the floor near him. During the rest of the session, he made little eye contact with his therapist or other adults and did not respond to their initiations or the initiations of other children in the group.

Sammy's therapist noted that Jane had difficulty reuniting with Sammy. She would frequently enter the room and, without greeting Sammy, pick him up and begin talking with his therapist about her own experiences in the adult group. Sammy's therapist worked with Jane and Sammy to facilitate their separations and reunions. By speaking for Sammy (e.g., "Bye, bye mom, I'll miss you"), the therapist helped Jane became more aware of her son's feeling states. Eventually, she began saying good-bye to her son, giving him a hug and telling him, "Mommy will be back soon." The therapist also spoke for Sammy during reunions ("Oh, Mom, it is so good to see you! I've been busy playing, but I really like it when you come back here to be with me!").

During the course of the group, Sammy, at age 9 to 12 months, became more focused and more interested in interacting with adults and peers in the group. Interestingly, the nature of his increased involvement with peers tended to be aggressive and rough. For example, on one occasion he bit a child who was playing with a toy he wanted. He also became more aware of what he could make happen with objects, (e.g., banging toys together, putting nesting cubes inside each other, and began using pop-up toys successfully).

Dyadic work and the father's involvement

Jane and Sammy also benefited from the dyadic portion of the group. The therapist's role during dyadic group activities is multifaceted. Therapists offer support and praise, amplify positive affect and behavior, reflect, model, and provide structure. They use strategies such as speaking for the infants and engaging mothers in the process of wondering about the meaning of their infants' cues or behavior. Again, the therapist responds to each member of the dyad, enabling each partner to respond better to the other.

After the first three group sessions, when a trusting relationship had been established with the adult and infant group therapists, Jane met with one of the therapists from the mothers' group and with Sammy's therapist to develop an individualized mother-infant dyadic therapy plan for the dyadic component of the group. This plan drew on observations of Jane and Sammy during the evaluation and the first three group sessions, as well as on Jane's responses to questionnaires and Sammy's developmental assessment. The plan included primary issues to be addressed observations and assessments of therapy, goals for the remaining group sessions, and strategies and approaches to be implemented. In addition, the written plan included a section for recording results; this was completed by the therapist at the follow-up session after the conclusion of the group experience.

The individualized mother-infant dyadic therapy plan for Jane and Sammy included the following:

1. Issue: Jane has her own issues to deal with and at times could be overwhelmed by them, becoming diffuse, unfocused, and self absorbed.

   Goal: To increase Jane's awareness of Sammy's emotional and developmental needs.

Strategies: To maintain focus on Sammy in dyadic therapy, and wonder along with Jane what Sammy may be feeling. To speak for Sammy, to help Jane read Sammy's cues, and respond to them in a sensitive, appropriate gentle manner.

2. Issue: Sammy has a tendency to behave roughly in group.

Goal: Help Jane to be with Sammy in a quiet, gentle way. Help her to play with him in a nonstimulating, calm manner. Help her to find less intrusive ways of interacting.

Strategies: Coach Jane to be gentle with, and emotionally available to, Sammy and to follow his lead. Help her to use facial expressions and a soft tone of voice to help Sammy know he has her attention, and need not interact with her in aggressive ways.

3. Issue: Sammy's infrequent verbalizations in group.

Goal: To amplify and mirror Sammy's vocalizations in children's group. Help Jane to mirror his vocalizations in dyadic therapy.

Strategies: Wonder along with Jane about what Sammy may be communicating and help her to understand the importance of recognizing and elaborating his verbalizations.

As stated earlier, the group model invites spouses or significant others to attend two of the 12 group sessions, which address depression and coping in the family and improving communication abilities. Fathers' involvement is critical, given the powerful role of the social environment in depressive illness. Therapists provide fathers with information aimed at demystifying depression while providing them with support and strategies for increasing communication and problem-solving. This approach is designed to help fathers and family members to be more empathically understanding with and supportive to mothers and infants.

Rob attended both sessions with Jane and Sammy. His involvement in the group was very beneficial for Jane as she saw his support as a sign of strength and willingness to work on existing issues. In addition, during the triadic portion of the group, Rob interacted with Sammy in a physical, yet mutually satisfying, manner. Sammy was more engaged with his father than he usually was with adults and was able to engage in eye contact with both him and his mother during the session. For example, during a family activity that included one parent holding the child while the other parent rolled a ball to the child, Rob was able to engage Sammy in laughter by bouncing the ball and laughing with him. This resulted in Jane laughing along with Rob and Sammy reaching up toward his mother's face as she smiled. When Jane was asked the following week how she felt about the session, she commented, "We felt like a real family and it felt good to laugh again."

Rob's style of interacting with Sammy was a rough-and-tumble one. He often threw Sammy up in the air to catch him or held him upside down. At the second triadic session, the therapist taught Rob and Jane a family lullaby, to offer them a less stimulating, more gentle and quiet way to interact with Sammy. Rob commented that he rarely interacted with Sammy in a gentle manner as Jane usually puts him down for his nap and at night. When asked how it felt to sing a lullaby to Sammy, Rob commented, "I kind of like it—I wish that my father could have been there for me in that way." The following week, Jane reported that she and Rob had used a communication/problem-solving exercise provided in group to develop a plan that provided Jane with one night a week off to work on her business while Rob cared for Sammy. This arrangement provided him with an opportunity for quiet time with Sammy before bed.

Emerging diagnostic issues

As the therapists observed and worked with Jane and Sammy over time, they (and Jane) became more aware of the anger that lay beneath her depressive symptoms. In retrospect, her underinvolvement could be seen as a way of protecting Sammy from her aggression. As anger came increasingly to characterize not only Jane's interactions but Sammy's as well, the therapists addressed these issues in all three groups. Had we revisited our Axis II diagnosis midway through the 12-week group, we would have chosen a diagnosis of Mixed Relationship Disorder with underinvolved and angry/hostile tendencies; at the conclusion of the intervention their relationship, though still characterized by some tension, anger and ambivalence on both parts, was far less intense, anger occurred less frequently and for briefer periods of time, and thus did not warrant a diagnosis. Their PIR-GAS rating of 40 for Jane and Sammy, at this time reflecting a disturbed but not disordered relationship, also indicates that no relationship diagnosis is warranted, though Sammy did exhibit some developmental delays, sober, avoidant affect, and later some aggressive behavior, these concerns may warrant ruling out an Axis I diagnosis of Mixed Disorder of Emotional Expressiveness for him if his sober affect and aggressive behavior persist.

During the course of the mothers' group sessions, Jane identified the sources of her anger toward her parents. She said that the lack of nurturance and warmth she had endured as a child had been perhaps more painful than the physical abuse she had experienced. She realized that the adults to whom she had looked for trust and love had not been available emotionally or able to keep her safe. She talked about the time months before when she shook Sammy when he wouldn't stop crying and the great deal of guilt she has regarding her fears of harming him. The therapist engaged her in wondering about what Sammy's crying meant to her, if she felt criticized by him as she was by her mother or perhaps she was identifying with his unmet needs. Over the course of the group, Jane became more aware of her need to keep herself distant from Sammy to protect him from her anger. She realized that because she did not have a nurturing role model she only knew to walk away from him, rather than harm him.

In the dyadic group we saw evidence that Jane's preoccupation with her relationship with her negative, controlling, and emotionally neglectful mother, and her generally painful internal working models of attachment relationships left her unable to focus on her relationship with her son in these sessions. She would often become self-absorbed, diffuse, and unfocused when interacting with him. As a result, Sammy's affective expressions often appeared unregulated or he became very sober, withdrawn, and even less communicative than usual. During one dyadic session, Sammy, then age 10 months, pulled his mother's hair. When she responded, "Ouch!," he laughed and kept on pulling. Jane talked about feeling more frustrated and angry toward Sammy; there was more irritability noted in her interactions with Sammy.

In the infant developmental therapy group, Sammy began biting and hitting other children. Sammy's parents were able to recognize his increased anger and aggression and were helped to understand both his frustration and the healthy aspect of his assertiveness and aggression. Sammy responded in group to his therapist's gentle hand on his back to calm and redirect him. In addition, Jane and Rob expressed interest in continuing to work on ways of interacting with Sammy that were sensitive and gentle. They both developed capacities to remain engaged, positive, and modulated in their interactions with their son.

Post-group assessments

Following his group experience, Sammy was assessed using the Bayley Scales of Infant Development (Bayley, 1993). Sammy was active, interested, and motivated during the assessment. His performance at 12 months indicated that his development remained on track, with an MDI=102, the same score he had achieved when tested 3 1/2 months earlier. This course contrasts with the experience of many infants of depressed mothers considered to be psychologically at risk, whose scores tend to fall as assessment protocols begin to include more items requiring verbal skills and self-initiation verbal and initiating items at the 12-month-level. He demonstrated an increased interest in his environment and the testing materials. This interest was illustrated by his tendency to pass items that depended on his initiation or exploration of the stimuli, such as unwrapping a cube (10.5 months), pushing a car along (11.3 months), and dangling a ring from a string (12.4 months), rather than items that required imitation of the examiner. Sammy appeared more verbal, as well, vocalizing during the testing session. His mother reported that he had begun saying some words at home. Interestingly, Sammy's motor development improved over the course of his therapeutic involvement (Pre-motor Scale=96, Post-motor Scale=111 I). His improved coordination in motor functioning was apparent in his ability to stand alone (I 1.0 months), walk unassisted (11.7 months), and get to a standing position from a supine position by first rolling over onto his stomach (12.6 months).

A follow-up assessment of Jane also revealed lessening of symptoms. After the group experience, she reported significantly fewer depressive symptoms and an overall decrease in hostility, although her hostility scale scores on the SCL-90 remained in the clinical range. Her postgroup scores on the Parenting Stress Index indicated less overall stress in the parenting role. She reported improved interactions with both her son and his father.

Our observations confirmed that Jane's interactions with Sammy improved following group. She expressed more positive affect with her son, demonstrated enjoyment and pleasure toward him, and initiated social initiatives and responded sensitively and appropriately to his cues. Sammy's interaction with his mother revealed improvements following their participation in the group. Although Sammy did not yet initiate social interaction with his mother on a regular basis, he did respond to her more often than in their pregroup interactions. He smiled more, and they engaged in more mutual eye contact and play. As a dyad, Sammy and Jane demonstrated increased joint attention to activities and reciprocity and regulation in their interactions, although the affective tone was still constricted.

Prognosis and discussion

The prognosis for the relationships among Jane, Sammy, and Rob is fair to good. In a participant-satisfaction questionnaire that group members are asked to complete following their involvement with the group, Jane reported that she found the group extremely helpful in improving her relationship with Sammy. She wrote, "I pick up his cues better and have learned better ways of interacting with him." Jane's anger towards her mother and, at times, towards Rob, remained of concern. Continued individual therapy was recommended, and since Jane seems committed to the process, the prognosis is fair to good.

The prognosis for her relationship with Sammy is good as well. Through insights developed in group, Jane became more aware of the feelings of psychological abandonment and fear that stemmed from her relationship with her own parents. She recognized her mother's anger towards her and how sad and angry she felt in return. She wanted Sammy to be spared that pain. Jane also realized that she felt rage when Sammy cried or expressed his needs in other ways because his demands reminded her of her father's needs, which always came first in her family. As she began to be able to see her son as a separate individual, with developmentally appropriate needs, Jane wanted to protect him from her rage. She could also see that her physical and emotional distance from both Sammy and Rob could be explained in part by her lack of a nurturing role model. By the end of group, Jane was better able to read her son's cues and continued to work on responding to those cues sensitively and appropriately. Her capacity for insight and her wish to be a better mother for Sammy bode well for them.

During the group experience, Jane also gained a renewed sense of commitment to her, relationship with Rob, whom she experienced as a source of support. She and Rob agreed to attend couples' therapy to identify and address ongoing issues in their own relationship as they were making plans to marry.

References

Abidin, R.R. (1986,1990). *Parenting Stress Index*. Charlottesville, VA: Pediatric Psychology Press.

Achenbach, T. M., & Edelbrock, C. (1983). *Manual for the Child Behavior Checklist* and Revised Child Behavior Profile. Burlington, Vermont: University of Vermont Department of Psychiatry.

Bayley, N. (1993). Bayley Scales of Infant Development: Second edition. *Manual*. San Antonio, Texas: Psychological Corp.

Beck, A. T., Ward, C. H., Mendelson, M., Mock, J., & Erbaugh, J. (1961). An inventory for measuring depression. *Archives of General Psychiatry*, 4, 561-571.

Bowlby, J. (1982). *Attachment and loss. Vol. I: Attachment (2nd ed.)*. New York: Basic Books.

Bretherton, I. (1987). New perspectives on attachment relations in infancy: Security, communication and internal working models. In J. D. Osofsky (ed.), *Handbook of Infant Development* (2nd ed.),1061-1100, New York: Wiley.

Caldwell, B.M. & Bradley, R.H. (1978). *Manual for the HOME Observation for Measurement of the Environment*. Little Rock, Arkansas: University of Arkansas.

Cicchetti, D. (1987). Developmental psychopathology in infancy: Illustration from the study of maltreated youngsters. *Journal of Consulting and Clinical Psychology*, 55 (6), 837-845.

Clark, R. (1986). *Psychosocial and Developmental Screener*. Madison, WI: Department of Psychiatry, University of Wisconsin-Madison.

Clark, R. (1985). The *Parent-Child Early Relational Assessment*. Madison, WI: Department of Psychiatry, University of Wisconsin-Madison.

Clark, R., Keller, A.D., Fedderly, S.S., & Paulson, A.W. (1993). Treating the relationships affected by postpartum depression: A group therapy model. *Zero to Three*,13,16-23.

Clark, R., Paulson, A. & Conlin, S. (1993). Assessment of developmental status and parent-infant relationships: The therapeutic process of evaluation. In C. Zeanah (Ed.), *Handbook of Infant Mental Health* (pp.191-209). New York: Guilford Press.

Committee on the Family, Group for the Advancement of Psychiatry (1995). A model for the classification and diagnosis of relational disorders. *Psychiatric Services*. 46 (9), 926- 931).

Derogatis, L. R., Lipman, R. S., & Covi, L. (1973). SCL-90: An outpatient psychiatric rating scale—a preliminary report. *Psychopharmacology Bulletin*, 9(1),13-28.

Fraiberg, S., Adelson, E., & Shapiro, V. (1980). Ghosts in the nursery: A psychoanalytic approach to the problems of impaired infant-mother relationships. *Clinical Studies in Infant Mental Health: The First Year of Life*,164-197. New York: Basic Books.

Lieberman, A. F. (1985). Infant mental health: A model for service delivery. Journal of *Clinical Child Psychology* ,14(3),196-201.

Lieberman, A. F., & Zeanah, C. H. (1995). Disorders of attachment in infancy. In K. Minde & M. Lewis (ed.), *Infant Psychiatry Child and Adolescent Clinics of North America*, Vol. 4, No. 3 (pp. 571-587). Orlando, FL: W. B. Saunders Co.

Main, M., Kaplan, N., & Cassidy, J. (1985). Security in infancy, childhood, and adulthood: A move to the level of representation. In I. Bretherton & E. Waters (eds.), Growing points of attachment theory and research. *Monographs of the Society for Research in Child Development*, 50, (Nos.1-2, Serial No. 209), 66-104.

Rothbart, M. K. (1986). Longitudinal observation of infant temperament. *Developmental Psychology*, 22, 356-365.

The Safe Home Checklist (1986). Massachusetts Department of Public Health.

Sameroff, A.J. & Emde, R.N. (1989). *Relationship disturbances in early childhood.* Basic Books: New York.

Spanier, G.B. (1976). Measuring dyadic adjustment: New scales for assessing the quality of marriage and similar dyads. *Journal of Marriage and the Family,* 38,15-28.

Spitzer, R. L., Williams, J. B. W., Gibbon, M., & First, M. B. (1987). *The Structured Clinical Interview for DSM-III-R (SCID-I & II).* New York, Biometrics Research, New York State Psychiatric Institute.

Stern, D. (1985). *The Interpersonal World of the Infant.* New York: Basic Books.

Thorndike, R. L., Hagen, E. P., & Sattler, J. M. (1986). Stanford-Binet intelligence scale: Fourth edition. *Technical Manual.* Chicago: Riverside Publishing.

Winnicott, D. W. (1965). *The Maturational Process and the Facilitating Environmnent.* New York: International Universities Press.

ZERO TO THREE (1994). *Diagnostic Classification of Mental Health and Developmental Disorders of Infancy and Early Childhood.* Arlington, VA: ZERO TO THREE/National Center for Clinical Infant Programs.

Contributors

Judith Ahrano, M.D., is a developmental/behavioral pediatrician and medical director of the Child Development Clinic of the Utah State Department of Health's Children with Special Health Care Needs Bureau, which serves children birth to five with developmental disabilities and their families. She has an adjunct clinical faculty appointment with the Department of Pediatrics at the University of Utah Health Sciences Center. Her primary interests are the medical, neurobiological, neuropsychological, family, and environmental issues that contribute to emotional, functional and behavioral problems, and planning effective intervention to address these issues.

Lois M. Black, Ph.D., is a child clinical psychologist and child neuropsychologist in private practice in Brooklyn, New York. She specializes in comprehensive neuropsychological-psychodynamic evaluations and psychotherapy with children of all ages and their families. She has a long-standing interest in understanding the emotional and behavioral sequelae of various forms of neuropsycholgical dysfunction. Her research has been on the social-emotional problems concomitant to developmental language disorders in preschool-aged children.

Irene Chatoor, M.D., is a Professor of Psychiatry at the George Washington University School of Medicine. She also serves as Vice Chair of the Department of Psychiatry at the Children's National Medical Center, Washington, D.C. Dr. Chatoor has a special research interest in eating disorders in infants, toddlers and adolescents and has written on feeding disorders for several major psychiatry textbooks.

Roseanne Clark, Ph.D., is Assistant Professor in the Department of Psychiatry at the University of Wisconsin Medical School and Director of its Parent-Infant and Early Childhood Clinics. Dr. Clark developed the *Parent-Child Early Relational Assessment*, an instrument used to measure the affective and behavioral quality of parent-child relationships through ratings of videotaped interactions and video replay interview with parents. Dr. Clark's interests include assessment and treatment of early relational disturbances, maternal depression, and maternal employment characteristics and mother-child relational quality.

Susan W. Coates, Ph.D. is Associate Clinical Professor of Medical Psychology in the Department of Psychiatry, College of Physicians and Surgeons, Columbia University, New York City, and is a faculty member at both the Center for Psychoanalytic Training and Research at Columbia University, and at the Department of Psychiatry at St. Luke's Roosevelt-Hospital Center. In addition to her interest in gender, Dr. Coates also has a long-standing interest in issues relating to the development of a sense of self. A primary focus of her work has been to develop effective strategies for therapeutic intervention with children and their parents based on an integration of psychoanalytic and attachment theories.

Karen Frankel, Ph.D., is a pediatric psychologist practicing at the University of Colorado School of Medicine and at the National Jewish Medical and Research Center, Denver, Colorado. She is the Co-Director of the Infant Psychiatry Clinic at UCSM, the Associate Director of the Kempe Center Therapeutic Preschool and the Irving Harris Training Program in Child Development and Infant Mental Health. She has a long-standing interest in infant mental health and is currently focusing on developmental psychopathology and clinical intervention.

Theodore J. Gaensbauer, M.D., is in private practice in Denver, Colorado, and is Associate Clinical Professor in the Department of Psychiatry at the University of Colorado Health Sciences Center. He has had a long-standing interest in adaptive and maladaptive emotional regulation in infancy and in the impact of traumatic experience on early development. Several recent publications have addressed the developmental effects of trauma in the pre-verbal period.

Robert J. Harmon, M.D. is Director of the Infant Psychiatry Program at the University of Colorado School of Medicine. Director of the Irving Harris Training Program in Child Development and Infant Mental Health, a member of ZERO TO THREE's Board of Directors and Diagnostic Classification Task Force, and a member of local, national and international professional associations, he has worked to bring about greater understanding and more effective practice in the areas of infant mental health, parent education and pregnancy loss.

Barbara Kalmanson, Ph.D., is a psychologist and special educator at the Infant-Parent Program, Department of Psychiatry, University of California, at San Francisco General Hospital. She has a private practice in San Francisco. Her teaching and publications focus on affective development, supportive parent-provider relationships, and innovative comprehensive intervention for young children with difficulties relating and communicating.

Sharon Y. Levy received her Ph.D. in clinical psychology from Syracuse University and performed her clinical internship at the University of Colorado Health Sciences Center. Currently, Dr. Levy is a post-doctoral research fellow at the National Jewish Medical and Research Center in Denver, Colorado, investigating parent-physician interactions and the medical management of children with severe chronic asthma.

Alicia F. Lieberman, Ph.D., is Professor of Psychology, Department of Psychiatry, University of California San Francisco. She is Director of the Child Trauma Research Project and Senior Psychologist, Infant-Parent Program, at the San Francisco General Hospital. She is the author of *The Emotional Life of the Toddler* and numerous articles on disorders of attachment, infant-parent psychotherapy and the role of cultural factors in infant mental health interventions.

J. Martín Maldonado-Durán, M.D., is a member of the faculty of the Karl Menninger School of Psychiatry, and an investigator at the Child and Family Center, Menninger Clinic, Topeka, Kansas. Dr. Maldonado specializes in infant mental health problems. His research concerns investigation of symptom patterns and their correlation with attachment issues.

Klaus Minde, M.D., F.R.C.P. (C) is Professor of Psychiatry and Pediatrics at McGill University, Montreal, Quebec, and the Chairman of the Division of Child Psychiatry. He is also the Director of the Department of Psychiatry of the Montreal Children's Hospital, co-chair of the Infancy Committee of the American Academy of Child and Adolescent Psychiatry, and editor of the annual issue of child psychiatry in the *Canadian Journal of Psychiatry*. Dr. Minde's research has focused on aggression and sleep disorders in infants and toddlers and, most recently, on the effect of psychosocially sensitive perinatal care on parenting behavior in high-risk families.

Andrew Paulson, Ph.D.. is a psychologist in private practice and a clinical instructor and supervisor of psychology interns in the Parent-Infant Clinic, Department of Psychiatry, University of Wisconsin Medical School, Madison, Wisconsin. Dr. Paulson also provides consultation to a number of agencies serving families with young children ages birth to three.

Judith H. Pekarsky, Ph.D., is Clinical Coordinator of the Infant-Parent Program at San Francisco General Hospital and Associate Clinical Professor in the Department of Psychiatry, University of California, San Francisco. A clinician and supervisor in programs offering psychotherapeutic intervention in difficulties in the relationships between children under three and their parents since 1975, she has long been interested in understanding the nature of the transactions between infants, toddlers, and parents and the internal experience of the child.

Mary Seidl, M.S., is a school psychologist at the Parent-Infant Clinic at the University of Wisconsin Medical School. Her areas of interest include assessment of infants and young children, therapeutic group interventions for preschool and school-age children, and facilitating home-school collaborations.

Rebecca Shahmoon-Shanok, M.S.W., Ph.D., serves as Director of the new Institute for Clinical Studies of Infants, Toddlers and Parents and the Early Childhood Group Therapy Service and Training Programs, both at the Child Development Center, Jewish Board of Family and Children's Services, New York City. Trained and experienced as an early childhood teacher, social worker and clinical psychologist, she is interested in transdisciplinary practice, supervision and training; development from conception through age 7; the interface between mental health and education; and prevention-intervention programs, especially in inner-city environments.

Robin C. Silverman, M.A., is a Doctoral candidate in clinical psychology at the Wright Institute in Berkeley, California. She is a child-parent therapist and clinical researcher at the University of California San Francisco Child Trauma Research Project, which offers clinical intervention to young children and their families who are experiencing domestic violence.

Jean M. Thomas, M.D., M.S.W., is Director of the Department of Child and Adolescent Psychiatry and Director of the Early Development Program, Cardinal Glennon Children's Hospital, St. Louis, Missouri, and Associate Professor of Psychiatry and Pediatrics at St. Louis University School of Medicine. She is the co-chair of the American Academy of Child and Adolescent Psychiatry's Infancy Committee and principal author of its Practice Parameters for the Psychiatric Assessment of Infants and Toddlers; she is also a member of ZERO TO THREE's Diagnostic Classification Task Force. A special research interest is clarification of the heterogeneity of risk factors and diagnoses of young children with hyperactive and disruptive behavior.

Lee Tidmarsh, M.D.C.M, F.R.C.P (C), directs a multi-disciplinary team that evaluates and treats families with very young children experiencing emotional disturbances and is Assistant Professor of Psychiatry at McGill University, Montreal, Quebec. She has particular interests in mental health assessment and diagnosis of the zero-to-three population and in promoting early childhood intervention by community-based health professionals.

Gambi White-Tennant, M.S., Ed., is Associate Director of Project ERA (Enhancing Resilience & Adaptation) in pediatric rehabilitation at the John F. Kennedy Medical Center, Edison, New Jersey and Adjunct Professor at Essex County College, Newark, New Jersey. She consults to intervention programs in the areas of infant/toddler assessment, individual development plans, dyadic intervention, and play therapy.

Serena Wieder, Ph.D., is a clinical psychologist in private practice in Silver Spring, Maryland. She is a consultant to research and clinical centers in the United States and Israel and serves as Associate Director of the Interdisciplinary Council for Developmental and Learning Disorders. A member of the Board of Directors of ZERO TO THREE: National Center for Infants, Toddlers, and Families, Dr. Wieder has served as Co-Chair (with Stanley I. Greenspan) and Clinical Director of the organization's Diagnostic Classification Task Force, editor of ZERO TO THREE's *Diagnostic Classification of Mental Health and Developmental Disorders of Infancy and Early Childhood (DC: 0-3)*, and clinical supervisor in the Developmental Specialist in Pediatric Practice project.

G. Gordon Williamson, Ph.D., O.T.R., is the director of several research and training projects in pediatric rehabilitation at the John F. Kennedy Medical Center, Edison, New Jersey, and is Associate Clinical Professor in the Rehabilitation Medicine Department at Columbia University, New York City. A member of ZERO TO THREE's Board of Directors, he has a long-term interest in fostering the adaptive and social development of young children and in supporting their families. This commitment is reflected in his most recent book, *Coping in Young Children: Early Intervention Practices to Enhance Adaptive Behavior and Resilience*.

Molly Romer Witten, Ph.D., works as a psychologist in the areas of infant mental health and family treatment with young children, in her private practice in Chicago, Illinois. Her clinical focus involves individuals and families with infants and toddlers, referred for trauma- and attachment- related regulatory issues. She has published in the areas of family therapy, autism, child maltreatment, evaluation of attachment disorders in foster children under age five, as well as depression in infancy. She teaches at Northwestern University.

Sabrina M. Wolfe, Ph.D., is Clinical Instructor in the Department of Psychiatry, College of Physicians and Surgeons, Columbia University, New York City and is a psychotherapy supervisor in the Department of Psychiatry at St. Luke's Roosevelt-Hospital Center. In addition to her interest in gender, she also has a long-standing interest in developing ways of assessing and intervening with children with developmental and learning disabilities, with a particular interest in helping families to foster resiliency in their vulnerable children.